POLITICAL POWER AND
SOCIAL THEORY

POLITICAL POWER AND SOCIAL THEORY

Series Editor: Julian Go

Recent Volumes:

Volume 1: 1980
Volume 2: 1981
Volume 3: 1982
Volume 4: 1984
Volume 5: 1985
Volume 6: 1987
Volume 7: 1989
Volume 8: 1994
Volume 9: 1995
Volume 10: 1996
Volume 11: 1997
Volume 12: 1998
Volume 13: 1999
Volume 14: 2000
Volume 15: 2002
Volume 16: 2004
Volume 17: 2005
Volume 18: 2006
Volume 19: 2008
Volume 20: 2009
Volume 21: 2010
Volume 22: 2011

POLITICAL POWER AND SOCIAL THEORY   VOLUME 23

POLITICAL POWER AND SOCIAL THEORY

EDITED BY

JULIAN GO

Boston University, Boston, MA, USA

United Kingdom – North America – Japan
India – Malaysia – China

Emerald Group Publishing Limited
Howard House, Wagon Lane, Bingley BD16 1WA, UK

First edition 2012

Copyright © 2012 Emerald Group Publishing Limited

Reprints and permission service
Contact: permissions@emeraldinsight.com

No part of this book may be reproduced, stored in a retrieval system, transmitted in any form or by any means electronic, mechanical, photocopying, recording or otherwise without either the prior written permission of the publisher or a licence permitting restricted copying issued in the UK by The Copyright Licensing Agency and in the USA by The Copyright Clearance Center. No responsibility is accepted for the accuracy of information contained in the text, illustrations or advertisements. The opinions expressed in these chapters are not necessarily those of the Editor or the publisher.

British Library Cataloguing in Publication Data
A catalogue record for this book is available from the British Library

ISBN: 978-1-78052-866-3
ISSN: 0198-8719 (Series)

ISOQAR certified Management Systems, awarded to Emerald for adherence to Quality and Environmental standards ISO 9001:2008 and 14001:2004, respectively

Certificate Number 1985
ISO 9001
ISO 14001

INVESTOR IN PEOPLE

CONTENTS

LIST OF CONTRIBUTORS *vii*

SENIOR EDITORIAL BOARD *ix*

EDITORIAL STATEMENT *xi*

EDITOR'S INTRODUCTION *xiii*

PART I: TRANSFORMATIONS AND POLITICS

FREE RIDING ON REVOLUTION: CONSERVATISM AND SOCIAL CHANGE
Robin Archer 3

PARTIES AND THE ARTICULATION OF NEOLIBERALISM: FROM "THE EMERGENCY" TO REFORMS IN INDIA, 1975–1991
Manali Desai 27

"A NEW HEALTH ORDER AS PART OF THE NEW SOCIAL ORDER": THE STRATEGIC RESPONSE OF THE WHO TO ITS MEMBER STATES
Nitsan Chorev 65

PART II: POLITICS AND IDENTITIES

THE RECONFIGURATION OF THE PALESTINIAN NATIONAL QUESTION: THE INDIRECT RULE ROUTE AND THE CIVIL SOCIETY ROUTE
Silvia Pasquetti 103

TRANSFORMING CITIZENSHIP: THE SUBJECTIVE
CONSEQUENCES OF LOCAL POLITICAL
MOBILIZATION
  Rachel Meyer   147

POLITICAL FIELDS AND RELIGIOUS MOVEMENTS:
THE EXCLUSION OF THE AHMADIYYA
COMMUNITY IN PAKISTAN
  Sadia Saeed   189

RACIALIZED CLASS FORMATION: BLACKS IN THE
PROFESSIONAL MIDDLE CLASS IN THE POST-CIVIL
RIGHTS ERA
  Eric S. Brown   225

PART III: SCHOLARLY CONTROVERSY: VARIETIES OF CAPITALISM

VARIETIES OF WHAT? SHOULD WE STILL BE USING
THE CONCEPT OF CAPITALISM?
  Fred Block   269

A POLANYIAN ANALYSIS OF CAPITALISM: A
COMMENTARY ON FRED BLOCK
  Nina Bandelj   293

MARX, WEBER, AND THE "CEASELESS
ACCUMULATION OF CAPITAL"
  Ho-Fung Hung   303

ON FRED BLOCK, VARIETIES OF WHAT? SHOULD
WE STILL BE USING THE CONCEPT OF
CAPITALISM?
  Wolfgang Streeck   311

THERE WAS NO BABY IN THIS BATHWATER: A
REPLY TO THE CRITICS
  Fred Block   323

LIST OF CONTRIBUTORS

Robin Archer	Department of Sociology, London School of Economics, London, UK
Nina Bandelj	Department of Sociology, University of California-Irvine, Irvine, CA, USA
Fred Block	Department of Sociology, University of California-Davis, Davis, CA, USA
Eric S. Brown	Department of Sociology, University of Missouri, Columbia, MO, USA
Nitsan Chorev	Department of Sociology, Brown University, Providence, RI, USA
Manali Desai	Department of Sociology, London School of Economics, London, UK
Ho-Fung Hung	Department of Sociology, Johns Hopkins University, Baltimore, MD, USA
Rachel Meyer	Department of Sociology, Harvard University, Cambridge, MA, USA
Silvia Pasquetti	Department of Sociology, University of Cambridge, Cambridge, UK
Sadia Saeed	Department of Sociology, Yale University, New Haven, CT, USA
Wolfgang Streeck	Max Planck Institute for the Study of Societies, Cologne, Germany

SENIOR EDITORIAL BOARD

Ronald Aminzade
University of Minnesota

Eduardo Bonilla-Silva
Duke University

Michael Burawoy
University of California-Berkeley

Nitsan Chorev
Brown University

John Coatsworth
Columbia University

Diane E. Davis
Harvard University

Susan Eckstein
Boston University

Peter Evans
University of California-Berkeley

Nora Hamilton
University of Southern California

Eiko Ikegami
New School University Graduate Faculty

Howard Kimeldorf
University of Michigan-Ann Arbor

Florencia Mallon
University of Wisconsin-Madison

Jill Quadagno
Florida State University

Ian Roxborough
State University of New York-Stony Brook

Michael Schwartz
State University of New York-Stony Brook

George Steinmetz
University of Michigan

John D. Stephens
University of North Carolina-Chapel Hill

Maurice Zeitlin
University of California-Los Angeles

Sharon Zukin
City University of New York

STUDENT EDITORIAL BOARD

Cara Bowman
Zophia Edwards
Kiri Gurd
Adrienne Lemon
David Levy
Megan O'Leary
Itai Vardi

EDITORIAL STATEMENT

Political Power and Social Theory is a peer-reviewed annual journal committed to advancing the interdisciplinary understanding of the linkages between political power, social relations, and historical development. The journal welcomes both empirical and theoretical work and is willing to consider papers of substantial length. Publication decisions are made by the editor in consultation with members of the editorial board and anonymous reviewers. For information on submissions, please see the journal website at http://www.bu.edu/sociology/ppst.

EDITOR'S INTRODUCTION

I am honored to present Volume 23 of *Political Power and Social Theory*. I do so amid tumultuous times. It is now spring 2012. Fiscal uncertainty and economic stagnation freeze the globe, racial division continues to plague political discourse in the United States (witness the case of Trayvon Martin), new social movements like Occupy proliferate and resurface while war, revolution, and political instability unsettle the Middle East. The essays in this volume do not directly address these specific issues but they do offer informed research and theoretical reflection on the larger themes the more specific issues invoke. Robin Archer's thoughts on revolution "Free Riding on Revolution" invites reflection in the wake of the revolutions that still grip the world's attention and perhaps, too, on the Occupy movement. Manali Desai's essay on the origins of neoliberalism in India offers some historical context to rising criticisms of neoliberalism around the world while also revealing the importance of national political parties in the formulation of globally circulating policies. Nitsan Chorev's essay on the World Health Organization illuminates how health programs are challenged and reformulated in response to political pressure from different parts of the world; an important observation given that international organizations face the prospect of dwindling revenues amid the current economic crisis.

The essays in Part II address questions of identity formation; however, each in different contexts. Rachel Meyer's essay, "Transforming Citizenship: The Subjective Consequences of Local Political Mobilization," reminds us of the power of local social movements upon identity formation despite continued globalization. In "The Reconfiguration of the Palestinian National Question," Silvia Pasquetti unveils how colonial state strategies have shaped group formation and nationalism in Palestine. In "Political Fields and Religious Movements: The Exclusion of the Ahmadiyya Community in Pakistan," Sadia Saeed redeploys Bourdieu's field theory to explain how and why the Pakistan state shifted from accommodating the heterodox Ahmadiyya community, a self-defined minority sect of Islam, to excluding it. Finally, Eric Brown discusses the black middle class in the United States – this at a time when the presidency of Barack Obama has invited renewed reflection on race and class in America.

A lively debate on Fred Block's essay "Varieties of What? Should We Still be Using the Concept of Capitalism" constitutes this volume's Scholarly Controversy part. The debate is timely. As the global economic system stagnates, as countries around the world face unprecedented austerity regimes, and as protests against current economic conditions proliferate around the globe – from Wall Street to Barcelona to Manila – global capitalism appears to be entering a new period of crisis. But Block asks if the term "capitalism" is useful at all. Does "market society," taken from Karl Polyani, work better? The question is as vital as it is timely. As Block reminds us, Paul Potter insisted in his famous speech on the Vietnam War in 1965: "we must name the system." To make sense of the crisis we face today, this question is all the more relevant. Incisive commentaries from Nina Bandelj, Ho-Fung Hung, and Wolfgang Streeck agree with Potter that we must "name the system," but they disagree with Block that we should *re*name it. The debate continues.

My thanks to Fred and all of the commentators, as well as the other contributors, for making this volume of PPST such an exciting one. Also thanks to Emma Bruun and the rest of the team at Emerald for their continued support and expertise.

PART I
TRANSFORMATIONS AND POLITICS

FREE RIDING ON REVOLUTION: CONSERVATISM AND SOCIAL CHANGE

Robin Archer

ABSTRACT

There are a number of reasons for thinking that the pursuit of change through revolution is fundamentally flawed. Indeed, after over two centuries of debate, Burkean conservatives seem to have won the argument. They have made a strong case against revolutionary change by demonstrating how it has regularly produced some of the worst atrocities we have known. They point out that despite the fact that revolutionary movements have often been the repositories of some of our highest aspirations, their unintended consequences have produced enormous human suffering. And they show how the pursuit of gradual change in some countries brought about the very same goals to which revolutionaries aspired in others, but with far less bloodshed and suffering.

But are the conservatives right? In this article, I consider various problems with their argument. One of the biggest is that the gradual changes they admire were closely entwined with the revolutions they deplore. Not only did revolutions provide incrementalists with a kind of compass that set the direction of change, but they also induced fear in powerful elites: fear that gave these elites an incentive to accept incremental changes they would otherwise have resisted. Indeed, because of these kinds of effects, countries that are usually seen as paradigm examples of the virtues of conservative change may have ultimately been among the major beneficiaries of revolution. In short, there is a good case for arguing that modern conservatism has been free riding on revolution.

Nobody now worries much about revolutions in the established capitalist democracies. Yet revolutions – both the fear of them and the hopes invested in them – have been one of the defining concerns of the last two centuries. I want to use the current relative lack of passion about revolutions to reassess some aspects of their long-term impact and to draw attention to some frequently overlooked effects. One reason for the current lack of concern is that there now seems to be widespread agreement that the pursuit of change through revolution is fundamentally flawed. In this article, I will begin by setting out three problems that have helped to foster this conclusion. Even those with some sympathy for revolutionary projects recognize that there are major problems, and here I will start by briefly considering two of these. I will then turn to a third critique that has typically been made by conservative opponents of revolution. This conservative critique is the most important, long-standing, and influential argument in the case against revolution, and it will be the main focus of this article. It is not my intention to challenge all of its conclusions. But I do want to reexamine some important elements of it.

DILEMMAS AND PARADOXES

The first problem I want to consider is what I will call the "revolutionary dilemma." This dilemma confronts movements seeking to establish a democratic order in the face of powerful resistance from a strong authoritarian establishment with the capacity and will to use harsh repressive measures. Such a movement has little choice but to establish tightly disciplined internally autocratic organizational structures if it is to have any chance of succeeding. If it does not, it will not be able to survive, and will have no chance of achieving its democratic goals. But if it does do this, and then manages to overthrow the old regime, these very organizational structures will carry an authoritarian incubus into the new regime. Unless it limits internal openness, pluralism and democracy under the old regime, it is sure to be crushed and it will have no hope of democratizing the political order. But if it does limit these things, it will develop an authoritarian internal organizational culture that, if it succeeds, it will then carry with it into the heart of the new political order. In short, the political opportunity structure of highly autocratic regimes tends to reproduce autocracy even when revolutionary movements succeed in overthrowing them.

The Russian Revolution provides a familiar example of this kind of political opportunity structure. The Bolsheviks had little chance of surviving Czarist repression without adopting an authoritarian internal party organization, which, in an attempt to square the circle, they called "democratic centralism." Indeed, it was partly for this reason that the Bolshevik approach seemed more viable to a majority in the broader Russian social democratic movement from which they emerged. However, when the Bolsheviks succeeded in seizing power, and set about establishing a new social and political order, they carried with them the organizational norms that they had established in opposition: a process that was reinforced by the insecure nature of the new regime during the chaos and flux of the early post-revolutionary years and the civil war.[1] In effect the party became the vehicle for transmitting the authoritarianism of the old regime into the heart of the new.

Some will doubt that the Bolsheviks ever aspired to establish a form of democracy in the first place. Long ago, for example, Plamenatz (1954, pp. 317–320) argued for a sharp distinction between "German Marxism" and "Russian Communism" on this very point. And the revolutionary dilemma is certainly not the only reason for Bolshevik authoritarianism. Seeking to rule in the name and interests of industrial workers in a society in which these remain a small minority does not sit easily with democratic norms. But whether or not the Bolsheviks really did have democratic aspirations, the revolutionary dilemma is a genuine one for democrats facing strongly autocratic regimes. It will be difficult for them to democratize the state without adopting an organizational culture that will tend to undermine the very goal they are seeking to achieve.[2]

The second problem I want to consider is what I will call the "freezing paradox." When revolutionaries set about establishing a new social and political order, they do not change each and every institution. Their focus is typically on particular institutional and legal changes that seem to them central. This is partly because it is just not possible to change everything at once, and partly because there are some features of the old regime that seem unimportant or unobjectionable to them. But once the new order is successfully established, the revolution that brought it about serves to legitimize all the institutions of the new regime, including those that have been simply carried over from the old. And once they have been legitimized (or relegitimized) in this way, all these institutions become entrenched (or re-entrenched) and difficult to change. In effect then, revolutions actually serve to preserve some institutions and norms, giving them a new lease of life that protects them from change and projects them far into the future.

The American Revolution provides a clear example of this. Having thrown off British colonial rule, the leaders of the revolution sought to make the executive arm of government accountable by ensuring that the President (in lieu of the monarch) was elected (albeit indirectly through an electoral college). Now there is no doubt that this was a radical departure from the British pattern of government, and one that involved substantially greater democracy. But in the process of transforming some of the institutions and norms of eighteenth century British government, the revolutionaries carried over a great many others. Take the monarchy. In Britain, in the absence of a revolution, the formal structure of the monarchy was maintained. But in the course of the following century, as democratic norms and demands became ever stronger, the monarchy lost its executive function and gradually took on a purely symbolic role. In the United States, the revolutionaries made a sharp break. In a sense, they opted to elect the monarch. But by doing so they simultaneously preserved a kind of executive monarchy. More generally, the American Revolution froze in place the balance of power between the Commons, the Lords, and the King, which many influential eighteenth century thinkers, like Blackstone and Montesquieu, thought to be one of the main virtues of the British system of government. In Britain itself, the House of Commons gradually became preeminent under the influence of democratizing pressures throughout the nineteenth century. In the United States, the revolution produced a significantly more democratic lower house, but it preserved and entrenched the idea that this democratic arm of the government should be contained and counterbalanced by the upper house and the executive.

Similar examples can be seen in other great revolutions. The French Revolution fundamentally changed the locus of sovereignty from the monarch to the people – or rather to all adult men – but in the process it carried over and helped entrench the highly centralized state that had been built up under the old regime. The Russian Revolution over threw the Czars, but the "Union of Soviet Socialist Republics" preserved the imperial territorial domain that the Czars had established. Unlike other contemporary land-based empires in Europe – those of the Habsburgs and the Ottomans – the Russian Empire was preserved for as long as the Soviet system itself remained intact.

The revolutionary dilemma and the freezing paradox raise serious doubts about the likely long-term consequences of revolutionary change. The first points to the propensity of revolutions to fail to produce change, and to instead reproduce a version of the status quo. The second points to their propensity to make change in the future more difficult. But in most discussions of revolution, it is a third critique that looms largest. I will call this the "conservative critique" in recognition of its main proponents. For the proponents of this critique, the main problem with revolutions is not the failure to facilitate change, but the dire consequences of the change that is brought about.

THE CONSERVATIVE CRITIQUE

The conservative tradition has from the outset been stimulated by and defined itself in opposition to fundamental social change in general and revolution in particular. The *locus classicus* is Edmund Burke's *Reflections on the Revolution in France*. Reacting to events in France, or, more precisely, to the claim by the dissenting cleric Richard Price that Britain might find some inspiration in these events, Burke made the case for resisting calls for reform and preserving the basic features of the existing social and political order. At the center of his argument is what he sees as the dire threat posed by human initiatives to pursue fundamental change. The outcome of such initiatives is invariably a dreadful calamity that compels people "to wade through blood and tumult." Revolution he describes as "this fond election of evil." The result is "treasons, robberies, rapes, assassinations, slaughters and burnings" (Burke, 1968 [1790], pp. 126–127). Burke's belief in the inevitability of these consequences is closely connected to his skepticism about human reason and theories, and his valorization, instead, of experience and historically accumulated customs, traditions, and prejudices, especially those embodied in established political and religious institutions (Burke, 1968, pp. 152, 183). In a characteristically rhetorical passage, he compares the revolutionaries with children, who, finding their father wounded, "are prompt rashly to hack that aged parent in pieces, and put him into the kettle of magicians, in hopes that by their poisonous weeds, and wild incantations, they may regenerate the paternal constitution, and renovate their father's life" (Burke, 1968, p. 194).

But conservatives are not hostile to all change. On the contrary they argue that gradual step-by-step change can safely be pursued, especially when it takes the form of organic growth that works with the grain of existing institutions.[3] Indeed, Burke (1968, p. 106) famously argues that the preservation of the existing social order sometimes requires this kind of change: "A State without the means of some change is without the means of its conservation. Without such means it might even risk the loss of that part of the constitution which it wished the most religiously to preserve." The central point, then, is not that all change should be repudiated, but that change should only be pursued with "circumspection and caution ... by a slow but well-sustained progress" that enables each step to be carefully studied and the costs and benefits evaluated before moving on to take another (Burke, 1968, pp. 280–281).

Later conservatives have developed this position further to argue that this slow step-by-step approach eventually managed to produce many of the changes that radicals and revolutionaries promised but without the terrible costs (Quinton, 1993, p. 254). Britain, for example, through a series of reforms implemented over a period of more than a century, eventually matched the promise of the French Revolution to remove property qualifications on voting, but without the degree of chaos and bloodshed that ensued in France. This revised Burkean conservatism is not Burke's own position. For it enables contemporary conservatives to embrace some substantive changes – like Price's call for parliamentary democratic reforms – that Burke (1968, p. 99) himself firmly deprecated. But it is broadly in the spirit of a Burkean interpretation of conservatism as a "counsel for caution in change." And while it deals with only one aspect of the conservative tradition (Hampsher-Monk, 1992), it is widely seen as capturing one of its central characteristics (Quinton, 1993, pp. 145, 154; Freeden, 1996, pp. 333, 344).

After more than two centuries of experience of revolution and its consequences, these neo-Burkean conservatives seem to have the better part of the argument. Indeed, one could almost say that there is now a kind of neo-Burkean consensus. The conservative position has a strong prima facie plausibility because, despite the fact that revolutionary movements have often been the repositories of some of our highest aspirations, each of the great revolutions has invariably been accompanied by terrible bloodshed and suffering. Moreover, conservatives have been able to show that some of the most important goals to which revolutionaries aspired have been achieved in those societies that rejected the revolutionary route. Countries that followed their counsel for caution in change not only avoided the costs of change, but eventually gained the benefits too.

But are the conservatives really right? There are a number of problems with their argument. I will briefly mention three of them. However, it is the third on which I then propose to focus.

The first problem concerns the tendency of conservatives to ignore or discount suffering and despotism in the pre-revolutionary social order: the suffering of the status quo. Burke (1968, p. 173), for example, simply insists that broadly speaking Europe "was in a flourishing condition" prior to the French Revolution, and this kind of complacency has been a regular feature of conservative arguments ever since. Fast forward to the civil rights era and you find Samuel Huntington (1957, p. 473) and other conservatives appealing to similar arguments to resist any rapid changes in the American South. This tendency to focus on some sources of suffering and unfreedom while ignoring others was noticed immediately by writers like Thomas Paine and Mary Wollstonecraft who were among Burke's most important early critics (Kramnick, 1983, p. 191).[4] However, recognizing this problem leaves us with an invidious task. It suggests that it is not enough simply to denounce the horrors attendant on revolutions, rather these must be weighed against other horrors. In a sense, then, it calls for a balance of horrors: scales that can weigh both different kinds of horrors and horrors at different times.

A second problem concerns the strangely inconsistent attitude of conservatives to the similarly catastrophic consequences of different kinds of collective human actions and initiatives. The most striking example of this is the different attitude that conservatives typically have to the consequences of war. Even if we limit ourselves to the last 250 years, it seems likely that war has led to the decimation of more societies and has produced far more suffering than has the relatively infrequent occurrence of revolution.[5] Yet, conservatives have not merely ignored the consequences of this category of human initiatives, but have frequently been among the main supporters of these initiatives. In Britain, for example, it was those who were most likely to sympathize with the French Revolution, who were most hostile to the costs of war, whereas conservative opponents of the revolution were among the war's most strident supporters. Indeed, according to Linda Colley (2005), war – both before and after the French Revolution – played a crucial role in forging the national sentiment that held together the British constitutional settlement of 1688 that Burke and the conservatives so valued. Given the emphasis they place on preserving the fabric of existing social orders and avoiding the potentially disastrous unintended consequences of dramatic human initiatives, it is odd how infrequently conservatives sympathize with pacifism.[6] In some respects revolutions are a bit like wars. It is difficult to wholly reject either in principle. But given the disruption and destruction that typically ensue, it is also difficult to support either, except as a last resort. Yet, the right and left sometimes seem to hold positions that are the mirror image of each other. It is strange how often conservatives have been for war but against revolution, and it is interesting how often radicals have been sympathetic to revolution but hostile to war. Often, indeed, this sympathy has been connected to the desire to stop war.[7]

A third problem with the conservative argument stems from the tendency of conservatives to ignore the transnational consequences of revolutions. Conservatives treat the gradual changes in the countries whose histories they admire as unconnected with the revolutions that they deprecate in other countries. But, what if these gradual changes were actually fostered by revolutions elsewhere? What if the countries that avoided revolutions ended up being the beneficiaries of them? In the rest of this article, I want to explore whether this was so.

To do this, I will examine two historical cases of reform, each of which is often thought to provide a paradigm example of the strengths of the conservative case against revolution and for gradual incremental change. These cases are also of special importance because they involve a reassessment of the classic great revolutions in the late eighteenth century – the revolutions that gave rise to the conservative tradition, and the critique of which remains a basic point of reference for much conservative thought. The first case concerns the achievement of parliamentary and electoral reforms in Britain, where, as we have already seen, conservatives emphasize how democratization was achieved over time but without the century or more of chaos unleashed by the French Revolution. The second concerns the achievement of self-government in Australia, where this was accomplished through a gradual negotiated process within the framework of British imperial rule but without the upheaval and destruction of the American Revolution.[8]

The first of these is arguably *the* paradigm case for conservatives. The second perhaps warrants a brief further comment, for it is not the kind of example to which *American* conservatives would be likely to appeal.[9] There is a tendency for American conservatives to apply their arguments to all revolutions except their own. This became especially marked after the elapse of a century or so, although in this they mimic Burke and the founders of British conservatism who saw themselves as carrying the flag for the Glorious Revolution. Indeed, even some French conservatives were eventually able to embrace their revolution toward the end of the nineteenth century (Gildea, 2008). But it remains the case that, like other great revolutions, if not always to the same extent, the American Revolution led to the kind of bloodshed, displacement, and suffering that is usually anathema to conservatives.

BRITISH DEMOCRACY AND THE FRENCH REVOLUTION

Parliamentary reform and universal manhood suffrage were achieved in Britain through a long drawn out series of reforms that unfolded over a period of over a century. The process began with failed bills in the 1790s, and it was not until 1832 that the first great reform act was passed. This was followed by further reform acts, each of which further expanded the suffrage in 1867, 1884, and 1918. Women's suffrage was introduced in 1918, but only for those who were at least 30 years old, a qualification that was removed in 1928. Unlike in France, these reforms were brought about without the outbreak of revolution. But, what impact did the French Revolution have on the reform movement in Britain?

The impact of the French Revolution in Britain unfolded in three stages.[10] The first stage was marked by a surge of interest in political reform in the early 1790s. A major debate took place about the revolution and its significance for Britain.[11] Burke's response to Price elicited replies in return, of which Thomas Paine's *Rights of Man* was just the most influential of numerous books and pamphlets. Various associations were formed to press for reform. Some, like the Society of the Friends of the People, were groups of established Whig liberals. Others, like the London Corresponding Society and similar bodies elsewhere, attracted the membership of large numbers of urban artisans for the first time.

The second stage was marked by repression, war, and popular loyalism. The onset of war with France in 1793 facilitated both government repression of the reform movement and the growth of a popular loyalist response. The Pitt government began implementing repressive measures even before the onset of war, although the war made it easier to strengthen and legitimize them. Books and pamphlets were banned, reform associations were broken up, and some leading figures were tried, jailed, and occasionally executed. Paine himself was sentenced to death *in absentia*. Britain had been at war with (Catholic, despotic) France for much of the previous century, and the conflict had played an important role in establishing a British identity (Colley, 2005). In this context, loyalist tracts proved popular and loyalist associations succeeded in mobilizing significant opposition to radicals and their reform demands.

The third stage was marked by the revival of radicalism. With the end of the Napoleonic wars in 1815, the reform movement reasserted itself. Agitation for reform was further fostered by the economic crisis and social unrest that the war left in its wake, and reform was established as the most contentious issue on the political agenda. After various unsuccessful attempts, the 1832 "Great Reform Act" was finally passed. It followed a wave of reforms removing discrimination against Protestant dissenters and Catholics, and the fall of Wellington and the Tory government that had ruled since the revolution.

The French Revolution helped to bring about reform in Britain in at least two important ways. The first concerns the realm of ideas. The second, the realm of interests.

In the realm of ideas, the revolution helped to set the political agenda and establish the terms of debate. Ideas like popular sovereignty and manhood suffrage set down markers of what would constitute progress, and provided British reformers with a kind of compass that helped to establish the direction of travel for the reform movement. British conservatives could block reform, but they could not shape the direction that reform would take should it become uncontainable. It was the radicals who did that. The Burkean legacy was clear that any change should be slow and incremental, but it left conservatives with no ideological resources for favoring one direction over another. All they could do was to react to the agenda set by the radicals. This does not mean that conservatives were passive participants in the British debate about the French Revolution. On the contrary, much recent scholarship has emphasized the vigor and popular appeal of much of the loyalist response to radical claims (Colley, 2005; Emsley, 2000). And some have argued that the conservatives actually "won" the debate, at least for a period (Dickinson, 1985; Dinwiddy, 1991). All this is compatible with the claim here. The issue is not who won the debate in the 1790s, but who established the main characteristics that defined political space – who, that is, constituted what would count as reform.

As E. P. Thompson (1968) and others have emphasized, there was already a long-standing English radical tradition before the French Revolution. The impact of the revolution was not the result of importing a set of wholly new ideas, rather it built on older arguments raised by Wilkesite radicals in the 1760s and those who sympathized with the American colonists in the 1770s and 1780s. However, the revolution not only revived these arguments, but radicalized them and gave them a greatly heightened salience that placed them at the center of political controversy. It polarized British politics around a set of issues that redefined the main axis of political space.[12] This was reflected in the widespread impact of the ideological debate between Burke, Paine, and others. Perhaps 200,000 copies of *Rights of Man* were sold before it was banned (Briggs, 2000, p. 115; Philp, 1991, p. 5). It was also reflected in the realignment of the party system that occurred as the old

Whig party split over the issue of the French Revolution. Its more conservative wing joined with Pitt to form the basis of the new Tory party, leaving the Whig opposition in the hands of a rump of more reform-minded politicians (Emsley, 2000, pp. 21–25). And it was reflected in the popular mobilization of reform associations and their loyalist opponents, which, for the first time, drew large numbers of artisans and members of the emerging working class into organized political debate.

In the realm of interests, the French Revolution encouraged radical artisans to organize and push for reforms and it induced fear in powerful elites: fear that gave them an incentive to accept incremental changes that many would otherwise have resisted. Conservatism as a body of thought might in principle recognize the importance of some gradual change. But that in itself did not give real-life conservatives an interest in giving up some of their power, wealth, or status. The French Revolution gave them such an interest. By suggesting that they faced a credible threat to their position, it gave them an incentive to compromise. There has been a debate among historians about whether revolution was a real possibility in Britain during these years (Christie, 1991; Well, 1991). But what matters here is only that the ruling elites *feared* that it was a danger: a point about which there is little dispute. After all, in 1795–1796 and again in 1800–1801, Britain experienced the most serious and widespread food riots in its history (Dickinson, 1999, p. 36). Those in power could hardly help but be aware of the catalytic role that food riots had played in the French Revolution itself.

This claim about the effects of the revolution requires some qualification. For the effects produced by the fear of revolution could pull in different directions. In particular, this fear could also help to induce a backlash against reforms. And this was certainly one of the effects that occurred in Britain. Fear of revolution induced conservatives to reach for the tools of repression, and it provided an ideological opportunity to rally a popular loyalist response. Conservatives could denounce calls for reform as threatening French-style anarchy, bloodshed, and tyranny,[13] and especially during invasion scares they could draw on a wave of patriotic sentiment (Dickinson, 1985, pp. 63–64; Thompson, 1968, pp. 111–116). This backlash was at its strongest during the second stage of the reaction to the revolution, following the start of war with France. But the war itself also stoked popular resentment against rising taxes, debt, and economic disruption, as well as against conscription, war profiteering, and military incompetence (Dickinson, 1985, pp. 64–65; Stevenson, 1992, pp. 183–87, 208–12). Once it ended, loyalist sentiments became more difficult to mobilize and repressive measures more difficult to legitimize and sustain, and the underlying incentive for conservatives to compromise with moderate reformers reasserted itself. Least, anyone doubt that revolution still posed a credible threat, another revolution occurred in France in 1830. The passage of the first reform act followed soon after.

It is clear that social and economic developments within Britain and especially the shifting balance of class power were also at work in generating pressure for political reform. In particular, the growth of an urban working class and the pressure that they, along with their sometime middle-class allies, were able to bring to bear played a critical role.[14] Extra-parliamentary pressure of this sort was both an important background condition and a critical strategic resource at various points during the great struggle for the first reform act (Briggs, 2000, pp. 218–220; Hilton, 2006, pp. 421, 422, 426–429). And with the subsequent emergence of Chartism, its importance only grew. But the example of the French Revolution made the threat facing ruling elites far more credible and immediate, and the potential dangers far greater and more dramatic. Moreover, this credibility could be established on the cheap – without either incurring or imposing the costs of the massive domestic upheaval that would otherwise be required to establish it.

Potential revolutionary dangers were regularly invoked not just in the implicit threats of radicals but also often by moderate reformers seeking to convince recalcitrant conservatives. They were invoked from the outbreak of the revolution onward. In November 1789, Richard Price (1789, p. 51) ended the sermon that so agitated Burke: "Tremble all ye oppressors of the world! Take warning all ye supporters of slavish governments, and slavish hierarchies! ... Restore to mankind their rights; and consent to the correction of abuses, before they and you are destroyed together." In the early 1790s, liberal Whigs in the Society of the Friends of the People argued that timely concessions on parliamentary reform would enable Britain to avoid the scenes being witnessed in France (Dickinson, 1985, p. 7, 8). During the food riots of 1800, notices appeared with threats like "Peace and large bread or a King without a head," despite the repressive measures then in force (Emsley, 1989, p. 53, 2000, pp. 104–106). Resurgent reformers renewed their warnings following the end of the war. And throughout the whole period, the governing elites suffered from a constant sensation of fear – above all of French-style revolution (Hilton, 2006, p. 31).

This general context of fear played an important role in the eventual passage of the Great Reform Act. Fear of revolution could also be invoked by opponents of reform. But it led a significant – and eventually decisive – section of the elite to conclude that resistance to reform was likely to result in a disastrous social breakdown (Fisher, 2009, p. 234; Molesworth, 1865, p. 161). Prudential considerations of this sort had already led Wellington, Peel, and the Tories to reverse themselves and support Catholic emancipation, and similar considerations were now central to the arguments of the (equally aristocratic) Whigs who were driving through what proved to be the first installment of democratic reform.

Fear of revolution can be seen at work in every stage of the process. It helped frame the argument for the original Reform Bill from the outset. Introducing the Bill in the House of Commons, Lord John Russell emphasized that it was aimed not only at remedying abuses but also at "the convulsion we hope to avoid" as well as the preservation of the "British Constitution" (Molesworth, 1865, pp. 103, 117–19). The new Prime Minister, Earl Grey, told the King that "it cannot be resisted without the greatest danger of leaving the government in a situation in which it would be deprived of all authority and strength," and similar arguments were used to convince the King to allow the early dissolution of Parliament so that the government could overcome opposition by taking the issue to the electorate (Briggs, 2000, pp. 207, 215). After this election, the Bill was easily passed by the House of Commons. But arguments about the danger of revolution reappeared with renewed urgency, now bolstered by the growing strength and assertiveness of extra-parliamentary organizations, in the struggle to stop the House of Lords from blocking the Bill and to force the King to appoint new peers if they refused to do so.[15] Macaulay and other supporters "threatened recalcitrant anti-reform peers with the fate of the French aristocracy" (Beloff, 1989, p. 91). And for many in the predominantly pro-reform press, the issue then boiled down to "Reform or Revolution" (Royle, 2000, p. 74). Even after the Act was passed, and passions had begun to subside, key protagonists continued to insist that, in securing reform, one of their main achievements had been "salvation from revolution" (Briggs, 2000, p. 225; Smith, 1992, p. 112).

The tenor of the standard position is well captured in a cartoon drawn at the height of the agitation (Colley, 2005, p. 340). In it a large bull dog – "John Bull" – representing the British people places his paw on a squirming rat. In the caption he says: "Reform Yourselves – Leave it not for me to do – My method may not suit you."

AUSTRALIAN SELF-GOVERNMENT AND THE AMERICAN REVOLUTION

The achievement of self-government in the Australian colonies also seems to be a prime instance of the kind of incremental change of which conservatives approve. Indeed, constitutional change has been so slow and incremental that, given the ongoing symbolic role of the British monarch as head of state, some doubt whether the process is finished yet. Nevertheless, it is clear that by the middle of the nineteenth century a system of autonomous, representative, and responsible self-government was achieved both in the oldest colony of New South Wales (NSW) and in its main sister colonies, and that this was achieved without the upheaval and suffering of the American Revolution. The drive for self-government in NSW, which will be my main focus here, was broadly supported by both conservatives and liberals in the colony. But it is important to note that it was entwined with a second struggle about the extent to which the institutions of self-government would be democratic. On this issue, there was substantial conflict between colonial conservatives, who sought a restricted franchise, a rural gerrymander, and an upper house that would protect their interests, and colonial liberals and radicals who opposed these measures.

Let me begin with a very brief sketch of the steps that led to self-government.[16] In the early 1820s, the British parliament, reacting in part to demands from within the colonies, established a NSW Legislative Council composed of nominees to advise the colony's Governor, and later that decade they gave the Council the right to initiate and veto local legislation. A new British Act in 1842 established a "blended" Council in which two-thirds of the members were elected by men meeting a property qualification. This marked the beginning of a form of representative government. But it failed to still demands for full autonomy. In place of a system in which the executive was responsible to the Colonial Office in London, the colonists demanded a system of responsible government in which the executive would be accountable to a NSW legislature that would have full authority to make laws on all bar Empire-wide matters.

The issue came to a head in the early 1850s.[17] In the late 1840s, the Colonial Secretary, Earl Grey, had proposed an indirectly elected chamber with limited powers.[18] This caused outrage in NSW and was abandoned. The simultaneous attempt by Grey to reintroduce the transportation of convicts, and a decision to grant a measure of responsible government to Canada (in the wake of rebellions in both English and French provinces) strengthened the Australian response.[19] Throughout 1851 and 1852, the NSW Legislative Council sent a series of increasingly assertive petitions and demands to Westminster. Grey rejected these, but at the end of 1852 his successors changed course and decided to concede self-government. The colonial legislatures were then asked to produce draft constitutions that were enacted in Westminster with some amendments in 1855. The elections the following year inaugurated the new era of self-government. The central conflict now shifted to divisions within NSW between conservatives and liberals over voting rights (which the drafting process had brought to the fore): a conflict that the liberals won decisively at the end of the 1850s.

All this was achieved without any of the upheaval and destruction that accompanied the American Revolution, and yet the American Revolution itself helped to bring this outcome about. As in the previous case, it did this in at least two ways.

First, it helped to establish self-government as a desirable and plausible goal, and, more generally, to provide a vision of the future and a direction of travel. Some radicals argued for a full-fledged Declaration of Independence and hoped to play the role of an Australian Jefferson, Franklin, or Paine (Headon & Perkins, 1998, pp. 2, 11; Hirst, 1988, pp. 9, 51; Lang, 1857). But most Australians wanted to maintain ties with Britain once self-government was achieved. Like the Americans who originally raised these demands, they principally saw themselves as claiming rights and freedoms they were entitled to as Britons. However, as a society with common origins as a group of British settler colonies, the idea that Australia was destined to be a "future America" or a "second America" had a widespread currency (Bell and Bell, 1993, pp. 17–20, p. 28). And in a more general way, the idea of America as an appealing model of the kind of power and prestige to which the maturing colonies could aspire had a nebulous but diffuse effect on the political culture and aspirations of the Australian colonists.

Second, the American Revolution provided the colonists with a thinly veiled threat that helped to maintain the pressure for reform. More or less explicit use of this rhetoric accompanied each stage of the process. It was part of the initial wave of agitation that led to the establishment of a legislative council in the 1820s. In 1819, W.C. Wentworth, who became a central figure in NSW politics for 40 years, published a call for constitutional reform least the colonists "be goaded into rebellion," a prospect he claimed was neither "problematical nor remote" (McMinn, 1979, p. 16; Melbourne, 1934, p. 67). And in 1826, a public meeting that gathered to vote an address of welcome to an incoming Governor, amended it to warn of the dangers of taxation without representation, and to declare that such a system "will never command the confidence of His Majesty's subjects in this quarter of the globe" (Melbourne, 1934, p. 132).

Similar claims recurred repeatedly thereafter. They were made by all segments of political opinion, from radicals to conservatives. The radicals were important because of their agenda-setting role. They were not marginal figures. The leading radical, J. D. Lang, was a Presbyterian Minister who played a prominent role in public life and elected office. In 1851, he topped the poll to win the first of three seats representing the city of Sydney: the largest, most representative, and most closely watched constituency in the election (Hirst, 1988, pp. 27–28). The conservatives were important because they dominated the existing Legislative Council. They were close to the interests of large pastoralists and merchants, and many actually thought of themselves as liberals, although not as democrats. Over time, W. C. Wentworth drew close to this camp, and eventually became their leading figure.

This common appeal to the experience of the American Revolution can be seen in the culmination of the agitation for self-government in the early 1850s. In 1850, Lang gave a series of lectures to packed houses in Sydney on "The Coming Event" in which he argued the case for independence and the establishment of the "United Provinces of Australia."[20] Having reviewed the costly and indefensible attempt by Britain to deny self-government to its American colonies, he argued that "if that right is not conceded peacefully [in Australia], those from whom it is unjustly withheld will only be acting in accordance with the great law of self-preservation, if they wrest it from their oppressors on the first favourable opportunity." "Does Great Britain require that instructive lesson to be taught her in the Southern Hemisphere, as it was in the Northern?," he continued in his next lecture. "It would appear that she does ...." Statements like these were continually punctuated by "great applause," "strong expressions of assent," and "cheers, long and loud." Lang gave the lectures around Australia and then developed them into a book, *Freedom and Independence for the Golden Lands of Australia*.

The language of the conservative-dominated Legislative Council, and its leading figure, W. C. Wentworth, was more official and less strident, but it implied the same basic threat.[21] In 1851, the Legislative Council sent a "Declaration, Protest and Remonstrance" to London setting out its demands for self-government. They argued that "whilst we are most anxious to strengthen and perpetuate the connexion which still happily subsists with our Fatherland," it would "be impossible much longer to maintain the authority" of the current system of colonial government (Clark, 1955, p. 325). When this was rejected by Colonial Secretary Grey, they sent a more strongly worded response in 1852 that made clear the parallels between their situation and that which led to the American Revolution. They noted that "similar grievances in America" had led to "the celebrated Declaration of Independence," and that the British "ministers who drove America to rebellion were as talented, and exemplary, and in every way as highly gifted as Earl Grey, but by their obstinacy they drove the American colonies to rebellion" (Oldfield, 1999, p. 150). Finally, they topped this off by threatening to withhold supply (Melbourne, 1934, pp. 389–391).

These kinds of threats were not the only source of pressure for change. Domestic social and economic developments were also playing a major role. Again, the changing balance of class power was particularly important. An alliance of the growing urban working and middle classes helped build support for self-government, and was critical, in the face of opposition from the previously dominant landed class of pastoralists and their allies, in ensuring that it took a democratic form (Gollan, 1960, pp. 7–9 & *passim*; Irving, 2006). More generally, the gold rushes of the early 1850s markedly increased both the population and wealth of the Australian colonies, and reinforced the pressure for change.

Nevertheless it is clear that the invocation of the American Revolution and associated threats had a significant effect in London. The effect can be seen in the arguments of colonial reformers and debates in the Colonial Office: arguments and debates that in turn shaped the decisions of Ministers and the British parliament. Colonial reformers saw concessions as a way of safeguarding the British Empire (Gollan, 1960, pp. 3, 4). Faced with increasingly intransigent demands from Australia, as well as in Canada and South Africa, they argued that the current British (Whig) government was in danger of making the same mistakes that had led to the loss of America. It was these reformers who blocked the attempt by Colonial Secretary Grey to impose colonial constitutions that fell well short of self-government. Some liberal Members of Parliament who were influenced by their arguments threatened to join with leading Tories to vote against the government (Hirst, 1988, pp. 23, 24).

The influence of similar debates within the Colonial Office can be seen particularly clearly in the change of policy that followed the departure of Grey.[22] The proximate cause of this change was a memorandum written for the new Colonial Secretary, Pakington, by his Permanent Under-Secretary – the top civil servant in the Colonial Office – Herman Merivale. The memorandum helped convince the Colonial Secretary to change position and accept the need for self-government. Merivale had taken over from an influential predecessor a few years earlier, and his memorandum reflected a developing understanding within the Colonial Office that it was no longer feasible to try to rule the settler colonies from London. He convinced the Colonial Secretary that conceding colonial demands would do less damage to British interests than continued resistance.[23] This message was no doubt reinforced by reports sent back to the Colonial Office by some of the colonial Governors. NSW Governor Fitzroy, for example, wrote that the Colonial Secretary "would be well advised to make concessions ... rather than prolong a controversy, which would undermine the loyalty of the people and destroy the power of government in the colony" (Melbourne, 1934, pp. 387, 391).[24] *The Times* of London concurred, arguing that "the fullest powers of self-government" would have to be granted "whether we wish it or not ... . It only remains for us to say whether this shall be gracefully conceded, or wrested from us by tumult and violence" (Thompson, 2006, p. 254). According to the Law Officer at the Colonial Office, Frederick Rogers, the eventual outcome of these concessions was "little less than a legislative Declaration of Independence on the part of the Australian colonies," designed to accomplish "the eventual parting of company on good terms" (Melbourne, 1934, pp. 419, 420).

Most Australian colonists purported to be upholding the spirit of British institutions and ideals. But whether many really wanted a revolutionary break with Britain was not what mattered. What mattered was that the American Revolution had established this as a real possibility: a danger that Britain might plausibly face if substantial reforms were not conceded. In this context, it was reform that promised order, and those who resisted it that threatened disorder and British interests. The new Colonial Secretary who conceded the principle of self-government was a conservative. Conservatives were concerned to make changes only when prudent. But the combination of colonial pressure and American precedent had changed what it was prudent to do.

CONCLUSION

Conservatives have placed great emphasis on the negative byproducts of revolution, but there are other byproducts that they have tended to ignore. They point out that revolutions have regularly produced immense bloodshed and suffering, and argue that the history of countries like Britain and Australia shows that gradual incremental change has been able to produce the very goals to which revolutionaries have aspired, but without these terrible costs. Thus, counter-revolutionary Britain achieved the democratization aspired to by revolutionary France. And largely loyalist Australia achieved the self-government for which the American revolutionaries fought.

The problem for conservatives is that the gradual changes they admire were closely entwined with the revolutions they deplore. Not only did revolutions provide incrementalists with a kind of compass that set the direction of change, but they also induced fear in powerful elites: fear which gave these elites an incentive to accept incremental changes that many would otherwise have resisted. Indeed, because of these kinds of effects, countries like Britain and Australia – which have some of the most stable polities in the world – may have ultimately been among the major beneficiaries of revolution. In short, there is a good case for arguing that modern conservatism has been free riding on revolution.

Of course, the effects of revolution in one country on reform efforts in another are not simple or unidirectional. There were periods, for example, especially during wartime, when the revolution in France helped British conservatives to mobilize a popular backlash that inhibited reform. Indeed, it is notable that the positive effects of revolution on reform are often felt after some decades. Perhaps there is an optimum moment when fear among hostile elites remains real, but is insufficient in the society as a whole to rally popular opposition to reform.

What do these findings mean for contemporary reform efforts? One of the defining characteristics of the present is the lack of any revolutionary threat in the established capitalist democracies. Throughout much of the twentieth century, the Russian Revolution loomed large, just as the American and French Revolutions had before. An optimistic interpretation might see the collapse of the Soviet system as beneficial, not just, as it surely was, for those who suffered under its rule, but also for Western progressives, since it made it harder for the opponents of reform to whip up antireform hysteria. But there is a good case for suggesting that fear of the Russian Revolution strengthened the hand of social democrats in Western Europe and beyond. It is not difficult to see why business elites and their political supporters would be more keen to concede demands to develop the welfare state or to increase industrial democracy when they were fearful of more fundamental changes. And it is striking that the era of retrenchment in these areas has broadly coincided with the decline and disappearance of any such threat. It may be that the present lack of any revolutionary threat goes some way toward explaining the current parlous state of the Western left.

However, whether a general argument can be made about the transnational effects of revolutions (including twentieth-century revolutions) is beyond the remit of this article. There have certainly been cases that show analogous effects to those of the classic revolutions I have been considering. In Southeast Asia, fear of Chinese (and Vietnamese) style revolutions sometimes helped to foster transitions to self-government and independence. In Malaya, for example, fear of revolutionary insurgency on the part of the British colonial authorities gave nationalist reformers leverage and a critical strategic position that led to a relatively orderly handover of power (Goodwin, 2001, pp. 116, 117, 123–128). Yet at other times, like in

Indonesia under General Suharto, this fear helped justify repression and authoritarian rule. Any general argument would have to acknowledge that the transnational effects of revolutions are mediated by a number of other factors including the international environment (and especially the capacities and interests of Great Powers), the development of civil society (and especially the balance of power between different classes), and the strength of any indigenous revolutionary tradition.

My aim here has not been to argue for a new historical generalization about the relationship between revolution and reform, but rather to reconsider some central elements of the conservative critique of revolution. This critique, along with the conservative tradition as a whole, grew out of a particular assessment of the consequences of the great revolutions of the late eighteenth century. So my principal concern here has been to reassess the effects of revolution in these paradigmatic cases. The evidence suggests that in these cases the conservative critique is flawed in important respects. Not only does it discount the suffering of the status quo and maintain an inconsistent attitude to the terrible costs of war, but it ignores the positive transnational effects of revolution. For the incremental reforms that conservatives admire, and to which they have long appealed, were in fact partly a product of the very revolutions they so strenuously opposed.

NOTES

1. See Goldstone (1991, pp. 479–480) who emphasizes the general importance of this problem. Revolution, he says, leads to a breakdown of order, which leads to a strengthening of militarism.
2. Arguably, the "negotiated revolutions" of the late twentieth century in Poland, Hungary, South Africa, and elsewhere point to a partial way out of this dilemma (Lawson, 2005, pp. 225–236).
3. On the importance of this organic conception of social order in conservative thought, see Quinton (1993, p. 245) and Freeden (1996, p. 334).
4. See also Moore (1966, pp. 505–506) who raises a similar issue.
5. See, for example, Sen and Dreze (1991, pp. 274–275) on war and famine.
6. Perhaps a conservative might argue that, if war is helping to constitute and maintain the social fabric, there is less of an inconsistency. However, the fact remains that war is the kind of dramatic initiative that conservatives deprecate and is quite contrary to the small step-by-step approach they favor. It is more like a high stakes gamble than one of the small practical experiments that Burke favors.
7. As in the classic position of the Second International before the First World War, and of the communist movement that grew out of both the abandonment of this position and the Russian Revolution (with its slogan of "Bread, Land, and

Peace"). In this argument, war serves as one of the preexisting (and potential future) horrors that outweigh the potential horrors of revolution itself.

8. There are, of course, other cases of failed reform, including those in which the conservative resistance to fundamental change has itself helped to produce appalling horrors on its own. The resistance of German conservatives to democratization before and after the First World War is one example. But these are not the sort of cases that conservatives are wont to invoke.

9. And Burke himself, of course, sympathized with the American colonists.

10. Summary narratives can be found in Dickinson (1985), Emsley (1989, 2000), and elsewhere.

11. It was arguably "the most passionate and widespread political debate since the mid-seventeenth century" (Hilton, 2006, p. 31).

12. There is a wide consensus on these points. See, for example, Briggs (2000, pp. 117–118), Dickinson (1985, pp. 1, 5, 6), Emsley (1989, pp. 54, 59), and Philp (1991, p. 12).

13. Indeed, in some respects, this negative interpretation of the French Revolution was common to radicals and conservatives, with conservatives denouncing radicals as Jacobins, and radicals denouncing the conservative government's "reign of terror" and branding Pitt as "The English Robespierre" (Emsley, 1989, p. 54).

14. Note, however, that organized working-class pressure for political reform was itself stimulated by the revolution (Dickinson, 1985, p. 8; Philp, 1991, pp. 1–2; Emsley, 1989, p. 60; Thompson, 1968). Indeed, paradoxically the very fact that the government had felt the need to mobilize popular loyalist support fostered a kind of backdoor democratization of political culture, if not of political institutions, by acknowledging and legitimizing the participation of ordinary people in political life (Eastwood, 1991, pp. 150, 168). See also Dickinson, 1985, pp. 12, 13; Emsley, 2000, p. 74; and Philp, 1991, pp. 16, 17).

15. On this, ultimately successful, struggle, see Briggs (2000, pp. 218–225), Hilton (2006, pp. 421–429), Royle (2000, pp. 70), Royle and Walvin (1982, pp. 144–148), and Thomis and Holt (1977, pp. 86–99).

16. Fuller accounts can be found in Melbourne (1934), Ward (1976), McMinn (1979), Hirst (1988), Hogan, Muir, and Golder (2007), and Thompson (2006).

17. For full treatments of this period, see Ward (1958), Irving (2006), Cochrane (2006), and Twomey (2004), and Thompson (2006).

18. Note that this Earl Grey was not the Prime Minister discussed earlier whose government brought in the Great Reform Act, but his son.

19. On transportation, see Hirst (1988, pp. 20, 21). On Canada, see McMinn (1979, pp. 48–51), Oldfield (1999, pp. 41–65), and Moore (2010, pp. 210–297). The rebellions happened in 1837 and 1838, and a form of responsible government was conceded there in 1848. The rebels were transported to Australia.

20. For the text of these lectures, see Headon and Perkins (1998, pp. 16–28). For the tone of the meetings, see Hirst (1988, pp. 22–23). For his book length treatment, see Lang (1857 [1852]).

21. Although the conservatives denounced Lang's explicit republicanism, they still knew how to participate in "the complex political dance of withdrawal of loyalty if concessions were not made, and assurances of loyalty when they were made" (Oldfield, 1999, pp. 141, 150–151).

22. For the following paragraph, see Melbourne (1934, pp. 398–399), Dickey (1974, p. 217), Ward (1976, pp. 296–298, 305–306, 310–311), Morrell (1966, pp. 382–384), and McMinn (1979, pp. 46, 50).
23. Some of these ideas were already apparent in lectures that Merivale (1861) had given earlier in Oxford.
24. This report is from 1852. For similar arguments in 1855 from Victorian Governor Hotham, see Clark (1955, p. 330).

REFERENCES

Bell, P., & Bell, R. (1993). *Implicated: The United States in Australia*. Melbourne, Australia: Oxford University Press.
Beloff, L. (1989). The Impact of the French revolution on British statecraft, 1789–1921. In C. Crossley & I. Small (Eds.).
Briggs, A. (2000). *The age of improvement* (2nd ed.). London: Longman.
Burke, E. (1968). *Reflections on the revolution in France*. Harmondsworth: Penguin Books.
Christie, I. R. (1991). Conservatism and stability in British society. In M. Philp (Ed.).
Clark, M. (1955). *Select documents in Australian history, 1851–1900*. Sydney: Angus and Robertson.
Cochrane, P. (2006). *The friends of liberty*. Melbourne: Melbourne University Press.
Colley, L. (2005). *Britons: Forging the nation, 1707–1837* (2nd ed.). New Haven, CT: Yale University Press.
Crossley, C., & Small, I. (Eds.). (1989). *The French Revolution and British culture*. Oxford: Oxford University Press.
Dickey, B. (1974). Responsible government in New South Wales: The transfer of power in a colony of settlement. *Journal of the Royal Australian Historical Society*, 60(4), 217–242.
Dickinson, H. T. (1985). *British radicalism and the French Revolution, 1789–1815*. Oxford: Basil Blackwell.
Dickinson, H. T. (1999). Democracy. In I. McCalman (Ed.), *An Oxford companion to the romantic age, British culture 1776–1832*. Oxford: Oxford University Press.
Dinwiddy, J. (1991). Interpretations of anti-Jacobinism. In M. Philp (Ed.).
Eastwood, D. (1991). Patriotism and the English state in the 1790s. In M. Philp (Ed.).
Emsley, C. (1989). The impact of the French Revolution on British politics and society. In C. Crossley & I. Small (Eds.).
Emsley, C. (2000). *Britain and the French Revolution*. Harlow: Pearson Education.
Fisher, D. R. (2009). *The History of Parliament: The House of Commons 1820–1832, I Introductory survey*. Cambridge: Cambridge University Press.
Freeden, M. (1996). *Ideologies and political theory*. Oxford: Clarendon Press.
Gildea, R. (2008). *Children of the revolution: The French 1799–1914*. London: Penguin.
Goldstone, J. A. (1991). *Revolution and rebellion in the early modern world*. Berkeley, CA: University of California Press.
Gollan, R. (1960). *Radical and working class politics: A study of eastern Australia, 1850–1910*. Melbourne: Melbourne University Press.
Goodwin, J. (2001). *No other way out: States and revolutionary movements, 1945–1991*. Cambridge: Cambridge University Press.
Hampsher-Monk, I. (1992). *A history of modern political thought*. Oxford: Blackwell.

Headon, D., & Perkins, E. (Eds.). (1998). *Our first Republicans*. Sydney: Federation Press.
Hilton, B. (2006). *A mad, bad, and dangerous people?* Oxford: Oxford University Press.
Hirst, J. B. (1988). *The strange birth of colonial democracy*. Sydney: Allen and Unwin.
Hogan, M., Muir, L., & Golder, H. (Eds.). (2007). *The people's choice: Electoral politics in colonial New South Wales*. Sydney: The Federation Press.
Huntington, S. P. (1957). Conservatism as an ideology. *American Review of Political Science, 51*(2).
Irving, T. H. (2006). *The southern tree of liberty: The democratic movement in New South Wales before 1856*. Sydney: Federation Press.
Kramnick, I. (1983). The Left and Edmund Burke. *Political Theory, 11*(2), 189–214.
Lang, J. D. (1857). *Freedom and independence for the golden lands of Australia*. Sydney: F. Cunningham.
Lawson, G. (2005). *Negotiated revolutions: The Czech Republic, South Africa and Chile*. London: Ashgate.
McMinn, W. G. (1979). *A constitutional history of Australia*. Melbourne: Oxford University Press.
Melbourne, A. C. V. (1934). *Early constitutional development in Australia: New South Wales 1788–1856*. London: Oxford University Press.
Merivale, H. (1861). *Lectures on colonization and colonies* (new edition). London: Longman, Green, Longman and Roberts.
Molesworth, W. N. (1865). *The history of the Reform Bill of 1832*. London: Chapman and Hall.
Moore, B. (1966). *Social origins of dictatorship and democracy*. Harmondsworth: Penguin.
Moore, T. (2010). *Death or liberty: Rebels and radicals transported to Australia 1788–1868*. Sydney: Murdoch Books.
Morrell, W. P. (1966). *British colonial policy in the age of Peel and Russell*. London: Frank Cass.
Oldfield, A. (1999). *The Great Republic of the Southern Seas*. Sydney: Hale and Iremonger.
Paine, T. (1984). *Rights of man*. Harmondsworth: Penguin.
Philp, M. (Ed.). (1991). *The French Revolution and British popular politics*. Cambridge: Cambridge University Press.
Plamenatz, J. (1954). *German Marxism and Russian communism*. London: Longmans, Green and Co.
Price, R. (1789). *A discourse on the love of our country*. London: George Stafford.
Quinton, A. (1993). Conservatism. In R. E. Goodin & P. Pettit (Eds.), *A companion to contemporary political philosophy*. Oxford: Blackwell.
Royle, E. (2000). *Revolutionary Britannia? Reflections on the threat of revolution in Britain 1789–1848*. Manchester: Manchester University Press.
Royle, E., & Walvin, J. (1982). *English radicals and reformers 1760–1848*. Brighton: Harvester Press.
Sen, A., & Dreze, J. (1991). *Hunger and public action*. Oxford: Oxford University Press.
Smith, E. A. (1992). *Reform or revolution? A diary of reform in England, 1830–32*. Stroud: Allan Sutton.
Stevenson, J. (1992). *Popular disturbances in England, 1700–1832* (2nd ed.). London: Longman.
Thomis, M. I., & Holt, P. (1977). *The treats of revolution in Britain 1789–1848*. London: Macmillan.
Thompson, E. P. (1968). *The making of the English working class*. Harmondsworth: Penguin.
Thompson, M. M. H. (2006). *The seeds of democracy: Early elections in Colonial New South Wales*. Sydney: The Federation Press.

Twomey, A. (2004). *The Constitution of New South Wales*. Sydney: Federation Press.
Ward, J. M. (1958). *Earl Grey and the Australian colonies, 1846–1857*. Melbourne: Melbourne University Press.
Ward, J. M. (1976). *Colonial self-government: The British experience, 1759–1856*. London: Macmillan.
Well, R. (1991). English society and revolutionary politics in the 1790s: The case for insurrection. In M. Philp (Ed.).

PARTIES AND THE ARTICULATION OF NEOLIBERALISM: FROM "THE EMERGENCY" TO REFORMS IN INDIA, 1975–1991

Manali Desai

ABSTRACT

This chapter enquires into the political struggles that have led to the gradual institutionalization of neoliberal policies in India. As India witnessed a surge in democratization since the 1980s, the state sought to implement a policy regime of privatization and liberalization, albeit with mixed success. This chapter's contribution is to focus on the party-movement relationships that were integral to establishing this new political economy. To this end the chapter undertakes an "event-centered" analysis of the failed authoritarian interlude of 1975–1977 (the Emergency) and its aftermath. Subsequent to this turning point, the chapter argues the two key political parties – the Bharatiya Janata Party (BJP) and Congress – converged upon and shaped support for a neoliberal project. In particular, the chapter traces the mechanisms by which the BJP seized the political opportunity opened during the wave of democratization that occurred from the Emergency period onward, gradually constructing a political bloc in opposition to socialism. Together with Congress Party policies "from above," the populist mobilization led by the Hindu Right sought to embed neoliberalism by eroding the disciplinary power of the middle classes. In making this argument, the chapter offers a theory of neoliberalism as a political project that, even as it is led by particular agents such as sections of the capitalist class, technocrats, and/or organized global interests, nevertheless must be embedded through democratic processes.

INTRODUCTION

This chapter asks how party-movement relationships from India's failed authoritarian interlude of 1975–1977 to the "second democratic upsurge" of the 1990s shaped support for neoliberal policies in India. Beginning in 1991 after a serious balance of payments crisis, a "pro-business"[1] policy regime that included the privatization of state-owned enterprises, reforms of the labor market and welfare policies, and industrial deregulation and liberalization was swiftly implemented by successive parties in power (Nayar, 2001; Sachs, Varshney, & Bajpai, 1999). These policies initially faced resistance not simply from the organized working classes, farmers, and new social movements as might be expected, but also from sections of the ruling party and major opposition parties, and sections of the bureaucracy (Jenkins, 2003; Varshney, 1998). Yet, since the first reforms were put in place, a broader consensus has emerged among the ruling parties, state elite, sections of the intelligentsia, and the urban middle classes regarding the "commonsensical" character of neoliberal reforms (Chopra, 2003; see also Chatterjee, 2004; Kapur & Mehta, 2004, 2006). However, because these reforms remain ideologically contested among the wider population, privatization of state enterprises and land grab for multinational investments, for example, have often been pushed back by popular protests. Moreover, since 2004 the Congress-led government has initiated a series of policies designed to promote "pro-poor" welfare in areas of health, access to school meals, employment guarantees, and food security. Yet, recognizing that neoliberal regimes are variable and hybrid, and do not appear as finished projects (Peck, 2010), there is little doubt that the predominant impulse of India's policy regime is a neoliberalizing rather than developmental one.[2] Of particular interest for this chapter is the fact that this post-1991 policy regime was implemented in the context of the unprecedented democratic mobilization of actors who challenged the caste and class structures of dominance by the party (Congress) that led the reforms

(Hansen, 1999; Jaffrelot, 2003; Yadav, 2004). This chapter argues that the political project of neoliberalization was attempted by two contending parties whose policies increasingly converged, albeit through different pathways, in the face of democratic mobilization and whose tactics in the face of democratic mobilization constitute an essential part of the explanation for this neoliberal turn.

India's market transition is viewed as a paradigmatic case of similar transitions in mixed or socialist economies, and given its timing, the emergence of "neoliberalism as doxa" (Chopra, 2003) has been widely attributed to the seismic global ideological shifts and crisis of state-led development during the 1970s. The Indian transition offers a useful corrective to this assumption for several reasons. First, as this chapter shows, the institutionalization of neoliberal policies cannot be understood without a focus on the domestic political struggles that began during the Emergency period (1975–1977). The Emergency was a brief and somewhat unsuccessful authoritarian attempt to suppress popular mobilization in the context of an economic crisis that had brought about large-scale food scarcities, growing unemployment, and a leadership crisis within the ruling Congress Party. The failure (or abandonment) of this interlude paved the way for a broader transformation of the political sphere during which the self-mobilization of lower castes and classes succeeded in breaking apart Congress Party hegemony and clientelist politics dominated by the upper castes and state elite (see Corbridge & Harriss, 2000; Hasan, 2002). This chapter shows how this "second democratic upsurge" (Yadav, 2004) that broke apart the nexus between Congress dominance and socialist ideology, had the unintentional consequence of simultaneously paving the way for social forces seeking to implement a neoliberal project. Indeed, the Congress-led state had begun a hesitant liberalization of the economy and accompanying political restructuring during the Emergency in response to the threat posed by mass movements among middle and working classes, and a domestic economic crisis. Yet, at that stage liberalization could only proceed hesitantly, because the regime's legitimacy was codified on the basis of Nehruvian socialism rather than market capitalism. This consensus was so firm that the pro-liberalization faction of the Congress Party in fact found itself in a minority. It is therefore useful to examine how this regime was ideologically dismantled and a new intra- and interparty consensus constructed. Additionally, attention to domestic struggles offers us an important perspective on the tenuous and contested nature of this neoliberal project. Rather than employing the metaphor of a "sweep" (see Harvey, 2007, p. 2)[3] neoliberalism should in fact be considered a slow and cautious project that encounters unexpected resistance to which states must continually adapt even as they seek to advance this project[4] (see also Peck, 2010; Brenner & Theodore, 2002).

The substantive argument of this chapter is that the gradual legitimization of the market transition initiated during the 1970s involved a protracted process of popular struggle against Congress Party dominance, which arguably rendered the political field the most fluid and open it had been since independence. One particular actor and participant in the mass mobilizations of the 1970s, namely the core party of the broadly constituted Hindu Right (first known as the Jan Sangh, then the BJP), drew on its superior organizational strength and seized the opportunity to become the most powerful opposition to the dominant Congress Party by the early 1990s. The form of political articulation carried out by the Hindu Right involved not only a strong ideological challenge to Nehruvian socialism, but the transformation of a culturally embedded rhetoric of self-sufficiency (*swadeshi*) and Gandhian socialism toward a pro-market ideology. How this transformation was effected forms the crux of the analysis presented in this chapter.

Drawing attention to the role of the Hindu Right in this way contradicts the argument that neoliberal reforms were pushed through by elites because mass politics was "preoccupied" with identity issues, among which lower caste assertion and Hindu revivalism are the most commonly cited (Varhsney, 2000). While "elite" politics of economic reform and policy are conducted in a different sphere from the rough and tumble of mass politics, the democratic upsurge that began during the 1980s and continued through the 1990s made such a separation, once de rigeur under Congress rule, in fact rather difficult. All parties turned increasingly toward populism, seeking electoral majorities in an increasingly competitive field. In tracing the complex process through which the Hindu Right gained ascendancy under these circumstances, the chapter argues that its success in forging a broader neoliberal consensus (that moved beyond the high elite and rarefied circles of the state and intelligentsia) cannot be understood outside its participation in these ongoing political struggles. The aim of the Hindu Right from the 1980s onward was to expand its electoral majority and construct a political project that promised order and the restoration of dominance to its constituency of the upper caste, urban middle classes. The contingent success of its ideology and political practices was owed, this chapter argues, in part also to the vacillating stance of the Congress-led regime on liberalization and its relationship to the legacy of Nehruvian socialism – a legacy that the BJP tried to create a break from. This substantive analysis suggests, then, that neoliberalism has to be understood as more than an elite or technocratic project imposed "from above." It argues that "political articulation," defined as the process by which parties integrate "disparate interests and identities into coherent sociopolitical blocs" (De Leon, Desai, & Tugal, 2009, p. 195) is equally critical to understanding how neoliberal ideas and practices come to be embedded, thwarted, and/or redefined. The concept of political articulation captures the active work required to construct such a consensus, often known as "hegemony" in the Gramscian sense. This work involves more than a mere reflection of ongoing political struggles; rather, it captures the process by which cleavages are named and defined, the alliances between different sectors that are drawn, and the manner in which the field of the conflict itself is defined. In conceptual terms a focus on articulation brings neoliberalism squarely into the political field rather than treating it as a matter of state policy (as the narrow term "economic reforms" implies), and allows us to trace how interests and identities are constructed, not merely reflected, in the making of this contingent and incomplete project.

IMPLEMENTING NEOLIBERALISM: EXISTING APPROACHES

Broadly considered, the literature on neoliberalism outlines two distinct mechanisms accounting for its institutionalization. The first is a "top-down" approach that characterizes elites – intellectuals, technocrats, global institutions such as the IMF and domestic and international capitalists – as the primary agents of neoliberal ideas and policies (Babb, 2001; Babb & Fourcade-Gourinchas, 2002; Campbell & Pederson, 2001; Prasad, 2006). While some scholars have paid less attention to the domestic context in which these agents have to embed their ideas, for "new institutionalists," the ideas and policies pursued by these agents gain traction only when the domestic balance of forces is favorable.[5] For example, Babb and Fourcade-Gourinchas (2002) argue that where working classes have been relatively strong, states have employed what they call an "ideological" neoliberal intervention to circumvent this institutional balance of power. Conversely, where working class movements have been relatively weak and/or there has been institutional consensus on the role of the technocracy, the pathway has been "technocratic," led by strong interventionist states (*ibid.*). Although new institutionalists hold that domestic institutions are key to explaining how neoliberalism is instituted, the dominant mechanism in their explanations is nevertheless "top-down" insofar as their theoretical frameworks do not problematize the question of how mass parties balance the demands of electoral majorities and neoliberal policies.

A second theoretical framework pays closer attention to the political struggles through which neoliberalism is instituted by focusing on the relationships between sections of capital, labor, and agrarian classes (some examples of a wide literature include Bardhan, 1999; Chibber, 2003; Evans, 1995; Kohli, 2004, 2006a, 2006b; Weiss, 1998). The relative balance of forces among these classes is seen as being reflected in the state's policy orientation such as "developmentalism" or "neoliberalism." Certainly, there is considerable variation among these perspectives. Some theorists adopt a more Weberian approach to the state, and examine state cohesion and autonomy as distinct and key variables in their explanations (Evans, 1995; Kohli, 2004), while others focus more on the balance of class power and the ability of the state to mediate these relations (Chibber, 2003). Although these explanations will be considered in greater detail in the discussion of the Indian case it is worth emphasizing that several neo-Marxist and neo-Weberian theorists emphasize *both* top-down and bottom-up mechanisms in their explanatory frameworks.

In the substantive theory of Indian neoliberalism developed in this chapter I will argue that while both theoretical frameworks have something important to offer, their explanations could be made more robust by the inclusion of the role of parties in articulating social blocs in support of neoliberal policies. Although this contention is developed through the analysis of a historical sequence in a single case, methodologically such an approach can be invaluable in putting established theories to the test (Abbott, 1988, 1992; Ragin, 1992). By analyzing a historical sequence that is often underappreciated in explanations of Indian neoliberalization, I argue for a greater focus on the role of political parties in embedding neoliberalism in mobilized democracies. State-centered theorists subsume the role of parties under the state, by focusing on the question of whether states are withdrawing or facilitating neoliberalism. This, however, leads to a critical neglect of how interparty competition and opposition parties in conjunction with social movements can mobilize popular support, as discussed subsequently in the case of India. Among those emphasizing top-down or bottom-up class struggles, the crucial role of parties in facilitating class formation, redirecting these struggles, and forging cross-class articulations remain relatively under-theorized. This chapter shows that parties can play a critical role in institutionalizing neoliberalism through their ability, at moments of flux and crisis, to forge political blocs that either support a neoliberal turn, or at least disorganize the social forces that may oppose it.

STATE, CLASS, AND NEOLIBERALISM IN INDIA: EXISTING EXPLANATIONS

The dominant explanations of the turn to neoliberal reforms in India hold that the crisis of Nehruvian state planning, including inadequate economic growth began to unravel by the late 1970s, creating a crisis in the dominant coalition of bureaucrats, agrarian and industrial bourgeoisie underpinning the "license-permit raj" (Bardhan, 1999). Pursuing a version of rational choice Marxism, Bardhan's explanation focuses on how each of these class actors had pursued their own interests within the larger state planning complex, seeking tax, credit, and other subsidies. This entirely rational but narrow pursuit of self-interest had the collective effect of draining the state of crucial fiscal resources needed to build investments and carry out the Nehruvian developmental agenda.

The "dominant coalition" thesis is a good example of theories that treat state policies largely as expressions of underlying class interests (see Jenkins, 1999, p. 38). In Bardhan's theory developmentalism was stymied by a dominant coalition of classes pursuing their own interests through the state. Two problems emerge from this when seeking to explain the neoliberal turn of the 1990s: first, such a framework cannot explain the "pro-business" turn of Indian state, instead treating this policy choice as a consequence of the collapse of the preceding alliances (Kohli, 2007). Second, it cannot explain the timing or pace of subsequent neoliberalizing policies because of a somewhat underdeveloped theory of the state. The pro-business orientation of the Indian state is, in fact, a consequence of a longer-term failure of the Indian state to discipline capital (Chibber, 2003) and whose origins have to be sought in the political process by which Nehruvian socialism as a set of ideas and institutions gradually came to be dismantled. Furthermore, greater attention is needed to the sequence of timing, the hesitant moves toward liberalization during the 1970s and 1980s, and its acceleration during the 1990s. As Kohli (1987, p. 242) notes: "[o]veremphasis on the role of those who benefit – social groups or classes – at the expense of those who make policies – state authorities – creates a serious methodological problem: how does one explain short-term policy changes in view of the fact that the class structure of a society alters only over the long term?"

Instead of Bardhan's rational choice institutionalist theory of reforms, Kohli (2007) offers a "state autonomy" explanation of the "slow but steady embrace of Indian capital as the main ruling ally" after the economic crisis of the 1970s. His argument is that as the economic crisis preceding the Emergency period deepened, the Indian state pursued a vigorous pro-business and antilabor strategy, singling out economic growth rather than equity as its primary goal. Then Prime Minister Indira Gandhi staffed committees with pro-business bureaucrats, facilitating a "remarkable convergence of views between the government and Indian big business," namely, that the key barriers to growth were the inefficient public sector, labor activism, lack of sufficient government support for business and weak infrastructure (*ibid.*, p. 96).[6] In adopting this stance, he argues, Indira Gandhi tried to forge a distinctly anti-redistribution regime and pull away from its prevalent socialist orientation. For a popularly elected party, however, this created the dilemma of "how to win the support of the majority, which is poor or near-poor, as the rhetoric of socialism and *garibi hatao* (abolish poverty) are being put aside" (*ibid.*, p. 100). This is a crucial question. Kohli's argument is that Indira Gandhi cynically employed ethnic populism to legitimize her increasing withdrawal of socialist language and policies in a largely poor country. As he puts it: "Indira Gandhi's flirtation with ethnic politics in this period, especially Hindu chauvinism and interfering with Sikh politics, marked the new political economy ..." (*ibid.*). This, however, raises the inevitable question of why political techniques should have taken the form of ethnic populism during this period – a question Kohli leaves largely unanswered.

The clearest link between neoliberal reforms and mass (identity) politics is put forward by Varshney (2000) who argues that it is *precisely* the rise of ethnic conflict between Hindus and Muslims during the 1990s, and the mass politics of caste reservations that allowed political parties to push through economic reforms. For, in his view, these issues dominated the attention of voters and gave reformers a "niche" to push through measures "that might otherwise generate considerable political resistance" (*ibid.*, p. 229). Issues that touched upon ascriptive identities such as religion or caste were of much greater interest to the masses compared with, say, capital markets or trade policy – in his words, the "political logic induced by explosions of communal passions gave the reformers room to push for reforms" (*ibid.*, p. 225).[7] It is thus that initial reforms were pushed through under the minority government of the Congress Party led by Narasimha Rao in 1991; notably these policies did not directly touch upon mass interests such as labor market reforms, privatization of land, and wages and price reforms that were left until later. Since 1991 governments have, in fact, been slow to implement such reforms for fear of losing elections.

Varshney is right to suggest that the two critical arenas of political activity – one elite (reforms), the other mass (identity politics) – although seemingly apart, are in fact related.[8] But how are they connected? It is stretching the point rather too far to suggest that the masses are *more* interested in ethnicity or religion than privatization, inequality, unemployment or shifting conditions of employment – all of which are consequences of the neoliberal policies that were undertaken. Indeed, while the finer points of economic policy debated in English language newspapers and elite forums are inaccessible to the masses, reforms can be grasped in terms of employment opportunities, potential sources of capital for entrepreneurship, avenues for upward mobility and not least the withdrawal of state subsidies, welfare programs and other antipoverty programs.[9] Rather than assume that the essential interest of the Indian masses lies in primordial and ascriptive identity politics, the approach of this chapter is to view such political expressions as products of political articulations. In other words, how individuals identify their interests, and which political identities become salient at particular historical moments are the product of their mobilization in specific political projects (on this see De Leon et al., 2009). Concretely, this means that the turn to ethnicized politics during the 1980s and 1990s has to be explained not simply by referring to an ubiquitous feature of Hindu or casteist identity concerns, but as a component of broader political strategies led by different parties.

EXPLAINING THE INDIAN CASE

The adoption of a historical perspective in this chapter, taking the timeline back to the Emergency (1975–1977) rather than the beginning of major reforms in 1991, is necessary to grasp the political work necessary to embed neoliberalism as a policy orientation in Indian democracy. During this period there was a spike in popular protest against food scarcity and rising prices, and a rise in levels of organization and action among the industrial working classes. Under similar conditions in Britain and Chile, Babb and Fourcade-Gourinchas (2002) argue, the state pursued an "ideological intervention" from above in order to push through neoliberal reforms.[10] Clearly, Indira Gandhi's attempts to staff her bureaucracies with "pro-business" people and the growth in influence of pro-market intelligentsia in her administration point toward such an attempt. However, it is unclear whether the working classes posed such an obstacle to implementing neoliberal reforms – in comparison to Britain and Chile the industrial working classes in India have had historically lower levels of political power. This is partly because of numerical weakness – organized workers have constituted a small minority of the total population of Indian workers (no more than 3–5%). Over time this influence has further subsided – trade union density in India (the percentage of the nonagricultural labor force organized into unions) showed a drop from 6.6% in 1980 to 5.4% in 1994 (ILO Labour Statistics Database, 1997; Fig. 1).[11] Despite the spike in organizing activity before the Emergency, the Emergency-era repression of strikes and union organization further reduced the threat posed by the organized working classes; consequently, a sharp decline in the organizational strength and militancy of workers in the formal sectors has been evident since the late 1970s (see Fig. 1).

Indeed, the crucial point is that despite some initial pro-market reforms, the Indian state pursued the reform agenda very cautiously through the late 1970s and 1980s. Given the relatively low and declining levels of working class organization during this period, an explanation of the initial caution followed by a more decisive stance in 1991, would have to look at additional

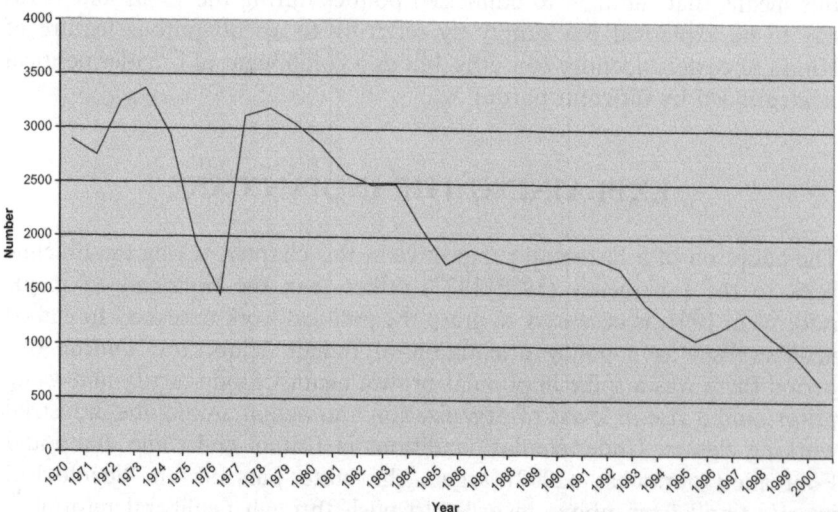

Fig. 1. Strikes and Lockouts in India, 1970–2000. *Source*: Data from ILO Labour Statistics Database (1997). Copyright © International Labour Organization (ILO Department of Statistics, http://laborsta.ilo.org/).

factors. Certainly, there is evidence that workers in the banking, insurance, and manufacturing sectors, and some bureaucrats and small businesses opposed to deregulation and increased competition, were able to exercise pressure on the pace of reforms on privatization of public sector units (PSUs), privatization of insurance sectors, and trade liberalization for example (Uba, 2008). Resistance by workers in these industries certainly accounts for some of the hesitation and relatively weak liberalization efforts of the Indian state in these sectors of the economy (Sachs et al., 1999). But given the longer-term decline of the political power of the working classes, it is unclear whether it can be seen as a sufficient source of resistance to the neoliberal policy orientation of the state.

To explain this neoliberal orientation Chibber (2003) takes a long historical perspective, locating the abandonment of developmentalism in the inability of the Nehruvian state (of the 1960s) to stem increasingly aggressive demands on the part of capitalists to dismantle the regulatory regime of state controls on private investment. The weakness of the state, he argues, opened the way to a neoliberal resolution in the face of periodic economic crises such as the 1991 balance of payments crisis and fiscal deficit. Indeed, this argument is entirely consistent with the earlier observation about the declining power of the working classes, whose inability to exercise influence on the direction of economic policy further eroded the state's disciplinary capacity. This argument posits India's neoliberal policy regime as a product of capitalist class organization working through a weak state, suggesting that the crucial mechanisms driving India's neoliberalization are the "hidden" means by which capital has sought influence on state policy.[12]

Without minimizing the importance of stealth and secrecy on the part of capitalist classes to push through difficult neoliberal reforms (see Sassen, 2006), this chapter seeks to sharpen our conceptualization of the mechanisms that are employed in the democratic sphere where popular mobilization can threaten the viability of reforms. Focusing on stealth does not take into sufficient account the arena of competitive party democracy within which parties win ascendancy and capture state power. Between the capitalist class and the organized, but small proportion of workers, lie the middle classes and assorted subaltern sectors who, as I subsequently argue, can play a decisive role in determining the character of the state and its policies. Under these conditions what capitalists can win is tempered by mass politics, just as mass politics can become the site for gradually embedding the legitimacy of reforms. This point will become particularly evident when we examine the Emergency period during which mass movements that pitted themselves against the Congress-led state proved unable to discipline the state's growing neoliberal orientation, and were tapped by the BJP to articulate mass opposition to Nehruvian socialism.

INDIA, 1975–1977: CRISIS AND "THE EMERGENCY" AS SOLUTION

The Emergency in India constituted a "turning point" for the rise of a new political economy in part as it opened the political field to new and previously marginal actors seeking to dismantle the Congress hold on political institutions. Not least, the Hindu Right gained its first real political opportunity during the growing protests against Congress rule, and the uncertainty surrounding the fate of the party.[13] Writing in 1976, an observer described the situation in India thus: "in the last two to three years an appalling situation came to prevail, a situation of utter laxity, alarming flabbiness, near complete erosion of the ethos of work and impermissible disregard for the financial disciplines necessary for a country like India" (Dutt, 1976, p. 1125). In 1975, Indira Gandhi, the prime minister of India and leader of the ruling Congress Party, had declared Emergency Rule in the wake of spreading protests across the country, a growing economic crisis, and internal party opposition to her leadership. Growing social violence and popular mobilization against price increases in the western state of Gujarat and northeastern state of Bihar, including the famous railways workers' strike of 1974, threatened to bring about the collapse of the government.

The protests against the "corrupt" state were led by a veteran of the anticolonial movement and Gandhian leader, Jayaprakash Narayan, whose aim was to bring the country to a standstill through strikes, demonstrations, and violent disruptions (henceforth referred to as the JP movement) (Chandra, 2003). The Emergency executive order resulted in the detention of thousands of opposition members and activists. A gag order on the press and a widespread culture of fear and secrecy accompanied campaigns to clear urban slums and sterilize large numbers of poor and lower middle class males (Prashad, 1996; Selbourne, 1977; Tarlo, 2003). Strikes among railway workers and employees of the public sector Indian Airlines and Life Insurance Corporation were swiftly repressed. The wider intention of these campaigns was to stem the crisis in India by purging the nation of its perceived excesses – of population, urban poverty, and strikes and demonstrations; in Indira Gandhi's words they were necessary to "bring ... discipline and order back to Indian society." To this end a range of repressive legislations and new bodies with extrajudicial power were deployed to suppress the growth of popular opposition to the government. These included (1) the erosion of state-level government powers and a shift to the executive, including the appropriation of city-level governance from popular control; (2) laws such as Maintenance of Internal Security Act (MISA) allowing the police to search and detain suspects without producing evidence in a court, and (3) the authorization and expansion of bodies accountable only to the executive such as the Research and Action Wing (RAW), Central Reserve Police Force (CRPF), and the Border Security Force (BSF) (Wiener, 1976, p. 898).

The perception of a crisis was widely acknowledged by those to the left and right of the Congress Party, which may partly account for the initial absence of serious opposition to the Emergency. The two communist parties (CPI and CPM) did not participate in the JP movement and likewise their affiliated trade unions did not join the movement; the CPI, however, supported the Emergency as a necessary step to curb illegal hoarding and corruption (Hewitt, 2008). Initially the stated aim of the Emergency was to defend Nehruvian socialism, not to promote the market or favor capital. Indira Gandhi, in fact, argued that opposition to her policies had emerged primarily from the "privileged" (Palmer, 1977, p. 161). These included the "organized workers" who lacked discipline and the "urban educated" who she described as "anti-democratic."[14]

Unlike authoritarian regimes such as that of Pinochet, however, Indira Gandhi sought to appropriate the language of democracy from the opposition, and redefine the state as the protector of democratic rights against a "fascistic" opposition. She defined democracy as "political order" in the face of antidemocratic or fascistic disruption. In a speech to the Parliament on July 22, 1975, Gandhi stated that "political liberty and political rights can only exist so long as political order remains... every right that the State concedes to the individual imposes an obligation on them" (Ministry of Information and Broadcasting, 1981, p. 33). To Gandhi democracy was under immediate threat from these mobilizations. Thus, her private secretary P.N. Dhar stated in a private communication to the U.S. Deputy Assistant Secretary that while the Emergency was in part motivated by the court case against Mrs. Gandhi, the underlying reason for it was that "the Indian governmental system had ceased to be a problem-solving one," and was increasingly held hostage by disruptive labor and individual politicians.[15] He drew a comparison with Britain as similarly besieged by strikes and sabotage; India was in need of a radical solution similar to that led by Thatcher. Nevertheless, just as Indira Gandhi did not make overt references to private property, the "sign" of democracy was central to her justification for the Emergency. In her view, democracy referred to "participation by the 'people'," yet it was also to be "disciplined and orderly."[16] As she stated: "there is only one magic which can remove poverty, and that is hard work sustained by clear vision, iron will, and the strictest discipline ..." (*ibid.*, p. 5). In her speech broadcast to the All India Radio on July 1, 1975, the key words were "land reforms," "ceiling law implementation," "ownership rights for landless laborers," "dealing with speculation in land," "socialization of urban and urbanizable land." Each term represents an attempt to *resist* the imperative of privatization.

A striking aspect of this historical moment was that the actors arrayed in opposition to each other – the broad church of the JP movement and the Congress-led government – voiced their point of view through the language of socialism, with no expressed intentions of dismantling its mandate. The Emergency 20-Point plan declared by Indira Gandhi, in fact, reabsorbed many of the demands of the JP movement, including the liquidation of rural debt, extension of credit to small farmers and rural artisans, abolition of bonded labor, raising minimum wages for agricultural labor, house sites for landless laborers and a host of concessions to students and middle income groups (Chandra, 2003, p. 176). Given that Indira Gandhi wanted to switch the economy onto a different track and create a more disciplined social base, this rhetoric was predictably unstable. She simultaneously began to make explicit references to the need to increase private sector participation in the economy, arguing that "daring ventures" were necessary for growth.[17] Thus despite the expressly socialist avowals of this period, and a turn for the better in economic growth and stability as a result of Emergency-era discipline (Kohli, 2006a, 2006b), the 1980s eventually began to see an intensification of market ideology and practices. To a large extent it was Indira Gandhi who, while professing socialism, created a greater role for the private sector by reducing state-imposed controls, tariffs, and reforming laws such as FERA (Foreign Exchange Regulation Act) (Chandra, 2003, p. 225). Her regime thus tottered on a series of mixed signs and messages, and there is little evidence to suggest that a coherent ideology of neoliberalism had found an anchor in India during the 1970s or even during the 1980s.[18] Instead, at this turning point there was simply a shift in the political field that began to erode the legitimacy of Nehruvian socialism and open up new political possibilities.

NEW POLITICAL ARTICULATIONS: CODING THE EROSION OF STATE LEGITIMACY

The growth of political possibilities during the 1980s were intimately related to a general decline in the legitimacy of parliamentary politics and institutions. The Emergency played a large part in contributing to a growing cynicism of institutional politics (Hewitt, 2008; Kapur & Mehta, 2006; Palmer, 1977).[19] But deinstitutionalization was also a product of the fact both the Congress Party and emerging social movements increasingly employed extra-parliamentary tactics of struggle, with the latter drawing on repertoires of protest from the anticolonial movement, including total strikes (*bandhs*), stopping road traffic (*rasta roko*), and civil disobedience, explicitly denouncing the Parliament as an instrument of oppression (Hansen, 1999, p. 141). Indira Gandhi also used the Emergency as a way of seizing control of decision-making to the executive, and by relying on a small coterie of loyal politicians and unelected leaders such as her son Sanjay Gandhi, encouraged the rise of personalistic and arbitrary power within the party and the growth of new zones of power such as the Youth Congress (Hewitt, 2008).

In the context of deinstitutionalization, the Congress regime initiated a series of shifts in their strategy of rule that directly courted the middle classes. Among the crucial shifts were (1) penalization of culprit groups from the poor or lower middle classes, represented in the male sterilization and slum removal campaigns in urban areas, (2) various forms of tax relief and incipient liberalization, and (3) moving rhetorical and policy emphasis from *garibi hatao* (or "remove poverty") toward a politics of rural clientelism and patrimonialism. The first two shifts represented a strategy to shape an urban, middle class constituency, and were owed in no small part to her son Sanjay Gandhi, who took personal responsibility for the slum clearance and sterilization campaigns (Mehta, 1978; Selbourne, 1977; Tarlo, 2003). His influence on Congress politics was brief but nevertheless critical in pushing forward a "pro-American" and anti-Soviet vision within the Congress Party (Prashad, 1996; Selbourne, 1977). While this influence should not be exaggerated, it is evident that he represented a small, yet influential opinion on the necessity for a pro-liberalization policy, and the necessity of using any means to "clean up" Indian society (Selbourne, 1977). It was a concept of politics that sought to bypass the state and take direct action; liberalization was understood as an aspect of this conception of "getting things done" without bureaucratic red-tapism.

While the first two aspects of Congress Party strategy were largely urban, the third shift in their strategy of addressing the crisis aimed at courting the allegiance of newly ascendant farmers, a product of the Green Revolution launched during the 1960s. According to Nayar (2001, p. 115) both the urban middle classes and rich farmers had become "alienated from the public sector" because of its perceived failure to perform and because it was seen as the source of the economic crisis, one that drew on high taxes from these two classes. The attempt to court both these classes was linked to a broader strategy of promoting growth – as the Minister of Finance in 1976–1977, C. Subramanyam stated, "let us also remind ourselves that the problems of poverty in our country cannot be solved by merely holding the price line. We can meet them only through growth. A rapidly growing economy is the best insurance against perpetuation of poverty; *indeed, it is the only solution* (my emphasis)."[20] The budgets of 1975–1976 and 1976–1977 reveal the variety of measures aimed at stimulating growth: these included a greater emphasis on the interests of middle peasants, such as reducing prices of fertilizers, emphasis on technology, credit, and high-yielding variety seeds.[21]

The Congress-led reforms of the Emergency period clearly demonstrated a shift in emphasis from the poorest sectors to sections of the middle classes. A strict categorization of "middle class" is an enormously difficult task in a country beset with class heterogeneity; however, scholars in India have tended to include in this overall category the "petty bourgeoisie," namely small businessmen and traders, as well as white collar employees, middle tanks of professionals and civil services, and the rich peasants or farmers (Corbridge & Harriss, 2000, p. 123). The role of these classes or sectors in forging or preventing a developmentalist path has generally been neglected in theories of "development," which tend to focus on the extremes of the social structure. Diane Davis (2004) has argued that salaried employees, small producers, farmers, petty bourgeoisie, and shopkeepers potentially play a key role by disciplining the excesses of capital and labor. A precondition for the middle classes' disciplinary role, Davis (2004, p. 23) argues, is its political independence from the upper and working classes; where they are absent or politically weak, states are less likely to impose discipline and more likely to accommodate the demands of rent-seeking and short-term profit maximization (they become "accommodating regimes"). On the other hand where they are politically independent, for example, in South Korea, the rural middle classes have formed the basis of an accumulation strategy.[22]

In India, conversely, it is possible to locate the turn *away* from a developmentalist logic after the Emergency period, and a strategy of "accommodation" that granted the urban and rural middle classes the possibility of joining the developing ascendancy of the agrarian and urban bourgeoisie (Rudolph & Rudolph, 1987). This involved the removal of the disciplinary restraints that accompanied the middle classes' identification with Nehruvian developmentalism. As one author argued: "[a] new category had arisen in India – ... the *nouveau* capitalists – concerned not merely with keeping a party in office for its own sake but also because they and that party had developed a symbiotic relationship with one another. Sanjay Gandhi, [Indira Gandhi's son and protagonist of the worst Emergency-era excesses] became their 'man' in Mrs. Gandhi's regime because he grasped their importance as a force to be reckoned with, a new political resource essential to the maintenance of the party and to a government preoccupied with regional hegemony and building the military-industrial complex ..." (Gould, 1986, p. 637). A strategy of "accommodation" between the middle classes and bourgeoisie was thus initiated and pursued by the Congress Party-led state, as growing middle class resentment against inflation, shortages, and a widely perceived failure of the state revealed the limits of the prevalent political economy. The Congress government, interpreted the growth in protests among the middle classes as evidence of its disillusionment with socialist policies, and therefore as a mandate to privatize and liberalize the economy (Nayar, 2001, p. 115). Among the enticements of deregulation and liberalization was the consumer revolution that began during the 1970s and accelerated during the 1980s, bringing cars, gadgets, computers, and a variety of luxury goods not just to the urban middle classes, but to prosperous rural groups as well (Hansen, 1999, p. 139).

While the urban middle classes, in particular, began to develop a material stake in the incipient reforms, it is not clear that the middle classes as a whole adopted an unambiguous pro-liberalization stance. As I go on to show, the JP movement attracted many of them precisely because it revived rather than discarded the Gandhian legacy of self-sufficiency, anticorruption, and even anti-westernization. The space occupied by the middle classes was ideologically conflicted and newer identities of globalized aspirations as yet incipient. This was the classic terrain for the growth of a populist movement or party. As theorists of populism have argued, a core feature of this form of politics is the appeal of new or previously marginal actors who articulate broad-based discontent with the status quo, and who promise a cleansing of the corruption and impurities of politics-as-usual (Laclau, 2005; Roberts, 2002, 2007). Populism is also inherently ambiguous as it eschews the traditional polarities of left vs right, which explains its ability to attach to a variety of political ideologies (Panizza, 2005). The JP movement gained its popularity during a period of growing uncertainty, when state-led liberalization appealed to a section of the middle classes, yet politically and ideologically the prevalence of socialist affiliations, the critique of political corruption and the perception of crisis contributed to the appeal of populist ideas and repertoires of protest.

In the second part of this chapter I discuss how the JP movement tapped this populist potential, yet also unintentionally served as an incubator for the growth of an electorally viable national Hindu Right. Hindu nationalists played a critical role in coding the mass mobilizations to create a growing discursive break with socialism, and normalizing the turn to market ideology through the language of "people's struggle." This discourse seized on the ambiguities of the Congress-led state's discourse, allowing the Hindu Right to expose the contradictions and fallacies of Congress socialism, and redefine a form of communitarianism from the detritus of failed socialism. In doing so the Hindu Right did not merely reflect an underlying coherent middle class interest – it played a critical role in shaping it.

CODING DISSENT: JP MOVEMENT AND THE HINDU RIGHT

Much like the popular anti-regime protests in Iran, Egypt, South Korea, and parts of southeast Asia during the 1970s, the social base of the JP movement was largely the rural and urban "middle" sectors-students, lawyers, urban professionals, peasants, and intellectuals, rather than the poor. Many of these participants were strongly opposed to Indira Gandhi's pro-capitalist turn, and have remained fiercely critical of neoliberalism since then. The charismatic leadership of J. P. Narayan in the context of the widely felt dissatisfaction with Indira Gandhi's cronyism and the Emergency-era excesses proved a significant force among these sectors. His main argument was that corruption and inequality had perverted the search for socialist justice, and that a return to the ideals of decentralization and nonviolent Gandhian principles ("total revolution") was the necessary antidote. This revolution, in his view, would dismantle the state and replace it with people's committees who would implement a radically new system of democracy.

Yet, if the Emergency had failed as a strategy of addressing the crisis "from above" then the JP movement as a "middle sector" movement failed, at least in terms of its own professed aims (Chandra, 2003; Chandhoke, 2000; Dhar, 2000). First, the movement had clear organizational limitations because its leadership explicitly rejected the party form as a vehicle for radical change.

This meant that when J. P. Narayan sought to expand the movement at an opportune time he was forced to rely overwhelmingly upon the superior organizational capacities of the Hindu Right party known as the Jan Sangh.[23] This had specific consequences for the ascendancy of the Hindu Right, a point that I discuss below. A second point, however, is that this reliance not only had ideological consequences, but limited the movement's growth beyond the northern states where the Hindu Right had a more entrenched social base during the 1970s – in the southern, western, and eastern states the weakness of the Jan Sangh, and two other regional northern parties upon whom J. P. Narayan relied, left the movement weak (Chandra, 2003, p. 105).

The organizational weakness and ideologically nebulous character of the JP movement might lead us to believe that it was a historical relic. Yet despite its limitations, I argue that the movement is of crucial significance because it left in its aftermath a fragmented democratic terrain from which two key elements emerged as significant. These were the Hindu Right (made up of the Jan Sangh and assorted associations), and Socialists who formed a temporary and strategic alliance under the Janata Party and constituted the main opposition to the Congress Party during the 1980s. Their social bases were different – the Socialists drew support from the agrarian small holders and lower middle castes, while the Hindu nationalists were primarily based among the urban petty bourgeoisie and an upper caste rural and urban constituency. In a complicated series of twists and turns, in 1980 the JP movement split into its two contradictory components, each leading movements that broke apart the dominance of the Congress Party and shattered the Nehruvian consensus.[24]

A key political opportunity for the Hindu Right arose in 1977 when Indira Gandhi abruptly decided to end the Emergency and in a serious miscalculation of its prospects, decided to call for elections. As a result, the Congress Party was defeated by the Janata Party, which then formed the government. Beneath this apparent victory, it was the Hindu Right that dominated the ideological debates of this period; the socialists, as Jaffrelot (2003) argues, were stricken by factionalism and incessant internal disagreements. It was therefore the Hindu Right that eventually seized the opportunity created by the electoral victory of the Janata Party in 1977, taking advantage of the political fragmentation and ideological disorientation of the socialists to attempt to become a "truly national alternative." This was an extraordinary feat for a party viewed with suspicion by the political establishment because of its associations with the RSS, which was widely held responsible for the assassination of Mahatma Gandhi in 1948.

Referring to this crucial political opportunity, L. K. Advani, then a participant in the JP movement and future leader of the Bharatiya Janata Party (BJP), noted:

> The biggest contribution made towards removing Jan Sangh's stigma of political untouchability was made by Jayaprakash Narayan. Repeatedly he was confronted with situations where Jan Sangh's participation in his movement seemed to provide an excuse for someone else to keep out. He could have one or the other, but he couldn't have both, he was told. And he made the choice unhesitatingly (Advani, 1979, p. 76).

The ideologically more extreme and secretive Rashtriya Swayamsevak Sangh (RSS), although abstaining from direct participation in the Janata Party, played a significant role in pushing the Hindu nationalists to prominence during the JP movement and after. Its front party, the Jan Sangh, almost entirely organized the anti-price rise riots in Gujarat (western India) during the 1970s, and seized control of the student movement.

As the dominant political tendency to emerge from the mass mobilizations of the 1970s, the Jan Sangh (and then the BJP which emerged from the Jan Sangh in 1980) played a key role in framing a powerful oppositional discourse to Nehruvian socialism and in evolving a "commonsense" about the moral bankruptcy of the Congress-led state, socialist planning, and communist party-led organized labor. First, the Jan Sangh framed its political discourse in terms of tapping into a revolutionary people's movement, with talk of "direct action" and "people's power." As Jan Sangh leader Nanaji Deshmukh asserted: "It is people's power in action ... [we] cannot keep away from such an upsurge of the masses."[25] This insurgent rhetoric was a key part of the attempt to take leadership of a movement that sought to discredit the state as the carrier of a covertly authoritarian project. The leader of the Jan Sangh and future prime minister of India, A. B. Vajpayee, denounced Parliament as a tool of the ruling elite, arguing that parliamentary activities had limited scope, and was "no longer a tool to bring about radical socioeconomic change,"[26] The parliamentary "technique" should be used to "expose the government," they argued, while "militant mass mobilization" would assert the "people's will and power."[27]

The rapid political ascendancy of the Hindu Right during the late 1970s and early 1980s (as Jan Sangh and then BJP) was both a consequence of its participation in the antistate struggles of this period, as well as crucially, its distinctive organizational capacity. The use of the party form, in particular, marked it as distinct from the other assorted associations and political currents within the JP movement, as did the discipline and cohesion exhibited by its leadership. In 1980 the Jan Sangh expressed dissatisfaction with the coalition it had entered into with the Socialists under the Janata Party, arguing that the party had weakened itself by "opening its doors to anyone who opposed the Emergency."[28] Such a "flabby" party, they feared, would be quickly opposed by a "militant communist movement," in which case the country would be "left to choose between those left, lefter, and leftist, a wholly unnatural arrangement in a country basically moderate and middle of the road."[29]

Mirroring the ruling party's reluctance to make a public break with the language of socialism, in the realms of popular mobilization the Hindu Right also continued to make its claims under the broader frame of socialism. An editorial in the Jan Sangh newspaper, the *Organizer*, named the government and big business as the enemies of socialism.[30] They advocated a strict policy of *swadeshi* or self-reliance (developed first by Gandhi during the anticolonial movement), opposing foreign investment and imports in general (Hansen, 1999, p. 130). Much like comparable nationalist or right-wing populisms, however, the Hindu Right was equally a bitter critic of organized labor and the communists who they regarded as a threat to order and stability. This effort to forge a "middle of the road" discourse thus sought to remove the right-left distinction from politics altogether. Instead, Gandhian "trusteeship," they argued, was the "middle way" between capitalism and socialism, fitting the Janata government's policy of decentralization of the economy.[31] This was very similar to the statement of the extra-parliamentary wing of the Hindu Right (RSS), that it was "neither capitalist nor socialist ... neither pro-business, nor pro-labour ... [but] ... only for the Indian masses, and not for any particular ideology."[32]

The employment of this "middle-of-the-road" discourse in fact demonstrated the beginnings of a growing public detachment from a socialist frame by projecting the responsibility for failed socialism onto the Congress Party.[33] "The gist of their public statements showed a particular concern with critiquing the state-ruling party nexus and the putative effects an accelerated liberalization policy would have upon this nexus. A "truly radical" and alternative policy, they argued, would begin by "dismantling the monstrous edifice of licenses and permits through which the politicians and bureaucrats have been lining their pockets."[34] The ability of the Hindu Right to code the dismantling of socialist planning as an act of democratic dissent undoubtedly allowed it to forge itself as a powerful alternative to the Congress Party. By the time the political field had begun to incorporate these new sectors more decisively, in the 1984 state assembly elections the BJP (the former Jan Sangh, which was renamed in 1980) had emerged as a clear front-runner among the opposition parties.

The Congress Party emerged from the wilderness of the Emergency period with Indira Gandhi returning to power in 1980, and by taking advantage of the perceived weaknesses of the Janata Party and a string of political scandals under their administration. Extending liberalization reforms that she had begun during the Emergency period, and then after her assassination in 1984, her son Rajiv Gandhi accelerated the dismantling of state licensing and regulatory structures. Rajiv Gandhi's tenure marked the most decisive break with the language and tradition of socialism, and a broader legitimization of liberalization despite skepticism and protests from public sector workers, bureaucrats, and some party officials. And it was under the Congress Party that market reforms were decisively implemented after a foreign exchange reserves crisis in 1991, breaking finally with the earlier Nehruvian model. The reforms of 1991 have thus been rightly seen as a decisive break with Nehruvian socialism. Yet, as this chapter has argued thus far, the 1991 reforms were undertaken at the end of a longer historical process marked by ever-broadening sociopolitical mobilization. The initial phase of this mobilization during the 1970s and early 1980s, I have argued, was appropriated and coded by the BJP in its quest for hegemony, even while critical opposition to market policies developed through this phase of mobilization. The "second democratic upsurge" of primarily lower castes (also known as Other Backward Castes or OBCs) that occurred during the mid-late 1980s and 1990s, on the other hand, was led in part by the socialists. This upsurge created an interesting paradox: the party (Congress) that put India on a new track to growth was organizationally exhausted and eventually defeated by the challenge of these democratic mobilizations, and only briefly reappeared until its coalition victory in the 2004 (and more recently 2009) elections. To explain the deepening of neoliberalization through this period, we have to continue to look at the political techniques adopted by the BJP which was reacting to the mobilization of lower castes.

CONSOLIDATING NEOLIBERALISM? PARTIES AND MOBILIZATION POST-1991

This section of the chapter focuses on how the BJP consolidated a neoliberal policy line after 1991, bringing itself increasingly into agreement with the Congress Party which had initiated these reforms in the first place. While this convergence could in theory be explained as a product of global ideological shifts and interparty competition, the move from an ideology of national self-sufficiency (*swadeshi*) toward one embracing neoliberal reforms requires explanation. Indeed, although the Congress Party had initiated these reforms in 1991, a significant period of neoliberalization was subsequently led by the BJP which formed the government through coalition with other parties, intermittently between 1996 and 2004. In some areas of policy, crucially the import of consumer goods and trade liberalization the BJP-led governments were far more radical than previous Congress-led governments (Table 1).[35]

Although its primary base among upper castes and the urban middle classes would suggest a clear interest in market reforms, the BJP had to pursue a logic of broad majorities to win elections and emerge as a national alternative. In the context of the democratic mobilizations of this period, the BJP evolved political techniques of articulating broad sectors. Even though this met with varying regional success, it allowed them to build a political bloc that brought them to power for several years. This political project, which was not without its contradictions, involved a populist logic that sought to widen its support among lower castes, OBCs, industrial workers and tribal communities depending on the region concerned. Given the upper caste orientation of the BJP, this would appear highly counterintuitive and yet, it is in these crisscrossing and contradictory alliances that one can locate the populist logic of the BJPs' political articulation project. For example, the BJP's affiliated workers' organization (Bharatiya Mazdoor Sangh, BMS), whose membership is largely drawn from the RSS, now claims the second largest membership of all trade unions.[36] By blending a nationalist appeal with working class interests, the BMS has taken the contradictory position of favoring privatization and liberalization, rejecting class conflict in favor of the "national interest" (Saxena, 1993). Despite this inherent antipathy to adopting a militant stance (the BMS views communism or left ideologies as subservient to the West), its ability to take up the interests of workers through strikes and protests, and to organize welfare for families faced with

Table 1. Major Governments in India, Post-Liberalization.

Congress:	1991–1996
BJP:	May 16–31, 1996
Congress-UF:	1996–1998
BJP-NDA:	March 19–October 23, 1998
BJP-NDA:	October 13, 1999–May 13, 2004
Congress-UPA:	2004–Present

Source: Various.

job losses has enabled it to gather a large membership. A similar effort at articulating different classes through a nationalist frame has been attempted in the realm of caste. Again, this shows important regional differences as I discuss below. In the state of Gujarat and other parts of India such as Orissa, for example, the BJP and affiliated Hindu Right organizations recruit among tribals, former untouchables (*dalits*), and marginalized groups, seeking to bring them into the Hindu fold by creating a network of voluntary and welfare associations in education, health, and child welfare (Yagnik, 2002; Shah, 1998). The incorporation of tribal communities and former untouchables into a high-caste led project is only possible through such political mediation; the incessant indoctrination of these communities is based upon the appeal of defining a new sense of community against an opposition (Muslims and Christians). The promise of equality with other castes is not based on substantive reforms (redistribution of land, income, or generation of employment), but rather the symbolic overture of joining a political community devoted to regional pride and nativist sentiments, wedded together with some welfare programs disseminated through religious charities.[37] The participation of tribals and *dalits* in violence against Muslims and Christians has been well documented, and there is much evidence to suggest that *dalits* (former untouchables) in urban Gujarat, in particular, have been growing increasingly affiliated to Hindutva politics.[38] Voting and pre-poll data in Gujarat, a BJP-led state, shows some of the effects of this articulation, even as it reveals the limits of the BJP's influence among lower castes and classes.

Two points about this table are noteworthy: first, while the caste complexion of the BJP is clearly drawn from the upper strata, among the OBCs who were traditionally discriminated against by the upper castes and were ritually just above the former untouchables, the BJP's support exceeds that of the Congress Party. OBCs had initially supported the Janata Party, whose leader V. P. Singh had attempted to implement a comprehensive affirmative action policy (also known as Mandal reforms) in 1991 while briefly in power. This attempt that included the reservation of government jobs for OBCs, was fiercely contested by the upper castes and all other political parties. The BJP initially supported the Mandal reforms, but ultimately withdrew its support, in line with its upper caste constituency. The resulting inherent contradiction of interests between these two caste groups raises important questions about why sections of the OBCs would support the BJP. This factor can only be attributed to a desire for attaining higher status by virtue of associating with a dominant socio-economic group and its political projects, namely, Hindutva.[39] Among tribals and *dalits*, the

Congress's traditional base has held strong, but the BJP is clearly a force to contend with.[40] The evidence of political articulation across socio-economic strata is even stronger when one looks at voting data by class (Tables 2 and 3) where moving from the "middle" to "lower" classes the BJP share of the vote is either higher or equivalent to the Congress, despite its getting the majority of the upper class vote. In other words, while the BJP appears clearly as a party of the upper caste, higher income groups, its support among those lower down the strata is not insubstantial.

If the Hindu Right acquired a resilient social base in states such as Gujarat, and embedded themselves as a distinct competitive force through alliances with other parties in Maharashtra, Karnataka, Rajasthan, and Madhya Pradesh, they struggled to establish substantial political influence

Table 2. Economic Class and Party Votes in Gujarat.

Economic Class	Votes (%)	
	BJP	Congress
Rich	66	25
Upper middle	61	26
Middle	49	37
Lower	45	41
Poor	41	44

Source: Centre for the Study of Developing Societies (CSDS) pre-poll survey, 2002 (Kumar, 2003, p. 272).

Table 3. Caste and Voting Pattern in Gujarat.

Caste	Votes (%)	
	BJP	Congress
Patidar	82	9
Other upper castes	76	24
Kshatriya	61	38
Koli	57	41
Other OBC	54	39
Adivasi	34	49
Dalit	27	67
Muslim	10	69

Source: CSDS post-poll survey 2002 (Kumar, 2003, p. 275).

in the northern states such as Uttar Pradesh and Bihar. In these northern regions lower and "backward" castes are represented by strong political parties (BSP and SP) that have successfully held back the BJP (Jaffrelot, 1996, 2003). A large number of upper castes had, over the course of the late 1980s and early 1990s, switched support from the Socialists to the BJP because of the former's support for job reservations for lower castes (Corbridge & Harriss, 2000, p. 125). In 1991, the BJP deployed this upper caste backlash to win elections in the crucial state of Uttar Pradesh, but was then defeated in the 1993 and 1996 elections by increasingly assertive lower caste and OBC parties. In the midst of this *intercaste* struggle, the BJP's strategy was to articulate a Hindu political bloc *without* including the lower castes. Its tactics were to take to the streets, neighborhoods, carnivals, and festivals in public spaces, in order to articulate a righteous middle class-upper caste cultural and political backlash. Religious revivalism was used to disseminate political messages, through the increasingly sophisticated use of popular media such as television serials (Ramayana), and the distribution of cassettes with hate speeches directed at Muslims (Basu, Datta, Sarkar, Sarkar, & Sen, 1993; Hansen, 1999; Jaffrelot, 1996; Rajagopal, 2001). A core element of the Hindu Right's mobilizing strategy also involved the use of violence – as an extensive literature has documented, communal riots aimed at Muslims sought to project a feeling of victimhood and injury among middle class Hindus, while projecting an aggressive and masculine image of Hinduism (Basu et al., 1993; Brass, 2003; Hansen, 1999). As survey research has shown, moreover, support for the demolition of a mosque in northern India (Babri Masjid) in 1992 was drawn largely from the urban middle classes – traders, small business people, and white collar workers (Chhibber & Misra, 1993). The employment of violence and intimidation in a series of spectacular events including the destruction of the Babri Masjid and later communal riots and pogroms (such as in Gujarat 2002) was a distinct *reaction* to the democratization of lower castes, rather than a component of this democratization. It was aimed at the restoration of order, discipline and cleanliness to politics against the perceived plebianization generated by the democratic upsurge, and was equally directed in a morally charged campaign against the corruption of Congress rule.

The fused coding of a Hindu nationalist ideology and accompanying practices with a more avowedly neoliberal orientation by the early 1990s was not an automatic transition for the BJP. Rooted in the struggles of the Emergency period, the BJP was, until the early 1990s, proclaiming a nationalist, quasi-socialist rhetoric, and upholding economic sovereignty and non-dependency on the West. This nationalist rhetoric conformed easily with the anti-liberalization stance of sections of the party that were drawn from the militant RSS (non-parliamentary wing of the Hindu Right from which some of the core leadership of the BJP is drawn). The BJP advocated opposition to modern technology and multinational investment, and argued that market reforms were making "the rich richer and the poor poorer."[41] However by the early 1990s it made a decisive discursive break with socialist language and economic nationalism. At its Plenary Session in 1991 the BJP declared that "the time has now come for a thorough review of the planning model ... [it was time] ... to move away from the Nehruvian model of development."[42] Similarly, it declared, "the BJP has consistently asked for abolition of the License-Permit-Quota Raj right since [its] Jan Sangh days," and "we are far too dependent on government for our needs ... the people should be the engine of growth, not the government."[43] The gradual dissolution of its anti-liberalization ideology during the 1990s is certainly a function of having to compete with the Congress Party, and broaden support beyond its traditional base, among whom traders and small businesses stood to lose from the opening of trade policy and deregulation. The dividends of a broader constituency were too big to ignore. The party's share of the vote doubled from 11.5% to 21% in the 1991 elections, and it was now the second largest party in the nation. By 1996, the BJP's rhetoric had joined the dots linking its earlier "people's socialism" to a more neoliberal one – its 1996 election manifesto declared that it would "introduce a system of allowing lateral entry of personnel from the private sector, NGOs, and educational/research institutes into government."[44] Likewise, it promised to "cut back on bureaucracy, shed controls and regulations, and reequip itself for its new role in providing a framework for free market operations for growth ...."[45] Accompanying the search for electoral majorities, however, is the fact that the BJP's transformation from quasi-socialist to pro-market ideology formed part of a longer historical process during which it evolved a political bloc in support of dismantling Nehruvian socialism. But there was no historical necessity driving the conjoining of Hindu, anti-Nehruvian, and neoliberal ideologies that underpinned this bloc; rather, these became conjoined in the course of encountering various forms of resistance from lower caste movements and parties (where they could not be absorbed. Crucially, this effort to dismantle the Nehruvian consensus had support from a different strand of the same political movement that spawned the BJP, namely, the Janata Dal (consisting of socialists from the JP movement). However, their opposition to Congress rule took the form of Mandalization, that is, caste reservations and recognition-based politics, which sought to reform the distribution of power in the state rather than the market. Given this alternative strand of politics that constitutes one pole of the field of Indian politics, we can see how contingent the success of the BJP's political articulation was. Indeed, at different points in time other political alternatives were possible. Not least, the Emergency period offered political opportunities to multiple social forces and movements; a stronger socialist party, better strategic leadership of the JP movement, and/or a different pattern of alliances between the left parties and the JP movement might have altered the subsequent political field in which a neoliberal project might have faced greater resistance.

CONCLUSION

The chapter began by noting the constraints faced by institutionalist theories in accounting for substantial transformations of preexisting institutions toward embedded neoliberalism. As a general theoretical and methodological orientation, the new institutionalist turn was effective in emphasizing how interests are shaped, mediated, represented, indeed constructed within specific symbolic and normative contexts (see, for example, Immergut, 1998; Steinmo, Thelen, & Longstreth, 1992). Yet, one criticism that has been leveled at historical institutionalists is that they are better at explaining longer-term continuities rather than ruptures (Lieberman, 2002; Orren, 1995; Schmidt, 2008). Ruptures and crises involve a rearticulation of political forces that seek to establish the hegemony of certain worldviews. Scholars have argued for the need to bring ideas to a more central place to counter the "static and overly deterministic nature of institutions" in their explanations (Schmidt, 2008, p. 304).

The dominant sociological paradigms of market transitions tend to treat discourse as largely residual, to be invoked when other variables cannot do the explaining. Instead, there is a tendency to emphasize how socioeconomic interests find political vehicles at moments of crisis in order to promote the dominance of their interests and world views, for example, the capture of political parties by corporate capital. The account presented in this chapter is slightly different – I argue that interests (including that of corporate capital, which are by no means self-evidently homogeneous) are politically constructed, articulated and legitmized, and parties play a crucial role in this process. Rather than being merely epiphenomenal, discourse is in fact central to this process. In the arena of democratic politics and mobilization, the framing of national, sectoral, class, and other interests

Parties and the Articulation of Neoliberalism 55

and the coding of these interests is crucial in producing key articulations. There is, in fact, very little to be gained by pitting "surface-level" discourse against "real" structurally driven politics.[46] These, as I hope I have succeeded in showing, are imbricated, not ontologically opposed.

Utilizing this theoretical perspective, this chapter has sought to develop a substantive theory linking two political projects – the authoritarian Emergency "from above" and middle sector insurgency – to the neoliberal transition in India. While it has been argued that India's trajectory resulted from the collapse of the dominant coalition and weakening state autonomy respectively, this chapter argues that these preceding conditions had to be successfully framed through a pro-globalization and liberalization lens that involved legitimizing a shift from "poverty eradication" to "growth." In forging this "sacred consensus" a discursive shift was enacted through the messy realities of mass mobilization in which several movements, parties, and ideologies competed for dominance. The victory of market-based discourse was not simply given in the nature of the global shift or underlying political economy; the emerging consensus was subject to resistance and reinterpretation, several shifts, and adjustments. In turn, "actually existing neoliberalism" in India is a contingent and ever-adjusting policy complex in which actors who emerged during the JP movement – former socialists among them – have resisted the nexus of unfettered markets and Hindu nationalism as attempted before 2004 by the ruling BJP (and that led to their electoral defeat for two successive terms).

The chapter's substantive argument is that disciplined party-led mobilization under the Hindu Right that began during the Emergency strongly contributed to the embedding of neoliberalism among the middle sectors and sections of subaltern actors. This offers an account of the making of neoliberalism that focuses upon "middle sector" actors, as well as the rise of political parties and forms of mobilization that draw upon ethnic (or religious or racialized discourses as the case may be). In doing so, it extends the insights of existing political-economic approaches that largely focus upon the state and/or capitalists and working classes by including a fuller range of actors whose political affiliations and identities are crucial battlegrounds for major parties. The chapter thus highlights the "relative autonomy of politics," that is, the extent to which party practices are critical determinants in the process of reorienting existing regimes and breaking with the ideas and institutions that preceded neoliberalism. An ethnicized discourse helped the BJP construct a counterintuitive and contingent alliance of castes and classes whose anti-Congress orientation was key to the delegitimization of the prior Nehruvian consensus. Middling categories such as sections of the OBCs and the urban middle classes shifted their allegiance increasingly away from Congress socialism toward support, however implicit, for the BJP's market orientation. The OBCs were in fact a crucial battleground for parties that sought to promote a state-centered model of equity through affirmative action and anti-casteism (Mandal), and a religious nationalism centered on strident market reforms (Mandir). These political struggles must be understood as *relatively* autonomous from structural conditions, because they are not solely determined by them. Yet, these underlying structures constrain such party practices and make it difficult for parties to secure a complete break with oppositional ideologies. Thus, for example, there are real limits to how far the BJP or Congress can articulate tribals, *dalits*, or the working classes with those who stand to benefit the most from neoliberalization. In highlighting such relatively autonomous practices the chapter argues that the party-movement dynamics of the post-1975 period are crucial for understanding the conjoining of market and democratic discourse in India. Because they took leadership of a mass movement at a crucial time, the Hindu Right could begin to evolve beyond their narrow base among traders and business people in northern India and begin to construct a wider national articulation opposing Congress socialism and its political "authoritarianism." Their success rested upon the evolution of political techniques of articulating different sectors, in part by appropriating political tactics from rival parties, and in part by incorporating populist movement repertoires and discourses. These political techniques, this chapter argues, should be given analytical autonomy in the analysis of neoliberal transitions whose shape and trajectory are not simply the product of crises, underlying class interests, or institutional "rules of the game." Instead, party-led movements, their repertoires, and efforts to pursue specific strategies against alternative, competing movements and discourses are a key part of any explanation of why transitions take the shape they do, and in turn offer important clues as to where the contingencies and fragilities of these new formations might be located.

NOTES

1. Kohli (2007) makes a useful distinction between pro-market and pro-business orientations, arguing that they are often collapsed in popular and scholarly discussions of development. While pro-market policies favor the entrance of new actors and increased competition, pro-business strategies largely favor established groups.

2. This point clearly merits a much longer discussion than is possible here. Kohli (2004) draws a compelling distinction between India's weak developmentalism and social democratic development, arguing that the former was determined by its fragmented, multi-class politics that the state failed to harness toward investment and sustainable, equitable growth. Arguably the turn toward the market since the early 1990s has embedded these tendencies further, welfare programs notwithstanding. Overall, expenditures on health, education, welfare, and agriculture have been declining steadily since 1991 (see "Beating Retreat," *The Times of India*, August 14, 2010), while the state is withdrawing from ownership of land, water, and other resources such as minerals. The weakening of state capacity has been exacerbated by what Kohli (2010) calls India's "pro-business" policies.

3. In Harvey's (2007) words: "[n]eoliberalism has in effect swept across the world like a vast tidal wave of institutional reform and discursive adjustment, and while there is plenty of evidence of its uneven geographical development, no place can claim total immunity … (p. 2).

4. The recent implementation of pro-poor welfare policies framed in the language of rights, such as the National Rural Employment Guarantee Act (NREGA), Mid-Day Meal Schemes, Rural Health, Right to Food, as well as legislation on land acquisition and rights of tribal communities to forest produce, mineral mining in Mines and Minerals Acts, and Land Acquisition Acts are evidence of an attempt to shape a more inclusive growth strategy and to broaden consensus for market reforms. The growth of a Maoist insurgency and their influence among tribal communities in large parts of India have so alarmed the Congress government that they have responded by restricting the rights and access of large corporations in the mining sector. There is enough evidence to suggest that the Congress Party is retreating and reshaping the earlier policies of the BJP, seeking to consolidate a base among the poor. These turns in policy require a more extended treatment than is possible here, but they suggest how crucial the domestic context is for understanding the implementation of neoliberalism (and its many varieties).

5. Among new institutionalists existing institutional arrangements are considered more important than global structural imperatives in determining how states will respond to the demands of international capital, multilateral agencies, and economic crisis. The domestic institutional balance of power is seen as offering a specific set of constraints and opportunities for policymakers, intellectuals, and think tanks to introduce neoliberal ideas and practices "from above" (Babb, 2001).

6. This pro-business orientation was also a product of successful lobbying by sections of the capitalist classes, who found a new sympathy within the Congress Party after a long period of hostility. I am grateful to an anonymous reviewer for emphasizing this point.

7. An authoritative survey of mass attitudes in 1996 showed that only 19% of the electorate had any knowledge of economic reforms, with only 14% of the rural electorate having any such knowledge. This was compared with 75–80% of the electorate that was aware of the ongoing religious conflict over the mosque demolition in 1992, and caste-based affirmative action (Varshney, 2000, p. 225). However, the surveys measure the extent of knowledge the public possesses about the policies, and does not measure the putative effects of these reforms (direct or indirect) upon their lives.

8. One may argue that the fine details of economic policy are rarely debated outside elite circles in most other countries, and not just in India – the rarefied readership circles of *The Financial Times or The Wall Street Journal* are perhaps their equivalents who read the *The Times of India or The Economic Times*.

9. This argument underpins the views of influential *dalit* (former untouchable) leaders, for example, who argue that Congress socialism offered fewer opportunities for the destruction of caste than do India's current liberalization policies (see Bhan Prasad, 2008).

10. As Babb and Fourcade-Gourinchas argue, the failure of the state to contain ongoing labor unrest in the context of failed economic policies and inflation turned labor and capital against the state. This opened the door to existing think tanks and political groups that pushed for monetarist policies (2002, p. 539).

11. This is in sharp contrast to South Africa, for example, where trade union density increased from 15.5% to 21.8% during the same period.

12. I am grateful to a reviewer for suggesting this important distinction between the means by which capital pushes forth its interests, and for forcing me to think more clearly about the implications of these mechanisms.

13. As Arvind Rajagopal (2003) notes, the importance of the Emergency in the growth of the Hindu Right "needs to be emphasized because it helps place Hindutva in a wider historical process .... With the Opposition leaders in jail (and a section of the parliamentary Left supporting the Emergency), [it] was ... one of the major grassroots organizations with a national reach."

14. "Strangely enough it is often the urban educated who promote anti-democratic organizations" (Ministry of Information and Broadcasting, 1978, p. 23). In another interview Indira Gandhi stated that the opposition had failed to gather mass support, and "their movement is largely confined to upper middle class [sic] – the peasantry was not involved, the industrial workers were not involved, the poorer sections of rural areas or urban areas were not involved" (*ibid.*, p. 162).

15. "Stability in South Asia: Justification for the Emergency," From American Embassy, New Delhi to Secretary of State, Washington DC, Secret File New Delhi 14119, U.S. Department of State Declassified Files (July 6, 2006).

16. Central Foreign Policy Files, Confidential File New Delhi 14117 221749Z, Declassified U.S. Department of State Files.

17. *Indian Express*, January 1, 1974.

18. This is despite the existence of a powerful capitalist lobby dating back to the Bombay Plan of the 1950s, and a relatively well-established intellectual critique of state planning by economists, many of them located in academic institutions outside India.

19. One simple measure of the declining importance of parliament has been the steady decline in the number of sessions since the 1950s, from an annual average of 122 sittings in 1952–1961 to 92.7 in 1982–1991 to 79 in 2002–2003 (Kapur & Mehta, 2006, p. 18). Similar numbers are revealed in an examination of number of bills passed and the numbers of sessions disrupted without closing of business (*ibid.*).

20. Speech of Shri C. Subramanyam, Minister of Finance, introducing the budget for the year 1976–1977, Retrieved from http://indiabudget.nic.in/bspeech.htm. Accessed on April 21, 2010.

Parties and the Articulation of Neoliberalism 59

21. Ministry of Finance, Government of India. Economic Survey, 1976–1977 Retrieved from http://indiabudget.nic.in/es1976-77/esmain.htm. Accessed on April 30, 2010.

22. In South Korea, this was enabled by a state project of instilling values of self-help, cooperation, and hard work among the small farmers (the project was known as *Saemul Undong*). Eventually this socio-cultural project was extended to the cities where the importance of self-discipline and austerity was impressed upon the rapidly growing middle classes.

23. A U.S. Department of State (2009) confidential report noted that the respectable turnout of between 100,000 and 200,000 marchers to Delhi in June 1976 was in large part owed to the Jan Sangh, evident also in the overwhelming representation of students and middle-class Hindus (Department of State, R061415Z, March 1975).

24. It is beyond the scope of this chapter to adequately discuss the role of socialists in political developments of the 1980s and 1990s. Their central role in leading lower caste mobilization for affirmative action and introducing caste into mainstream politics has been discussed at length elsewhere (Jaffrelot, 2003).

25. *Organizer*, July 6, 1974.
26. *Organizer*, January 18, 1975.
27. *Ibid.*, August 17, 1974.
28. *Ibid.*, July 23, 1977.
29. *Ibid.*
30. *Ibid.*
31. Decentralization has a long history within Indian political and economic discourse, and of specific interest is the revival of this discourse within the contours of a broad market transition. It draws on suspicion of big government and bureaucracy, and is embraced by all mainstream parties as an alternative to the latter.

32. *Organizer*, November 21, 1977.
33. In 1984, the BJP stated that "[t]he Congress Party, which professed socialism policy-wise, actually resorted to capitalism action-wise. This will be evident from one single fact. Fifty percent farmers who own land up to 1 hectare had only 10% of the total land available in the country, while 4% of the farmers owning 10 hectares or more of land own 30% of the total land available in the country .... [This] lack of political will to implement land ceiling laws has created a new class of kulaks ... who are exploiting the rural peasantry through distress sale of small holdings ...." (BJP National Council Resolution, 1984 in BJP (2000).

34. *Organizer*, January 8, 1978.
35. Between 1998 and 1999, during BJP rule, the import of consumer goods was completely liberalized, and by 2001 very few tariffs were in place to support domestic producers. Likewise, the BJP government drastically lowered import controls and quantitative restrictions, in some instances going beyond the WTO's requirements. This was a policy that directly benefited those who were rich and had secure livelihoods rather than the poor whose employment opportunities depended on the viability of smaller domestic producers (Chandrasekhar & Ghosh, 2002, p. 116).

36. This claim requires verification and as of 1989 the figure appeared exaggerated (Saxena, 1993, p. 694).

37. These charities have been extensively documented in the report titled *The Foreign Exchange of Hate: IDRF and the American Funding of Hindutva* (2002), which was written by several activist organizations and based upon interviews, newspaper sources, judicial enquiry commissions, and citizen panels among others.

38. Personal communication with *dalit* leader Martin Macwan and leading social activist Achyut Yagnik, Ahmedabad, September 2010.

39. During the Ram Janambhoomi movement led by the BJP, OBCs and some scheduled castes joined the activists (*kar sevaks*) seeing it as an "opportunity to be included in the greater Hindu family from which they had been excluded for so long" (Gupta, 2007, p. 123).

40. The support of sections of tribals and *dalits* for Hindutva politics is similar to that of the OBCs – a desire to raise one's social standing through political affiliations with dominant caste-class projects.

41. 1985 National Executive meeting in Bhopal (BJP, 2000, p. 61).

42. *Ibid.*

43. *Ibid.*

44. BJP 1991 Election Manifesto (BJP, 2000, p. 14).

45. *Ibid.*, p. 19.

46. As I have made clear throughout the discussion, it is of course problematic to reify discourse without specifying the conditions under which particular discourses have particular effects on social structures and institutions. Put differently, political discourse is ineffective without specific forms of action and strategy, and its communicative power is a function not only of its coherence, but also the strength of the organizational and strategic entity it is conveyed through, and the political practices it is harnessed to.

REFERENCES

Abbott, A. (1988). Transcending general reality. *Sociological Theory, 6*(2), 169–186.

Abbott, A. (1992). From causes to events: Notes on narrative positivism. *Sociological Methods and Research, 20*(4), 428–455.

Advani, L. K. (1979). *The people betrayed.* New Delhi: Vision Books.

Babb, S. (2001). *Managing Mexico: Economists from nationalism to neoliberalism.* Princeton, NJ: Princeton University Press.

Babb, S., & Fourcade-Gourinchas, M. (2002). The rebirth of the liberal creed: Paths to neoliberalism in four countries. *American Journal of Sociology, 108*(3), 533–579.

Bardhan, P. (1999). *The political economy of reform in India.* Oxford: Oxford University Press.

Basu, T., Datta, P., Sarkar, S., Sarkar, T., & Sen, S. (1993). *Khaki shorts and saffron flags.* Delhi: Orient Longman.

Bhan Prasad, C. (2008). *Markets and Manu: Economic reforms and its impact on caste in India.* CASI Working Papers Number 08-01.

Bharatiya Janta Party (BJP). (2000). *BJP economic resolutions, 1980–1999.* Delhi, India: BJP.

Brass, P. (2003). *The production of Hindu-Muslim violence in contemporary India.* Seattle, WA: University of Washington Press.

Brenner, N., & Theodore, N. (2002). *Spaces of neoliberalism: Urban restructuring in North America and Europe.* Oxford: Blackwell.

Campbell, J. L., & Pedersen, O. K. (2001). *The rise of neoliberalism and institutional analysis.* Princeton, NJ: Princeton University Press.
Chandhoke, N. (2000). The lessons of the JP movement. *The Hindu*, June 23. Retrieved from www.hindu.com. Accessed on January 15, 2011.
Chandra, B. (2003). *In the name of democracy: JP movement and the emergency.* New Delhi: Penguin.
Chandrasekhar, C. P., & Ghosh, J. (2002). *The market that failed: A decade of neoliberal reforms in India.* New Delhi: Leftword Books.
Chatterjee, P..(2004). *The politics of the governed.* New York, NY: Columbia University Press.
Chhibber, P., & Misra, S. (1993). Hindus and the Babri Masjid: The sectional basis of communal attitudes. *Asian Survey, 33*(7), 665–672.
Chibber, V. (2003). *Locked in place: State-building and late industrialization in India.* Princeton, NJ: Princeton University Press.
Chopra, R. (2003). Neoliberalism as Doxa: Bourdieu's theory of the state and the contemporary Indian discourse on globalization and liberalization. *Cultural Studies, 17*(3–4), 419–444.
Corbridge, S., & Harriss, J. (2000). *Reinventing India: Liberalization, Hindu nationalism and popular democracy.* Malden, MA: Polity.
Davis, D. (2004). *Discipline and development: Middle classes and prosperity in East Asia and Latin America.* Cambridge: Cambridge University Press.
De Leon, C., Desai, M., & Tugal, C. (2009). Political articulation: Parties and the constitution of cleavages in the U.S., India and Turkey. *Sociological Theory, 27*(3), 193–219.
Dhar, P. N. (2000). *Indira Gandhi, the "emergency," and Indian democracy.* New Delhi: Oxford University Press.
Dutt, V. P. (1976). Emergency in India: Background and rationale. *Asian Survey, 16*(12), 1124–1138.
Evans, P. (1995). *Embedded autonomy: States and industrial transformation.* Princeton, NJ: Princeton University Press.
Gould, H. (1986). A sociological perspective on the eighth general election in India. *Asian Survey, 26*(6), 630–652.
Gupta, S. (2007). The rise and fall of Hindutva in Uttar Pradesh, 1989–2004. In S. Pai (Ed.), *Political Process in Uttar Pradesh: Identity, economic reforms and governance* (pp. 110–135). New Delhi: Pearson Education.
Hansen, T. B. (1999). *The saffron wave: Democracy and Hindu nationalism in modern India.* Oxford: Oxford University Press.
Harvey, D. (2007). Neoliberalism as creative destruction. *Interfacehs, 2*(4), 1–28.
Hasan, Z. (Ed.). (2002). *Parties and party politics in India.* Oxford: Oxford University Press.
Hewitt, V. (2008). *Political mobilization and democracy in India: States of emergency.* London: Routledge.
ILO. (1997). Strikes and lockouts, by economic activity in India. Retrieved from http://laborsta.ilo.org. Accessed on July 26, 2010.
Immergut, E. (1998). The theoretical core of the new institutionalism. *Politics and Society, 26*(1), 5–34.
Jaffrelot, C. (1996). *The Hindu nationalist movement and Indian politics.* London: Hurst.
Jaffrelot, C. (2003). *India's silent revolution: The rise of the lower castes.* London: Hurst.
Jenkins, R. (1999). *Democratic politics and economic reform in India.* Cambridge: Cambridge University Press.

Jenkins, R. (2003). International development institutions and national-economic contexts: Neoliberalism encounters India's indigenous political traditions. *Economy and Society*, *32*(4), 584–610.
Kapur, D., & Mehta, P. B. (2004). *Indian higher education reform: From half-baked socialism to half-baked capitalism*. CID Working Paper No. 108. Center for International Development at Harvard University, Cambridge.
Kapur, D., & Mehta, P. B. (2006). *Indian parliament as an institution of accountability*. UNRISD Program Paper No. 23. UNRISD, Geneva, Switzerland.
Kohli, A. (1987). The political economy of development strategies. *Review Article, Comparative Politics*, *19*(2), 233–246.
Kohli, A. (2004). *State-directed development*. Cambridge: Cambridge University Press.
Kohli, A. (2006a). Politics of economic growth in India: Part 1: The 1980s. *Economic and Political Weekly*, April 1.
Kohli, A. (2006b). Politics of economic growth in India: Part 2: post-1991. *Economic and Political Weekly*, April 7.
Kohli, A. (2007). State, business, and economic growth in India. *Studies in Comparative International Development*, *42*, 87–114.
Kohli, A. (2010). *Democracy and development in India: From socialism to pro-business*. Oxford: Oxford University Press.
Kumar, S. (2003). Gujarat assembly elections 2002. *Economic and Political Weekly*, January 25, pp. 270–275.
Laclau, E. (2005). Populism: What's in a name? In F. Panizza (Ed.), *Populism and the mirror of democracy*. London: Verso.
Lieberman, R. (2002). Ideas, institutions, and political order: Explaining political change. *American Political Science Review*, *96*(4), 697–712.
Mehta, V. (1978). *The Sanjay story: From Anand Bhavan to Amethi*. Bombay: Jaico.
Ministry of Information and Broadcasting. (1978). *Democracy and discipline: Speeches of Shrimati Indira Gandhi*. New Delhi: Ministry of Information and Broadcasting.
Nayar, B. R. (2001). *Globalization and nationalism: The changing balance in India's economic policy 1950–2000*. New Delhi: Sage.
Orren, K. (1995). Ideas and institutions. *Polity*, *28*(1), 97–101.
Palmer, D. (1977). India in 1976. The politics of depoliticization. *Asian Survey*, *17*(2), 160–180.
Panizza, F. (Ed.). (2005). *Populism and the mirror of democracy*. London: Verso.
Peck, J. (2010). *Constructions of neoliberal reason*. Oxford: Oxford University Press.
Prasad, M. (2006). *Politics of free markets: The rise of neoliberal economic policies in Britain, France, Germany, and the United States*. Chicago, IL: University of Chicago Press.
Prashad, V. (1996). Emergency assessments. *Social Scientist*, *24*(9/10), 36–68.
Ragin, C. (1992). Introduction: Cases of "what is a case?". In C. Ragin & H. Becker (Eds.), *What is a Case? Exploring the foundations of sociohistorical enquiry*. Cambridge: Cambridge University Press.
Rajagopal, A. (2001). *Politics after television: Religious nationalism and the reshaping of the Indian public sphere*. Cambridge: Cambridge University Press.
Rajagopal, A. (2003). The emergency and the Sangh. *The Hindu*, June 13. Retrieved from www.hindu.com. Accessed on January 15, 2010.
Roberts, K. (2002). Social inequalities without class cleavages in Latin America's neoliberal era. *Studies in Comparative International Development*, *36*(4), 3–33.
Roberts, K. (2007). Latin America's populist revival. *SAIS Review*, *XXVII*(1), 3–15.

Rudolph, L., & Rudolph, S. (1987). *In pursuit of Lakshmi*. Chicago, IL: University of Chicago Press.
Sachs, J., Varshney, A., & Bajpai, N. (Eds.). (1999). *India in the era of market reforms*. New Delhi: Oxford University Press.
Sassen, S. (2006). *Territory, authority, rights*. Princeton, NJ: Princeton University Press.
Saxena, K. (1993). The Hindu trade union movement in India: The Bharatiya Mazdoor Sangh. *Asian Survey, 33*(7), 685–696.
Schmidt, V. (2008). Discursive institutionalism: The explanatory power of ideas and discourse. *Annual Review of Political Science, 11*, 303–326.
Selbourne, D. (1977). *An eye to India*. Harmondsworth: Penguin.
Shah, G. (1998). The BJP's riddle in Gujarat: Caste, factionalism and Hindutva. In T. B. Hansen & C. Jaffrelot (Eds.), *The BJP and the compulsions of politics in India*. Delhi: Oxford University Press.
Steinmo, S., Thelen, K., & Longstreth, F. (Eds.). (1992). *Structuring politics: Historical institutionalism in comparative analysis*. Cambridge: Cambridge University Press.
Tarlo, E. (2003). *Unsettling memories: Narratives of the emergency in Delhi*. London: Hurst.
Uba, K. (2008). Political protest and policy change: The direct impacts of Indian anti-privatization mobilizations, 1999–2003. *Mobilization, 10*(3), 383–396.
U.S. Department of State (2009). *U.S. central foreign policy files (declassified), 7/1/1973–12/31/1975*. Retrieved from http://www.aad.gov/archiveswww.aad.gov/archives. Accessed on June 15, 2009.
Varshney, A. (1998). Mass politics or elite politics? India's economic reforms in comparative perspective. *Policy Reform, 2*(3), 301–335.
Varshney, A. (2000). Is India becoming more democratic? *The Journal of Asian Studies, 59*(1), 3–25.
Weiss, L. (1998). *The myth of the powerless state*. Ithaca, NY: Cornell University Press.
Wiener, M. (1976). India's new political institutions. *Asian Survey, 16*(19), 898–901.
Yadav, Y. (2004). Radical shift in the social basis of power. *The Hindu*, May 20.
Yagnik, A. (2002). The pathology of Gujarat. *Seminar*, May.

"A NEW HEALTH ORDER AS PART OF THE NEW SOCIAL ORDER": THE STRATEGIC RESPONSE OF THE WHO TO ITS MEMBER STATES

Nitsan Chorev

ABSTRACT

This article explores the range of responses available to international bureaucracies when confronted with demands made by their member states through the study of the World Health Organization (WHO) during the 1970s and 1980s. I show that the WHO bureaucracy successfully addressed the demands of developing countries for health policies compatible with a more equitable world economic order, but in a way that preserved the bureaucracy's own agenda and without upsetting the opposite coalition of wealthy countries. Drawing on insights from the sociology of organizations, this article shows that externally dependent international bureaucracies are able to preserve their autonomous agenda by strategically reframing countries' demands before responding to them.

INTRODUCTION

The World Health Organization (WHO), which was established in 1948 as a specialized agency of the United Nations (UN), is the UN's "directing and coordinating authority for health."[1] The stated mission of the WHO, as defined in its founding constitution, is "the attainment by all peoples of the highest possible level of health" (WHO, 1958: Annex. 1). Hence, the constitution considers universal access to quality health services the principal objective of the WHO.

This progressive mission was assigned to a layered organization, consisting of the World Health Assembly, which is attended by representatives of all UN member states, an executive board of experts, and a secretariat. During the first two decades of its operation, the World Health Assembly included only a relatively small number of member states that, while divided between West and East, were mostly industrial countries, with a relatively similar level of economic development and a comparable approach to public health (Manela, 2010). In line with those countries' approach, during that period the WHO's operational assistance for poor countries focused on vertical interventions that relied on "magic bullets" for targeted diseases (Smith & Bryant, 1988, p. 911). During those years, the WHO launched mass campaigns against tuberculosis (1947–1951), malaria (1955–1970), yaws (1955–1970), and the exceptionally successful eradication program of smallpox (1967–1980) (Lee, 2009, p. 48).

Decolonization, however, radically changed the composition of the World Health Assembly and, as a result, the "external environment" in which the WHO secretariat functioned.[2] With decolonization, the beneficiaries of WHO programs were no longer passive recipients of decisions outside their control but – as rightful UN members – active participants in the deliberations. Certainly, rich countries, which funded the organization, still had major influence over initiatives, but developing countries now had a majority of votes at the World Health Assembly that they could use to influence decisions and support policies that were compatible with their own perceptions and interests.

By analyzing the era during the 1970s and early 1980s in which developing countries pressed the WHO to introduce radically new policies and programs, this article examines how international bureaucracies respond to external pressures, specifically, how they respond to demands that are potentially opposed to the bureaucracy's own material or ideational interests. Building on insights from the sociology of organizations, this article draws attention to the capacity of even externally dependent organizations to preserve their goals and priorities. I argue that international bureaucracies do not always passively submit to external demands they oppose but they also cannot simply resist or ignore them. Instead, the case of the WHO reveals the capacity of international bureaucracies to respond to members' expectations strategically, which enable these bureaucracies to win policies that satisfy the external demands while also addressing their own independent goals.

The following section discusses the nature of international bureaucracies and identifies the range of strategic responses that are available to them. Following an analysis of the WHO case, the conclusion discusses one condition underlying the capacity of international bureaucracies to engage in strategic responses, that of leadership, and the limitations of such strategies.

INTERNATIONAL BUREAUCRACIES: AUTONOMY, CAPACITY, AND ADAPTIVE STRATEGIES

How do international bureaucracies respond to demands made by member states? The conventional literature on international relations, especially neorealism, perceives international organizations as arenas, and their bureaucracies are not expected to have autonomous positions. The view most common in the literature, instead, is that policies made by international organizations reflect the position of the more powerful member countries (Mearsheimer, 1994). This, however, was not the WHO experience. Poor countries made explicit their expectations that the WHO develop programs more in line with their perceptions, and the WHO bureaucracy, at times against the explicit position of rich countries, responded, at least in part, to those demands. Moreover, when the WHO bureaucracy deviated from the expectations of developing countries, it was often in attempt to advance the bureaucracy's own preferences rather than those of rich countries.

Other schools of thought, including neoliberal institutionalism, allow international policies to be the outcome of a compromise between negotiating states under certain conditions, so that rather than a reflection of the interests of the powerful states, international policies may address at least some of the preferences and interests of the weaker states (Keohane, 1984; Keohane & Martin, 1995). But WHO policies during the 1970s and 1980s were not a compromise negotiated between rich and poor countries. First, most of the WHO policies were designed and advocated by the WHO bureaucracy, and negotiations, when they occurred, were between the bureaucracy and member states rather than among member states. Second, in those discussions, the WHO bureaucracy did not serve as the mouthpiece of countries (whether rich or poor) and the main objective of the bureaucracy was not reaching a compromise between member states but, rather, promoting the bureaucracy's own agenda. In short, the case of the WHO suggests the possibility for an *autonomous* organization that has the *capacity* to pursue at least some of its preferred agenda.

The argument that organizations, including international bureaucracies, have autonomous interests has been convincingly made by sociologists of organizations, and, in the literature on international organizations, by principal-agent theorists and constructivists. In organizational sociology, early articulations of neo-institutionalist theory that suggested that organizations conformed to the dictates of their environments (DiMaggio, 1983; Powell, 1988) were later revised as scholars recognized the possibility of organizations for strategic choice (Scott, 2008, p. 430; see also DiMaggio, 1991). Constructivist and principal-agent theories similarly view international bureaucracies as holding independent goals (Barnett & Finnemore, 2004; Hawkins, Lake, Nielson, & Tierney, 2006; Nielson & Tierney, 2003). These goals reflect international bureaucracies' material interests and ideational principles. International bureaucracies' material goals include an interest in having sufficient (and expanding) authority to act and sufficient (and growing) funds to act effectively (Barnett & Coleman, 2005). International bureaucracies' ideational position – the principles that guide bureaucracies' perceptions of their missions and their understandings of the best way to achieve their missions (Albert & Whetton, 1985; Jepperson, 1991) – may be drawn from a number of resources, including historical and therefore path-dependent sources, such as the organization's foundational texts (Harris & Ogbonna, 1999), or contemporary and potentially path-breaking sources, such as new fashions in a relevant professional field (Glynn, 2000).

Autonomous interests, however, do not necessarily come with capacity to act to achieve those interests. Indeed, international bureaucracies are heavily constrained due to their dependence upon their member states for resources, votes, and legitimacy. Resource dependence stems from the fact that most international organizations rely on external contributions, mostly from their member states (Pfeffer & Salancik, 1978). Because contributions to UN agencies are based on member states' capacity to pay, the UN and the UN specialized agencies are disproportionately dependent upon the United States and other wealthy countries. However, when member states are represented in a governing body that follows a one-country, one-vote rule, international bureaucracies are vulnerable not only to the power of rich member states to withhold funds but also to the power of poor states to withhold votes. With decolonization, the UN and its specialized agencies have become procedurally dependent on a voting majority of poor countries. Finally, an international organization's mission and programs have to be accepted as legitimate by rich and poor countries alike (Barnett & Finnemore, 2004, pp. 166–170; Hurd, 2007; Suchman, 1995).

The literature on international bureaucracies is surprisingly quiet on how such dependence limits their ability to act. General formulations of the constructivist view acknowledge and identify the external constraints that limit the authority and powers of international bureaucracies (Barnett & Finnemore, 2004, p. 12). In many empirical analyses, however, constructivists avoid the need to analyze the potential tension between an organization's independent goals and these external constraints by studying international organizations' autonomous action in instances in which external forces were supportive, indifferent, or uninformed of the action (Abdelal, 2007; Barnett & Finnemore, 2004; Chwieroth, 2008). There is scant empirical attention to cases involving explicit or even potential tension. As a result of this bias in the selection of case studies, many constructivist accounts tend to overstate the autonomy and power available to international organizations and downplay the role of external constraints. As Nielson and Tierney (2003, pp. 244, 245) have described with a colorful metaphor: "For organizational theorists ... [international organizations] are like global Frankensteins terrorizing (or more often benefiting) the international countryside. Once [international organizations] have been created, they take on a life of their own and are largely beyond the control of their creators." Some constructivists have conceded that "the virtue of a focus on the characteristics of the organization for explaining organizational change is also its vice: The emphasis on the organization can lead to the neglect of the environment" (Barnett & Coleman, 2005, p. 594). However, this does not imply that constructivist accounts have necessarily overstated the capacity of international bureaucracies to act autonomously. Rather, their oversight has been in neglecting to explore the factors that enable international organizations to advance their independent interests *even when these interests clash with external demands.* The potential for a conflict between the international bureaucracy and member states or other actors cannot be ignored if we are to understand the capacity of a bureaucracy to act on its autonomous wishes.

Principal-agent scholars have similarly ignored instances of actual clashes. The principal-agent analysis holds that an international organization (the agent) "can exhibit significant independence" because member states (the principals) are impeded by the complications of "collective principal," "multiple principals," and "chain of delegation," which limit their effective supervision (Nielson & Tierney, 2003). While this formulation reflects greater attentiveness to inevitable tensions between member states and international organizations than many constructivist accounts, the principal-agent literature has mostly focused on identifying the characteristics of principals that allow for more or less effective supervision. As a result, by these scholars' own admission, the analysis "contains a remarkably thin view of agent behavior" (Hawkins & Jacoby, 2006, p. 1999).

Hence, both constructivist and principal-agent theories have rightly identified the partial autonomy of international organizations, but they have yet to develop a more complete understanding of the capacity of international bureaucracies to protect their goals when these clash with the preferences of member states or other external pressures. To identify the conditions under which international bureaucracies can protect their goals and preferences when those are in conflict with member states, we need to look at the capacity of these bureaucracies for strategic responses.

My analysis of the strategic responses available to international bureaucracies builds on earlier explorations by sociologists of organizations (for example, Goodrick & Salancik, 1996; Goodstein, 1994). Most systematically, Christine Oliver (1991) has offered a list of five possible responses by organizational actors to exogenous pressures. Briefly, the possible responses include acquiescence (acceding to pressures), compromise (exacting concessions), avoidance (attempting to preclude the necessity of conformity), defiance (rejecting expectations), and manipulation (attempting to actively change the content of the expectations). Barnett and Coleman (2005) have argued that the same range of strategies was available also to international organizations and suggested a sixth response, that of strategic social construction (tailoring the environment so that it is consistent with the organization's goals); Weaver (2008) has described in detail the use of avoidance (or "organized hypocrisy") as a central strategy of the World Bank (also Luken, 2009).[3]

In these works, scholars have analyzed the responses available to organizations as if they followed a linear logic, varying "from passive conformity to active resistance" (Oliver, 1991, p. 146). But the two dichotomies – passive/active and conformity/resistance – do not neatly overlap. What makes a response passive or active is not whether it conforms to or resists the exogenous demands. Rather, it is whether the response includes an attempt to alter the meaning of those demands, be this part of either conforming to or resisting them. (What Oliver calls active responses I refer to from now on as "strategic.") For example, Oliver lists manipulation – the attempt to co-opt, influence, or control institutional pressures in order to change the content of the expectations – as resistance, because it is "the most active response to these pressures" (Oliver, 1991, p. 157). If due to manipulation the organization is able to avoid compliance with the original demands, then manipulation should indeed be viewed as a form of resistance. However, if after manipulating the content of the demands the organization adheres to the altered expectations *in a way that satisfies the original demands*, manipulation should instead be viewed as a form of strategic compliance. Lumping the two dichotomies together prevents an independent assessment of passive and strategic responses as distinct from compliance and resistance, which is fundamental for understanding the ability of international bureaucracies to successfully deviate from exogenous prescriptions.

Table 1 displays the different types of responses that emerge if we maintain a distinction between the two dichotomies, so that the categories are based on (1) whether the responses employed lead to changes that satisfy the exogenous forces (compliance) or whether the responses employed avoid changes or lead to changes that do not satisfy the exogenous forces (resistance), and (2) whether the organizations take the pressures "as a given constraint to be obeyed or defied" (passive) or whether they attempt to redefine – "alter, re-create, or control" – the meaning of the exogenous pressures (strategic) (Oliver, 1991, p. 159).

This categorization creates four types of possible responses. Passive responses are those that accept the demands as given and include *passive compliance*, when the international bureaucracy adheres to the original expectations, and *passive resistance*, when the international bureaucracy explicitly disobeys the exogenous demands. The familiar dichotomy between compliance and resistance refers, in fact, to these passive categories. However, I argue that the more common responses to external demands are adaptive responses, of strategic compliance and strategic resistance. Both strategic responses involve altering the meaning of the demands but with different intentions.

Table 1. Types of Response to Exogenous Pressures.

	Compliance	Resistance
Passive	Adherence to original expectations	Disobedience
Strategic	Adherence to reinterpreted expectations	Voidance

When *strategically complying* with exogenous demands, an international bureaucracy adheres to the demands of member states but only after giving those demands a meaning that, while compatible with the original expectations, could be reconciled with the bureaucracy's independent goals. The reinterpreting of expectations (altering the meaning of the demands) is not the same as changing expectations (altering the demands), which should be considered an act of resistance rather than compliance. Hence, strategic compliance is not about making the exogenous forces change their demands but about convincing those forces that the original demands were met. By offering an acceptable reframing of the demands – the challenge is exactly in making such reframing acceptable – international bureaucracies make a distorted compliance look complete.

When *strategically resisting* exogenous demands, an international bureaucracy reframes the demands so that it is no longer expected to conform to them. Strategic resistance does not entail rejection of the external demands but rather reliance on the logic underlying the demands to legitimate refusal to comply. Such justifications may allow an international bureaucracy to void the expectation to comply, thereby rendering what member states might have viewed as provocative (passive) resistance into an agreeable action.

While passive responses – compliance and resistance – are the ones most often described in the literature (Scott, 2008), the more common responses of international bureaucracies to external demands are strategic ones. The reason is risk avoidance. Passive compliance undermines the organization's material and/or ideational goals and passive resistance threatens its resources, votes, and/or legitimacy. In contrast, altering the meaning of the external demands before adhering to them reduces the extent to which the organization's principles and goals are sacrificed, and being able to convincingly justify resistance lowers the risk of being penalized for it.

The capacity of international bureaucracies to strategically adapt to external pressures means that international policies do not emerge out of unmediated negotiations between member states. Rather, the international organization's leadership and staff – those who plan the budget, rank program priorities, author position papers, formulate arguments, and advocate policies to member states – can heavily influence policy outcomes. These international bureaucracies are not mouthpieces for the most powerful states, nor are they neutral mediators merely helping to find a workable compromise. Rather, international bureaucracies attempt to incorporate their own independent goals into the policies they help formulate by either strategically complying or strategically resisting the external demands.

In the narrative that follows I show that when the demands of developing countries for a new international economic order (NIEO) conflicted with the preferences of the WHO bureaucracy, the secretariat took authorship over the organization's response. The WHO bureaucracy was able to redefine the NIEO core principles of development, equity and self-reliance in a way that allowed it to comply with the demands of developing countries by launching programs, such as Health for All and primary health care, that also addressed the bureaucracy's own agenda; and the WHO bureaucracy relied on the NIEO principle of national sovereignty to oppose initiatives against multinational companies. In the course of strategically responding to the external demands, the WHO programs changed substantially and its bureaucracy could not always avoid the sacrifice of its goals or the dissatisfaction of at least some member states. Nonetheless, the gap between the NIEO logic and WHO programs attests to the ability of international organizations to significantly maneuver their political environment and actively contribute to the decision-making process.

THE WHO'S STRATEGIC ADAPTATION TO THE NIEO

In the early 1970s, global political conditions radically transformed. Decolonization led to the establishment of a large number of independent states, and Third World countries, as they were then called, became the majority in the UN and its specialized agencies, and therefore an influential force in shaping international policies. Latin American, Asian, and African countries – grouped under the Non-Aligned Movement and, later, the Group of 77 (G-77) – formulated a common criticism of how developed countries and transnational enterprises exploited the developing world, which, they argued, had impeded poor countries' potential for economic growth.

Developing countries were determined to exploit their majority of votes at the UN to shape international policies and programs and force a more equitable distribution of global resources. In May 1974, the Sixth Special Session of the UN General Assembly adopted the "Declaration on the Establishment of a New International Economic Order." The Declaration "solemnly proclaim[ed]" the "united determination" of member states:

> To work urgently for the establishment of a New International Economic Order ... which shall correct inequalities and redress existing injustices, make it possible to eliminate the widening gap between the developed and the developing countries and

ensure steadily accelerating economic and social development and peace and justice for present and future generations.[4]

The General Assembly subsequently passed a number of additional declarations that articulated the essence of the envisioned new order, including a "Programme of Action on the Establishment of a New International Economic Order," the "Charter of Economic Rights and Duties of States," and a resolution on "Development and International Economic Cooperation."[5]

These resolutions committed UN member states to a number of principles that were to remedy the injustice of the existing system: (1) The new international order was to be based on *equity among nations*, "whereby the prevailing disparities in the world may be banished and prosperity secured for all."[6] (2) The main objective of the new order was to enhance worldwide cooperation toward steadily accelerating *economic and social development*. In particular, the G-77 called for increased industrialization and for improved access to foreign markets for their primary commodities. (3) The NIEO extended the principles of self-determination and political sovereignty to the economic realm. *Economic sovereignty* – the rejection of foreign influence – was aimed both at other states and at multinational corporations, due to concerns that reliance on foreign capital prevented states' real development and maintained their dependent position in the world economy. (4) In an attempt to reverse the uneven influence in the process of decision-making at the international level, Third World countries tried to shift authority from the World Bank, the International Monetary Fund, and the General Agreement on Tariffs and Trade to universal international organizations that followed the one-country/one-vote rule. Third World countries wanted these organizations to regulate interstate relations and states' relations with multinational companies, including through *international codes of conduct*. (5) Because inequalities among states had been the outcome of past and contemporary economic relations of exploitation, the G-77 held that developed countries had the *duty to support* developing countries. Among other initiatives, developing countries called for an international code of conduct on the transfer of technology that would provide developing countries access to Western know-how. (6) Finally, although most NIEO principles accepted that economic growth in poor countries depended on engagement with the industrial world, some developing countries considered *collective self-reliance* among developing countries the only sure basis upon which they could make development plans.

Developing countries made explicit their expectation that the specialized agencies of the UN launch projects compatible with the principles of the NIEO (Murphy, 1984, p. 131). In the political-economic environment of the 1970s, the institutional arrangements of UN agencies made them uncharacteristically vulnerable to developing countries, which used their unified votes to impose their agenda. But the influence of developing countries was tamed by these agencies' dependence on resources provided by wealthy countries, who opposed what they considered the "politicization" of technical international organizations and the expectation that they should pay for developing countries' political demands. In addition to the need to satisfy both coalitions, international bureaucracies had their own organizational and professional agendas to defend. How did the WHO bureaucracy respond to these competing pressures?

A New International Order in Health

In response to the demands of developing countries for a more just economic order, the WHO, like other specialized agencies, adopted radically new initiatives and programs. The new agenda was deliberately celebrated as a loyal representation of the NIEO spirit. A 1980 WHO report, "Technical Discussions on the Contribution of Health to the New International Economic Order," which reviewed the WHO's activities in the previous years, forcefully argued that "the philosophy, policy, principles and practices recently adopted in the world health sector correspond fully with the aims of the NIEO and with the means for achieving them," and contended that "the health sector is giving the lead in showing how the theory of the NIEO can be put into practice, and is providing models for other sectors" (WHO, 1980). In referring to the WHO new flagship programs – Health for All by the Year 2000 and primary health care – the report described the affinity between NIEO principles and the WHO programs in the following way:

> The characteristics inherent in the strategy of health for all by the year 2000, based on primary health care ... are precisely those demanded by the NIEO. Examples are: multisectoral coordination, with the mutual contribution to development of actions in the health and relevant socioeconomic sectors; the transfer of technology (as in the policy of appropriate technology for health); redistribution of resources on a more equitable basis, leading to universal accessibility of primary heath care and its supporting services; increased self-reliance (as in the policy of technical cooperation among developing countries); and mass participation, ensuring involvement of the community in shaping its own health and socioeconomic future. (WHO, 1980)

The evidence offered in the report to indicate WHO's conformity with the NIEO hints at the means by which the WHO bureaucracy responded to the exogenous expectations. First, the report proudly presents the radical changes in the agenda of the WHO as faithfully conforming to NIEO principles and fully addressing the demands of developing countries. Second, however, the report's description of the NIEO principles to which the WHO conformed modifies those principles. In the passage quoted above, for example, the report qualifies the transfer of technology to appropriate technology, it turns equitable distribution to universal accessibility, and it emphasizes self-reliance rather than duties of developed states. In the remainder of the article, I show that this reinterpretation of the original principles expressed the attempt of the WHO leadership and staff to promote policies, principles, and practices that were acceptable to developing countries but that also preserved the bureaucracy's ideational and material concerns.

The WHO bureaucracy's ideational goals, as frequently and vigorously expressed by the WHO Director-General Dr. Halfdan T. Mahler, were largely based on the WHO founding constitution and on contemporary trends in public health knowledge.[7] Mahler, who acquired a reputation as "a strong idealist"[8] and someone who approached "his task with a vigor and missionary zeal,"[9] believed that "the attainment of all peoples of the highest possible level of health" was the only objective of the WHO constitution,[10] and he made the pursuit of this objective the central mission of the organization. Mahler's reading of the WHO constitution – particularly his emphasis on "of all peoples" – made the WHO under his leadership prioritize the needs of the poor and support comprehensive, rather than targeted, health care programs.

Mahler's idealism, however, was accompanied by an astute pragmatism and an acute awareness of the WHO's vulnerabilities. Developing countries' political achievements in the UN led to growing tensions with developed countries, which complained of the "rapid growth in the activities and budgets of the main Specialized Agencies and the accompanying decline in our influence,"[11] and were reluctant to pay for advancing an international order they did not support. Compliance with developing countries' expectations could undermine the support of wealthy countries of the WHO and threaten the organization's material interests. While promoting the NIEO logic as a guide for WHO policies, Mahler warned member states that "the Organization should have a clear vision of its goal, but unless it was pragmatic in its approach it would fail to achieve it."[12] In regard to resolutions condemning Israel or South Africa, for example, Mahler worried that such resolutions, which the United States vigorously opposed, might "blow up our Organization," and pleaded member states not "to be lured astray into fields beyond our constitutional competence" (cited in Williams, 1987, p. 63). The WHO bureaucracy's need to appeal to rich countries should not be confused, however, with the organization being a mere mouthpiece of these countries. First, the WHO bureaucracy considered its financial dependence as only one among a number of priorities. Second, as we will see, the WHO bureaucracy was able to respond strategically to the expectations of rich countries as to those of the poor. Hence, while the material interests of the WHO bureaucracy made it attentive to the demands of rich countries, the bureaucracy developed an agenda that also incorporated other considerations, both material and ideational.

The following sections describe four central initiatives that were advocated by the WHO bureaucracy in the years following the call for an NIEO: health for all by the year 2000, primary health care, essential drugs list, and the regulation of marketing practices. The analysis shows that to preserve its ideational and material interests while addressing the demands made by a majority of its member states, the WHO bureaucracy found a way to interpret the NIEO principles so that complying with them would be compatible with its own goals or, in other cases, found a way to successfully justify its resistance by drawing on the NIEO logic.

Health for All by the Year 2000

At the Thirtieth World Health Assembly, in 1977, member states agreed on an all-encompassing new goal for the organization. Resolution WHA30.43 declared that "the main social target of governments and WHO in the coming two decades should be the attainment by all citizens of the world by the year 2000 of a level of health that will permit them to lead a socially and economically productive life." This resolution expressed a radical departure from the WHO's previous programs. Rather than the piecemeal targeting of specific diseases based on available technological advances, the WHO was now committed to the overall improvement in health conditions.

With Health for All, the WHO staff was able to formulate and advocate an agenda that reflected its ideational position as the new program promised to steer the organization back to its constitutional call for the highest possible level of health to all peoples. According to Mahler, the goal of Health for All by the Year 2000 "embodied" the WHO's central constitutional objective.[13] A board member expressed a common view when he stated that the only innovative aspect of the goal of health for all when compared to the constitution was its setting of a deadline.[14]

But Health for All was also the WHO bureaucracy's key attempt to address the demands of developing countries for a NIEO and it was celebrated as a faithful articulation of the NIEO in the field of health. In 1975, in a number of presentations to member states of the concept of health for all, Mahler stated:

> I have chosen as my subject "Health for all by the year 2000!" because it permits me to express my views on how you and your Organization might make a contribution to the New Economic Order.[15]

A report of a WHO expert committee similarly linked Health for All back to the NIEO:

> The commitment of the Member States of WHO to the goal of health for all by the year 2000 has been presaged by the General Assembly of the United Nations which proclaimed in 1974 ... its united determination to work urgently for the establishment of a New International Economic Order.[16]

With Health for All, the WHO bureaucracy responded to the NIEO by embracing two of its most fundamental principles: development and equity. In doing so, however, the WHO bureaucracy strategically adapted to the external demands by interpreting these notions to better fit its own values. Specifically, the WHO bureaucracy strategically complied with the NIEO by prioritizing social over economic development, and intrastate over than interstate equity.

Development

The WHO report made the claim that "the recognition of the close relationship between health and development ... led the ... Assembly to decide" on the Health for All goal (WHO, 1980). This "close relationship" was articulated in a number of ways, including that "a healthy people [is] the most essential cause and effect of development," and, therefore, that "health development [is] a viable strategy for development planners to pursue" (WHO, 1980). However, when the WHO staff referred to development, they did not mean economic development, which was the most pressing concern of developing countries, but social development, namely, improved access to shelter, health, education and productive employment. The NIEO stressed the fundamental importance of economic development and that it was to be achieved through industrialization and technology transfer. In the realm of health, focus on industrialization and technology transfer would have meant investment in sophisticated health infrastructure through the utilization of

A New Health Order as Part of the New Social Order 79

advanced Western medical technology (for example, to allow for the local manufacturing of medicines). Such programs would have relied on aid from developed countries, through both funds and technology, but could have arguably contributed to the economic development of the countries investing in such infrastructure. The WHO's Health for All, on the contrary, focused on social development through improvements in living conditions and quality of life *under conditions of scarce resources.* Hence, the WHO bureaucracy rejected the assumption made in the call for an NIEO that social development could only be achieved through economic development, and WHO reports defined development almost solely in social terms: "Development implies continuing improvements in the living conditions and quality of life of people" (WHO, 1980). Once the goal became social development, the claim of central role of health could also be made: "The quality of life depends directly upon the level of health. Health development is therefore essential for social and economic development" (WHO, 1980). In short, in response to the NIEO, the WHO shifted its central attention to the issue of development, as developing countries demanded. By strategically emphasizing social rather than economic development, however, the WHO secretariat offered a notion of development that was in line with the WHO bureaucracy's own interests as well as principles.

The WHO staff used adaptive strategies to make the shift from economic to social development noncontroversial. Most often, the concern with social development was offered as a welcome corrective to the dominant focus on economic development, explicitly asserting that "development cannot be equated with economic growth alone" (WHO, 1980). The WHO staff emphasized the importance of non-quantitative measures of social poverty and insisted that the goal should be the "improvement in the living conditions and quality of life of the people" (WHO, 1980). Mahler told member states that he would "personally ... prefer" to call the New Economic Order a "New Development Order," disclosing his displeasure with a narrowly economic emphasis.[17]

These claims convinced member states that in addressing social development, Health for All could contribute to the new international order in significant ways. A draft resolution, jointly sponsored by 16 non-Western countries, asserted: "the New International Economic Order ... can only be effectively set in motion when due attention is paid to social as well as economic development, of which health is an integral part."[18]

Equity
The WHO staff was able to present Health for All as compatible with the NIEO logic by relying on the selective interpretation of not only

development but also equity. One of the legacies of colonial medical services was a skewed resource allocation, and health care in many poor countries was still limited to urban areas so that the majority of the population, who was living in suburban and rural areas, had no access to health care resources (Mamdani, 1992). Health for All was meant to improve access to and quality of health services for the very poor. Echoing the NIEO, this concern was framed in terms of equity. According to Mahler, "The question of social equity, the possibility of realizing oneself as a fundamental right, was the most important concept in the goal of health for all by the year 2000."[19] However, the WHO staff focused on inequities among populations within poor countries, which most governments of developing countries would have preferred not to discuss at the international level, rather than inequities between poor countries and rich ones, which was developing countries' main concern in calling for a new international order. Mahler asserted, "The time is now long overdue for a reduction of the growing disparity in the distribution of health resources not only between counties but also within countries."[20]

To broaden the concept of equity as it was defined by developing countries, the WHO staff questioned the assumption that the benefits of an international restructuring of the economic system would automatically translate into social improvements, including improvements in health, and stated that a sole focus on international equity was insufficient.[21] For social improvements, a WHO report argued that "there needs to be equity [also] in the intra-national distribution of resources" (WHO, 1980). The Health for All campaign against "the disparities existing within countries" was the WHO's model for bridging between international and intra-national equities.[22]

Also in regard to equity, therefore, the WHO's Health for All goal adhered to NIEO principles, but only after altering their meaning. In a piece published in a WHO magazine, *World Health*, Mahler reiterated the affinity between the inter-national and intra-national equity: "For ... governments do have responsibility for the health and socio-economic development of all their people, and not only of the elite in the main cities. This implies distributing resources for health more evenly, and to do so means giving top priority to the socially under-privileged." Mahler then added, "This applies within countries, but it also applies internationally, since the more fortunate countries have a double responsibility – to their own people and to those in countries in less fortunate circumstances."[23]

In short, the signature program of the WHO in the 1970s, Health for All, conformed to the two fundamental demands in the call for an NIEO, development and equity. However, by insisting on *social* development and *intra*state equity, the WHO leadership was able to promote an agenda that, while acceptable to poor states, closely reflected the ideational position of the bureaucracy. The success of this strategic compliance is manifested in the endorsement of the General Assembly. In 1979, Resolution 34/58, entitled "Health as an Integral Part of Development," recalled the UN resolutions calling for an NIEO and welcomed "the important efforts of the World Health Organization ... associated with the effort to attain the goal of 'health for all by the year 2000'."[24]

Primary Health Care

In striking contrast to the vertical approaches favored by the WHO until then, in the late 1970s the WHO selected the primary health care approach as "the KEY to achieving the target of health for all" in one generation (WHO, 1980). The most important aspect of this approach was *universal* access to *essential* health care. Essential health care services were to be scientifically sound, socially acceptable, and at a cost that the community and country could afford to maintain. The primary health care approach relied on health workers, including auxiliaries and community workers, to provide the "basic" health needs of the population. This strategy was formulated by the WHO secretariat in response to the failure of previous disease-specific interventions sponsored by the WHO and in line with new trends in public health. Hence, it was a strategy that was developed by the WHO staff independently of external political pressures. But the choice of primary health care was also presented in a way that could satisfy the demands of developing countries for a new international order.

The rejection of vertical interventions followed the failure of the Malaria Eradication Program, which was launched in 1955 and abandoned by WHO member states in 1968 (Nájera, 1989; Packard, 1997). The malaria program failed for a variety of reasons (Packard, 1997, p. 286), but discussions at the WHO focused on one particular barrier: the lack of health service infrastructure, especially in rural areas (Newell, 1988, p. 903; Raviglione & Pio, 2002). In response, in the early 1970s, the WHO staff prepared a number of reports on basic health services that introduced the primary health care approach.[25] The reports and documents stated that the prevailing approach to the development of health services, namely, "the transfer of health technology from ... developed to developing as well as urban to rural," had failed and forcefully argued that developing primary health services at the community level was the "only way in which the health services can develop rapidly and effectively."[26]

Delegates from developing countries expressed support for the concept of primary health care. The representative from Kuwait summarized: "WHO's policy on primary health care was one of the most important landmarks in the philosophy of the organization. All delegates welcomed that endeavor."[27] Western industrial counties were also swayed (Gish, 1983). When the Chinese delegation suggested an international conference to exchange experience on the development of primary health care, the WHO leadership thought it premature and initially opposed it but Mahler eventually succumbed to members' demands and also accepted an offer by the Soviet Union to host the conference in the capital of the Soviet Republic of Kazakhstan, Alma-Ata.[28]

The International Conference on Primary Health Care took place in September 1978 and became the landmark event for primary health care (Brown, Cueto, & Fee, 2006, p. 67). By the end of the conference, the more than 3,000 attending delegates adopted the "Declaration of Alma-Ata International Conference on Primary Health Care" (WHO, 1978), which made the primary health care approach the central overarching logic of national, regional, and WHO health programs and the "centerpiece of WHO's effort to achieve its ambitious goal of health ... for all by year 2000."[29]

In justifying the primary health care approach, Section I of the Alma-Ata Declaration made explicit references to the principles of the WHO Constitution. Public pronouncements reiterated the same sentiment: member states agreed that "[the] strategies for health for all by the year 2000 [were] in perfect conformity with the spirit of the Constitution of WHO,"[30] and Mahler declared the Alma-Ata Declaration a contemporary roadmap for the constitution.[31] Sections II and III of the Declaration, in turn, drew on the NIEO principles of equity and development. As in discussions on Health for All, the link between primary health care and the NIEO was made possible by emphasizing inequities both across and within countries and then making the claim that the primary health care approach was fundamental to reducing such inequities. Hence, Section II announced, "The existing gross inequality in the health status of the people particularly between developed and developing countries as well as within countries is ... unacceptable." Section III declared:

> Economic and social development, based on a New International Economic Order, is of basic importance to the fullest attainment of health for all and to the reduction of the

A New Health Order as Part of the New Social Order 83

gap between the health status of the developing and developed countries. The promotion and protection of the health of the people is essential to sustained economic and social development and contributes to a better quality of life and to world peace.

References to inequality and the unequal distribution of resources were also made in other WHO documents on primary health care. Mahler often argued, for example, "In the field of health, the most important measure for reducing some of the cross-national and international differences that separate human beings is, perhaps, the promotion of primary health care."[32]

In addition to development and equity, the Alma-Ata Declaration made use of another central NIEO principle, claiming that primary health care was "in the spirit of self-reliance and self-determination." Speeches and programs suggest two ways by which the WHO interpreted the NIEO meaning of self-reliance. In some cases, self-reliance stood for reliance on a nation's own economic resources, which called for health services only "at a cost that the community and country can afford to maintain" (WHO, 1978). As an American report approvingly described: "One of Mahler's favorite themes is that developing countries themselves must provide 90 percent of the effort and resources needed for attaining WHO's goals."[33] However, Mahler insisted that "maximum national self-reliance in health matters" should not be confused with self-sufficiency.[34] Hence, Mahler maintained that developed countries had responsibility "to those in countries in less fortunate circumstances,"[35] but without giving away the developing countries' ownership of their programs.

Indeed, the second meaning of self-reliance was that of self-governance. A British official reported, "Dr. Mahler's ... message is ... loud and clear that it is the member States who have the key formative role in WHO's development."[36] In a speech before the Assembly, Mahler described how country health programming followed "the principle of attaining early national self-reliance" by providing the means "to develop the capacities within countries to clarify for themselves the reasons for their health underdevelopment and decide by themselves, through a process that is both rational and consonant with their culture, on the most appropriate policies and programs for developing the health of all their peoples."[37] Self-reliance was the WHO's response to the failure of vertical interventions, in which decisions were imposed from above with little consideration of the specific needs of different countries.[38] The term also accorded with the NIEO principles of collective self-reliance and sovereign will, although the locus of self-reliance shifted from the country level to the community level. The Alma-Ata Declaration called for "maximum community and individual self-reliance": communities and individuals, rather than national governments, were the relevant participants.

In short, the primary health care approach did not follow the conventional interpretation of the call for an NIEO. Rather than calling for the transfer of resources and technology from developed countries in order to make health services in the Third World match the quality of those services in wealthy countries, the WHO bureaucracy followed its own agenda and embraced health policies that focused on basic needs, community involvement, and that required minimal resources. By insisting on the capacity to improve public health under conditions of scarce resources, moreover, the WHO bureaucracy provocatively underplayed the need for economic development that was central to the demands of developing countries. But by reinterpreting the NIEO notions of development, equity and self-reliance, instead of merely defying them, the WHO bureaucracy was able to convincingly bridge the NIEO principles and its own preferred programs and thereby gain developing countries' support.

Essential Drugs

Developing countries' harsh criticism of multinational corporations often focused on the pharmaceutical sector. Studies showed that drug companies exported to poor countries harmful or ineffective medicines that had been withdrawn from other markets. Drug companies also used misleading labeling and information and failed to warn against serious and possibly fatal side effects, and they utilized ruthless methods of promotion in attempt to artificially create a demand for the most profitable of their patented drugs, with a limited relation to actual needs (Mamdani, 1992; Melrose, 1983).

In response, the WHO staff sought ways to rationalize national drug policies, including through the selection of essential drugs. The concept of essential drugs and the idea that the WHO could guide governments' procurement strategies for such drugs came from a report prepared by a meeting of experts in 1975.[39] The report defined essential drugs as "those considered to be of the utmost importance and hence basic, indispensible, and necessary for the health needs of the population." The report also recommended that the WHO draw up a model list of drugs considered essential. The World Health Assembly endorsed the recommendations. At the Fifth Non-Aligned Conference in Colombo, in 1976, developing countries again endorsed the plan (Lall, 1978, pp. 29, 30).

Subsequently, an expert panel convened by the WHO published a technical report, "WHO Expert Committee on the Selection of Essential

A New Health Order as Part of the New Social Order   85

Drugs,"[40] which included a model list of 224 essential drugs and vaccines as well as guidelines for preparing such a list at the national level.[41] The Alma-Ata Declaration considered the provision of essential medicines a key component of primary health care. By 1984, the WHO could proudly state that "more than 80 ... countries have already developed a list of essential drugs based on the WHO model list."[42]

A model list of essential drugs was a radical endeavor. In effect, the WHO suggested that governments should have the power to restrict the drugs available in the market or, at minimum, prioritize the purchasing of essential drugs over other drugs, including not only those deemed unsafe, but also those that were considered too expensive or were treating "nonbasic" medical needs. WHO staff presented the list of essential drugs as contributing to developing countries' self-reliance and to their social and economic development.[43] It was also claimed to support the transfer of "appropriate technology,"[44] which was framed as compatible with the NIEO's central tenet of transfer of technology, even though the NIEO did not distinguish between appropriate and inappropriate technologies.

The model list of essential drugs, which was promoted by the WHO staff as a way to address an important concern to the organization, was backed by developing countries, who found it compatible with the NIEO principles. The drug industry, however, considered it an unprecedented and illegitimate attempt to curtail its freedom of action in the production and marketing of drugs (Reich, 1987). The sector's trade journal, *SCRIP*, declared that the list was "completely unacceptable to the pharmaceutical industry" (cited in Mamdani, 1992, p. 19), and a formal statement by the Council of the International Federation of Pharmaceutical Manufacturers and Associations (IFPMA) expressed "serious reservations" and threatened that the report "would discourage investment by the pharmaceutical industry in research."[45] The WHO bureaucracy's response to the industry's opposition shows the autonomy of the WHO bureaucracy but also points at the limits of strategic adaptation.

One of the industry's objections was that by creating a list of essential drugs, the WHO secretariat effectively argued that all drugs not included in the list were nonessential.[46] The IFPMA noted that "it is particularly unfortunate if the inference is drawn from the use of the word 'essential' that all other drugs not so designated are unnecessary."[47] In spite of this objection, the WHO staff retained the term but to appease the industry they became intentionally ambiguous on whether essential drug policies were designed to promote essential drugs or to exclude certain nonessential drugs (Reich, 1987). Indeed, the executive vice-president of IFPMA was "glad to say that WHO ... made it clear that ... it was not indicating that drugs not included in the list were Non-Essential" (Peretz, 1983, p. 131). In turn, the International Organization of Consumers Unions (IOCU) complained that "the WHO's programme on essential drugs originally referred to the need to restrict the supply of conspicuously inessential drugs .... It no longer does" (Fazal, 1983, p. 267). Another objection of the pharmaceutical industry was the list's universal application. The industry insisted that if the model list was to be used at all, it should apply only for the least developed countries.[48] To quiet such objections, the WHO bureaucracy phrased its position in a way so that the IFPMA conceded that "WHO has clarified ... that the concept is 'directed primarily to the needs of developing countries' although they go on to say that it does 'have values in other contexts'" (Peretz, 1983, p. 131). These two modifications defused the industry's objections. By 1982, according to the Chairman of the Ad Hoc Committee on Drug Policies, "the manufacturers' associations ... appeared not only to accept but to support the concept of essential drugs."[49]

The WHO bureaucracy offered these concessions to pacify pharmaceutical companies and the wealthy governments behind them. In reaching this compromise, the WHO did not act strategically. The suggested modifications tried to appease the industry by adopting its preferred language, without much alteration. Importantly, however, while the literature would categorize the case as a compromise between developing countries and Western interests, the outcome was rather a set of two independent negotiations: one between developing countries and the WHO bureaucracy and the other between the WHO bureaucracy and the pharmaceutical sector. The concessions offered to the pharmaceutical sector did not compromise the interests of developing countries but rather the WHO secretariat's own goals, particularly its commitment to intrastate equity. WHO policies on essential drugs now applied only to the "have-nots," thereby giving up on the original understanding that Health for All would require changes in the health services available to the "haves" as well.

Regulating Multinational Companies

In its major programs, Health for All and Primary Health Care, the WHO bureaucracy strategically complied with developing countries. However, following the distressing experience of complying with an initiative to regulate the infant formula industry, the secretariat strategically resisted a similar code for the pharmaceutical sector.

The decision to have an international code that would restrict aggressive forms of marketing and advertising by companies selling breast-milk substitutes was made in a consensus resolution, WHA33.32, in which the World Health Assembly requested the director-general to draft such a code (Sethi, 1994; Sikkink, 1986). The resolution followed a joint WHO/UNICEF meeting, which took place in October 1979, where member governments, UN agencies, other intergovernmental organizations and professional experts, and the infant formula industry and its critics had met to discuss the issue.[50] The joint meeting affirmed the right of member states to collectively regulate the practices of multinational corporations. A statement of the meeting declared, "The problem [of poor infant-feeding practices] is part of the wider issues of poverty, lack of resources, social injustice and ecological degradation; it cannot be considered apart from social and economic development and the need for a new international economic order."[51]

Following contentious negotiations, on both substantive and procedural matters, in May 1981 the World Health Assembly adopted, in Resolution WHA34.22, a nonbinding International Code of Marketing of Breast-Milk Substitutes.[52] The Code passed by 118 votes in favor, 3 abstentions, and the US delegation against.

Despite the almost unanimity in voting for the code, for the WHO staff the negotiations over the code proved costly. The WHO's reputation and legitimacy were undermined, as the bureaucracy had been accused by developed countries of dealing with matters outside the scope of the organization's constitutional authority. Mahler found it necessary to publicly defend himself by explicitly denying that the WHO bureaucracy had its own agenda. The minutes of Committee A at the Thirty-Third Assembly describe Mahler's protestation:

> The Director-General said that he had come to the Committee meeting particularly because of accusations that he had been making the Organization play a role it should not be playing and that he had gone beyond his mandate. He thought that two World Health Assemblies had instructed the Director-General in unambiguous resolutions to deal with all problems having to do with infant feeding.... He invited the members of the Committee to read resolutions WHA27.43 and WHA31.47 and decide whether, in the light of these resolutions, it had not been a perfectly logical and necessary step to convene the joint WHO/UNICEF Meeting.[53]

Another statement by Mahler conveyed an even greater sense of distress.

> Throughout what was called the free press the Secretariat had been labeled as secretive United Nations bureaucrats marching under the banner of WHO. He had hoped,

however, that the Board would defend the Secretariat and see the proposals not as the Secretariat's policy but as the high degree of participatory democracy for which the Organization had been able to provide a platform in developing protection for children throughout the world.[54]

Mahler concluded that talk "by saying that the experience had not been pleasant for the Secretariat," and that "it had been a difficult climate in which to maneuver and keep its vision straight."[55]

In light of that experience, when developing countries called for a similar code for the pharmaceutical industry, Mahler was determined not to repeat the same mistake.

Support for a code of conduct for the marketing of pharmaceutical products was widespread among developing countries. Governments bitterly complained on pressures exerted on them by drug companies to purchase drugs and, already in 1978, the Assembly authorized the WHO to study strategies for reducing the prices of drugs, "including the development of a code of marketing practices."[56] A piece in the *Food Drug Cosmetic Law Journal* asserted, "The issues in this controversy are being framed within the context of the New International Economic Order ... [and] it appears that the pharmaceutical industry is destined to be a testing ground on which the future of this UN program will be decided" (Phelps, 1982, p. 2000). In 1984, a WHO Ad Hoc Committee on Drug Policies declared, "Where the WHO was concerned, the ultimate goal was the elaboration and application of a code which would govern the manufacture, marketing and handling of drugs."[57] Also in 1984, the Assembly passed a resolution that requested the director-general to convene a meeting of experts to "discuss the means and methods of ensuring the rational use of drugs ... and to discuss the role of marketing practices in this respect."

Such a meeting was clearly meant to resemble the expert meeting that had preceded the code on infant formula (Sikkink, 1986, p. 837), but the WHO leadership concluded that the importance of having a code for the pharmaceuticals market could not justify the damage the inevitable debate over pharmaceutical marketing might cause to the reputation of the organization. Already in 1982, Maher argued that "on the question of codes of practice, it was important to move forward in a spirit of cooperation, and not deliberately to seek confrontation, because to do so would be counterproductive."[58] In a meeting of UNCTAD's Trade and Development Board, in which the spokesman of the G-77 "stressed that the drawing up of norms and standards on marketing, promotion, distribution, trade and technology in the pharmaceutical sector continued

A New Health Order as Part of the New Social Order

to be one of [the G-77] major preoccupations,"[59] a WHO representative responded:

> The WHO secretariat was not lacking in courage, but it did try to exercise prudence .... There was deep-rooted concern in WHO and its governing bodies that the preoccupation with an independent code of marketing practice for pharmaceutical products could divert attention away from the constructive progress that had been made by member states in developing national policies on essential drugs and by the pharmaceutical industry in accepting its responsibilities within the framework of the Drug Action Programme. Much more needed to be done in an atmosphere of collaboration rather than confrontation.[60]

In trying to dissuade developing countries from forcing a code with their votes, the WHO strategically relied on NIEO principles to justify its opposition. First, the WHO leadership made the case that focusing on pharmaceutical marketing would undermine the NIEO concern with equity. Mahler stated:

> In most developing countries, there were between 5% and 10% of drug "haves" and from 90% to 95% of drug "have-nots." ... [Despite] sympathy for the minority, who might be supplied with too many or the wrong kind of drugs ... the action programme was primarily concerned ... that so many people had no regular access to essential drugs. It was therefore of little value becoming involved in marginal, conflictual issues while there were governments which had no national policy for essential drugs or were not implementing such a policy ... WHO must concern itself first and foremost with the "have-nots."[61]

Second, and more effectively, the WHO leadership passionately argued that turning the organization into a supranational authority violated the NIEO principle of sovereignty. A discussion paper by the director-general insisted, "It is not possible for WHO to enforce intercountry cooperation for health against the desires of the governments concerned since it is not a supranational organization but an international one."[62] In insisting that the WHO should not be used to impose rules on countries, the bureaucracy downplayed developing countries' call for strengthened universal international organization and highlighted the principles of self-reliance and sovereignty. Nonetheless, by drawing on the NIEO to oppose the code, the WHO bureaucracy avoided the seemingly inevitable confrontation passive resistance would have led to.

In November 1985, the WHO secretariat organized a conference of experts on the rational use of drugs, but supporters of the code criticized the staff for its reluctant efforts to make the conference successful. For example, critics viewed the decision to hold the conference in Kenya as an attempt to lower the profile of the meeting. They also criticized the decision to keep the list of invited participants secret and for asking those invited not to divulge the contents of the background papers in advance of the conference (Walt & Harnmeijer, 1992, pp. 37, 38; Kanji, Hardon, Harnmeijer, Mamdani, & Walt, 1992). These accusations made Mahler particularly upset, as he described before the Assembly in 1986:

> That decision [to arrange a meeting on the rational use of drugs] had given rise to a type of international social pathology the likes of which he has never experienced in his long career in WHO. It had threatened the very existence of the Organization, with passions running wild on all sides. Accusations had been made that the Secretariat was sabotaging the meeting .... Scandalously slanderous misinformation had been spread all over the world. Suspicions had been openly stated by one interest group that WHO was sold to the other and vice versa, and all seemed to be convinced that the meeting would only be a cover-up for predetermined conclusions – the opposite to the ones they wanted, of course![63]

At the meeting, however, the WHO bureaucracy's desire to avoid confrontation was satisfied as the experts rejected the possibility of an international code of conduct. In summing up the conference before the Assembly, Mahler described how: "There was a general understanding of WHO's international as opposed to supranational role. WHO is a cooperative of Member States and it is they who decide on its policy .... Policies can be defined in WHO but they cannot be imposed by WHO."[64]

The debate over a code of conduct for the marketing of pharmaceutical products highlights the WHO bureaucracy's vulnerability in the face of external disapproval and the fact that the secretariat's position was often informed by the need to maintain legitimacy. It also shows the capacity of the bureaucracy to strategically resist developing countries' demands, when those were seen to undermine the organization's standing.

CONCLUSION

The WHO, like other specialized agencies, was expected in the 1970s and early 1980s to contribute to the making of an NIEO, based on the principles of equity, development, self-reliance, and economic sovereignty. The WHO leadership developed in response new programs and set new priorities that were persuasively presented as the organization's adherence with the new order. In an address to the World Health Assembly, for example, Mahler referred to the Alma-Ata Declaration as "the New International Economic Order in the field of health, or – if you prefer – a new international order in health."[65]

However, the WHO secretariat's response to developing countries, which could use their voting majority to determine the fate of the proposed programs, was not a passive compliance that merely implemented programs favored by the G-77. Instead, the WHO bureaucracy was able to provide a meaning to the central NIEO principles so that the programs designed in compliance with those principles were also in line with the constitutional mission of the WHO, addressed the disillusionment of public health experts with vertical interventions, and could gain the support also of developed countries and multinational companies. The WHO bureaucracy was able to present its own perceptions as entirely compatible with the NIEO logic, largely by shifting the NIEO focus with economic development to the more relevant focus on social development, and redirecting the original concern with inequity among states to inequity within states. The principle of self-reliance was also broadened, in order to call for the participation of developing countries in the decision-making process of the WHO, to legitimate the participation of communities at the local level, and – when strategically resisting developing countries' demands – to justify a nation's reliance on its own economic resources and political will in making and implementing health programs. In turn, the principle of technology transfer was narrowed, to justify the WHO's support of essential drugs lists. Through such reframing, the WHO bureaucracy was able to promote the programs of Health for All, primary health care, and essential drugs lists, which were concerned with health disparities within poor countries and with improvements in living conditions and quality of life under conditions of scarce resources. Additionally, such reframing enabled the WHO bureaucracy to oppose developing countries' attempts to regulate pharmaceutical companies.

The response of the WHO staff to the demands of developing countries in the 1970s and early 1980s shows that international bureaucracies produce programs, plans, and policies that reflect the bureaucracies' own autonomous goals. In three of the four cases analyzed here – Health for All, primary health care, and essential drugs list – the initiatives came from the WHO bureaucracy rather than from member states, and they were not in response to external political pressures. Moreover, it illustrates the capacity of international bureaucracies to defend those programs, plans and policies even in situations in which they potentially clash with the expectations of member states.

In such situations, the WHO bureaucracy utilized strategic rather than passive responses. In the cases analyzed here, blind compliance with developing countries would have come at the expense of some the WHO's ideational principles and compromised its relations with developed countries. Resistance, in turn, could have failed, given developing countries' voting majority in the World Health Assembly. Instead, by complying with reinterpreted demands, which made cases of distorted compliance look complete, the WHO staff was able to satisfy the expectations of developing countries while lessening the potential sacrifices. In other cases, by presenting disobedience as adherence, the WHO staff strategically resisted the demands, which reduced the risk of failure or retaliation.

Leadership as a Condition for Strategic Response
While adaptive strategies such as those used by the WHO staff in the 1970s are common, international bureaucracies do not always choose such strategies. The WHO failed to act strategically, for example, toward the end of Mahler's tenure, when the negotiations over the NIEO collapsed and international organizations were expected instead to adopt policies in line with neoliberal economic principles that were supported by the US government. It was only in the late 1990s that the WHO, under the leadership of Gro Harlem Brundtland, adapted effectively to the neoliberal logic. Also during the 1970s, the response of international bureaucracies varied: the ILO and UNICEF strategically complied with the NIEO in a way similar to the WHO (Jolly, 1991; Melanson, 1979), but UNESCO complied with the demands of developing countries and its New International Information Order led to the withdrawal of the United States and others from the organization (Imber, 1989). While a comprehensive analysis of the conditions allowing international bureaucracies to strategically respond to external pressures requires a comparative study, the experience of the WHO in the 1970s points at one important factor influencing the choice of strategic response, that of leadership.[66] The experience of Director-General Mahler suggests that strategic adaptation is more likely when (1) the institutional conditions of the international organization allow for strong leadership, which provide the leader with the means to transform the organization without such attempts being paralyzed by external opposition or internal debates. At the WHO, directors-general prepare the budget and therefore influence the organization's priorities; additionally, they can often appoint new staff, create new divisions, and in other ways "layer" new priorities on top of old programs. These institutional arrangements allow directors-general to effectively shape the direction of the organization. Charismatic leaders like Mahler were especially able to use such authority for strategic responses. (2) The leadership is newly recruited and can therefore more easily rethink the organization's position and introduce strategic

changes to it. Even "strong" leaders are more likely to employ adaptive strategies successfully during their first years in office. Once new policies get institutionalized, however, they become barriers when exogenous conditions require a different response from the organization. Mahler became Director-General in 1974 and immediately mobilized the organization behind a new agenda. By the mid-1980s, however, he was arguably too committed to that agenda to be able to respond effectively to a transformed political context. (3) The new leaders are partially embedded in the exogenous environment so that the leaders can function as bridges between the bureaucracy and the broader environment (Thornton & Ocasio, 1999), although this may be the cause of some of the difficulties leaders have in responding effectively to new conditions in the later years of their tenure. Strategic responses are more likely when leaders are partially embedded in the exogenous environment because it allows them to accept, at least in part, the dominant ideas, and because it gives them sufficient knowledge of the environment to know how to manipulate it. Mahler spent many years as a WHO official in India and he had great respect to developing countries' demands for a more equal world order. This position greatly influenced the WHO's position in support of the NIEO, but also allowed the bureaucracy to successfully legitimate its distortions. Embeddedness, however, needs to be partial, as complete identification may lead to greater loyalty to the exogenous environment than to the organization and therefore to passive compliance.

Limits of Strategic Adaptation. Even under the most conducive conditions, including effective leadership, strategic responses have limits. First, my analysis highlights the significant policy changes that are often required in cases of strategic compliance, and also when the bureaucracy is able to protect its goals. Second, while reinterpretation of demands allows better protection of the bureaucracy's agenda, strategic responses are not about "duping" the environment. To be effective, the reframing has to make sense to the exogenous forces and therefore cannot stray too far from the original expectations. As a result, the possible success of a strategic response is limited by the logical boundaries of the original demands. Even when responding strategically, therefore, an international organization's new policies would be informed, at least in part, by the external demands. It is due to these limits that adaptive strategies are at times easy to confuse with "passive" compliance or resistance. Scholars who reject the capacity of international bureaucracies to act autonomously are able to read partial compatibility with external demands as instances of compliance; scholars who emphasize bureaucratic autonomy are able to overemphasize the independence of such actions. In contrast, this article emphasizes the interplay that is inherent in strategic adaptation and that allows for international bureaucracies to follow external expectations while protecting their autonomous agendas.

NOTES

1. See http://www.who.int/about/en
2. While both the World Health Assembly and the secretariat are integral parts of the organization, the analysis here focuses on the organization's *bureaucracy*, which experiences the demands and expectations of member states, including those conveyed at the World Health Assembly, as *external* demands.
3. In a study that builds on principal-agent theory, Hawkins and Jacoby (2006) atypically investigate not the characteristics of agents but the strategies these agents use to circumvent principals' controls. The scope of their analysis, however, is limited to strategies intended to influence the agent's level of autonomy, such as the reinterpretation of the international organization's mandates, and they do not discuss strategies used by agents within given levels of autonomy.
4. Declaration on the Establishment of a New International Economic Order. Sixth Special Session. May 1, 1974. A/RES/S-6/3201.
5. For accounts on the NIEO, see Frieden (2006), Krasner (1985), Murphy (1984), and Sauvant (1981).
6. Declaration on the Establishment of a New International Economic Order. Sixth Special Session. May 1, 1974. A/RES/S-6/3201.
7. The analysis here pays particular attention to formal reports and to speeches made by the WHO leadership, especially Director-General Mahler. This is not to deny the likelihood of internal opposition among the WHO staff. However, WHO reports and Mahler's statements reflect the formal position of the WHO bureaucracy – that is, the position that prevailed following internal negotiations and debates – and as such they represent the position of the WHO as it was presented to member states, which is the main concern of this article.
8. Note. "Dr. Halfdan Mahler, DG of the UN WHO." Attached to a memorandum from Robert Emrey, International Health Assessment Staff at the White House to Robert Bourne. July 6, 1977. Staff Offices, Bourne, Box 34, International Health 7/1/77–7/31/77. Carter Presidential Library.
9. Report. Steering Committee on International Organizations. WHO. *Report on the 27th WHA*. Geneva, May 7–23, 1974. Department of Health and Social Security. July 19, 1974. FCO 61/1208. UK National Archives.
10. "The constitutional mission of the World Health Organization." Address by Dr. H. Mahler, Director-General of the WHO in presenting his report for 1973 to the Twenty-Seventh World Health Assembly. May 8, 1974. WHO Library.
11. Note by the Foreign Office. "UN specialized agencies." October 2, 1964. OD 29/59. UK National Archives.
12. WHO Document. January 1982. EB69/SR/15. WHO Library.

A New Health Order as Part of the New Social Order 95

13. WHO Document. January 1980. EB65/SR/6. WHO Library.
14. WHO Document. January 1979. EB63/SR/19, p. 4. WHO Library.
15. "Health for all by the year 2000." Address delivered by Dr. H. Mahler, Director-General of the WHO to the Twenty-Sixth Session of the Regional Committee for the Western Pacific, Manila, September 1, 1975. WHO Library. Emphasis in original.
16. *Health manpower requirements for the achievement of Health for All by the year 2000 through primary health care.* 1985. Report of a WHO Expert Committee. WHO Technical Report Series 717. WHO Library.
17. "Health for all by the year 2000." Address delivered by Dr. H. Mahler, Director-General of the WHO to the Twenty-Sixth Session of the Regional Committee for the Western Pacific, Manila, September 1, 1975. WHO Library.
18. WHO Document. 1980. WHA33/A/SR/4. WHO Library.
19. WHO Document. January 1980. EB65/SR/6. WHO Library.
20. "Health for all by the year 2000." Address delivered by Dr. H. Mahler, Director-General of the WHO to the Twenty-Sixth Session of the Regional Committee for the Western Pacific, Manila, September 1, 1975. WHO Library.
21. WHO Document. January 1980. EB65/SR/5. WHO Library.
22. WHO Document. January 1976. EB57/SR/15. WHO Library.
23. Mahler, H. 1981. "What is Health for All?" *World Health.* WHO Library.
24. WHO Document. "Text of Resolution 34/58, Adopted by the United Nations General Assembly on 29 November 1979." A33/5, p. 11. PAHO Library.
25. At the time, Mahler was an assistant director-general, responsible for programs that were concerned with improving national capabilities in health planning, and as such at the center of the debate over alternatives to the eradication agenda (Cueto, 2004, p. 1865).
26. WHO Document. 1974. *Promotion of national health services. Report by the director-general.* EB55/9. WHO Library; also Litsios (2004).
27. WHO Document. 1976. A29/SR/20, p. 20. WHO Library.
28. The Soviets were likely motivated by an intra-communist ideological battle between the Chinese form of medical care that inspired the notion of primary health care and the more medically-oriented Soviet approach (Cueto, 2004, p. 1867).
29. Telegram. "31st World Health Assembly (May 8–24) – Third week." Department of Defense. May 1978. Staff Offices, Bourne, Box 38. International Health – TDR and other WHO related materials, 12/12–14/77–6/26/78. Carter Presidential Library.
30. WHO Document. 1979. WHA32/A/SR/15. WHO Library.
31. WHO Document. January 1980. EB65/SR/6. WHO Library.
32. Mahler, H. T. 1980. "Primary health care – An analysis of some constraints." Address delivered to the Special Congregation for the Conferment of an honorary degree on Dr. Halfdan T. Mahler at the University of Lagos on Saturday, October 20, 1979. University of Lagos Press. WHO Library.
33. Note. Department of State. "Mahler the man." Undated. Staff Offices, Bourne, Box 38. International Health – Undated Material [1]. Carter Presidential Library.
34. "World health target for basic human needs." Address by Dr. H. Mahler, Director-General of the WHO in presenting his eport for 1976 to the Thirtieth World Health Assembly. May 3, 1977. WHO Library.

35. Mahler, H. 1981. "What is health for all?" *World Health*. WHO Library.
36. WHO. 28th WHA. Geneva. May 13–30,1975. Department of Heath and Social Security. August 29, 1975. FCO 61/1351. UK National Archives.
37. "WHO's mission revisited." Address by Dr. H. Mahler, Director-General of the WHO in presenting his report for 1974 to the Twenty-Eighth World Health Assembly. May 15, 1975. WHO Library.
38. "Health for all by the year 2000." Address delivered by Dr. H. Mahler, Director-General of the WHO to the Twenty-Sixth Session of the Regional Committee for the Western Pacific, Manila, September 1, 1975. WHO Library.
39. WHO Document. 1975. *Prophylactic and therapeutic substances. Report by the director-general*. A28/11. PAHO Library.
40. WHO Document. 1977. Technical Report Series. No. 615. WHO Library.
41. WHO. 1978. Background document for reference and use at the technical discussions on "National policies and practices in regard to medicinal products, and related international problems." A31/Technical Discussions/1, p. 18. PAHO Library.
42. WHO Document. *DAP comments on ACC Task Force project proposal No. 3*. May 24, 1984. WHO Library.
43. WHO Document. 1975. *Prophylactic and therapeutic substances. Report by the director-general*. A28/11. PAHO Library.
44. As noted above, the Alma-Ata Declaration stated that one of the principles of primary health care was reliance on appropriate – that is, "scientifically sound and socially acceptable" – technology.
45. IFPMA. April 1978. *Statement as adopted by the IFPMA Council on the selection of essential drugs*. Report of a WHO Expert Committee Technical Report Series No. 615. WHO, Geneva, 1977. WHO Library.
46. Airmail from J. Richard Court, Director of Bureau of Drugs, Department of Health, Education and Welfare, USA to the Director, Division of Prophylactic, Diagnostic and Therapeutic Substances, WHO. February 9, 1978. WHO Library.
47. A note from Imperial Chemical Industries Limited, Pharmaceuticals Division, to Dr. Kilgour, Department of Health and Social Security. January 4, 1978. MH 148/1050. UK National Archives.
48. IFPMA. April 1978. *Statement as adopted by the IFPMA Council on the selection of essential drugs*. Report of a WHO Expert Committee Technical Report Series No. 615. WHO, Geneva, 1977. WHO Library.
49. WHO Document. 1982. EB69/SR/14. WHO Library.
50. On the domestic and international mobilization that had led to the joint meeting, see Jayasuriya, Griffiths, & Rigoni (1984), Sethi (1994), and Sikkink (1986).
51. *Statement and recommendations of the joint WHO/UNICEF meeting on infant and young child feeding*. Retrieved from http://www.unu.edu/Unupress/food/8F023e/8F023E04.htm
52. Many developed countries found the draft code "unrealistically extreme" and preferred the voluntary option that would have allowed them to avoid implementation of such obligations (Memorandum. *Draft international code of marketing of breastmilk substitutes*. External Affairs. July 15, 1980. RG25, Vol. 14977, file 46-4-WHO-1, 9, Canadian National Archives).

53. WHO Document. 1980. WHA33/A/7. WHO Library.
54. WHO Document. 1981. EB67/SR/24. WHO Library.
55. WHO Document. 1981. EB67/SR/24. WHO Library.
56. As with the code for infant formula, regulation was supported by a large group of activists. See Mamdani and Walker (1986), Reich (1987), and Walt and Harnmeijer (1992).
57. WHO Document. 1984. EB73/SR/15, p. 195. WHO Library.
58. WHO Document. 1982. EB69/SR/13. WHO Library.
59. Trade and Development Board. 28th Session. WHO Library.
60. Trade and Development Board. 28th Session. WHO Library.
61. WHO Document. 1984. EB73/SR/15. WHO Library.
62. WHO Document. 1985. *Global strategy for health for all by the year 2000: Political dimension.* Discussion Paper by the Director-General. EB24, Annex. 10, pp. 160, 161. WHO Library.
63. WHO Document. 1986. WHA39/A/SR/11. WHO Library.
64. WHO. 1986. A39/12. *Director-general's summing-up, at the conference of experts, of the issues, proceedings, and potential implications for WHO's programme.* Annex. 5. WHO Library.
65. "Action for health." Address by Dr. H. Mahler, Director-General of the WHO to the Thirty-Second World Health Assembly. May 8, 1979. WHO Library.
66. Scholars have argued that an organization's response to pressures is determined by the perceived cost to the organizational goals that compliance would require compared to the cost to the organization if it was panelized for its resistance (Barnett & Coleman, 2005; Oliver, 1991). Such calculations, however, are less relevant once strategic responses are available, since these significantly lower the potential costs. Instead, we need to consider what factors provide organizations the capacity for reducing these potential costs, that is, the capacity for strategic action.

ACKNOWLEDGMENTS

I would like to thank Greta Krippner, Andrew Schrank, Patrick Heller, Mark Blyth, Peter Andreas, James Jasper, Tim Bartley, Victoria Johnson, and the anonymous reviewers of *Political Power and Social Theory* for their helpful comments. This article has also benefited from the institutional support of Brown University and the Woodrow Wilson International Center for Scholars.

REFERENCES

Abdelal, R. (2007). *Capital rules: The construction of global finance.* Cambridge: Harvard University Press.
Albert, S., & Whetton, D. A. (1985). Organizational identity. *Research in Organizational Behavior, 7,* 263–295.

Barnett, M., & Coleman, L. (2005). Designing police: Interpol and the study of change in international organizations. *International Studies Quarterly, 49*, 593–619.

Barnett, M., & Finnemore, M. (2004). *Rules for the world: International organizations in global politics.* Ithaca, NY: Cornell University Press.

Brown, T. M., Cueto, M., & Fee, E. (2006). The World Health Organization and the transition from 'International' to 'Global' public health. *American Journal of Public Health, 96*(1), 62–72.

Chwieroth, J. (2008). Normative change from within: The international monetary fund's approach to capital account liberalization. *International Studies Quarterly, 52*, 129–158.

Cueto, M. (2004). The origins of primary health care and selective primary health care. *American Journal of Public Health, 94*, 1864–1874.

DiMaggio, P. J. (1983). State expansion and organizational fields. In R. H. Hall & R. E. Ouinn (Eds.), *Organizational theory and public policy* (pp. 147–161). Beverly Hills, CA: Sage.

DiMaggio, P. J. (1991). Constructing an organizational field as a professional project: U.S. Art Museums, 1920–1940. In W. W. Powell & P. J. DiMaggio (Eds.), *The new institutionalism in organizational analysis* (pp. 267–292). Chicago, IL: University of Chicago Press.

Fazal, A. (1983). The right pharmaceuticals at the right prices: Consumer perspectives. *World Development, 11*(3), 265–269.

Frieden, J. (2006). *Global capitalism: Its fall and rise in the twentieth century.* New York, NY: Norton.

Gish, O. (1983). The relation of the new international economic order to health. *Journal of Public Health Policy, 4*(2), 207–221.

Glynn, M. A. (2000). When cymbals become symbols: Conflict over organizational identity within a symphony orchestra. *Organization Science, 11*(3), 285–298.

Goodrick, E., & Salancik, G. R. (1996). Organizational discretion in responding to institutional practices: Hospitals and cesarean births. *Administrative Science Quarterly, 41*(1), 1–28.

Goodstein, J. D. (1994). Institutional pressures and strategic responsiveness: Employer involvement in work-family issues. *The Academy of Management Journal, 37*(2), 350–382.

Harris, L. C., & Ogbonna, E. (1999). The strategic legacy of company founders. *Long Range Planning, 32*(3), 333–343.

Hawkins, D. G., & Jacoby, W. (2006). How agents matter. In D. G. Hawkins, D. A. Lake, D. L. Nielson & M. J. Tierney (Eds.), *Delegation and agency in international organizations.* New York, NY: Cambridge University Press.

Hawkins, D. G., Lake, D. A., Nielson, D. L., & Tierney, M. J. (Eds.). (2006). *Delegation and agency in international organizations.* New York, NY: Cambridge University Press.

Hurd, I. (2007). *After anarchy: Legitimacy and power in the United Nations Security Council.* Princeton, NJ: Princeton University Press.

Imber, M. F. (1989). *The USA, ILO, UNESCO and IAEA: Politicization and withdrawal in the specialized agencies.* London: Macmillan.

Jayasuriya, D., Griffiths, A., & Rigoni, R. (1984). *Judgment reserved: Breast-feeding, bottle-feeding and the international code.* Nawala, Sri Lanka: Asian Pathfinder.

Jepperson, R. (1991). Institutions, institutional effects, and institutionalism. In W. W. Powell & P. DiMaggio (Eds.), *The new institutionalism in organizational analysis* (pp. 143–163). Chicago, IL: University of Chicago Press.

Jolly, R. (1991). Adjustment with a human face: A UNICEF record and perspective on the 1980s. *World Development, 19*(12), 1807–1821.

Kanji, N., Hardon, A., Harnmeijer, J. W., Mamdani, M., & Walt, G. (Eds.). (1992). *Drugs policy in developing countries*. London: Zed Books.
Keohane, R. (1984). *After hegemony: Cooperation and discord in the world political economy*. Princeton, NJ: Princeton University Press.
Keohane, R., & Martin, L. L. (1995). The promise of institutionalist theory. *International Security*, *20*(1), 39–51.
Krasner, S. D. (1985). *Structural conflict: The third world against global liberalism*. Berkeley, CA: University of California Press.
Lall, S. (1978). *The growth of the pharmaceutical industry in developing countries: Problems and prospects. ID/204*. Vienna: UNIDO.
Lee, K. (2009). *The World Health Organization (WHO)*. London: Routledge.
Litsios, S. (2004). The Christian medical commission and the development of the World Health Organization's primary health care approach. *American Journal of Public Health*, *94*(11), 1884–1893.
Luken, R. A. (2009). Greening an international organization: UNIDO's strategic responses. *Review of International Organizations*, *4*, 159–184.
Mamdani, M. (1992). Early initiatives in essential drugs policy. In N. Kanji, A. Hardon, J. W. Harnmeijer, M. Mamdani & G. Walt (Eds.), *Drugs policy in developing countries*. London: Zed Books.
Mamdani, M., & Walker, G. (1986). Essential drugs in the developing world. *Health Policy and Planning*, *1*(3), 187–201.
Manela, E. (2010). A pox on your narrative: Writing disease control into cold war history. *Diplomatic History*, *34*(2), 299–323.
Mearsheimer, J. (1994). The false promise of international institutions. *International Security*, *19*(3), 5–49.
Melanson, R. A. (1979). Human rights and the American withdrawal from the ILO. *Universal Human Rights*, *1*(1), 43–61.
Melrose, D. (1983). Double deprivation: Public and private drug distribution from the perspective of the third world poor. *World Development*, *11*(3), 181–186.
Murphy, C. (1984). *Emergence of the NIEO ideology*. Boulder, CO: Westview Press.
Nájera, J. A. (1989). Malaria and the work of WHO. *Bulletin of WHO*, *67*(3), 229–243.
Newell, K. (1988). Selective primary health care: The counter revolution. *Social Science and Medicine*, *26*(9), 903–906.
Nielson, D., & Tierney, M. (2003). Delegation to international organizations: Agency theory and world bank environmental reform. *International Organization*, *57*(2), 241–276.
Oliver, C. (1991). Strategic responses to institutional pressures. *Academy of Management Review*, *16*(1), 145–179.
Packard, R. (1997). Malaria dreams: Postwar visions of health and development in the third world. *Medical Anthropology*, *17*, 279–296.
Peretz, S. M. (1983). An industry view of restricted drugs formularies. *Journal of Social and Administrative Pharmacy*, *1*(3), 130–133.
Pfeffer, J., & Salancik, G. R. (1978). *The external control of organizations: A resource dependence perspective*. New York, NY: Harper & Row.
Phelps, J. R. (1982). The new international economic order and the pharmaceutical industry. *Food Drug Cosmetic Law Journal*, *37*, 200–211.

Powell, W. W. (1988). Institutional effects on organizational structure and performance. In L. G. Zucker (Ed.), *Institutional patterns and organizations: Culture and environment* (pp. 115–136). Cambridge: Ballinger.
Raviglione, M. C., & Pio, A. (2002). Evolution of WHO policies for tuberculosis control, 1948–2001. *The Lancet, 359*(9308), 775–780.
Reich, M. R. (1987). Essential drugs: Economics and politics in international health. *Health Policy, 8*, 39–57.
Sauvant, K. P. (Ed.). (1981). *Changing priorities on the international agenda: The new international economic order*. Oxford: Pergamon.
Scott, R. W. (2008). Approaching adulthood: The maturing of institutional theory. *Theory and Society, 37*, 427–442.
Sethi, S. P. (1994). *Multinational corporations and the impact of public advocacy on corporate strategy: Nestle and the infant formula controversy*. Boston, MA: Kluwer Academic Publishers.
Sikkink, K. (1986). Codes of conduct for transnational corporations: The case of the WHO/ UNICEF code. *International Organization, 40*(4), 815–840.
Smith, D., & Bryant, J. H. (1988). Building the infrastructure for primary health care: An overview of vertical and integrated approaches. *Social Science Medicine, 26*(9), 909–917.
Suchman, M. (1995). Managing legitimacy: Strategic and institutional approaches. *Academy of Management Review, 20*(3), 571–610.
Thornton, P. H., & Ocasio, W. (1999). Institutional logics and the historical contingency of power in organizations: Executive succession in the higher education publishing industry, 1958–1990. *American Journal of Sociology, 105*(3), 801–843.
Walt, G., & Harnmeijer, J. W. (1992). Formulating an essential drugs policy: WHO's role. In N. Kanji, A. Hardon, J. W. Harnmeijer, M. Mamdani & G. Walt (Eds.), *Drugs policy in developing countries*. London: Zed Books.
Weaver, C. (2008). *Hypocrisy trap: The World Bank and the poverty of reform*. Princeton, NJ: Princeton University Press.
WHO. (1958). *The first ten years of the World Health Organization*. Geneva: WHO.
WHO. (1978). Declaration of Alma Ata: International Conference on Primary Health Care, Alma Ata, USSR, September 6–12, 1978. Geneva: WHO.
WHO. (1980). Technical discussions on the contribution of health to the new international economic order. A33/Technical Discussions/1. Geneva: WHO Library.
Williams, D. (1987). *The specialized agencies for the United Nations: The system in crisis*. London: Hurst.

PART II
POLITICS AND IDENTITIES

THE RECONFIGURATION OF THE PALESTINIAN NATIONAL QUESTION: THE INDIRECT RULE ROUTE AND THE CIVIL SOCIETY ROUTE

Silvia Pasquetti

ABSTRACT

How are social groups unmade? Current theories identify the symbolic power of the state as a primary factor in the creation of social groups. Drawing on Gramsci's The Southern Question, *this chapter extends state-centered theories by exploring policies that are critical but undertheorized factors in group formation. These include the concession of material benefits as well as the use of coercive means. Further, while current theories focus on how social groups are made, a Gramscian perspective draws attention to how the state intervenes to prevent or neutralize group-making projects from below. This chapter explores a case of a decrease in national group solidarity. Specifically, this study explains how in the 1990s the Israeli state weakened national group formation among Palestinians by adopting two spatially distinct but coordinated strategies. First, the rearrangement of the military occupation of the Gaza Strip and the West Bank through the establishment of an authority of self-rule (the Palestinian Authority) demobilized and divided Palestinian residents of the Occupied Territories, especially along classcum-moral lines. Second, state practices and discourses centered on citizenship rights shifted the center of political activism among Palestinian citizens of Israel toward citizenship issues. I argue that these two routes, which I call the indirect rule route and the civil society route, were complementary components of a broader attempt to neutralize Palestinian collective mobilization around nationhood. Despite recent changes and contestations, these two strategies of rule continue to affect group formation and to create distinct experiences of politics among Palestinians under Israeli rule. Analysis of the Palestinian–Israeli case shows that the state can unmake groups through the distribution of interrelated policies that are specific to certain categories of people and places. Understanding the conditions under which certain policies of inclusion or exclusion affect group formation requires going beyond the analytic primacy currently given to the symbolic power of the state.*

In the 1970s and 1980s, Palestinians under Israeli rule mounted collective forms of protest against the Israeli state, ranging from mass protests against land confiscation in Israel to a sustained popular uprising against the Israeli military rule in the Occupied Palestinian Territories (El-Asmar, 1976; Hiltermann, 1985, 1991; Lockman & Beinin, 1989; Lustick, 1980, 1993a; MERIP, 1976; Nassar & Heacock, 1990; Rekhess, 2007; Rouhana, 1989; Yiftachel, 1996). National group solidarity was on the rise on both sides of the Green Line, the "border" that has separated Israel and the Occupied Palestinian Territories since 1967.[1] Collective mobilization around the question of land rights was central to the articulation and expression of nationalist feelings among both Palestinian citizens of Israel and residents of the West Bank and the Gaza Strip. Nationhood had the potential to become a source of solidarity between these two segments of Palestinians under Israeli rule, especially because, in the 1970s and 1980s, social contacts across the Green Line were relatively easy and the Israeli state reacted to popular protests on both sides of the Green Line with direct repression (Al-Haj, 2005; Yiftachel, 2000, 2006, pp. 170–171).[2]

This chapter examines how, in the early 1990s, the Israeli state weakened national group solidarity among Palestinians by adopting distinct policies and discourses toward different categories of Palestinians. Two spatially distinct but coordinated strategies emerge as particularly consequential for Palestinian national group formation. First, the rearrangement of the military occupation of the Gaza Strip and the West Bank through the establishment of an authority of self-rule (the Palestinian Authority, PA) demobilized and divided Palestinian residents of the Occupied Palestinian Territories, especially along class-cum-moral lines. Second, state practices and discourses centered on citizenship rights shifted the center of political activism among Palestinian citizens of Israel toward citizenship issues. I argue that these two routes, which I call the indirect rule route and the civil society route, were complementary components of a broader attempt to neutralize Palestinian collective mobilization around nationhood.

The analytic perspective on national group solidarity among Palestinians under Israeli rule developed in this chapter draws on Gramsci's writings (1995 [1926]) about the Italian "Southern Question." In the Italian context, "the Southern Question" refers to a still much relevant political and intellectual debate about the dualism between Northern and Southern regions since the unification of the state in 1861. Writing in the 1920s, Gramsci rejected the view that the underdevelopment of the Southern regions was mainly due to the cultural or racial backwardness of the Southern populations (D'Agostino, 2002);[3] he also criticized another dominant approach that disconnected the problems of the South from the broader history of Italy and called for economic and political reforms only in the South (Barbagallo, 1980; Petraccone, 2005; Salvadori, 1963). By situating the North–South interrelationship in Italy within the development of Italian capitalism, Gramsci examined how, during the Giolittian period (1900–1914), the Italian government used a distribution of different policies to neutralize the mounting pressure of mobilized popular sectors ranging from revolutionary socialism among workers in the North to peasant revolts in the South. These policies included a politics of reforms, concessions, and associationism for the Northern working class as well as the co-optation of key political and intellectual elites and the use of coercion against the peasantry in the South (Gramsci, 1995 [1926], pp. 29–30). Gramsci also discussed how these distinct but interconnected policies affected the symbolic and political relations between Northern workers and Southern peasants by reinforcing cultural and political differences between them.

This Gramscian perspective on the role of the state in affecting the definition of group membership and the articulation of political interests among workers and peasants in Italy is a useful tool for my study of the linkage between Israeli policies and national group solidarity among Palestinians under Israeli rule. Drawing on Gramsci, I discuss how the state can neutralize or channel group-making projects from below. Specifically, I explore how a single state can undermine group solidarity among different segments of a population under its rule, through the distribution of different but interrelated policies that are specific to certain categories of people and places.

I give particular attention to three elements of the process of weakening of Palestinian national group solidarity, which took place during the 1990s: (1) the popular demobilization and the estrangement between popular constituencies and political elites in the Occupied Palestinian Territories; (2) the increased salience of legal citizenship as an axis of symbolic and political distance; and (3) the emergence of the Israeli associational sphere as a new venue for professional opportunities and political activism for Palestinians in Israel. I situate these three elements within the broader process of physical separation between different segments of Palestinians, which was initiated by the Israeli state in the 1990s and which has intensified in the last decade via the introduction of new legal restrictions on Palestinian mobility, and via the construction of new physical obstacles between and within different areas of the Occupied Palestinian Territories.

On the one hand, I examine how the establishment of the PA undermined national solidarity among Palestinians in several regards. First, the emergence of new lifestyles centered on new forms of entertainment and consumption, especially in Ramallah, the "capital" of the PA and the new urban center of life for the emerging Palestinian middle class (Taraki, 2008a) engendered widespread feelings of resentment among poor Palestinians (Bucaille, 2004, pp. 56–57; Johnson, 2007). These feelings were strengthened by an everyday reality marked by uninterrupted Israeli military repression. Second, the PA infrastructure reactivated old lines of division among Gaza and West Bank Palestinians such as clan membership (*hamula*) that had been weakened during the First *Intifada* (Uprising, 1987–1993) (Frisch, 1997; Robinson, 1997; Roy, 2001). Third, the PA's power to create jobs and make appointments created new strains of social friction in poor communities such as refugee camps, which, while never devoid of internal divisions, had played an important role in cementing national solidarity in the 1970s and 1980s (Collins, 2004, pp. 195–197). The negative impact that the role of the PA as a distributor of political and economic favoritisms had on national group solidarity was reinforced by high levels of unemployment among poor Palestinians. Widespread unemployment was, in turn, mainly due to the Israeli decision to replace Gaza and West Bank Palestinian workers with foreign workers as main source of cheap labor (Farsakh, 2005; Rosenhek, 2003).

On the other hand, new policies and discourses around citizenship rights promoted by the judicial branch of the state, especially the Israeli Supreme

Court, strengthened the salience of citizenship for Palestinians inside Israel (Peled, 2005; Shafir & Peled, 2002) and shifted their political activism toward the Israeli courts and associational sphere (Payes, 2005; Sallon, 2009). This chapter draws attention to the timing of the adoption of the civil society route as a strategy of rule over Palestinian citizens, which coincided with the creation of a regime of indirect rule in the Occupied Palestinian Territories and with the introduction of a new regime of forced immobility for Gaza and West Bank Palestinians. I explore how, within this broader rearrangement of the Israeli system of rule in the 1990s, which introduced new spatial, political, and class divisions among Palestinians, the civil society route contributed to widen the gap in political interests and opportunities between Palestinian citizens and noncitizens as viewed by the Palestinian minority with Israeli citizenship.[4]

This goal of developing a single conceptual framework linking Israeli policies and Palestinian national group solidarity requires an important caveat. While I explain how certain Israeli policies contributed to a decrease in national group solidarity among Palestinians, this analysis is not by any means a final assessment of either Israeli policies or Palestinian nationhood. Indeed, as I will discuss at the end of my empirical investigation, far from being stable, the reorganization of Israeli rule over Palestinian citizens and noncitizens here examined has undergone several changes and contestations, especially after the beginning of the Second Palestinian *Intifada* in October 2000. Thus, for example, since 2000, Israeli governmental and parliamentary initiatives have attacked the citizenship rights of Palestinians in Israel, while direct Israeli military repression has greatly intensified in the Occupied Palestinian Territories. At the same time, recent initiatives among Palestinian citizens and noncitizens have attempted to reconnect different segments of Palestinians both symbolically and politically.

Yet, the divide between citizens and noncitizens remains a particularly important line of division among Palestinians; citizenship issues remain central to political activism among Palestinian citizens; and the old and new lines of divisions strengthened by the creation of the PA remain difficult obstacles in the path toward a more unified Palestinian national movement. Further, the legal and spatial restrictions imposed on Palestinian mobility greatly limit encounters and discussions across legal statuses and places of residence. This essay argues that these cleavages among Palestinians cannot be explained without an understanding of the workings of what I define as the indirect rule route and the civil society route.

The question of the long-term effects of these two strategies of rule is also relevant for the methodology that I use in this study. This chapter is based on an original reading of the vast amount of historical data and secondary sources available on the Israeli–Palestinian context in the 1990s. I also present data from my interviews and informal dialogue in villages and refugee camps of the West Bank and among young Palestinian activists, university students, and professionals in Israel. I collected these data between the years 2003 and 2008.[5] While Palestinians surely articulated their political views and concerns differently in the 1990s and after the Second *Intifada*, what is important to note is that in the post-Second *Intifada* period Palestinian citizens and noncitizens have continued to grapple with the effects of institutions and mechanisms introduced in the early 1990s. Take, for example, the estrangement between elites and popular constituencies among Palestinians in the Occupied Territories. In his interviews conducted in 1995 and 1996, Lønning (1998, p. 181) already documented the widespread frustration among Gaza and West Bank Palestinians against the PA leadership that I discuss in this chapter.[6] Along similar lines, Roy's (2001, pp. 8–9) study of the Gaza Strip in the 1990s already drew attention on the reemergence of clan politics (what she defines as "tribalism") under the PA. Thus, while I recognize and discuss the instability of the two strategies, I highlight how the articulation of political views among Palestinians – including the expression of emotions such as hope, frustration, and anger – captured by my data cannot be understood without a discussion of how the indirect rule route and the civil society route continue to create distinct experiences of politics among different segments of Palestinians under Israeli rule.

Theoretically, this chapter engages and extends state-centered theories of group formation (Bourdieu, 1989, 1991; Brubaker, 2004; Brubaker, Loveman, & Stamatov, 2004; Goldberg, 2003; Loveman, 2005) from a Gramscian perspective. These theories identify the symbolic power of the state as a primary factor in the creation of social groups. Further, they focus more on the making – rather than the unmaking – of social groups. This chapter argues that the analytic primacy given to symbolic mechanisms makes it difficult to pose the question of how social groups are unmade. Indeed, theorizing the unmaking of social groups requires investigating how social forces initiate group-making projects outside and against the symbolic categories of the state; it also requires studying how the state intervenes to neutralize these projects that challenge its symbolic power. Drawing on Gramsci's approach to group formation, I explore how the state unmakes social groups through strategies that remain under-theorized in the literature on group formation. These include the concession of material benefits as well as the use of coercive means.

The next section elaborates on my critique of existing state-centered theories of group formation. Second, through a review of the literature on Palestinians under Israeli rule, I highlight how an analytic focus on the state's symbolic power cannot explain processes of national group solidarity among different segments of Palestinians. Third, I discuss how, by contrast, Gramsci's *The Southern Question* offers an ideal framework to shed light on the interrelation of Israeli state strategies and Palestinian group formation across the divide between citizens and noncitizens. The fourth section of this chapter develops my empirical analysis of the workings of the indirect rule route and the civil society route. I conclude with a discussion of the implications of this chapter.

GROUP FORMATION BEYOND THE SYMBOLIC POWER OF THE STATE

How are social groups unmade? This question was not part of the research agenda of the early "primordialist" approach to social groups, which posited the "natural" existence of groups on the basis of "primordial" or "ascriptive" identities (Geertz, 1973; Horowitz, 1985; Shils, 1957). By contrast, the question of group formation is central to current constructivist approaches, which highlight how social groups can be constructed out of a multiplicity of potentially available principles of membership including class, ethnicity, race, and nationhood. Constructivism raises questions about which factors lead to the creation of groups and what determines the selection of a principle of membership over another.

The dominant constructivist perspective on group formation builds on Bourdieu's (1989, 1991) theory of group formation as the outcome of symbolic struggles over categorization. Bourdieu (1991, p. 221) identifies the state as a powerful "group marker" that is often able to "impose the legitimate definition of the divisions of the social world." Brubaker (2004) and Loveman (2005) expand this Bourdieusian framework to theorize how the symbolic power of the state – the state power to categorize people – creates social groups.[7] Brubaker (2004, p. 8) also contends that a focus on how the state symbolically creates groups works as an antidote against "groupism," that is, "the tendency to represent the social and cultural world as a multichrome mosaic of monochrome ethnic, racial, or cultural blocs." The main argument of this Bourdieusian approach is that "official categories can contribute to 'making up people' or 'nominating into existence' new kinds of persons ... Conversely, a policy of *not* classifying or counting by ethnicity or race can impede group formation" (Brubaker, 2009, p. 33, emphasis in original). This state-centered constructivist approach has significant explanatory power. Indeed, scholars have studied how state categorization practices (naming, recording, counting, documenting, and classifying) have affected peoples' subjectivities and involvement in political action (Loveman, 2005, 2007; Markowitz, 2007; Petersen, 1997; Scott, Tehranian, & Mathias, 2002; Starr, 1987, 1992). Extending the focus on the symbolic power of the state to colonial regimes, Mamdani (1996, 2001) has contended that colonial official categories developed by British and French rulers in colonial Africa shaped the political identities of the ruled and have also continued to affect politics in postcolonial societies. In his words: "There is a language particular to the modern state, including its colonial version. That is the language of law. Legal distinctions are different from all others in that they are enforced by the state, and then are in turn reproduced by institutions that structure citizen participation" (Mamdani, 2001, pp. 653–654). Recent works on colonial states have also examined how different actors within the colonial bureaucracies have engaged in classificatory struggles to categorize the ruled populations and to develop policies to manage them (Comaroff, 1998; Goh, 2007; Steinmetz, 2007).

Yet state actors do not always operate without resistance. Nor do they always rely on categorization practices to attempt to mold the political terrain on which they operate. The analytic primacy given to the state symbolic power tends to obfuscate the struggles over group-making projects between state and nonstate actors. This tendency is evident in the "cognitive turn" taken by these theories, which link people's cognitive dispositions to the available official categories while detaching them from the social and political struggles in which people take part (Brubaker et al., 2004; Hirschfeld, 1996).[8] Another analytic problem is that the neglect of the role of nonstate actors prevents the theorization of how, beyond their classificatory practices, states intervene to block group-making projects from below through the coordinated distribution of both policies of inclusion and exclusion. The critique here developed contributes to recent theorizing about group formation beyond the symbolic power of the state (Bailey, 2008; Tugal, 2009; Wimmer, 2008). It also resonates with works on the classificatory and political struggles between different segments of both the colonial rulers and the ruled populations (Demetriou, 2007; Go, 2007, 2008) and with Zinoman's (2000, 2001) analytic shift from categorization to coercion as a productive power in colonial Vietnam.[9] The specific contribution of this chapter is to examine how the state intervenes to unmake social groups, which have emerged outside and against the state's official structure of categories, thus challenging its "definition of the divisions of the social world." Drawing on Gramsci's *The Southern Question*, in this chapter, I give particular attention to the coordinated use of co-optation, concession of material benefits,[10] and coercion as strategies that the state deploys to unmake social groups.

NATIONAL GROUP FORMATION AMONG PALESTINIANS

The question of the limits of the symbolic power of the state to shape group formation clearly emerges from the case of Palestinians under Israeli rule. A couple of examples will suffice. The Israeli state's structure of official categories denies nationhood as a conceptual framework for Palestinian citizens of Israel. Precluded from symbolic access to nationhood, Palestinians in Israel are inserted into five ethnoreligious official categories: Muslims, Christians, Bedouins, Druze, and Circassians. Yet, since the 1970s, nationhood has become a salient principle for symbolic membership and political organizing for Palestinians in Israel (Ghanem, 2001; Pappé, 2011; Rouhana, 1997; Shafir & Peled, 2002). Along similar lines, shifting attention to the legal categorization of place, Eyal (1996, p. 420) shows that the categorization of Palestinian localities in Israel as "villages" did not prevent the urbanization of these places and their centrality as sites of grassroots organization around nationhood: "In 1976, Orientalists and government experts were completely taken by surprise, when the 'committee for national direction' (composed of 'village' mayors!) organized mass demonstrations to protest government plans to confiscate more Palestinian lands."[11]

The study of recent changes in the cognitive schemas of poor West Bank Palestinians also requires a theoretical framework encompassing not only the state structure of categories but also other social structures as explanatory factors of group formation. Indeed, while nationhood constituted a salient principle of collective membership and mobilization in the 1980s, especially during the First *Intifada*, the nationalizing discourse promoted by the PA – an officially recognized "national" authority of self-rule – since 1994, combined with the uninterrupted use of coercive means by the Israeli army, has engendered a resentful anti-elitist and classed counterdiscourse among poor Palestinian populations. Thus, explaining the cognitive dispositions of these populations requires not only a study of the conceptual categories available to them but also an examination of their deteriorating material situation and their exposure to new (middle-class) lifestyles under the PA.

Given these limits of the Israeli state's symbolic power to shape trajectories of group formation among Palestinians, the literature on Palestinians under Israeli rule has examined how the state has attempted to shape Palestinians' political identities and practices through other – mainly coercive – strategies including political surveillance (Cohen, 2010; Lustick, 1980; Sa'di, 2003; Zureik, 1979, 2001), differential access to state benefits (Kanaaneh, 2009), and mass arrests and incarceration (Hajjar, 2005; Nashif, 2008). Scholars have also conceptualized the PA as an institution through which the Israeli state exercises indirect rule over the Occupied Palestinian Territories (Ghanem, 2010; Gordon, 2008; Rabbani, 2006; Said, 1996, 2001, 2004; Usher, 1995; Weinberger, 2006). Further, recent works have linked the creation of the PA to the neoliberal turn of the Israeli economy (Bouillon, 2004; Clarno, 2008; Hanafi & Tabar, 2005; Lagerquist, 2003; Peled, 2004; Shafir & Peled, 2000). In other words, without explicitly engaging the theoretical literature on group formation, these works go beyond the symbolic power of the state and point to the different group-making effects of distinct coercive practices.[12]

However, this state-centered literature on Palestinians under Israeli rule does not examine the interrelation of state strategies toward different segments of Palestinian citizens and noncitizens. Thus, for example, scholars who have studied the PA as an institution of indirect rule have not explored how the creation of the PA relates to changes in state strategies toward Palestinian citizens of Israel (e.g., the decade of political liberalism in the 1990s). This shortcoming is mainly due to the implicit assumption that the legal statuses in which Palestinians are inserted – especially, citizenship for Palestinians in Israel and statelessness for Palestinians in the Occupied Territories – inevitably and invariably constitute salient lines of group membership and political interests (Al-Haj, 1993; Schölch, 1983). In this sense, the symbolic power of the state – specifically, the Israeli citizenship regime – reemerges as a privileged analytic perspective even if its explanatory power is limited.

This assumption, however, underestimates the historical variability of legal citizenship as a salient principle of social division for Palestinians under Israeli rule. It also prevents the study of how the Israeli state has worked to buttress this divide between Palestinian citizens and noncitizens during periods in which group solidarity across it intensified. This chapter aims to overcome this shortcoming by bringing into a single analytic framework, strategies of rule targeting different segments of Palestinian citizens and noncitizens and tracing their effects on their political and communal solidarities.

LESSONS FROM GRAMSCI'S *THE SOUTHERN QUESTION*

While the historiographical debate on the Giolittian period (1900–1914) remains open (Aquarone, 1981; Coppa, 1971; De Grand, 2001; Salomone, 1960; Salvemini, 2000), what interests me is that Gramsci's analysis of the Giolittian rule constitutes an excellent framework for this study for three main reasons. First, it shows how a single state can prevent, neutralize, or channel group-making projects from below via a distribution of different policies. For example, Gramsci contends that the Giolitti government reacted to popular pressure through the coordination of three main strategies. Specifically, its policy toward the Northern workers was "*a reformist policy on wages and trade union freedoms*" (1995 [1926], p. 29, emphasis added) while "the Mezzogiorno [South] ... was kept 'disciplined' by measures of two kinds. First, *police measures*: pitiless repression of every mass movement, with periodical massacres of peasants. Second, *political-police measures*: personal favors to the 'intellectual' stratum ... incorporation of the most active Southern elements 'individually' into the leading personnel of the State, with particular 'judicial' and bureaucratic privileges" (2003 [1971], p. 94, emphasis added).

Second, Gramsci offers an original perspective on the effects of distinct but coordinated policies on group formation. In the Italian case, the three-pronged distribution of strategies affected group formation among workers and peasants, by cementing "a capitalist/worker industrial bloc" and widening the gap between workers and peasants. Indeed, "the Northern workers believed that the Southerners were 'biologically inferior beings, either semi-barbarians or out and out barbarians by natural destiny'" (1995 [1926], p. 20). By contrast, the Southern peasants perceived the Northern workers as exploiters, as "cause of their ills and their misery" (1995 [1926], p. 34).

Third, Gramsci's analysis of the role that each of the three policies played in the prevention of a convergence between workers and peasants is rich with lessons for the Palestinian case.[13] For example, the case of the Southern intellectuals exemplifies the contribution that elite co-optation and corruption can bring to popular demobilization. In this sense, the Southern intellectuals contributed to the peasants' "inability to give a centralized expression to their aspirations and needs" (1995 [1926], p. 36). As a result of elite co-optation and corruption, "Southern discontent, for lack of leadership, did not succeed in assuming a normal political form; its manifestations, finding expression only in an anarchic turbulence, were presented as a 'matter for the police' and the courts" (2003 [1971], p. 94). Further, direct repression ("periodic massacres of peasants") also played a role in isolating and weakening the peasantry. At the same time, the convergence of interests and identities among capitalists and workers in the North was cemented through reformist policies toward the workers, including high wages, unionization, and the freedom to develop associations such as cooperatives and mutual aid societies (Bonfante & Sapelli, 1981, pp. 203–214). Thus, associationism emerges as an important aspect of the reformist approach toward the workers.[14]

To sum up, Gramsci' *The Southern Question* offers important lessons for filling the gaps in the literature on Palestinians under Israeli rule. Specifically, it provides a framework that bridges different state policies, studies how these policies introduce and build on differences among segments of a population under state rule, and analyzes the role of co-optation, coercion, and associationism in the unmaking of social groups.[15]

THE WEAKENING OF PALESTINIAN GROUP SOLIDARITY: TWO ROUTES

In summer 2004, during a conversation with me, Abu Mahmud,[16] a Palestinian refugee in his fifties living in Balata, a West Bank refugee camp, talked about his encounters with other Palestinians across the Green Line in the mid-1970s:

> I remember that as a college student I was very happy to go to summer camps organized by the Nazareth municipality [Palestinian town in Israel] and connect with Palestinians there ... I was doubtful because they were mainly members of the Israeli Communist Party while we had the PLO [Palestine Liberation Organization][17] but I was very pleased that there was a space for interaction between people, an area for debate, communication, and meetings ... We learned about land confiscation and house demolitions in the Galilee[18] and I felt that we had the same problems ... But now everything is gone (*kul ishi rāḥ*) ...

After a pause, he continued, shifting his attention to the present situation in the Occupied Palestinian Territories:

> And the same thing is now happening with Gaza, there are no more contacts, I'm afraid that I don't know anymore how Palestinians in Gaza feel about the [military] occupation, about Fatah and Hamas ... And here in the West Bank things are also

The Reconfiguration of the Palestinian National Question 115

difficult, people organize at the level of this village or that [refugee] camp but we don't have a sense of unity anymore.

Abu Mahmud's words capture different components of a decrease in national "groupness" among Palestinians. His nostalgia about his past contacts with other Palestinians across the Green Line quickly turns into a reflection about the current lack of unity among Palestinians in the West Bank and the Gaza Strip.

The same summer, during a meeting in Jerusalem organized by an Israeli human rights organization, I had a conversation with Ahmed, a Palestinian student in his early twenties enrolled in an Israeli university. Ahmed voiced a different concern:

> It is not in our interests [as citizens] to make a connection with what happens in the West Bank; if we make the connection then everything becomes about security and terrorism; what I want to do is to struggle for our rights as citizens and make a connection with other minorities around the world ... I think that my duty is to study law and to learn how to challenge the discrimination that there is against Palestinians inside Israel because we suffer discrimination in everything, jobs, education, urban planning.

While Abu Mahmud emphasizes his distress for the lack of unity among Palestinians, Ahmed's words point to the increased salience of citizenship. They also reveal Ahmed's attempt to formulate the problems of Palestinian citizens as outside the realm of "state security" and inside the legitimate boundaries of political discourse, with "security" and "legitimate politics" both defined and imposed by the Israeli state.[19]

This empirical section examines how different Israeli policies introduced in the 1990s – including the creation of the PA, the regime of immobility for West Bank and Gaza Palestinians, the "sealing off" of the Green Line, and the Israeli Supreme Court's discourse of individual rights for Israeli citizens – worked together to create a political terrain preventing Palestinians from meeting across legal status and place of residence and pushing them to develop different political interests.

THE INDIRECT RULE ROUTE: OLD AND NEW CLEAVAGES

Since the establishment of the PA in 1994,[20] the Israeli authorities have imposed increasingly strict restrictions on the movement of Palestinian residents of the Occupied Territories, effectively preventing them from entering East Jerusalem and Israel and barring them from traveling between the Gaza Strip and the West Bank. Further, the administrative division of the West Bank into three areas – areas A, B, and C – each associated with a different level of PA's formal control,[21] has created dozens of noncontiguous territorial enclaves within the West Bank. The establishment of Israeli military checkpoints on many West Bank roads and the construction of bypass roads to connect Jewish settlements[22] to the Israeli territory have intensified this process of territorial fragmentation. The Israeli state's decision to retain the power to determine who can be registered in the PA population registry, and who can transfer their place of residence from one part of the Occupied Palestinian Territories to another has further restricted the movement of Palestinian residents of the West Bank and the Gaza Strip (Zureik, 2001, pp. 217–218).[23] Since the Second *Intifada* (2000–2004), this process of territorial fragmentation has reached the micro level of localities with prolonged curfews and closures isolating specific refugee camps, villages, and towns. Additionally, the construction of a fortification system including fences and concrete walls in parts of East Jerusalem and the West Bank has further restricted the movement of West Bank Palestinians (Weizman, 2007).[24] Within this context of forced immobility, the struggle over political power between the two main Palestinian factions – Fatah and Hamas – has acquired a new territorial dimension with the split between a Fatah-dominated authority in the West Bank and a Hamas-run government in the Gaza Strip since June 2007.

While this ongoing process of territorial fragmentation and spatial immobility has generated scholarly interest (Falah, 2005; Farsakh, 2005; Hanafi, 2009; Parsons & Salter, 2008), less attention has been given to the link between Israeli spatial policies, the working of the PA, and national group solidarity among Palestinians. In this section I examine how the working of the PA in the West Bank within the spatial regime imposed by the Israeli authorities has affected group solidarity among Palestinians. Specifically, I investigate three lines of division: (1) a new class division between an expanding urban middle class oriented toward the PA institutions and increasingly concentrated in Ramallah, the de facto "capital" of the PA, and the majority of poor Palestinians who do not participate in the new lifestyles pursued by urban middle-class families;[25] (2) an old line of division – clan allegiance – which had been weakened during the 1970s and especially during the First *Intifada* with the rise of nationhood as primary source of collective solidarity but has been reactivated as a principle of social organization under the PA; and (3) and new divisions among poor Palestinians generated by the PA's power to distribute employment opportunities and other resources.

Class Polarization

> There are two types of Palestinians: those who stand and waste their time under the sun and the rain at the checkpoints and those who are VIPs and feel the wind of freedom in their face because they travel fast in their cars.

With these words, Nasser, an unemployed young villager living in a small West Bank enclave surrounded by fences and checkpoints, summarizes his perspective on how the system of travel permits built into the regime of indirect rule has divided Palestinians between those who have received VIP cards and can easily cross checkpoints and borders and the rest of the population who are left alone to face Israeli policies of "closure."[26] The VIP system of travel permits, which was institutionalized via diplomatic negotiations between the PA leadership and the Israeli government, includes three different categories of VIP cards, each carrying a different degree of individual immunity from the Israeli policies of closure (Bishara, 1998, pp. 220–222).[27] The main beneficiaries of these travel privileges are the high cadres of the PA, but there are also other PA officials, business executives, and merchants who benefit from less restrictive travel measures compared to ordinary Palestinians. The Israeli authorities have often explicitly linked their management of VIP cards – particularly the granting and withdrawal of these cards – to the security or political actions of PA officials. For example, on March 19, 1999, the Israeli Prime Minister revoked the VIP identification card of "three Palestinian Authority members" as a punishment of their involvement in "political activities" in Jerusalem.[28] Similarly, in February 2010, some PA officials belonging to Fatah had their VIP cards removed because of their participation in West Bank villages' protests against the Israeli fence (Waked, 2010). As Parsons and Salter (2008, p. 712) put it, "these documents are a clear example of the government of Israel defining the mobility of a particular segment of the Palestinian population – constituting the part of the population that can move and that part which cannot."

The frustration that ordinary Palestinians feel about an asphyxiating regime of travel permits translates into resentment toward those who are exempted from it. This resentment toward the PA leadership clearly emerges from comments like these that I often heard in refugee camps and villages:

> The *Sulṭa* (the authority, PA) is made of VIPs, not leaders.
>
> Those negotiators who came to Palestine[29] after the agreement were the unique beneficiaries; they have developed their trade, increased their bank balance and send

their children learning abroad without looking at the refugees in Jabalia, Jalazon, and Asker camps who can't even provide water and bread to their families.

Similar criticism was voiced by "ordinary" Palestinians even before the Second *Intifada*:

> I trust the chairman,[30] but not the people surrounding him, people like Nabil Sha'th, Abu Mazen, Abu Ala. They made the Oslo agreement and the other agreements, and created all our problems now. Who are they? They were never in jail, they were never stopped at checkpoints. They have VIP status and don't know what suffering is. (Lønning, 1998, p. 181)

This class-based sense of estrangement and even betrayal is not directed to a restricted circle of high-ranking PA officials with VIP cards but extends to the urban middle class that has expanded during the 1990s as a result of new employment opportunities offered by the PA institutions, by the growing NGO sector,[31] and by the private sector (Hilal & Khan, 2004).[32] This middle class is not a homogenous actor with the divide between "returnees"[33] and local families and the competition between PA officials and NGOs as its two most important fissures (Hammami, 1995; Hilal, 2003, 2006; Tamari, 2002). Despite their internal diversity, middle-class Palestinians share new urban lifestyles and consumption patterns. The town of Ramallah, the de facto "capital" of the PA, has also become the main center of life for this emerging middle class.[34] Thus, in Ramallah, "new spaces (mostly commercialized) were created to accommodate the new thirst for urban pleasures. Internet cafés sprang up, new hotels and restaurants were established, several swimming pools were opened, a number of upscale and more modest fitness centers were set up, and even a disco was allowed to operate" (Taraki, 2008a, p. 71).

In his critical perspective on Ramallah's "middle class enclave," Abourahme (2009, p. 505) characterizes the Palestinian urban middle class as "a class with an outward gaze and strong transnational links ... [A class] better linked to Amman, the Gulf, Europe, and North America than it is to the rest of the West Bank." He also argues that with the expansion of this class "new subjectivities premised on consumption as a social value have emerged and, as corollaries, discourses of non-violence and post-national/civil-society politics have been disseminated." Taraki (2008b, p. 77) gives insights into the dominant perspective from within this new urban middle class, which perceives itself as a force of modernity claiming the right to "a normal life" and pursuing "a new cultural hegemony in which the old-style austerity and Puritanism have no place." In other words, urban middle-class Palestinians are engaged in a project of critiquing and renewing "the culture of resistance" developed by Palestinians during the First *Intifada* and replacing it with a new understanding of "resistance" including "recreation and entertainment."

Yet, this middle-class project of redefinition of political practices has engendered a negative reaction among poor Palestinians. In the view of many Palestinians from camps, villages, and other towns, the new lifestyles that the urban middle class has introduced in Ramallah make the outcome of the First *Intifada* even more difficult to accept. As Collins (2004, pp. 203–207) shows, "freedom" and "justice" were the main expectations of most Palestinians who mobilized during the First *Intifada*. Thus, in the post-Oslo period, while middle-class families in Ramallah started complaining about "loitering" and "sexual harassment" committed by youth from nearby camps and villages who roamed around in the streets of Ramallah (Taraki, 2008a, p. 71), residents of camps and villages started voicing very different concerns and complaints by mixing a class-based discourse of lack of justice and a discourse of moral corruption:

> The harvest is always for the rich. (Collins, 2004, p. 197)

> Moral dissolution has increased greatly in the city and restaurants and places where male and female youth behave in an immoral way because of an absence of law to call them to account. (Johnson, 2007, p. 612)

This resentment toward the new lifestyles introduced by the urban middle class has at times found expression in acts of vandalism toward Ramallah's new restaurants and pubs (Taraki, 2008b, p. 72). For example, in June 2006, I had an e-mail exchange with Ashraf, who, at that time, was working for an NGO in a refugee camp near Ramallah. To my question about his birthday party, he wrote me:

> It didn't work out easily, I was planning to have it at Sangrias [the name of a famous restaurant in Ramallah] but all restaurants in Ramallah (Sangrias, Stones, Al-Makan, Al-Matal, Al-Bardoni, etc.) were destroyed [vandalized] by people from the camp, the people I am working with, it is ridiculous, it is as if I knew that it would happen, I called all the restaurants and none were open ... In any case Billy [a foreigner] invited me to have the party at his place, it was nice.

In a follow-up phone conversation, Ashraf explained that just a few days before, Force 17 (a security force tied to the PA Presidency) had established a checkpoint at the entrance of the camp in order to conduct an arrest. Eventually, a 17-year-old boy was chased down in the camp and was killed during an exchange of fire and crowds of young men from the camp expressed their anger and frustration by vandalizing Ramallah's main restaurants.

These perceptions of class privilege and moral corruption also color how poor Palestinians interpret and react to political initiatives run by middle-class Palestinians. For example, Allen (2006, pp. 289–292) shows how poor Palestinians negatively reacted to a campaign against suicide bombings initiated by urban intellectuals based in Ramallah through a petition printed in *Al-Quds* newspaper in June 2002. While suicide bombing remains a controversial issue within the wider Palestinian society, this particular petition against suicide bombing was interpreted as an example of self-interested behavior by the petitioners who want to preserve their "good life," and as an indication of their detachment from the suffering of the majority of Palestinians.

The mutual estrangement between middle-class Palestinians and poor Palestinians is also reflected in their diverging temporal and political trajectories. Urban middle classes perceive themselves as the backbone of a new project of modernity, cosmopolitanism, and redefinition of political resistance. By contrast, poor Palestinians who are excluded from this project, which is mainly centered on expensive consumption patterns, also grapple with the PA regime's reactivation of "pre-modern" forms of membership such as clan allegiances that had been weakened during the 1980s and the First *Intifada*.

Clan Allegiances

The PA regime has strengthened the salience of kin-based politics among Palestinians of the Occupied Territories (Abdo, 1999; Bowman, 2001; Brynen, 1995; Frisch, 1997; Roy, 2001; Rubenberg, 2001). This is particularly evident in the expanding activities of clans inside refugee camps. In 1948, refugees came from different villages and towns and grouped inside the camps according to their places of origin. Thus, clan membership was transplanted as an important principle of collective identity and social organization for the refugees, despite their general dislocation. In the 1970s and even more so in the 1980s, nationhood had increasingly subsumed clan identities as the main source of both symbolic membership and political organizing. However, the PA's reliance on clan politics as a tool of rule and extraction of consent has reversed this trend. For example, clans have expanded and formalized their activities through the establishment of "Village Associations," which are named after different villages of origin. Each association is managed by one or more clans and each provides services or intervenes in favor of refugees who are members of that clan.

Thus, during my fieldwork in Jalazon camp in 2007, several clans were in the process of buying land or constructing new buildings for their associations. They had also registered their associations at the PA's "Ministry of Interior."

Many refugees voiced the view that the expanded role of these associations in camps was a troubling symptom of a decrease in national solidarity. This position was particularly strong among men in their forties who participated in the First *Intifada* and among a new generation of youth who resented their lack of legitimacy within kin-based organizations because of their age. In the words of Mahmud, a student in his early twenties:

> The [Village] Associations encourage the clans more than giving new benefits to our society ... So what happens is that a person who is, for example, from Nabalah's clan (*hamula*) becomes committed to the Nabalah's Association ... But there is no need [for the Associations] to speak about Beit Nabalah [a village of origin for some refugees in Mahmud's camp] if I am from Beit Nabalah. We need to talk about Palestine.

Similarly, Khaled, a man in his mid-forties, contrasted the First *Intifada* as a factor that "opened people's brains (minds)" with the creation of the PA as a factor that pushed people "backward" toward kin-based forms of associations.

Shifting their critique toward the political factions, other camp dwellers pointed to the interrelation between the crisis of legitimacy experienced by Fatah and Hamas – the two main political movements in the Occupied Palestinian Territories – especially after the Second *Intifada* and the increased role of Village Associations inside the refugee camps. Speaking about the current political impasse in the Occupied Palestinian Territories, a refugee told me: "People stopped trusting the political parties. That's why they started to communicate with the [Village] Associations."

Indeed, Village Associations present themselves as an alternative group membership to the political factions whose infighting threatens to tear apart Palestinian families, which often include members belonging to different factions. In filling this role, these associations have expanded their activities dramatically. For example, instead of holding occasional gatherings for important social events like weddings or periods of mourning, they have taken on a frequent presence through after school programs and explicitly political practices such as the commemoration of clan "martyrs."[35]

Yet, rather than offering an alternative to the current predicament of marginality experienced by poor Palestinians, the expansion of kin-based politics has been dictated by the PA's use of clans as channels for the distribution of power and resources. Indeed, among poor Palestinians – including those who are not critical of the activities of kin-based associations – there is a widespread belief that membership in a clan with family and political connections with the PA plays a crucial role in shaping the outcome of internal disputes. For example, in describing a case of conflict between two families in his village, Sami, a middle-aged man who does not belong to either clan, pointed to the negative role of the PA in mediating between the two clans:

> The governor (*muḥāfiz*)[36] came but he only visited and listened to one side [clan] because they have a relationship with the Authority (the PA)... And so he didn't get a clear picture of what had happened.

The role played by powerful clans in mediating access to the PA's institutions and resources has introduced new internal tensions in places such as refugee camps, where (moral) practices aimed at the fair distribution of resources had previously intertwined with discourses about shared and unalloyed suffering to cement social cohesion under conditions of material scarcity and political oppression.

Divisions among Poor Palestinians

The poor Palestinians I have encountered have generally directed their negative moral judgments about new materialist lifestyles outward, toward the PA elites and the urban middle classes. However, they still resent the decrease in their communal ethos of suffering. There is an acute awareness that, as many Palestinians repeatedly told me, "Under the PA, you are someone only if you have money," or that "Being poor under the PA is a disgrace." Thus, the PA has pushed poor Palestinians to improve their individual material conditions through political or family connections with PA officials. This pressure has only been amplified by the PA's use of clans as channels for the provision of resources and by its blatant stigmatization of poverty. The culmination of this pressure – to survive at the micro level of the individual, the family, and clan connections without sabotaging the communal ethos of solidarity – results in a dangerous state of social cohesion in these poor communities. In her interviews with Gaza Palestinians in the mid-1990s, Roy (2001, p. 8) cogently captures this tension between escaping poverty and preserving social cohesion at its onset in the Gaza Strip, where the PA first established its rule:

> During the [First] Intifada, the ways in which we must now behave would have been *haram* [forbidden]... What are we suppose to do? If we don't pay a bribe, we don't get a phone, a license, health insurance, or a job. Those who try to be "good" are lost. People

The Reconfiguration of the Palestinian National Question

see how the PA cheats and extorts and becomes rich. Why should the poor guy from a refugee camp with many mouths to feed do any better? What is the point in trying to do the right thing when the only reward for doing so is more suffering? The longer-term implications are, of course, frightening, but who has time to worry about them when one's children are hungry.

About 10 years after Roy's work, during my fieldwork in the West Bank, I also documented how, according to many poor Palestinian villagers and camp dwellers, the PA has substituted the previously dominant ethos of collective solidarity and shared suffering with a new discourse of personal material achievement. There is a widespread perception among poor Palestinians that the PA's emphasis on status and wealth ("money," *maṣārī*) constitutes a threat to their communal solidarity. For example, during a conversation with me, Khaled, a retired English teacher from a village that over the years has lost most of its land to a nearby Jewish settlement, questioned his own decision to invest some of his savings into the tuition and transportation expenses necessary to enroll his youngest son, a teenager, into an English course taught in one of Ramallah's private schools:

> My neighbor is unemployed and struggles to feed his family and I send my son to expensive English lessons ... This is not fair, I don't like it.

This tension between the pressure felt to improve one's material conditions by using means and connections unavailable to one's neighbors and the concerns for the decrease in practices and feelings of solidarity within poor communities has deepened with the increased importance of the PA as a distributor of employment opportunities for semiskilled and unskilled workers. From 1967 to the early 1990s, Palestinian workers from the Gaza Strip and the West Bank constituted the main source of cheap labor inside Israel. By contrast, since the early 1990s the Israeli state has drastically reduced the number of work permits granted to Palestinians and has started relying on migrant workers as main source of cheap labor (Rosenhek, 2003). As a result of this change at the bottom of the Israeli labor market, many unskilled and semiskilled Palestinians have turned toward the PA as an employer, aiming especially at the lower ranks of its multiple police and security units (Usher, 1996). Thus, the PA's power to create and distribute jobs has become an important factor in creating a material and symbolic distance between those who have connections with the PA and those who do not (Collins, 2004, pp. 195–197). First, working in the PA's police and security forces pushes one up in the class ladder in a poor community such as a refugee camp; this becomes especially striking in comparison to the everyday lives of the unemployed or the daily laborers who work in Jewish settlements or who "illegally" cross the Green Line to work in the Israeli construction and agriculture industries. Second, given the political infighting between Fatah and Hamas, employment in the police forces of the Fatah-dominated PA also generates frictions between friends and family members belonging to different political movements, especially when the PA forces arrest members of other factions.

At the same time, Israeli forms of direct military rule ranging from prolonged curfews to "administrative detention,"[37] to military invasions and arrests have continued to target disproportionally poor Palestinians, especially those living in refugee camps. For example, in a revealing comparison between Amari refugee camp, which is located within the city of Ramallah, and two other districts of the city, Johnson (2005, p. 92) highlights how, during the Second *Intifada*, the refugee camp and the city had distinct experiences of Israeli military repression with camp dwellers reporting significantly higher percentages of family members who had been arrested, injured, severely maimed, or killed by the Israeli army.[38]

This differential treatment by the Israeli army has contributed to widen the gap between the everyday experiences of poor Palestinians and middle-class Palestinians. By contrast, protracted exposure to Israeli military repression has attenuated the frictions within poor communities here examined by reinforcing their shared experiences of suffering and their sense of shared destiny.

Of the distribution of policies that Gramsci discusses in the Italian case, the indirect rule route analyzed in this section is reminiscent of Gramsci's "Southern route." According to Gramsci (1995 [1926], p. 36), the Southern route, which was based on direct repression of the peasantry and co-optation of key political and intellectual elites, produced "a great social disintegration" in the South and prevented the peasantry from giving "centralized expression to their aspirations and needs." In the Palestinian case, the creation of a regime of indirect rule as a component of a broader matrix of military control including the creation of territorial enclaves and continued measures of military repression disproportionally targeting specific towns and refugee camps, has undermined national group solidarity among Palestinians of the Occupied Territories by distancing popular constituencies from their leaders, by introducing new class divisions, and by reactivating clan allegiances. In the next section I examine how, by contrast, the civil society route toward Palestinian citizens has shaped the latter' political interests and opportunities via a politics of concessions and associationism and, thus, roughly resembles Gramsci's "Northern route" toward the workers.

THE CIVIL SOCIETY ROUTE: CITIZENSHIP, "LAWYERING," AND ASSOCIATIONISM

While Palestinians in the Occupied Territories have become preoccupied with territorial, political, class, and moral divisions, Palestinian citizens of Israel have turned their attention toward their legal citizenship. Certainly, the creation of the PA played an important role in highlighting legal citizenship as an axis of divisions among Palestinians. But so did a new discourse of citizenship rights promoted by the judicial branch of the Israeli state.

Many Palestinian citizens have come to perceive the PA as both weak in relation to the Israeli army and authoritarian in relation to Palestinians of the Occupied Territories. In the early 1990s, Israeli politicians and high-rank military officials had already explicitly emphasized their view of the PA's security role:

> I hope that we will find a partner responsible in Gaza in the internal Palestinian problems. It will deal with Gaza without the problems of the [Israeli] High Court of Justice, without the problems of *B'tselem* [Israeli human rights organization], and without the problems of all kinds of sensitive souls and all kinds of mothers and fathers.[39]

> They [The Palestinian police force] will also have an intelligence outfit in order to control the Palestinian street.[40]

> The idea of Oslo was to find a strong dictator to keep the Palestinians under control.[41]

In the 1990s, the creation of the PA within a security-oriented discourse promoted by Israeli political and military leaders was matched by the growing intervention of the Israeli Supreme Court in contentious issues within Israeli society. Indeed, under the influence of Former Chief Justice Aharon Barak, the Supreme Court presented itself as a new forum for addressing social and political controversies in two interrelated ways. First, the Supreme Court's jurisprudence recognized two new Basic Laws on human rights, which were adopted in 1992, as constitutional laws; at this time, the court also affirmed its right to decide the constitutionality of other existing laws through judicial review (Barzilai, 1999; Galnoor, 2003).[42]

Second, the Court developed an individualistic perspective on citizenship rights. In both his academic writings (1995, 1998, 2006) and legal opinions, Barak offered a legal model of improved civil rights for "non-Jewish" citizens considered as an aggregate of single individuals. Barak's legal model did not recognize Palestinians inside the state as bearers of distinct communal or national rights. By contrast, it considered them as individuals "entitled to full equality" within "a Jewish nation-state." Thus, for example, in the Qa'dan case (HC 6698/1995) the Israeli Supreme Court ruled that the Qa'dan family – Palestinians with Israeli citizenship – had the right to buy a house in Katzir, an Israeli community that had prevented them from buying a house by arguing that Katzir was a Jewish communal village. As Jabareen (2002, p. 205) contends in his critique of this decision, the Qa'dan family did not make particular claims to equality or land ownership as members of a national group or a native population. This is the main reason why their request for "a better quality of life" resonated with the Supreme Court's discourse of individual rights: "they sought – and are still seeking – to live in a place with a different quality of life and standard of living from those where they are currently living."

While denying nationhood as a principle of membership for Palestinians inside Israel, the new individualistic discourse of civil rights markedly highlighted their status as citizens. This is particularly evident when this discourse of civil rights directed toward Palestinian citizens is compared to the Supreme Court's acceptance of a security-based legal discourse for the Palestinians of the Occupied Territories (Hajjar, 2005, pp. 57–58; Kretzmer, 2002). Thus, in the Occupied Territories, the Israeli Supreme Court has not interfered with the decisions of the Israeli military courts and has sanctioned practices such as expulsions, deportation, curfews, detention without trial, extrajudicial executions, and punitive house demolition (Sultany, 2007, pp. 84–85).

This difference between the security-based orientation toward the Palestinians of the Occupied Territories – as expressed both by the PA's security role and by the almost unrestricted power of the Israeli army – and the discourse of civil rights toward Palestinian citizens has shaped the latter's perceptions of their political interests and opportunities. Specifically, during my conversations with young Palestinian students and activists volunteering or working for human rights organizations in Israel, citizenship emerged as a crucial factor of difference between the political opportunities of Palestinian citizens and those of noncitizens:

> They have the [military] occupation; we are struggling for our civil rights.

> The PA is not democratic and is not a state; that is the challenge for the Palestinians in Gaza and the West Bank; they have to democratize the PA and turn it into a state; we [citizens] have a different challenge, we have to make Israel more democratic.

> There are many similarities: there are house demolitions in the West Bank and in the Negev;[43] the state doesn't want Palestinians there [West Bank] and it doesn't want us [Palestinians] here [inside the state] but we are citizens so for us it's different.

The Reconfiguration of the Palestinian National Question 127

Look, I go to all the demonstrations against the occupation, I express my solidarity with the Palestinians in Gaza, but ... I feel bad because at times I would like us to be like other minorities in other states, without the problem of the occupation, the PA, and Hamas ... Then we could focus on our rights as citizens.

My interviewees expressed their awareness that certain Israeli policies such as land confiscation and house demolitions target both segments of Palestinians under Israeli rule. Yet, they felt uneasy about linking their problems with those of Palestinian noncitizens. Together with continued forms of coercion against Palestinian noncitizens – exercised both directly by the Israeli army and indirectly through the PA – the political liberalism toward citizens' individual rights, which was promoted by the Israeli courts in the 1990s, contributed to this process of distancing from Palestinian noncitizens and their problems.

At the same time, citizenship has become a resource for Palestinian citizens to mobilize through forms of direct engagement with the Israeli judicial branch and civil society (Jamal, 2007a, 2008). Many Palestinian citizens, especially the younger generation of educated Palestinians, perceive that they have distinct political opportunities in struggling against state discrimination through court-based political activism. The above-mentioned decision by the Supreme Court to exercise judicial review of primary legislation – what Barak (1995, p. 16) defined as a "constitutional revolution" – has transformed the Court into a primary arena available for Israeli citizens to raise human and civil rights issues. In this context, litigation has become an important form of political action among educated Palestinian citizens and lawyers have assumed a prominent role in articulating and expressing political claims (Sallon, 2009, pp. 169–171).[44] Another interrelated aspect of the predominance of court-based political activism is the steady rise in associations, and especially legal NGOs, among Palestinian citizens as a privileged channel to pursue collective rights (Gidron, Bar, & Kats, 2004; Haklai, 2009; Payes, 2005). Indeed, the rate of registration of associations created by Palestinian citizens increased dramatically in the 1990s and "approximately 80 per cent of all PAI [Palestinian Israeli] civil society associations were formed since 1988" (Haklai, 2009, p. 879). In 1998 there were about 1,000 registered Palestinian NGOs inside Israel representing about 4 percent of the total 20,700 NGOs in Israel (Payes, 2005, p. 62).

The importance of engaging the Israeli courts and developing associations emerges, albeit in different forms, both from my dialogue with educated Palestinians and from my fieldwork among poor, uneducated Palestinians.

For example, Suad, a human rights activist and law student in her midtwenties, refers to her father's political activism with these words:

> My father always speaks about the land and the homeland, he has always been a nationalist, our national identity as Palestinians is important for me too, but I know more than him about how to protect our rights as citizens, they [the Israeli state] use the legal system to discriminate against us, and we have to use it to improve our condition.

If, like many Palestinian citizens of her generation, Suad identifies the courts as the main arena to struggle for Palestinian citizens' individual and group rights, many poor Palestinians in Lod, an Israeli town where I conducted ethnographic fieldwork in 2008, repeatedly expressed their frustration with the scarcity of available tools to struggle against house demolitions and police brutality, two of their most urgent concerns.[45] On the one hand, many residents of Lod often commented on their hopes that their children would become lawyers and "understand what the law says," for example, about house demolition. They also resented their failed attempts at creating local associations and pressuring local authorities via court-based activism. On the other hand, some poor Palestinians in Lod have developed an anti-intellectual stance, considering local initiatives to establish NGOs as "empty words" (*ḥakī fāḍī*).

While Gaza and West Bank Palestinians were placed under the PA within a regime of forced immobility and the Green Line was "closed," the shift toward citizenship issues among Palestinians in Israel was initially buttressed by material concessions. The Rabin government (1992–1995) implemented affirmative action programs to hire Palestinian citizens in the public sector; the Ministry of Interior increased the budgets for Arab local councils; and the Ministry of Education increased the budget for Arab education (Rouhana, 1997, p. 102). These concessions were particularly meaningful for young educated Palestinians. For example, a Palestinian lawyer in her early thirties told me that when she was a law student, she was very impressed by the new hiring policy in the judicial system: "there was this really big wave of nominations of Arab lawyers and judges." While subsequent governments put an end to these material concessions, associational development and court-based activism have continued to provide opportunities for individual social mobility and professional achievement for a new generation of educated Palestinians (Haidar, 1997).

Interestingly, I conducted my fieldwork after the October 2000's mass protests among Palestinian citizens in solidarity with Palestinian demonstrators in the Occupied Territories.[46] The protests were repressed by the Israeli security and police forces with the use of live ammunition resulting in the killing of 13 unarmed protestors. These protests are often considered a turning point in the relationship between the Palestinian minority and the Israeli state (Bishara, 2001; Peled, 2005; Rabinowitz & Abu-Baker, 2005). After all, they were an expression of national solidarity with Palestinians of the Occupied Territories and the Israeli police and security forces treated demonstrators in the same way that they regularly treat Palestinian noncitizens: with military repression. However, while the Second *Intifada* among Gaza and West Bank Palestinians quickly lost its popular constituencies to become militarized (Johnson & Kuttab, 2001; Hammami & Tamari, 2001), the campaign for citizenship rights among Palestinian citizens has continued to be based on forms of direct engagement with the Israeli courts and associational arena. While generating a widespread sense of disillusion with Israeli institutions among Palestinian citizens, the brutal repression of the mass demonstrations in 2000 also worked as a threatening reminder that, like in the past, when Palestinian citizens were put under military rule, the state can and does resort to direct repression to police the boundaries of legitimate political discourse and practices among Palestinians with Israeli citizenship. In this sense, the legal restrictions and physical obstacles continue to prevent the interaction between citizens and noncitizens and at the same time the threat of state coercion merges with the limited civic agenda to push Palestinian citizens' political orientation away from Gaza and West Bank Palestinians and toward the Israeli courts and associational arena.

THE INDIRECT RULE ROUTE AND THE CIVIL SOCIETY ROUTE: PRESENT AND FUTURE

Palestinian nationalist forces have historically struggled against powerful actors in their pursuit of nationhood as a principle of collective membership (Khalidi, 1997, 2007). This chapter has drawn attention to how differently situated Palestinians under Israeli rule face distinct (and shifting) combinations of liberal, illiberal, and colonial forms of rule. This empirical section has focused on two strategies of rule – the indirect rule route and the civil society route – that informed the reorganization of Israeli rule in the 1990s and it has examined their effects on national group solidarity among different segments of Palestinians. However, this reorganization is neither stable nor uncontested. A cursory look at the current situation shows that the two routes here examined have undergone changes and contestations.

These changes and contestations open new questions about future trajectories of power and resistance in the Israeli–Palestinian context.

In the Post-Second *Intifada* period, Jewish ethnonationalism has clearly taken the upper hand on the civic agenda in the formulation and application of Israeli policies toward Palestinian citizens (Blecher, 2005; Jamal, 2007b; Peled, 2007; Rouhana & Sultany, 2003; Sultany, 2003, 2004, 2005). This is evident in recent legislative and governmental initiatives aimed to revoke citizenship for those citizens involved in "terrorist" acts and to introduce "loyalty oaths" to the state for all citizens (Cook, 2006, p. 165; Kanaaneh, 2009, p. 29).[47] Another recent measure that has deeply infringed on Palestinian citizens' rights is an amendment to the Israeli Nationality Law that bars Gaza and West Bank Palestinians married to Israeli citizens from obtaining legal permits to live with their spouses in Israel. In 2006, by a narrow majority of six-to-five, the Israeli Supreme Court upheld this amendment. Chief Justice, Aharon Barak, who had initiated the "liberalizing" trend in the early 1990s and who voted with the minority, declared that "the law is a violation of the right of Arab citizens of Israel to equality." By contrast, Deputy Chief Judge, Michael Cheshin, who voted with the majority stated that "the residents of the Palestinian Territories are de facto enemy nationals, and as such they are a group that presents a risk to the citizens and residents of Israel."[48]

It is interesting to compare this decision on "mixed" marriages between Palestinian citizens and noncitizens with the recommendations made by the commission of inquiry headed by the Supreme Court judge Theodore Or[49] – the Or Commission – in regard to the killings of Palestinian citizens during the protests of 2000. While in the case of "mixed" marriages the majority of judges sided with other state actors justifying the infringement on the family rights of Palestinian citizens, in the case of police repression of Palestinian citizens' demonstrations, the Or Commission criticized the Israeli police for treating Palestinian citizens as enemies rather than citizens (implicitly drawing a line between the treatment of citizens' protests and the protests of Palestinian noncitizens). With a focus on the interactions between Palestinians in Israel and Palestinians in the Occupied Palestinian Territories, this ban on "mixed marriage" constitutes another layer in the regime of legal and physical separation between these two segments of Palestinians. It also clearly labels all Gaza and West Bank Palestinians as "enemy nationals" which, allegedly for security reasons,[50] are permanently excluded from the Israeli citizenship regime.

While this label of "enemy nationals" unites Gaza and West Bank Palestinians in their predicament of exclusion, the strategies of rule in the

West Bank and in the Gaza Strip have diverged. In the West Bank, the Fatah-dominated PA is currently pursuing a project of "statehood-by-2011," which, in line with its operation in the 1990s, centers on institution-building and economic projects through international donor funding in West Bank cities, especially Ramallah (Khalidi & Samour, 2011).[51] By contrast, since the takeover of the Gaza Strip by Hamas in 2007, Gaza Palestinians have been subject to direct forms of Israeli military repression, including blockades, attacks, and air bombardments (Finkelstein, 2010).

This chapter invites more empirical investigations into how these recent changes – the attacks to the civil society route and the bifurcation between PA's "statehood" in the West Bank and military siege in the Gaza Strip – might affect social relations among Palestinians. Further attention must also be paid to the ongoing attempts by several forces among Palestinians across legal status and place of residence[52] to address the need for representative bodies and venues where different voices and concerns can be heard (Bishara, 2003; Bisharat & Doumani, 2006; Doumani, 2007; Nabulsi, 2006).

STRATEGIES OF RULE AND THE UNMAKING OF SOCIAL GROUPS: CONCLUSIVE REMARKS

This chapter has examined how in the 1990s the Israeli state responded to rising popular mobilization among Palestinians on both sides of the Green Line by attempting to cement old divisions and introduce new ones among different segments of Palestinian citizens and noncitizens. I have investigated the workings of distinct state strategies ranging from the combination of military coercion and indirect rule toward stateless Gaza and West Bank Palestinians to a limited civic agenda toward Palestinians with Israeli citizenship. I have argued that, when combined, these strategies of rule weakened national group solidarity among Palestinians. My analysis has also drawn attention to how this rearrangement of Israeli rule remains unstable and has been recently contested from both within the state and below it.

In theoretical terms, this essay has shifted away from the emphasis on the making of groups through state symbolic mechanisms. Instead, drawing on Gramsci's *The Southern Question*, I have posed the question of how the state unmakes social groups. A Gramscian perspective is particularly well suited to pose this question for three interrelated reasons. First, it draws attention to the limits of the symbolic power of the state to shape people's cognitive processes. As Gramsci (1963, p. 180) argues, "identity in concrete reality determines identity of thought, and not vice versa."[53] Second, it gives analytic relevance to how social forces initiate group-making projects outside and against the state structure of categories. Third, it suggests that state actors might intervene to neutralize these projects from below through the coordinated use of distinct strategies ranging from the concession of material benefits to the use of coercion.

An important argument for advancing the theoretical agenda on group formation and deformation emerges from my Gramscian analysis of the weakening of national group solidarity among Palestinians under Israeli rule: modern states use different strategies of exclusion and inclusion in their attempts to block the formation of social groups that challenge their power to define and control people's social and political lives. Thus, understanding the conditions under which certain policies of inclusion or exclusion affect group formation requires going beyond the analytic primacy currently given to the symbolic power of the state.

NOTES

1. Since 1967 the Israeli state has ruled over two segments of the Palestinians: the minority of Palestinians, who managed to remain inside the newly formed state and were given Israeli citizenship in 1948, and the Palestinians of the West Bank and the Gaza Strip, that is the territories that Israel occupied in 1967. Another segment of Palestinians under Israeli rule are those living in East Jerusalem who have a distinct legal status of "permanent residents" of the city after East Jerusalem was annexed by Israel in 1967. Palestinian residents of Jerusalem do not enjoy full rights of citizens.

2. From 1967 to the early 1990s, movement across these different places (Gaza, West Bank, East Jerusalem, and Israel) was allowed for all categories of Palestinians. Further, in the 1970s and 1980s national and land issues were the basis for popular protests on both sides of the Green Line. In particular, land expropriation was a common concern for all Palestinians under Israeli rule and was central to a similar interaction between Palestinians and the Israeli state: collective protests against land expropriation and state repression of these protests.

3. This view is still current. For example, Putnam (1993) differentiates between Italy's Northern "civic regions," whose inhabitants collectively value associationism and engage in practices of mutual trust, and its Southern regions, which have developed a culture lacking all the "virtuous" characteristics of civic life in the North. From a Gramscian perspective, the main shortcoming of Putnam's culturalist account is that it does not take into consideration the role of the state in creating or at least strengthening social, cultural, and economic differences between the South and the North.

4. I do not argue that the civil society route undermined national consciousness among Palestinian citizens. Yet, I also disagree with Rabinowitz's and Abu-Baker's argument (2005) that the shift toward citizenship rights among Palestinian citizens in

the 1990s was the product of an increase in national consciousness. Indeed, albeit not expressed in the language of citizenship and civil society, collective mobilization around nationhood among Palestinian citizens was already strong and on the rise in the 1970s and the 1980s. What mainly changed was the modality of expression of nationalist feelings; a change that had important consequences for the relations between Palestinian citizens and noncitizens and their national group solidarity.

5. In the summers of 2003, 2004, and 2005, I conducted fieldwork in several villages and refugee camps of the West Bank. I met with members of village councils and camp popular committees. I spent many hours speaking informally with families at night. I accompanied students in their daily commute to their universities. In the same period, I participated in meetings, forums, and conferences organized by major Palestinian NGOs and activist groups in Israel. Further, in February 2008, I completed eight months of ethnographic work in a West Bank refugee camp. From March to August 2008, I conducted ethnography in a poor Palestinian minority district inside an Israeli town. This chapter draws on my broader comparative study of political activism and group formation among Palestinian residents of the Occupied Territories and Palestinian citizens of Israel. In this chapter, the quotes that are not explicitly attributed to other scholars come from my interviews and informal conversations. I conducted some of these interviews and conversations in English and some in Palestinian Arabic. I tape-recorded some of the interviews, while in other cases I took notes during or just after the conversations.

6. For example, Lønning (1998, p. 181) argued that resentful attitudes toward the PA leadership were already widespread in the mid-1990s. In his view, the following statement made by one of his interviewees, a young man who had participated in the First *Intifada* (1987–1993) was representative of broader perceptions among Gaza and West Bank Palestinians: "Well, as I told you, Palestinian leaders have become more and more remote from the people as they sit behind closed office doors surrounded by security guards. But people still need leaders. We have a saying in Arabic, that if you find three men walking together towards a junction, they would all choose different directions if one of them failed to assume leadership. This saying, I believe, reflects human nature."

7. Brubaker (2004, p. 12) defines a social group as "a mutually interacting, mutually recognizing, mutually oriented, effectively communicating, bounded collectivity with a sense of solidarity, corporate identity, and capacity for concerted action."

8. Riley (2006, p. 383) draws attention to how "the post-Lukácsian-Marxist tradition" already worked from a "non-groupist" assumption. In addition to a privileged focus on class over ethnicity, the main difference between this tradition and the current state-centered theories of group formation is that the former studied the effects of "social structure" on group formation, while the latter focuses on how the state "structure of categories" creates social groups.

9. Zinoman contends that the colonial prison had the unintended consequence of giving unity to different segments of the Vietnamese population, including "petty criminals," and turning them into "revolutionaries."

10. Brubaker (2009, p. 33) mentions but does not elaborate on the role of "tangible benefits" in buttressing the effectiveness of the state's structure of categories.

11. According to Eyal, Israeli authorities have continued to mobilize "the discourse on the Arab village" despite its failure to control political change among

Palestinians because its primary goal is not to control Palestinians but to create a separate ("Western-modern") Israeli identity for the Jewish citizens of the state. While this line of inquiry is interesting, this chapter draws attention to how different state strategies have attempted to create separate identities *among* Palestinians (both within and across legal statuses).

12. Nashif (2008) shows how Israeli coercive strategies can have unintended effects by examining how Israeli prisons have become laboratories for group solidarity among Palestinian prisoners from the Occupied Palestinian Territories. By contrast, Kanaaneh (2009) examines the weakening of group solidarity among Palestinian citizens due to their different relations to the Israeli army and border police: Muslim and Christian Palestinians are excluded from the Israeli security apparatus while Bedouin Palestinians can volunteer in specific "ethnic" units inside the Israeli army and Druze Palestinians are subject to mandatory conscription.

13. While there are of course historical and political differences between the Italian case at the turn of the 20th century and the Palestinian case in the 1990s, as the empirical section of this chapter will show, the policies that Gramsci discusses are also relevant for the Palestinian–Israeli context.

14. For a Gramscian vision of the associational sphere as an important site of struggle in hegemonic regimes, see Riley (2005, 2010).

15. Other scholars have built on Gramsci to discuss the Israeli state's ideological hegemony and its control practices as well as political organizing among Palestinians and the role of civil society in the broader Arab region (Al-Sharif, 1988; Beinin, 1990; Bishara, 2000, 2003; Lustick, 1993b; Said, 1979; Swedenburg, 1995; Yiftachel & Ghanem, 2004). However, these works have not used Gramsci's *The Southern Question* to discuss the link between Israeli policies and group solidarity among Palestinians in both the Occupied Territories and Israel.

16. All names of people are fictitious. I have also changed the names of villages and refugee camps where I conducted fieldwork.

17. Abu Mahmud refers here to the different political orientations of Palestinian citizens of Israel and Palestinian residents of the West Bank and the Gaza Strip. On the one hand, the Israeli Communist Party (*Maki*), which was founded in 1948 with a platform of Jewish–Arab cooperation, and especially the New Communist List (*Rakah*), which was established inside Israel in 1965 with a pan-Arab agenda, played an important role in the political lives of Palestinian citizens. On the other hand, Palestinians of the Gaza Strip and the West Bank considered the PLO (Palestine Liberation Organization) as their political representative in exile. The PLO had been established in 1964 by the Arab League (a regional organization of Arab states) but had then quickly become an independent actor in expressing and supporting Palestinian nationalism.

18. The Galilee is a northern region inside Israel with a large Palestinian population.

19. Palestinian citizens have historically been treated as a security threat by the Israeli security apparatuses. From 1948 to 1966, they were placed under military rule that entailed strict restrictions on their freedom of movement and on their political activism. Political surveillance has continued after the abolition of the military government. Thus, Ahmed's words also reflect a widespread awareness among Palestinian citizens that their legal citizenship does not protect them from military and other coercive measures. In this sense, Ahmed perceives that taking distance

from the problems of Gaza and West Bank Palestinians can reduce the risk of being reduced to and treated as a security threat.

20. As the result of secret diplomatic negotiations, in 1993 the PLO and the Rabin government signed an agreement, the Oslo Accords, which led to the creation of the PA as an authority of self-rule for the Palestinians of the West Bank and the Gaza Strip. The Israeli government also recognized the PLO as the legitimate representative of the Palestinians and allowed many PLO officials to return with their families to the Occupied Palestinian Territories. A subsequent agreement, the 1994 Gaza–Jericho agreement, identified the Gaza Strip and the West Bank town of Jericho as the first two places where the PA could operate as an authority of self-rule.

21. The Oslo Interim Agreement, which was signed by the PA and the Israeli government in 1995, limited the area of Palestinian self-rule, area A, to the main West Bank towns, while most West Bank villages and camps remained under joint PA–Israeli control (area B) and the area in proximity of Israeli settlements remained under full Israeli control (area C).

22. The number of Jewish settlers in the West Bank more than doubled during the 1990s.

23. For example, Palestinians from the Gaza Strip who live in the West Bank have been collectively denied the possibility of transferring their legal residence there. Further, in April 2010, an Israeli military order defined tens of thousands of Palestinians from Gaza living in the West bank as "infiltrators" subject to deportation to the Gaza Strip. While the Israeli army has not systematically attempted to enforce the order, its mere existence adds another layer of uncertainty and anxiety to the lives of Palestinians who are registered as residents in Gaza though they live in the West Bank.

24. The structure that is currently under construction in parts of the West Bank and East Jerusalem – what is often called as "separation wall" or "separation fence" – is in reality a complex fortification system made of concrete wall, electrified fencing, deep trenches, buffer zones, patrol roads, video cameras, sniper towers, and razor wire. This structure complements the system of checkpoints, roadblocks, and by-pass roads that has fragmented the West Bank into noncontiguous areas since the beginning of the 1990s.

25. I conducted my fieldwork mainly among poor Palestinians living in villages and refugee camps. Thus, I cannot generalize my findings to the urban poor. However, my sites also included one refugee camp within the municipal boundaries of Ramallah. In this sense, the camp dwellers of this camp are part of the urban poor of the city. Other sites include refugee camps and villages only a few miles away from Ramallah. While more research on the urban poor is surely needed, I provisionally say that, given their inability to partake in the consumption patterns of the urban middle class, the urban poor might express similar classed subjectivities to those I document in this chapter.

26. As Hass (2002, p. 6) puts it, "'closure' ... means to deprive the Palestinian inhabitants [of the Occupied Territories] of their right to free movement. It involves a pass system first introduced in early 1991 and which has been refined and perfected ever since." The Israeli policy of closure is mainly based on curfews, designation of certain villages or agricultural areas as closed military zones, roadblocks, checkpoints, and a system of travel permits.

27. According to the 1995 Oslo Interim Agreement, only one category of these three VIPs cards (VIP 1) exempts the carrier from all Israeli restrictions.

28. See announcement by the Prime Minister's Media Adviser on the website of the Ministry of Foreign Affairs. Retrieved from http://www.mfa.gov.il/MFA/Government/Communiques/1999/Israel%20Withdraws%20VIP%20Status%20from%20Three%20Palestinian. Accessed on July 26, 2011.

29. The interviewee is referring here to the PLO officials who returned to the Palestinian Territories as a result of the Oslo agreement. These PLO members and their families are often defined as "returnees" in the literature on Palestinian society (on these "returnees," see footnote 33).

30. By "chairman," the interviewee refers to Yasser Arafat, the PA president from 1996 to his death in 2004 after being confined under siege by the Israeli army in the PA governmental compound in Ramallah. Arafat, who was the chairman of the Executive Committee of the PLO from 1969 to 2004, can be considered as the symbol of the Palestinian national struggle for four decades.

31. In the 1970s and 1980s, popular grassroots organizations were central forces in the Palestinian political mobilization. Under the PA, these organizations were disempowered and replaced by a plethora of NGOs without any links with popular constituencies. These new NGOs, which are run by urban middle-class Palestinians, are perceived by the majority of poor Palestinians as forces that have depoliticized the Palestinian national cause under the pressure of international, especially Western donors (Challand, 2009; Jad, 2007; Taraki, 1989).

32. "The new middle class is composed of a number of sections. First, there are those in the higher echelons of the PA bureaucracy, and in public services. Second are the directors of Palestinian and international NGOs, as well as university teachers and administrators. Thirdly, there are those in management of the new enterprises, banks, and companies" (Hilal, 2003, p. 169).

33. The returnees are Palestinians who spent most of their lives abroad and who returned to the Palestinian Territories when the PA was established. Most of them had worked as high-rank officials in the PLO while they were abroad. The returnees in general come from middle-class families who emigrated mainly because the Israeli economy in the 1970s and 1980s absorbed Palestinian unskilled and manual workers but did not offer opportunities to middle-class Palestinians.

34. The internal migration of educated and professional Palestinians toward Ramallah greatly contributed to the high percentage of Ramallah residents who were born in other parts of the West Bank. Taraki and Giacaman (2006, p. 44) find that "50 percent of Ramallah residents at the time of the [1997] census reported that they had moved from another place to Ramallah city, compared to 27 percent for Nablus and only 13 percent for Hebron."

35. According to Palestinians, "martyrs" are all the men, women, and children whose death is caused by the Israeli military occupation. Photographs, posters, murals, and calendars are all ways through which Palestinians commemorate "martyrs." On the commemoration of "martyrs" in Palestinian society, see Khalili (2007).

36. The PA has divided the West Bank in several "Governorates," each under an appointed "Governor." These "governors" are the most powerful PA figures in the different noncontiguous areas of the West Bank under formal PA control.

37. "Administrative detention" is a type of imprisonment that does not include a trial and lasts for six months renewable. Israeli military judges sentence Palestinians to "administrative detention" on the basis of secret evidence provided by the Israeli army or security apparatuses. This evidence is never shared with the prisoner.

38. Doumani (2004) offers an ethnographic study of the Israeli army's differential treatment of urban Palestinians and camp Palestinians in the West Bank city of Nablus. Israeli army also targets different West Bank cities in different ways. For example, "Hebron city spent a quarter of its time under curfew in a three-year period from 2002 to 2005, compared to 20 percent in Nablus and a mere 11 percent in Ramallah" (Taraki & Giacaman, 2006, p. 46).

39. This is how the then Israeli Prime Minister Rabin commented on the creation of the PA in Gaza and the West Bank in the newspaper *Yediot Aharonot* in an interview on March 3, 1993 (quoted in Kretzmer, 2002, p. 2).

40. This is what the then Deputy Chief of staff of the Israeli army, Lipkin-Shahak, stated in a 1994 interview (quoted in Johnson & Kuttab, 2001, p. 23).

41. This is a comment made by former Israeli minister Natan Sharansky, who was actually critical of the shift toward indirect rule because he did not trust the PLO leadership (quoted in Finkelstein, 2010, p. 19).

42. These two laws are the Basic Law on Human Dignity and Freedom and the Basic Law on Freedom of Occupation. It is interesting to note that Israel is a country that lacks a written constitution and that the jurisprudence of the Supreme Court, in its capacity as a High Court of Justice, has granted constitutional relevance to these two Basic Laws as well as other Basic Laws previously adopted by the Knesset, the Israeli Parliament.

43. The Negev is a desert area in southern Israel where there are dozens of villages inhabited by Palestinian Bedouins that the Israeli state does not officially recognize and that therefore live an everyday reality of house demolition and lack of public services. On the question of Palestinian Bedouin villages in the Negev, see Abu-Saad (2008).

44. It is also important to note that some Palestinian legal NGOs explicitly tackle the question of the limits of litigation as a tool for social change. For a discussion of the potential and the limits of litigation, see Esmeir (2000).

45. Lod is an Israeli town with a Jewish majority and a Palestinian minority. Before the Arab–Israeli war of 1948, Lod – then called Lydda – was a Palestinian town but most of its inhabitants were expelled during the war (Yacobi, 2009). The reconstitution of the Palestinian population in the town after 1948 took place with several waves of migrants or internally displaced Palestinians. These families often settled and built houses and shacks on state-owned land. Almost half of Palestinians in the town live in houses that are subject to demolition.

46. At the beginning of the Second *Intifada* in October 2000, many unarmed Palestinian demonstrators in the West Bank and the Gaza Strip were killed by the Israeli army. The mass protests among Palestinian citizens in solidarity of Palestinians of the Occupied Territories lasted for 10 days.

47. The criminalization of Palestinian citizens' political practices has deepened after Palestinian legal NGOs and research centers in Israel formulated proposals suggesting a constitution based on the principle of equality among citizens rather than on the distribution of rights according to ethnoreligious membership.

48. The texts of the minority and majority decisions are available at the Supreme Court's website: http://elyon1.court.gov.il/files_eng/03/520/070/a47/03070520.a47. pdf. Accessed on July 30, 2011.

49. This committee was part of the judiciary branch of the state. As Peled (2005, p. 103, note 1) puts it, "although state commissions of inquiry are set up by the cabinet, their members are appointed by the Chief Justice and they are presided over by a judge."

50. In addition to "security" reasons, Israeli state officials have often given demographic reasons in support of the ban. For example, in 2006 Zeev Boim, the current Israeli Minister for Immigration Absorption, stated: "We have to maintain the state's democratic nature, but also its Jewish nature. The extent of entry of Arabs [Palestinian spouses] into Israel is intolerable" (quoted in Cook, 2006, p. 127).

51. Khalidi and Samour (2011, p. 8) argue that the program pursued by the PA "is inspired by a model of neoliberal governance increasingly widespread in the region" and that it "recalls the PA's promotion of Gaza in the mid-1990s as the next Singapore."

52. This chapter does not discuss another important segment of the Palestinian population, which was politically marginalized in the 1990s: Palestinian refugees and exiles.

53. See Mac-Laughlin and Agnew (1986, p. 248) for full citation.

ACKNOWLEDGMENTS

I thank Dylan Riley for his invaluable help and advice at each stage of this chapter's development. I am also grateful to Michael Burawoy who supervised the master's thesis from which this chapter originated. I also thank Jesse Nissim, Tom Pessah, Gretchen Purser, Cihan Tuğal, and Loïc Wacquant for the many useful comments and sharp critiques on earlier drafts. Finally, I thank the editor of and the three reviewers for PPST for their helpful insights and critical feedback.

REFERENCES

Abdo, N. (1999). Gender and politics under the Palestinian authority. *Journal of Palestine Studies, 28*(2), 38–51.

Abourahme, N. (2009). The Bantustan sublime: Reframing the colonial in Ramallah. *City, 13*(4), 500–509.

Abu-Saad, I. (2008). Spatial transformation and indigenous resistance. *American Behavioral Scientist, 51*(12), 1713–1754.

Al-Haj, M. (1993). The impact of the Intifada on the orientation of the Arabs in Israel: The case of a double periphery. In A. Cohen & G. Wolsfeld (Eds.), *Framing the Intifada: Media and people* (pp. 64–75). Norwood, NJ: Ablex Publishing Corporation.

Al-Haj, M. (2005). Whither the Green Line? Trends in the orientation of the Palestinians in Israel and the Territories. *Israel Affairs*, *11*(1), 183–206.

Allen, L. (2006). Palestinians debate "polite" resistance. In J. Beinin & R. L. Stein (Eds.), *The struggle for sovereignty: Palestine and Israel 1993–2005* (pp. 288–296). Stanford, CA: Stanford University Press.

Al-Sharif, M. (1988). *The communists and issues in the current national struggle*. Damascus, Syria: Center for Socialist Research and Study in the Arab world. [In Arabic].

Aquarone, A. (1981). *L'Italia Giolittiana (1896–1915)*. Bologna, Italy: IL Mulino.

Bailey, S. R. (2008). Unmixing for race making in Brazil. *American Journal of Sociology*, *114*(3), 577–614.

Barak, A. (1995). La Révolution Constitutionnelle: La Protection des Droits Fondamentaux. *Pouvoirs*, *72*, 17–35.

Barak, A. (1998). The role of the Supreme Court in a democracy. *Israel Studies*, *3*(2), 6–29.

Barak, A. (2006). *The judge in a democracy*. Princeton, NJ: Princeton University Press.

Barbagallo, F. (1980). *Mezzogiorno e Questione Meridionale (1860–1980)*. Naples, Italy: Guida.

Barzilai, G. (1999). Courts as hegemonic institutions: The Israeli Supreme Court in a comparative perspective. *Israel Affairs*, *5*(2), 15–33.

Beinin, J. (1990). *Was the red flag flying there? Marxist politics and the Arab-Israeli Conflict in Egypt and Israel, 1948–1965*. Berkeley, CA: University of California Press.

Bishara, A. (1998). Reflections on the realities of the Oslo process. In G. Giacaman & D. J. Lønning (Eds.), *After Oslo: New realities, old problems* (pp. 212–226). London: Pluto Press.

Bishara, A. (2000). *Civil society: A critical study* (In Arabic). Beirut, Lebanon: Center for Arab Unity Studies.

Bishara, A. (2001). Reflections on October 2000: A landmark in Jewish-Arab relations in Israel. *Journal of Palestine Studies*, *30*(3), 54–67.

Bishara, A. (2003). The quest for strategy. *Journal of Palestine Studies*, *32*(2), 41–49.

Bisharat, G., & Doumani, B. (2006). Open forum: Strategizing Palestine. *Journal of Palestine Studies*, *35*(3), 37–82.

Blecher, R. (2005). Citizens without sovereignty: Transfer and ethnic cleansing in Israel. *Comparative Studies in Society and History*, *47*(4), 725–754.

Bonfante, G., & Sapelli, G. (1981). *Il Movimento Cooperativo in Italia: Storia e Problemi*. Turin, Italy: Einaudi.

Bouillon, M. E. (2004). *The peace business: Money and power in the Palestine-Israel conflict*. London: Tauris.

Bourdieu, P. (1989). Social space and symbolic power. *Sociological Theory*, *7*(1), 14–25.

Bourdieu, P. (1991). *Language and symbolic power*. Cambridge, MA: Harvard University Press.

Bowman, G. (2001). The two deaths of Basem Rishmawi: Identity constructions and reconstructions in a Muslim-Christian Palestinian community. *Identities: Global Studies in Culture and Power*, *8*(1), 47–82.

Brubaker, R. (2004). *Ethnicity without groups*. Cambridge, MA: Harvard University Press.

Brubaker, R. (2009). Ethnicity, race, and nationalism. *Annual Review of Sociology*, *35*, 21–42.

Brubaker, R., Loveman, M., & Stamatov, P. (2004). Ethnicity as cognition. *Theory and Society*, *33*(1), 31–64.

Brynen, R. (1995). The Neopatrimonial dimension of Palestinian politics. *Journal of Palestine Studies*, *25*(1), 23–36.

Bucaille, L. (2004). *Growing up Palestinian: Israeli occupation and the Intifada generation.* Princeton, NJ: Princeton University Press.

Challand, B. (2009). *Palestinian civil society: Foreign donors and the power to promote and exclude.* London: Routledge.

Clarno, A. (2008). A tale of two walled cities: Neo-liberalization and enclosure in Johannesburg and Jerusalem. *Political Power and Social Theory, 19*, 159–205.

Cohen, H. (2010). *Good Arabs: The Israeli Security Agencies and the Israeli Arabs, 1948–1967.* Berkeley, CA: University of California Press.

Collins, J. (2004). *Occupied by memory: The Intifada generation and the Palestinian state of emergency.* New York, NY: New York University Press.

Comaroff, J. L. (1998). Reflections on the colonial state, in South Africa and elsewhere: Factions, fragments, facts and fictions. *Social Identities, 4*(3), 321–361.

Cook, J. (2006). *Blood and religion: The unmasking of the Jewish and democratic state.* London: Pluto Press.

Coppa, F. (1971). *Planning, protectionism, and politics in liberal Italy: Economics and politics in the Giolittian Age.* Washington, DC: Catholic University of America Press.

D'Agostino, P. (2002). Craniums, criminals, and the "Cursed Race": Italian anthropology in American Racial Thought, 1861–1924. *Comparative Studies in Society and History, 44*(2), 319–343.

De Grand, A. (2001). *The Hunchback's tailor: Giovanni Giolitti and Liberal Italy from the challenge of mass politics to the rise of Fascism, 1882–1922.* Westport, CT: Praeger.

Demetriou, C. (2007). Political violence and legitimation: The episode of Colonial Cyprus. *Qualitative Sociology, 30*(2), 171–193.

Doumani, B. (2004). Scenes from daily life: The view from Nablus. *Journal of Palestine Studies, 34*(1), 37–50.

Doumani, B. (2007). Palestine versus Palestinians? The iron laws and ironies of a peoplehood denied. *Journal of Palestine Studies, 36*(4), 49–64.

El-Asmar, F. (1976). Israel revisited 1976. *Journal of Palestine Studies, 6*(3), 47–65.

Esmeir, S. (2000). Resisting litigation in Umm el-Fahem. *Human Rights Dialogue, 2*(2), 15–33.

Eyal, G. (1996). The discursive origins of Israeli separatism: The case of the Arab village. *Theory and Society, 25*(3), 389–429.

Falah, G. (2005). The geopolitics of "Enclavisation" and the demise of a two-state solution to the Israeli-Palestinian conflict. *Third World Quarterly, 26*(8), 1341–1372.

Farsakh, L. (2005). *Palestinian labour migration to Israel: Labor, land, and occupation.* Abingdon, UK: Routledge.

Finkelstein, N. (2010). *This time we went too far.* New York, NY: OR Books.

Frisch, H. (1997). Modern Absolutist or Neopatriarchal state building? Customary law, extended families, and the Palestinian authority. *International Journal of Middle East Studies, 29*(3), 341–358.

Galnoor, I. (2003). The judicialization of the public sphere in Israel. *Israel Law Review, 37*(2), 500–542.

Geertz, C. (1973). The integrative revolution: Primordial sentiments and civil politics in the new states. In C. Geertz (Ed.), *The interpretation of cultures* (pp. 255–310). New York, NY: Basic Books.

Ghanem, As'ad. (2001). *The Palestinian-Arab Minority in Israel, 1948–2000: A political study.* Albany, NY: State University of New York Press.

Ghanem, As'ad. (2010). *Palestinian politics after Arafat: A failed national movement.* Bloomington, IN: Indiana University Press.
Gidron, B., Bar, M., & Kats, H. (2004). *The Israeli third sector: Between welfare state and civil society.* New York, NY: Kluwer Academic Publishers.
Go, J. (2007). The provinciality of American empire: "Liberal Exceptionalism" and U.S. Colonial Rule, 1898–1912. *Comparative Studies in Society and History, 49*(1), 74–108.
Go, J. (2008). *American empire and the politics of meaning: Elite political cultures in the Philippines and Puerto Rico during U.S. colonialism.* Durham, NC: Duke University Press.
Goh, D. (2007). States of ethnography: Colonialism, resistance, and cultural transcription in Malaya and the Philippines, 1890s–1930s. *Comparative Studies in Society and History, 49*(1), 109–142.
Goldberg, C. A. (2003). Haunted by the specter of communism: Collective identity and resource mobilization in the demise of the Workers Alliance of America. *Theory and Society, 32*(5), 725–773.
Gordon, N. (2008). *Israel's occupation.* Berkeley, CA: University of California Press.
Gramsci, A. (1963). *Il Materialismo Storico e la Filosofia di Benedetto Croce.* Turin, Italy: Einaudi.
Gramsci, A. (1995 [1926]). *The Southern Question* (P. Verdicchio, Ed. & Trans.). Toronto, Canada: Guernica Editions.
Gramsci, A. (2003 [1971]). *Selections from the Prison Notebooks of Antonio Gramsci* (Q. Hoare & G. N. Smith, Eds. & Trans.). London: Lawrence & Wishart.
Haidar, A. (1997). *The Palestinians in Israel and the Oslo Accords.* Beirut, Lebanon: Institute of Palestine Studies. [In Arabic].
Hajjar, L. (2005). *Courting the conflict: The Israeli Military Court System in the West Bank and Gaza.* Berkeley, CA: University of California Press.
Haklai, O. (2009). State mutability and ethnic civil society: The Palestinian Arab minority in Israel. *Ethnic and Racial Studies, 32*(5), 864–882.
Hammami, R. (1995). NGOs: The professionalization of politics. *Race & Class, 37*(2), 51–64.
Hammami, R., & Tamari, S. (2001). The second uprising: End or new beginning? *Journal of Palestine Studies, 30*(2), 5–25.
Hanafi, S. (2009). Spacio-cide: Colonial politics, invisibility and rezoning in Palestinian Territory. *Contemporary Arab Affairs, 2*(1), 106–121.
Hanafi, S., & Tabar, L. (2005). *The emergence of a Palestinian globalized elite: Donors, international organizations and local NGOs.* Jerusalem: Institute of Jerusalem Studies.
Hass, A. (2002). Israel's closure policy: An ineffective strategy of containment and repression. *Journal of Palestine Studies, 31*(3), 5–20.
Hilal, J. (2003). Problematizing democracy in Palestine. *Comparative Studies of South Asia, Africa and the Middle East, 23*(1), 163–172.
Hilal, J. (2006). Hamas's rise as charted in the polls, 1994–2005. *Journal of Palestine Studies, 35*(3), 6–19.
Hilal, J., & Khan, M. H. (2004). State formation under the PA: Potential outcomes and their viability. In M. H. Khan, G. Giacaman & I. Amundsen (Eds.), *State formation in Palestine. Viability and governance during a social transformation* (pp. 64–119). London: Routledge.
Hiltermann, J. R. (1985). Mass mobilization under occupation: The emerging trade union movement in the West Bank. *MERIP, 136/137,* 26–31.

Hiltermann, J. R. (1991). *Behind the Intifada: Labor and women's movements in the occupied territories*. Princeton, NJ: Princeton University Press.
Hirschfeld, L. A. (1996). *Race in the making: Cognition, culture, and the child's construction of human kinds*. Cambridge, MA: MIT Press.
Horowitz, D. (1985). *Ethnic groups in conflict*. Berkeley, CA: California University Press.
Jabareen, H. (2002). The future of Arab citizenship in Israel: Jewish-Zionist time in a place with no Palestinia memory. In D. Levy & Y. Weiss (Eds.), *Challenging ethnic citizenship: German and Israeli perspectives on immigration* (pp. 181–195). New York, NY: Berghahn Books.
Jad, I. (2007). NGOs: Between buzzwords and social movements. *Development in Practice*, *17*(4), 622–629.
Jamal, A. (2007a). Strategies of minority struggle for equality in ethnic states: Arab politics in Israel. *Citizenship Studies*, *11*(3), 263–282.
Jamal, A. (2007b). Nationalizing states and the constitution of "Hollow Citizenship": Israel and its Palestinian citizens. *Ethnopolitics*, *6*(4), 471–493.
Jamal, A. (2008). The counter-hegemonic role of civil society: Palestinian-Arab NGOs in Israel. *Citizenship Studies*, *12*(3), 283–306.
Johnson, P. (2005). Amari Refugee Camp in comparison with its neighbours: Stability, transformations, and vulnerability. *Review of Women's Studies*, *3*, 80–92.
Johnson, P. (2007). Tales of strength and danger: Sahar and the tactics of everyday life in Amari refugee camp, Palestine. *Signs: Journal of Women in Culture and Society*, *32*(3), 597–620.
Johnson, P., & Kuttab, E. (2001). Where have all the women (and men) gone? Reflections on gender and the Second Palestinian Intifada. *Feminist Review*, *69*, 21–43.
Kanaaneh, R. A. (2009). *Surrounded: Palestinian soldiers in the Israeli army*. Stanford, CA: Stanford University Press.
Khalidi, R. (1997). *Palestinian identity: The construction of modern national consciousness*. New York, NY: Columbia University Press.
Khalidi, R. (2007). *The Iron Cage: The story of the Palestinian struggle for statehood*. Boston, MA: Beacon Press.
Khalidi, R., & Samour, S. (2011). Neoliberalism as liberation: The Statehood Program and the remaking of the Palestinian national movement. *Journal of Palestine Studies*, *40*(2), 6–25.
Khalili, L. (2007). *Heroes and martyrs of Palestine: The politics of national commemoration*. Cambridge, UK: Cambridge University Press.
Kretzmer, D. (2002). *The occupation of justice: The Supreme Court of Israel and the Occupied Territories*. Albany, NY: State University of New York Press.
Lagerquist, P. (2003). Privatizing the occupation: The political economy of an Oslo Development Project. *Journal of Palestine Studies*, *32*, 5–20.
Lockman, Z., & Beinin, J. (1989). *Intifada: The Palestinian uprising against Israeli occupation*. Boston, MA: South End Press.
Lønning, D. J. (1998). Vision and reality diverging: Palestinian survival strategies in the Post-Oslo Era. In G. Giacaman & D. J. Lønning (Eds.), *After Oslo: New realities, old problems* (pp. 146–161). London: Pluto Press.
Loveman, M. (2005). The modern state and the primitive accumulation of symbolic power. *American Journal of Sociology*, *110*(6), 1651–1683.
Loveman, M. (2007). Blinded like a state: The revolt against civil registration in nineteenth-century Brazil. *Comparative Studies in Society and History*, *49*(1), 5–39.

Lustick, I. (1980). *Arabs in the Jewish state: Israel's control of a national minority*. Austin, TX: University of Texas Press.
Lustick, I. (1993a). Writing the Intifada: Collective action in the Occupied Territories. *World Politics, 45*(4), 560–594.
Lustick, I. (1993b). *Unsettled states, disputed lands: Britain and Ireland, France and Algeria, Israel and the West Bank–Gaza*. Ithaca, NY: Cornell University Press.
Mac-Laughlin, J., & Agnew, J. (1986). Hegemony and the regional question: The political geography of regional industrial policy in Northern Ireland, 1945–1972. *Annals of the Association of American Geographers, 76*(2), 247–261.
Mamdani, M. (1996). *Citizen and subject: Contemporary Africa and the legacy of late colonialism*. Princeton, NJ: Princeton University Press.
Mamdani, M. (2001). Beyond settler and native as political identities: Overcoming the political legacy of colonialism. *Comparative Studies in Society and History, 43*(4), 651–664.
Markowitz, F. (2007). Census and sensibilities in Sarajevo. *Comparative Studies in Society and History, 49*(1), 40–73.
MERIP. (1976). Arab Land Day: The file of 1948 has been reopened in their consciousness. *47*, 3–5.
Nabulsi, K. (2006). *Palestinians register: Laying foundations and setting directions*. Oxford, UK: Nuffield College University of Oxford.
Nashif, I. (2008). *Palestinian political prisoners: Identity and community*. London: Routledge.
Nassar, J., & Heacock, R. (1990). *Intifada: Palestine at the crossroads*. New York, NY: Praeger.
Pappé, I. (2011). *The forgotten Palestinians: A history of the Palestinians in Israel*. New Haven, CT: Yale University Press.
Parsons, N., & Salter, M. (2008). Israeli biopolitics: Closure, territorialisation and governmentality in the Occupied Palestinian Territories. *Geopolitics, 13*(4), 701–723.
Payes, S. (2005). *Palestinian NGOs in Israel: The politics of civil society*. London: Tauris Academic Studies.
Peled, Y. (2004). Profits or glory? *New Left Review, 29*, 47–72.
Peled, Y. (2005). Restoring ethnic democracy: The Or Commission and Palestinian citizenship in Israel. *Citizenship Studies, 9*(1), 89–105.
Peled, Y. (2007). Towards a post-citizenship society? A report from the front. *Citizenship Studies, 11*(1), 95–104.
Petersen, W. (1997). *Ethnicity counts*. New Brunswick, NJ: Transaction Publishers.
Petraccone, C. (2005). *Le "Due Italie:" La Questione Meridionale tra Realtà e Rappresentazione*. Rome, Italy: Laterza.
Putnam, R. (1993). *Making democracy work: Civic traditions in modern Italy*. Princeton, NJ: Princeton University Press.
Rabbani, M. (2006). Palestinian authority, Israeli rule. In J. Beinin & R. Stein (Eds.), *The struggle for sovereignty: Palestine and Israel 1993–2005* (pp. 75–83). Stanford, CA: Stanford University Press.
Rabinowitz, D., & Abu-Baker, K. (2005). *Coffins on our shoulders: The experience of the Palestinian citizens of Israel*. Berkeley, CA: University of California Press.
Rekhess, E. (2007). The evolvement of an Arab-Palestinian national minority in Israel. *Israel Studies, 12*(3), 1–28.
Riley, D. (2005). Civic associations and authoritarian regimes in interwar Europe: Italy and Spain in comparative perspective. *American Sociological Review, 70*(2), 228–310.

Riley, D. (2006). Waves of historical sociology. *International Journal of Comparative Sociology*, 47, 379–386.
Riley, D. (2010). *The civil foundations of Fascism in Europe: Italy, Spain, and Romania, 1870–1945*. Baltimore, MD: Johns Hopkins University Press.
Robinson, G. (1997). *Building a Palestinian state: The incomplete revolution*. Bloomington, IN: Indiana University Press.
Rosenhek, Z. (2003). The political dynamics of a segmented labour market: Palestinian citizens, Palestinians from the Occupied Territories, and migrant workers in Israel. *Acta Sociologica*, 46(3), 231–249.
Rouhana, N. (1989). The political transformation of the Palestinians in Israel: From acquiescence to challenge. *Journal of Palestine Studies*, 18(3), 38–59.
Rouhana, N. (1997). *Palestinian citizens in an ethnic Jewish state: Identities in conflict*. New Haven, CT: Yale University Press.
Rouhana, N., & Sultany, N. (2003). Redrawing the boundaries of citizenship: Israel's new hegemony. *Journal of Palestine Studies*, 33(1), 5–22.
Roy, S. (2001). Palestinian society and economy: The continued denial of possibility. *Journal of Palestine Studies*, 30(4), 5–20.
Rubenberg, C. (2001). *Palestinian women: Patriarchy and resistance in the West Bank*. Boulder, CO: Lynne Rienner Publishers.
Sa'di, A. (2003). The incorporation of the Palestinian minority by the Israeli state, 1948–1970: On the nature, transformation, and constraints of collaboration. *Social Text*, 21(2), 75–94.
Said, E. (1979). *The question of Palestine*. New York, NY: Times Books.
Said, E. (1996). *Peace and its discontents: Essays on Palestine in the Middle East Peace Process*. New York, NY: Vintage Books.
Said, E. (2001). *The end of the peace process: Oslo and after*. New York, NY: Vintage Books.
Said, E. (2004). *From Oslo to Iraq and the road map*. New York, NY: Pantheon Books.
Sallon, H. (2009). Lawyering for the cause of the Arab Minority in Israel: Litigation as means for collective action. In E. Marteu (Ed.), *Civil organizations and protest movements in Israel* (pp. 165–186). New York, NY: Palgrave-Macmillan.
Salomone, W. (1960). *Italy in the Giolittian Era: Italian democracy in the making, 1900–1914*. Philadelphia, PA: University of Pennsylvania Press.
Salvadori, M. (1963). *Il Mito del Buongoverno: La Questione Meridionale da Cavour a Gramsci*. Turin, Italy: Einaudi.
Salvemini, G. (2000). *Il Ministro della Mala Vita: Notizie e Documenti sulle Elezioni Giolittiane nell'Italia Meridionale*. Turin, Italy: Bollati Boringhieri.
Schölch, A. (1983). *Palestinians over the Green Line: Studies on the relations between Palestinians on Both Sides of the 1949 Armistice Line since 1967*. London: Ithaca Press.
Scott, J., Tehranian, J., & Mathias, J. (2002). The production of legal identities proper to states: The case of the permanent family surname. *Comparative Studies in Society and History*, 44(1), 4–44.
Shafir, G., & Peled, Y. (2000). *The New Israel: Peacemaking and liberalization*. Boulder, CO: Westview Press.
Shafir, G., & Peled, Y. (2002). *Being Israeli: The dynamics of multiple citizenship*. Cambridge, UK: Cambridge University Press.
Shils, E. (1957). Primordial, personal, sacred, and civil ties. *British Journal of Sociology*, 8, 130–145.

Starr, P. (1987). The sociology of official statistics. In W. Alonso & P. Starr (Eds.), *The politics of numbers* (pp. 7–58). New York, NY: Russell Sage Foundation.
Starr, P. (1992). Social categories and claims in the liberal state. In N. Goodman, M. Douglas & D. L. Hull (Eds.), *How classification works* (pp. 154–172). Edinburgh, Scotland: Edinburgh University Press.
Steinmetz, G. (2007). *The devil's handwriting: Precoloniality and the German Colonial State in Qingdao, Samoa, and Southwest Africa*. Chicago, IL: Chicago University Press.
Sultany, N. (2003). *Citizens without citizenship*. Haifa, Israel: Mada Arab Center for Applied Social Research.
Sultany, N. (2004). *Israel and the Palestinian Minority 2003*. Haifa, Israel: Mada Arab Center for Applied Social Research.
Sultany, N. (2005). *Israel and the Palestinian Minority 2004*. Haifa, Israel: Mada Arab Center for Applied Social Research.
Sultany, N. (2007). The legacy of Justice Aharon Barak: A critical review. *Harvard International Law Journal, 48*, 83–92.
Swedenburg, T. (1995). *Memories of revolt: The 1936–1939 rebellion and the Palestinian National Past*. Minneapolis, MN: University of Minnesota Press.
Tamari, S. (2002). Who rules Palestine? *Journal of Palestine Studies, 31*(4), 102–113.
Taraki, L. (1989). Mass organizations in the West Bank. In N. Aruri (Ed.), *Occupation: Israel over Palestine* (pp. 431–452). Belmont, MA: Association of Arab-American University Graduates.
Taraki, L. (2008a). Enclave Micropolis: The paradoxical case of Ramallah/al-Bireh. *Journal of Palestine Studies, 37*(4), 6–20.
Taraki, L. (2008b). Urban modernity on the periphery: A new middle class reinvents the Palestinian city. *Social Text, 26*(2), 61–81.
Taraki, L., & Giacaman, R. (2006). Modernity aborted and reborn: Ways of being urban in Palestine. In L. Taraki (Ed.), *Living Palestine: Family survival, resistance, and mobility under occupation* (pp. 1–50). Syracuse, NY: Syracuse University Press.
Tuğal, C. (2009). Transforming everyday Life: Islamism and social movement theory. *Theory and Society, 38*(5), 423–458.
Usher, G. (1995). Bantustanisation or Binationalism? An interview with Azmi Bishara. *Race & Class, 37*(2), 43–49.
Usher, G. (1996). The politics of internal security: The PA's new intelligence services. *Journal of Palestine Studies, 25*(2), 21–34.
Waked, A. (2010). Fatah official: Israel confiscated VIP IDs. *Y-net News*, February 26. Retrieved from http://www.ynetnews.com/articles/0,7340,L-3855040,00.html. Accessed on July 26, 2011.
Weinberger, P. (2006). *Co-opting the PLO: A critical reconstruction of the Oslo Accords, 1993–1995*. Lanham, MD: Lexington Books.
Weizman, E. (2007). *Hollow Land: Israel's architecture of occupation*. London: Verso.
Wimmer, A. (2008). The making and unmaking of ethnic boundaries: A multilevel process theory. *American Journal of Sociology, 113*(4), 970–1022.
Yacobi, H. (2009). *The Jewish-Arab City: Spatio-Politics in a mixed community*. London: Routledge.
Yiftachel, O. (1996). The political geography of ethnic protest: Nationalism, deprivation, and regionalism among Arabs in Israel. *Transactions: Institute of British Geographers, 22*(1), 91–110.

Yiftachel, O. (2000). "Ethnocracy" and its discontents: Minorities, protests, and the Israeli polity. *Critical Inquiry, 26,* 725–756.

Yiftachel, O. (2006). *Ethnocracy: Land and identity politics in Israel/Palestine.* Philadelphia, PA: University of Pennsylvania Press.

Yiftachel, O., & Ghanem, As'ad. (2004). Understanding "ethnocratic" regimes: The politics of seizing contested territories. *Political Geography, 23*(6), 647–676.

Zinoman, P. (2000). Colonial prisons and anti-colonial resistance in French Indochina: The Thai Nguyen Rebellion, 1917. *Modern Asian Studies, 34*(1), 57–98.

Zinoman, P. (2001). *The colonial Bastille: A history of imprisonment in Vietnam, 1862–1940.* Berkeley, CA: University of California Press.

Zureik, E. (1979). *The Palestinians in Israel: A study in internal colonialism.* London: Routledge & Kegan Paul.

Zureik, E. (2001). Constructing Palestine through surveillance practices. *British Journal of Middle Eastern Studies, 28*(2), 205–227.

TRANSFORMING CITIZENSHIP: THE SUBJECTIVE CONSEQUENCES OF LOCAL POLITICAL MOBILIZATION

Rachel Meyer

ABSTRACT

In a context of increasing globalization and neoliberal restructuring and with labor's power diminishing vis-à-vis employers, American workers have turned in recent years to community-based campaigns targeting local government. These mobilizations have received considerable attention from scholars who see this emerging community orientation as a significant strategic innovation. This study, alternatively, focuses on the subjective and ideological consequences of such mobilizations for those engaged in protest. In particular, it seeks to extend social movement theory regarding the transformative impact of collective action by asking: how do distinct forms of collective action bring about particular kinds of consciousness and identity among participants?

Scholars rooted in a variety of traditions – from theorists of "post-industrial" society and "new" social movements to state theorists and geographers – have suggested that identities fostered at the local level are characterized by a "defensive," "introverted," or "retrospective" quality.

This study examines a local mobilization, the case of a living wage campaign in Chicago, which deviates from these expectations. Through an analysis of interviews with participants, I find that instead of spurring defensiveness the campaign engendered a citizenship identity that was both active *and* inclusive. *In explaining why my findings diverge from existing theories of identity formation, my analysis highlights three conceptual deficiencies in the literature with respect to (1) the distinction between local versus transnational collective action, (2) the relationship between social movement goals/tactics and outcomes, and (3) the prioritization of "new" social movements over the labor movement. Examining the citizenship identities that developed during Chicago's living wage campaign is instructive, finally, for understanding the sources of counter-hegemonic subjectivity within a broader context of eroding citizenship rights and a dominant market fundamentalist ideology. More generally, this analysis paves the way for a more productive engagement among theories of social movements, citizenship, labor, and globalization.*

Although the traditional focus of social movement scholars has been on the causes of collective action, there has lately been increasing attention to its consequences. Recent scholarship has examined consequences that are external to the movement itself. The question of social movement success is addressed through analysis of macro-level structural outcomes including political, institutional, and cultural change (Amenta, 2006; Andrews, 2004; Gamson, 1990; Giugni, 1998; Giugni, McAdam, & Tilly, 1999; Zald, Morrill, & Rao, 2005). While this has proved to be a fruitful line of inquiry, some of the most profound effects of collective action lie elsewhere – in the subjective transformation of social movement participants themselves (Fantasia, 1988; Hirsch, 1990). Such transformations have been characterized as "explosions of consciousness" (Mann, 1973) or "moments of madness" (Zolberg, 1972), where new forms of consciousness and understanding are born.

Scholarship on the biographical and subjective consequences of social movements has been focused mainly on former student activists from the 1960s. In the tradition of McAdam's (1988) classic *Freedom Summer*, this research has examined the effects of activism on a variety of biographical outcomes, from marriage patterns to career choice (Fendrich, 1993; Fendrich & Turner, 1989; Jennings, 1987; Klatch, 1999; Marwell, Demerath, & Aiken, 1993; McAdam, 1989; Whalen & Flacks, 1989). Perhaps most importantly, these studies have shown that political attitudes and commitments forged in the heat of battle have tended to persist across the life course, contrary to popular predictions that youthful activists would become more conservative or apolitical with advancing age.

But how do distinct forms of collective action engender particular kinds of consciousness and understanding for those engaged in protest? Recent studies of democratically governed mobilizations have uncovered their capacity to instill in participants a lasting commitment to the values and goals of democratic, grassroots organizing (Markowitz, 2000; Polletta, 2002), but such research is minimal and many avenues of inquiry remain unexplored. This study, then, aims to enrich our understanding of how particular forms of collective action engender specific subjective consequences for participants.

The idea of there being a single, unitary subjectivity emerging from social conflict has plagued the labor movement in particular, given the Marxist legacy of positing a "true" versus "false" working-class consciousness. This legacy shapes even recent scholarship on working-class ideology, which has compared labor's "reformism" versus "radicalism" – with the latter including such traditional socialist party pillars as the "expropriation of private property" (Marks, Mbaye, & Kim, 2009). Some theorists, however, have moved beyond such formulations. Katznelson (1986), for example, critiques the imposition of "revolutionary" yardsticks of class consciousness, instead recognizing the rich variation in working-class formation. This study is couched within the theoretical framework of Katznelson and others (Marshall, 1983; Somers, 1997) who have emphasized how the content and contours of class formation in different historical contexts vary widely.

In examining how collective action experiences, specifically, shape class consciousness, we can contrast two modes of working-class mobilization that have come to the fore in response to neoliberal globalization: a transnational one and a local one. Transnational strategies have been seen as particularly important given the heightened mobility of capital, and because asserting workers' power within large multinational corporations is bolstered by the use of multiple pressure points (Bronfenbrenner, 2007; Evans, 2000, 2005; Gordon & Turner, 2000; Hathaway, 2000, pp. 169–196; Herod, 2003; Kay, 2005, 2011; Nash, 1998; Stillerman, 2003). There are, at the same time, significant trends in the opposite direction toward community-based labor organizing and the pursuit of social change through local government. Although community-based mobilizations are not necessarily articulated as a response to globalization, they nevertheless have emerged because of workers' weakened power on the job in the face of neoliberal restructuring and increased capital mobility.

Social movement scholars have recognized the "glocal" aspects of some contemporary protest. This is most prominently articulated by della Porta and Tarrow who emphasize the melding or linking of transnational and local protest – that is, both "the global in the local" and "the local in the global" (Tarrow, 2005a; also see della Porta, 2007 and Tarrow, 2005b). Nevertheless, with state power arguably bifurcating toward supra- and subnational scales in the post-Fordist era (Brenner, 1998; Brenner, Jessop, Jones, & MacLeod, 2003; Jessop, 1994; Swyngedouw, 2004), these become the loci of disparate forms of collective action that are empirically and analytically distinct. And while social movement scholarship has prioritized "complex internationalism," transnational collective action, and the "internationalization of contentious politics" (della Porta & Tarrow, 2005, p. 2, 16, 235), state theorists and geographers have emphasized the importance of social conflict manifesting at the local level in the contemporary political economic juncture (see, for example, Swyngedouw, 2004, p. 40; Brenner, 1998, p. 22).

Students of the labor movement have likewise recognized the increasing importance of local-level protest. Workers' use of community-based mobilizations has received significant attention from activists and academics alike. Its importance comes from the fact that, as Fine has argued, "low-wage workers in American society today have greater political than economic power" such that they have had more success achieving changes in public policy than addressing grievances through direct labor market intervention (2005, p. 156, also see Black, 2005, p. 31). With no national labor or workers' party in the United States, however, this political power has been exerted at the local level. The focus in the literature has been on opportunity structures (examining the structural conditions under which such campaigns have been viable) and also on what specific strategies "work," with an emphasis on coalition building and on union-community alliances (Dean & Reynolds, 2009; Dobbie, 2008; Nissen, 2000; Reynolds, 2004; Rhomberg & Simmons, 2005; Sciacchitano, 1998; Turner & Cornfield, 2007). As this literature demonstrates, community-based labor organizing has a clear *strategic* significance – offering leverage and even concrete material gain to workers whose power has been crippled in the face of global capital. What has gone unexamined, however, are the *subjective and ideological* consequences of these strategies for those involved in protest.

In this study I ask: what are the subjective and ideological consequences of locally based political mobilization? What kind of working-class identity is engendered? What kind of political vision is inspired? In order to answer these questions, I examine a case from the living wage movement – a movement that has been an icon of these local political strategies. Through in-depth interviews with participants in the Chicago Jobs and Living Wage Campaign, and an analysis of participant narratives, this study explores the subjective consequences of the campaign for those involved.

I find that participants emerged from their experience of collective action with a *reconceptualization of citizenship as both active and inclusive*. Although participants came to expect more from the state, at the same time they expected their struggles to continue. Their newfound citizenship identities revolved around the idea that they would only be able to extract concessions from the state if they continued to demand them. Local political mobilization also engendered an inclusive vision of citizenship and working-class solidarity that crossed previously entrenched social boundaries – in particular those of national origin and immigration status. These findings are important for understanding the contemporary American political landscape because of the increasing prominence of these community-based labor strategies. They also pose a theoretical puzzle given existing conceptualizations of citizenship and identity.

In particular, post-Fordist shifts in state power are associated with a "new authoritarianism": an erosion of democracy and participation through the "systematic exclusion or further disempowerment of politically and/or economically already weaker social groups" (Swyngedouw, 1996, p. 1499). This political disempowerment is bolstered by the dominance of market fundamentalist ideology, which has had a long-standing role in the erosion of citizenship rights (Somers, 2008). In a similar vein, theories of identity formation have posited that there has been a fading of citizenship identities paralleled by the emergence of more defensive and introverted subjectivities. Given these varied yet parallel arguments about the erosion of citizenship, the dominance of market fundamentalism, and the proliferation of defensive identities, the active and inclusive vision of citizenship uncovered in this study appears as something of a deviant case. As such it offers a lens through which to reevaluate our understanding of contemporary citizenship and identity.

"DEFENSIVE" LOCAL IDENTITIES IN A GLOBAL CONTEXT

When examining emergent subjectivity in Chicago's living wage campaign, it is instructive to draw on Melucci's concept of collective identity that "cannot be separated from the production of meaning in collective action" (1996, p. 69). Similarly, his conceptualization of the "relational dimension" of collective identity points to the larger social context in which collective identities emerge:

> Social movements develop collective identity in a circular relationship with a system of opportunities/constraints. Collective actors are able to identify themselves when they have learned to distinguish between themselves and the environment. Actor and system reciprocally constitute themselves, and a movement only becomes self-aware through a relation with its external environment, which offers to social action a field of opportunities and constraints, that in turn are recognized and defined as such by the actor. (1996, p. 73)

Citizenship identities in Chicago developed in dialogue with a specific context or "system" and its particular constellation of constraint and opportunity. Writ large, this context has been conceptualized as the "network" or "information" society, "post-Fordism," or as "flexibility." Regardless of the specific terminology or theoretical tradition, however, there is a common thread among scholars from these various perspectives emphasizing the defensive localism of collective identities that emerge in this context.

At the same time, there is potential for local community to foster both "progressive" and "regressive" identities. Melucci refers to the "two processes" of, for example, ethnic identity – one that may embody "self-determination" and the other that may resort to "violent forms of resistance" (1996, p. 159). The question, as posed by Mayo (2006), is if local communities are "heavens, havens or hells."[1]

In his second volume of *The Information Age*, Castells (2010 [1997]) outlines his vision of how identities are shaped in the context of the contemporary political economy. He recognizes the diversity of identities that may emerge and conceptualizes some contemporary expressions of identity, such as feminism and environmentalism, as "proactive" (2010 [1997], pp. 2, 8–10). Nevertheless, in his analysis it is "defensive" or "secluded" identities that are most salient in the context of what he calls the "network society":

> [T]he network society is based on the systemic disjunction between the local and the global for most individuals and social groups .... Under such new conditions, civil societies shrink and disarticulate because there is no longer continuity between the logic of power-making in the global network and the logic of association and representation in specific societies and cultures. The search for meaning takes place then in the reconstruction of *defensive identities* around communal principles. (2010 [1997], p. 11, emphasis mine)

Daunted by an inability to engage and resist global structures, civil society turns inward. These local community-based responses to increasingly global processes of capitalist development embody not a forward-thinking politics of social change but a retrenchment of traditional norms and practices. They are characterized by:

> ... an identity of retrenchment of the known against the unpredictability of the unknown and uncontrollable. Suddenly defenseless against a global whirlwind, people stuck to themselves .... [T]hese identities, in most cases, are defensive reactions against the impositions of global disorder and uncontrollable, fast-paced change. They do build havens, but not heavens. (2010 [1997], pp. 65, 68).

Castells explores a variety of these "defensive reactions" including Islamic and Christian fundamentalism, nationalism, and the American militia.

Castells' account is reflected in recent work by other prominent theorists of identity and globalization. Touraine (2000) offers a conceptualization of how emerging "global networks of production, consumption and communication" are accompanied by a "return to community":

> [T]hroughout the world there are more and more identity-based groupings and associations, sects, cults and nationalisms based on a common sense of belonging. ... *As it becomes more difficult in this globalized society to define oneself as a citizen or a worker*, it becomes more tempting to define oneself in terms of a cultural community such as an ethnic group, a religion or belief, a gender or a mode of behavior. (pp. 2, 31, emphasis mine)

For Touraine, these are "introverted" communities, "retrospective utopias" that are "turning in on themselves" (2000, pp. 4, 26, 34). As in Castells, local communities are seen as exhibiting defensive, reactionary tendencies:

> Hence the central paradox of our society: at the very time when the economy is being globalized and transformed rapidly by new technologies, the personality is no longer being projected into the future, and is looking, on the contrary, to the past or to an ahistorical desire for support. (Touraine, 2000, p. 39)

Where in the modern era there was an "extension of the public and political space," we are now driven to "defend our identity by turning to primary groups for support and by re-privatizing part, and sometimes all, of public life" (Touraine, 2000, p. 4).

This characterization of the local as particularistic and defensive spans a variety of theoretical traditions. It is not only expressed by these theorists of "post-industrial" society but is also found among state theorists and geographers, some falling within a broadly Marxist tradition. While prioritizing the local arena as a site of conflict, these state theorists at the same time emphasize the particularism of local struggles in which "local loyalties, identity politics and celebrating the different Other(s) attest to an impotence to embrace an emancipatory and empowering politics of scale" (Swyngedouw, 2004, p. 42). Swyngedouw's account resembles that of Castells and Touraine when he discusses how "the reclamation of territorial identity and homogeneity finds fertile ground among those who feel deeply and bitterly disempowered by the disabling strategies pursued by those occupying the loci of power" (2004, p. 29).[2] Harvey refers to "militant particularisms" that "are in some senses profoundly conservative because they rest on the perpetuation of patterns of social relations and community solidarities – loyalties – achieved under a certain kind of oppressive and uncaring industrial order" (1996, p. 40). When Brenner speculates about democratic possibilities he points to the supranational level of the European Union rather than the local level, although the focus of his discussion is on urban development (2003, p. 215).

Likewise, those who theorize about identity with reference to the increasing flexibility and "fluidity" of capitalism, such as Bauman (2000) and Sennett (1998), see a similar tendency to turn inward along with an erosion of solidarities and human bonds. For Bauman, insecurity and the "precariousness of social existence" erode connections between people and breed intolerance (2000, p. 164). Although the particular framing varies, underlying each of these accounts is the idea that the global, flexible economy has brought about local subjectivities that have a defensive, inward turning character.[3]

While local communities are presumed to breed defensiveness, a complement to this paradigm can be found in ideas about the benefits of a transnational countermovement. Such ideals have surfaced in work, for example, on the "global consciousness" of Zapatismo (Olesen, 2005) and the "prefigurative politics" of the World Social Forums (Smith et al., 2008). With respect to the labor movement in particular, the long-standing trope of international working-class solidarity has served as a rallying cry for labor progressives and left wing political parties since Marx pleaded for the workers of the world to unite in his *Manifesto of the Communist Party*. Taken together, these two perspectives – the defensiveness of local action and the counter-hegemonic potential of transnational action – seem convincing on theoretical, empirical, and intuitive levels.

But such defensiveness is not an outcome of the local community-based living wage campaign examined in this study. Why do the subjective consequences of that campaign differ from the defensive identities that would be predicted by existing theory? And how, then, can this discrepancy advance our theoretical understanding of identity, citizenship, and globalization? I will suggest the need for a reconceptualization of collective action at various scales, stemming from a greater appreciation of the ways in which local mobilizations are most amenable to grassroots action. They are arguably more likely, compared to transnational activism, to be "bottom-up," democratic, broad-based, and, ultimately, transformative for those involved.

THE CASE OF THE CHICAGO LIVING WAGE CAMPAIGN: RESEARCH DESIGN AND METHODS

The living wage movement in the United States exemplifies the trend toward pursuing local political solutions to economic problems rooted in global capitalism. The aim of a "living wage" is to keep working families above the poverty level – a goal that existing minimum wage laws have failed to secure. The intent is to hold public entities accountable for their labor practices, and to legislate a living wage for the employees of firms and organizations receiving public contracts or subsides. The first major living wage campaign succeeded in securing legislation in Baltimore in 1994 through extensive grassroots mobilization. The success in that city was soon replicated elsewhere, with campaigns springing up across the country and nearly 150 city or county ordinances in place (Living Wage Resource Center, 2007).

Not all living wage legislation is a product of extensive struggle. Living wage campaigns vary greatly in terms of their breadth, the degree of conflict, and the extent to which they rely on collective action and grassroots mobilization (Luce, 2004). Some campaigns are won relatively easily due to sympathetic politicians or a favorable political climate, and so require limited mobilization by supporters. Nevertheless, one of the key features of the living wage phenomenon has been its ability to mobilize people – in particular, those who have been left out of more traditional labor union strategies. The campaign that is the focus of this study consisted of an extensive grassroots effort that succeeded in mobilizing workers from many sectors of the economy and walks of life. In the case examined here, low-wage workers from the more "marginal" sectors of the working class clashed with – and won against – Chicago's powerful political machine. Mayor Daly had historically dominated city council such that the aldermen rarely went on record in opposition to the mayor. And so when Daly came out against the ordinance, the stage was set for a long and difficult battle.

Launched in June 1995, the Chicago Jobs and Living Wage Campaign involved a large and diverse coalition of organizations and workers coming at the issue from a variety of backgrounds and perspectives. More than 60 organizations were involved, from neighborhood groups to unions and community organizations. Spearheading the effort was the Chicago-based Illinois ACORN (the Association of Community Organizations for Reform Now), a grassroots membership-based organization. ACORN was joined in the campaign by its long time ally, the Service Employees International Union (SEIU) Local 880, a union of home care workers[4] and childcare providers, and by the Chicago Coalition for the Homeless (CCH), who brought shelter residents and day laborers into the campaign. Traditional labor unions were also brought into the fold. Thousands of people mobilized throughout the course of the campaign, with individual events drawing hundreds – and up to a thousand or more – demonstrators. The campaign employed a variety of grassroots tactics to put pressure on public officials, including many large rallies and demonstrations. Finally, after three long years of struggle, after countless meetings and marches and visits to aldermen, activists won passage of a living wage ordinance in July 1998 covering for-profit city contractors and subcontractors.[5]

This study uses semi-structured interviews with participants in the Chicago Jobs and Living Wage Campaign to get some purchase on how they experienced the campaign and the subjective transformations that ensued. The in-depth interviews were conducted with 24 respondents in the spring and summer of 2004. The study includes testimony from key activists, leaders, and staff, who were able to offer a birds-eye view of the subjective shifts afoot, as well as rank-and-file participants articulating their on-the-ground experiences.

There is a long-standing critique directed at the value of surveys for studying working-class consciousness, accompanied by arguments in favor ethnographic and other qualitative methods (see, for example, Blackburn & Mann, 1975, p. 156; Fantasia, 1988, pp. 6, 7; Glaberman, 1980, pp. 121, 129–131, 133; Marshall, 1983, pp. 289–293). In line with these critiques, this study aimed not for a statistically representative sample since the goal was depth more than breadth. That is, instead of offering a more superficial yet statistically significant account of subjectivity through survey methods, the point of this study is to dig more deeply into the meanings and interpretations of collective action experiences as understood by participants themselves. Respondents were mainly selected through snowball sampling using recommendations from participants, and then further screened to assure representativeness in terms of demographic characteristics and

Transforming Citizenship: Consequences of Local Political Mobilization 157

organizational affiliation. They were thus chosen because they were part of a particular group in order to ensure that perspectives were included from both leadership and the rank-and-file, from members of both unions and community groups, and from different demographic groups involved in the campaign. That respondents came from such a wide variety of perspectives serves to highlight the extent to which the commonalities in their narratives were a result of campaign participation rather than being due to affiliation with a particular group or organization.[6]

Given the dearth of research on the subjective outcomes of particular forms of collective action, the method of analysis was necessarily inductive. The subjectivities uncovered here did not frame the research proposal at the outset but, rather, emerged from respondents' testimony. The long interview format, where questions were relatively open-ended and followed up as necessary, was best suited to exploring consciousness and subjectivity and allowed a deeper probing of cultural meaning and resonance. The use of qualitative, semi-structured interviews opened up space for subjects to relate how they experienced and understood the campaign and to do so in their own words. Instead of imposing the traditional yardsticks of class consciousness, this more inductive, narrative approach allowed for exploration of how subjectivities were articulated by working-class people themselves.

Participants were asked direct yet open-ended questions about the subjective impact of the campaign and how it affected them more generally. Since skeptics have questioned the extent to which the subjective effects of collective action are lasting (Langford, 1994; Mann, 1973), there is an advantage to conducting interviews some years after the campaign occurred; in doing so we are better able to assess the enduring ideational consequences of collective action, not merely its transient and ephemeral effects.

Sociologists and oral historians alike, however, are well aware of the pitfalls associated with retrospective accounts – in particular with respect to how people view the past through the lens of the present. In this case, however, this supposed pitfall turns out to be a benefit since this study aims to uncover *how people understand the transformative events of their past in the present.* As articulated by Grele, this is precisely the value of retrospective or oral historical interviews, which indeed provide "evidence of the ways in which history live[s] on in the present" (2006, pp. 59, 61).

This study relies on archival material to reconstruct the overall context, specific events, and timelines.[7] It does not rely on retrospective accounts primarily to reconstruct or verify the factual sequence and character of events, which is arguably of dubious validity. Instead, it uses interview data to understand how past events – specifically, collective action events – endure and live on as a legacy in people's lives. Maynes, Pierce, and Laslett articulate how the "value of personal narratives is related precisely to their tendency to go beyond the simple facts: They tap into the realms of meaning, subjectivity, imagination, and emotion" (2008, p. 148). These authors suggest that narrative evidence is particularly useful for research that documents "the lifelong consequences of transformative experiences" (2008, p. 6). An understanding of the role of narrative is instructive, moreover, since it is difficult to separate some supposed "actual" subjective experience from the stories people tell about those experiences:

> Eventually the culturally shaped cognitive and linguistic processes that guide the self telling of life narratives achieve the power to structure perceptual experience, to organize memory, to segment and purpose-build the very "events" of a life. In the end we become the autobiographical narratives by which we "tell about" our lives. (Bruner quoted in Grele, 2006, p. 70)

In this study, respondents' narratives do not amount to a twisted, biased lens onto some other kind of factual data; instead, respondents' present understanding and interpretation of past events, and their reconstruction of such events in the present, is exactly the data that are being sought.[8]

THE SUBJECTIVE CONSEQUENCES OF LOCAL POLITICAL MOBILIZATION

One might argue that there was a certain degree of defensiveness, and concomitant narrowness of political vision, in the Chicago living wage campaign. Its goals, for example, were often couched by participants as stemming from an inability to keep up with the cost of living. Although these low-wage workers had a long history of marginalization, there was a sense that things were getting increasingly worse for them materially and that wages were on a consistent downward trend. The living wage campaign was about preventing them from falling further behind and, ideally, making up for some of this lost ground. The goal was to get a larger piece of the advanced capitalist pie.

The campaign, additionally, displayed a certain degree of parochialism in its tactics. This was exhibited by its focus on specific city council members and local politicians. Activists publicized, for example, which aldermen had supported the ordinance and which had not. And they held a large rally at the home of Ed Burke, a prominent alderman who was chair of the council's

Committee on Finance (which had been charged with the living wage issue), to demand hearings on the subject. Targeting Burke's private residence – knocking on neighbors' doors and asking them to phone Burke about supporting the living wage – betrayed a personalized approach to the problem.[9] Of course, the focus on specific aldermen, with the aim of influencing their position on the issue, made tactical sense since the city council ultimately held the power to enact a living wage ordinance (or not). Nevertheless, this focus on individual politicians might appear to lend a personalized, individualized, or circumscribed quality to the campaign.

But despite this apparent narrowness of both goals and tactics, the living wage campaign in fact underwrote an expanded vision of what could be expected from the state. Rather than fostering defensiveness or parochialism, the campaign betrayed the capacity of locally based political organizing to create an increasingly expansive political vision. Whereas Chicago's aldermen had traditionally been called upon to address relatively narrow concerns of their constituency, campaign participants came to see public officials as responsible for a much broader agenda. Tom,[10] an experienced SEIU staffer, described this transformation:

> [The living wage campaign] was also an attempt to have public officials accountable for more than just "do I get my garbage can?" ... I think the thing that was new was that the aldermen were now being asked to take a stand on a quality of life, quality of wages issue that they had never been asked to take a stand on. They are always asked, you know – garbage cans, this, that, and the other thing. The strongest issues in your aldermanic campaign [are] streets and sanitation, garbage, and that's it. But this was a new one where they were forcing their aldermen to take a stand on an issue that had to do with the type of jobs in the city of Chicago and what the city should be putting their money into. Should they be paying a living wage? And that just catapulted the whole – after we did the campaign, everybody was talking about living wage jobs. And you can see now, all the politicians when they run for office – even Republicans – are saying "we need jobs with living wages." Living wages was not even part of the political discourse prior to 96–97.

The living wage campaign offered a fresh take on the responsibilities of politicians and their obligations toward the citizenry. ACORN, for example, had lobbied politicians in the past, but the demands had been more limited and, moreover, they had never before focused on the entire city council.

Appealing to the state to address class-based grievances entails a different understanding of power structures and class relations: Who is the opposition? Where does power reside? And who is responsible for ensuring workers' well-being? The answers to these questions began to change for those who had been through the living wage campaign. As a long-time organizer, Tom was able to articulate the importance of this shift:

> It became much more real to people where the money really comes into the pipeline: that it's partially the boss, but it's also the state. And that it made the state a target much more than it has been probably prior to that. I think prior to that most people just naturally saw their boss as their enemy, or as the person that was keeping them from making a decent wage. And now: so it wasn't just the boss, it was the state. It can be the boss, but it wasn't just the boss; it was a missed situation, you know?

The experience of locally based political mobilization underwrote a fresh perspective on state power and governmental responsibility for workers' welfare.

Campaign participants thus began to see the state as responsible for workers' well-being, and so came to expect more from the politicians who represented them. This perspective was articulated by Lucy, a formerly homeless person who became involved with the campaign through the Coalition for the Homeless (CCH):

> *I:* Did anything change in terms of the community's relationship to politicians due to that campaign?
>
> *R:* I think so!
>
> *I:* How's that?
>
> *R:* I think, what happened was, community leaders and individuals *began to expect more from their politicians. I think they began to get a bigger picture and see that they could expect more.* They could make contact with their politicians and ask for things, and if they don't get it find out who can render these services. I definitely feel like it made a difference. Yeah, it made a difference. You know without involvement you basically just maybe sit back and just take whatever is handed to you. But when there is education and awareness, you begin to step up to the plate and not just take anything. You begin to put your request in. *Let your request be made known and expect to get it. Keep it winnable and expect to get it.* (emphasis mine)

For Lucy, the most salient change in the relationship between the community and politicians was the community's assumptions about what they could expect from elected officials. Instead of accepting what the political process handed to them, campaign participants came to embrace their own expanded vision of what the state could be expected to provide.

Particularly among people who lack institutional power and who have traditionally been left out of the political process, as is the case with the rank-and-file of Chicago's living wage campaign, the importance of increased expectations should not be underestimated. Expecting little from elites and from the political system, along with the acceptance of structural inequalities, is one crucial aspect of hegemony (Gaventa, 1980; Gramsci, 1971). Expecting that political elites should be doing something to address poverty and inequality – especially in the American context with its pervasive ideology of meritocracy and individualism – is thus more significant than it might at first appear to be.

The living wage campaign altered participants' ideas about what politicians were expected to provide for the citizenry. At the same time, and more important for our understanding of local subjectivities, it transformed *what it meant to be a citizen.* In particular, participants developed a citizenship identity that was both *active* and *inclusive.* Although an account focusing solely on goals and tactics might make the campaign appear narrow, defensive, or short sighted, a deeper analysis rooted in participants' narratives tells a very different story.

Active Citizenship

Campaign participants came to expect more from politicians, but at the same time they also learned that these expectations would not be easily met. Instead, participants came to embrace the idea that only through struggle could they achieve their goals in the political arena. When answering questions about the consequences of the campaign, what it accomplished, or what changed because of the campaign, participants explained that they came to embrace a more active role in the political process. They came to believe that even those with the least political power, such as the poor, the unemployed, and the homeless, had the ability to make their voice heard and to affect social change if they became *active citizens* who persisted in struggle.

While Lucy expected more from politicians, as articulated above, at the same time she came to embrace the idea that social change would come about only if it was demanded. She described how the campaign was a springboard for continued mobilization:

> I felt like I had won and made a difference in a large number of people's lives. So, I was real excited about that and I felt like, you know, the other delinquents that we're dealing with, we need to do the exact same thing. Mobilize and get out there and start screaming and hollering and yelling and bring about change.

This sentiment was echoed by Jill, another formerly homeless member of CCH, when describing the campaign's consequences:

> Politicians know that just because a person is homeless don't mean that they don't count. It doesn't mean that because they're homeless or because they're making very little

money that all of a sudden their voices can't be heard, *because now those people now know that all they have to do is get a group together and you gonna hear what I'm saying. One thing about it that I found out ... the squeaky wheel gets the oil. Being quiet doesn't get you anything. But you want to get something? Start making a ruckus.* (emphasis mine)

Participants came to embrace the idea that the way the political process "works" – the way that the voices of ordinary people are heard – is by groups of citizens "making a ruckus."

Citizenship, in short, became active rather than passive. As articulated by Margaret, an ACORN member, the living wage campaign demonstrated that citizenship was not about passively depending on the government, but about actively fighting for your rights and your community:

> *I:* What do you think the campaign accomplished?
>
> *R:* Well, I think it gave people a – it motivated us even more to know that, to reiterate the fact that you have to fight for what you want because if you depend on your city government or your politicians or whoever to give you your fair share, you're absolutely wrong. You have to fight for everything you get, and then you may not get it. So we learned from that experience. We found out that if you persevere, if you stick with what you know is rightfully something you should have, where there's numbers, there's power. ... It motivated people. It motivated the people to continue – not only to continue to be involved but to even get more involved in fighting for your community, for your rights.

This sentiment was echoed by Alejandro, an unemployed ACORN member who had worked in a company's shipping and receiving department, when asked if he thought differently about politicians since the campaign:

> As they say, if the benefit doesn't come to you, you have to go after the benefit. It's up to us to succeed in getting benefits. The politicians aren't going to come and do it. They'll offer us things during their election campaigns, but once they're in office, if we don't pressure them there's nothing. The politicians are only going to do what they want, what's happening that day. However, if twenty of us come to tell them that we want this and we want that, well that's where change happens. *Things have changed. Before, not many of us were involved. Now we are, and we go and get what we want. That is what has changed.* (emphasis mine)

Participants certainly became more politically savvy, coming to understand that politicians could not be trusted to defend citizens' interests, and that politicians might say one thing and do another. But the transformation involved went well beyond developing a mistrust of politicians. More importantly, as articulated by Margaret and Alejandro, participants in the living wage campaign came to embrace new ideas about what it meant to be a citizen and what citizens were expected to do in response to government intransigence. The testimony of living wage campaign participants betrays the development of activists engaged in the political process, willing to struggle on behalf of the marginalized and disenfranchised. This is how the campaign, long over, lived on in the present.

For those who are relatively powerless, feeling that one can become active in the political process amounts to a profound personal transformation. The changes that took place in Chicago were thus not merely about participants embracing new social norms, but about the transformation of personal identity – of everyday people into activists. Alejandro was asked if anything surprised him during the campaign, and he recounted his transformation from a regular community member into an activist who could take part in the public sphere:

> To tell you the truth, I was the one who was surprised. Because I was not prepared to be in charge of an agenda for the community, nor was I prepared to belong to an organization; then one doesn't understand how to reach a politician, one doesn't understand how to be a member, one doesn't understand how to talk to a politician, or to a leader. In other words, one doesn't understand anything. Then the surprised one was me, because I never believed that I could talk to the mayor, that I could talk to the governor, or that I could talk to some politicians.

From Alejandro's perspective this was a momentous, surprising turn of events; his understanding of self shifted from humble community member to politically savvy community leader.

Karen, who belonged to the neighborhood-based group Organization of the NorthEast (ONE), articulated the kinds of emotional and psychological changes that ensued when she discovered that she could affect social change:

> *I:* Did the campaign change you in any way?
>
> *R:* Yeah. It made me know that – I guess it reinforced my – it raised my self-esteem. It made me feel like I did have some power and that I wasn't powerless. And it gave me a new way of dealing with my anger. Instead of letting the anger eat on me, I used it in a way that was more effective. So having a voice and using that voice and knowing when to use it and knowing what the issue is and knowing how to give and take – you know what I'm saying?

As they became active citizens, participants like Karen found an outlet for their anger. Here Karen described how the campaign led her to deal with her anger in a new way, as an activist using her "voice" to make change. Her enhanced self-concept came from learning how to solve problems as an active citizen, strategically addressing the things that angered her through organizing and speaking up.[11]

The development of an active citizenship identity was a theme that united testimony from a variety of groups. The homeless, retirees, union members, home care workers, factory workers, day laborers, African Americans, and Latinos each brought unique perspectives to the campaign. But the experience of becoming active citizens was a common thread throughout participants' narratives. While Jill, quoted above, articulated this sentiment with reference to her experience of homelessness, other participants articulated it in terms of their own perspectives. Jorge, a middle-aged punch press operator and Spanish-speaking ACORN member, put it this way:

> *R:* The truth is that we must continue working. The bad thing about politicians is that they are like "anafres" as they say in Mexico. Do you know what an "anafre" is?
>
> *I:* No.
>
> *R:* An anafre is like a charcoal grill. The charcoal there is different than it is here. Here you light charcoal with a liquid and it catches fire. That's not the way it is in Mexico. In Mexico you have to put paper underneath and light it on top, and it's wood, and it catches fire little by little. If you don't act, the fire goes out. That's how the politicians are. If you're not on top of them, they die down and forget about the people. So the only way you can get them to continue to give services to the people is to put pressure on them, or move them around like you would charcoal, so that they get fired up again. Otherwise they die down and forget about the people. That's exactly what has happened.

Participants put the "lesson" of becoming active citizens into their own idiom. But the lesson itself was the same for each group in this diverse and broad-based campaign.

Participants described experiences of inspiration and enlightenment: "There was some learning moments – that moment when you like, ah-ha!" One of those learning moments, woven throughout participants' narratives, was the realization that citizens' collective efforts actually make a difference. The campaign's success underwrote a sense of collective efficacy – that is, a belief in the capacity to act as a group and the conviction that if the group does act they will succeed (Bandura, 1982; Freyberg, 1995; Penney, 2002). This belief proved to be a crucial element in the development of active citizenship. It emerged in Jorge's narrative, for example, when he described how the campaign affected him and changed his thinking:

> I know that when we organize we will be able to get justice and that is a positive thing. ... [I now think that] one can face the powerful now. One knows that the powerful can't be so arbitrary. ... That one can overcome the abuses committed by those in power. ... That we can face and stop those who abuse their power exploitatively because they have money. That they can't keep exploiting the people.

Jorge's sentiments were echoed by Susan, also an ACORN member, when discussing what she learned from the campaign and how "everyday people" can make a difference if they come together:

> I think that even when you face a politician that's against you, your issues, if you stand strong and you get people behind you, organized behind you, and you carry the effort

forward, I think you can turn them around. And I learned that people can make a difference – and this is everyday people. These are not people that you think about – middle class people. These are everyday working low-wage workers. They can make a difference if you get a number of them organized. ... [The campaign] gave people a sense of pride; a sense of accomplishment. They saw that they were able to accomplish something that, for the first time, that they were up against enormous forces and they were able to overcome these forces. ... I think it's important to emphasize that it was a grassroots campaign and it's important to emphasize that everyday people brought this about, collectively working together. I think that's very important. That if you say no more than that, that's what's important.

Susan emphasized how, working collectively, it was "everyday people" who secured passage of the Chicago living wage ordinance. It was not some force external to the movement. It was not luck or God or even, importantly, the politicians who eventually voted for the legislation. And she learned that when those everyday people are organized and "standing strong" they can "make a difference."

Marisol, a homemaker, described in similar terms the changes that took place during the course of the campaign:

Some of our neighborhoods used to say that it was an impossible task because we all know that Richard Daley is a very important man. They used to say: "how can we, the common people, fight with such a powerful individual?" We may be unimportant and common but the community understands now that we have some power, that we can mobilize many people under the auspices of ACORN. Daley knows that we will fight and protest.

That "common people" would feel powerless is of course not unique to Chicago. But in Chicago, where community members were under the thumb of Daley's strong political machine, feelings of powerlessness at the outset of the campaign had been arguably more acute. Even the 50-member strong city council – as democratically elected representatives, the supposed "voice" of the people – was afraid to move against the mayor no matter the extent of popular support they enjoyed. Through the living wage campaign, however, working-class Chicagoans learned that they too could wield power and work against the machine if they mobilized together.

Karen's narrative about the development of active citizens likewise emphasized how campaign participants learned that they could have a hand in making change if they worked together. In addition, it underscored the profound sense of impotency and cynicism normally experienced by America's working class and how that changed for those who struggled to secure a living wage. Gaining a sense of collective power through the living wage campaign thus amounted to "thinking outside the box":

> I think they realized – and I don't think they realized it before that – that their voice made a difference. And I think a lot of people feel powerless and feel like they can't make a difference, and you can sort of get just apathetic. You just – yeah, you know all of this is going on and you don't like it and you're pissed off, but then you don't do anything about it. You don't write letters, you don't make calls, you don't – you know what I'm saying? So I think the community felt energized that they could make a difference .... If you haven't been exposed to how to make a difference – you know, how do you approach your alderman, what you should be asking for – I don't think that's just something that people just know. So I think that whole movement really strengthened communities and the people that live in communities to get them to start thinking outside the box, like "wow, my voice is important, my vote is important; I can go to my church and start talking about this to people and get ..." – you know, so it was just a big movement where everybody had something to do and everybody was important. ... It made people feel really good. I think people felt good about working on the campaign. And definitely wanting to make a difference. Not just to be doing it, but definitely wanting to make a difference and wanting to be part of that movement to make a difference.

Although participants came to the campaign with a sense of powerlessness and even apathy, the campaign led them to believe that they could "make a difference." Being an active citizen thus came to be seen as an appropriate, and potentially fruitful, response to marginalization. Karen's account here, moreover, expresses the emotional component of this transformation. Being an active citizen "felt good" – and this feeling was something that endured in the aftermath of the campaign.

Active citizens embrace the idea that struggle is ongoing. Ron, a candy factory worker and ACORN member, articulated how learning that "we can do anything" led participants to envision new struggles and future battles. Being an active citizen was thus not a matter of campaign history or personal biography; instead, it was an ongoing orientation and a basis for future action:

> Say: "Hey, we got the living wage, let's work on the minimum wage." That let us know that we can go up to another level. So we got the state living wage, let's work on the federal living wage. Growth; growth would be the word. Once you start attacking little things, you figure you can conquer the world. ... Let us know that we can do anything. So we took on – after that, we took on predatory lending. After that we took on minimum wage. And now we've taken on Wells Fargo. We keep this up, we can take on Washington, DC!

Living wage campaign participants emerged from the campaign ready to take on other social issues of importance to them, and to mobilize at new levels and in new arenas of struggle. What emerges in Ron's narrative is how ostensibly "little" actions can lead to much larger ones – or to an ongoing activist stance. It highlights, in short, how the development of active citizens rested on prior *experience* with successful collective action.

Ann, a long-time ACORN staff person, expressed how those involved in collective action came to embrace an activist identity:

> How could you stop when you know what you can do? Alright, we can win a living wage, so why would we stop when we know we could raise the minimum wage statewide. And if we could do that, why would we stop when we know we could stop Wal-Mart? And if we could stop Household, then we could stop Wells Fargo. And it's these – being a part of ... it's sort of like *because I was there, I experienced that wonderful moment of power that led toward success. So I know that we can be successful in other ways because I've experienced it.* ... We've got a history of failure in this constituency, really everybody feels like they have no power – and *if you actually experience that wonderful moment of wielding power, Lord God, then you'll just take on anybody.* ... It's also that it is pretty much fun getting there. [laughs] I mean there's something about wielding power that feels good and solidarity where you got back up. That's a great, great feeling.

Through three long years of struggle, relying on little but the power of their own internal solidarity, it was the tangible, palpable, embodied nature of collective action that led participants to develop a genuine sense of their own collective power and to commit to ongoing struggle.

The campaign's ostensibly narrow goals and tactics did little to undermine this process. It was the experience of collective action – no matter that it took place at a local, community-based level – that led to the development of active citizens. In short, when participants in collective action succeed in achieving their goals, even if somewhat narrow or circumscribed ones, this experience can lead to more powerful and enduring activist identities (see Klandermans, 1997, p. 42; Schwartz & Paul, 1992). In working-class history in particular, narratives of labor struggle describe how the success of previous mobilization leads to the development of class consciousness, workers' sense of power, and ongoing activism (Juravich & Bronfenbrenner, 1999, pp. 199–206; Kimeldorf, 1988, p. 109; Penney, 2002).

Some labor unions have been putting more resources toward voter turnout and also toward financial contributions to political candidates in recent years. But the active citizenship conceptualized here is not primarily about electoral politics, about workers voting for Democrats or Republicans or independents. It is rather a shift toward workers embracing grassroots political mobilization. Indeed, the political successes of the labor movement in recent years come primarily from street heat rather than from voting booths where limited choices constrain political possibilities. Although the electoral process indeed offers pressure points and opportunities for activists, the new labor strategies may be best thought of as "politics without elections" (Reynolds, 1999). Such strategies more often entail grassroots mobilization targeting legislation around specific issues rather than getting out the vote in support of a particular political party or candidate.

The active citizenship that sprung from the living wage campaign embraced exactly this kind of "politics without elections." It was not the embodiment of some mainstream pluralist vision where a diversity of voices is represented in the halls of government. Rather, it was precisely the assumption that their voices would not be heard without a struggle that underwrote this active stance. For participants in the living wage campaign there was no assumption that elected officials would represent them or that the political process would take a variety of interests into account, particularly those of the marginalized and disadvantaged. Moreover, the ideals of citizenship that developed were not about civic organizations supporting the electoral process but were, instead, about collective action. Citizenship was not about voting, but about mobilization. On the pluralist view, social movements occur when there are flaws in the normal operation of institutional politics. For living wage campaign participants, alternatively, activism came to *define* citizenship. They had developed a politics of struggle and conflict.

Inclusive Citizenship

It is possible to have an active citizenry that has, at the same time, an exclusive vision of who those citizens are. In the Chicago living wage campaign, however, the development of an active citizenship was coupled with an *inclusive* vision of who should be counted as rights bearing citizens. This can be contrasted with the kind of defensive subjectivity that references a bounded community (often ethnic, religious, or national). Although "local" tends to imply something narrow or homogenous, as it does in the scholarly perspectives on defensive identity outlined above, a local mobilization that is based on broad-based grassroots action may embody something very different.[12]

The Chicago Jobs and Living Wage Campaign was intensely focused on the local level but it was, nevertheless, broad-based. The campaign was racially, ethnically, and linguistically diverse, with a strong base in both the African Americans and Latino communities. Participants were, moreover, drawn from the ranks of those with a history of being politically disempowered.

One of the hallmarks of community-based workers' movements is that they have been spearheaded by nontraditional workers. Participants have typically been, for example, workers doing part-time, informal, or contract work. The Chicago living wage campaign's targeted constituency – the city's low-wage workers – worked in all manner of nonstandard employment situations. Some were part-time. Some could be thought of as seasonal day laborers who worked the summertime festivals. The campaign's home care workers labored under uniquely difficult conditions, dispersed as they were in private homes, isolated from co-workers and with no common workplace. Many campaign participants lacked a stable employment situation. Particularly striking was the mass mobilization of those not even engaged in paid labor: retirees, the homeless, the unemployed, homemakers, and others outside the labor force. In its rich diversity, cutting across both demographic and occupational categories and including those outside the standard employment relationship, the campaign mobilized what Kelley has called "the new urban working class" (1997) who have traditionally been excluded from the house of labor.

When it comes to the question of citizenship in these local political mobilizations perhaps the most noteworthy development is the central role of immigrants. A key feature of community-based labor organizing in particular has been its inclusion of immigrant workers – documented and undocumented alike. Worker centers, an especially prominent example of these strategies, have found particularly fertile ground in immigrant communities (Fine, 2006). Day labor organizing, likewise, has revolved around immigrant workers in a local context, mobilizing in the community to affect public policy (Esbenshade, 2000). Through living wage campaigns, immigrant workers' centers, and day labor organizing, there has been a critique – sometimes implicit but more often explicit – of national boundaries and citizenship rights.

Crucially, in the Chicago living wage campaign the mobilization of immigrant workers was not merely about demographic diversity. Instead, immigrant mobilization led to a more inclusive understanding of who should be making demands on the state. Organizers from labor and community organizations alike noted how many of their rank-and-file members had come to the campaign with anti-immigrant sentiments, but that ideas about immigrant rights changed over the course of the campaign. An ACORN staffer, for example, recalled how Harriet, a retired African American member, began to question the teachings of her church:

> It's been phenomenal. ... Harriet's church was teaching her that a sign that it was the end of the world was that so many Latinos were moving in and taking our jobs and they were going to take everything away from us. And Harriet spoke up at a meeting and said, "You know what we need to do? We need to make sure that our Latino brothers and sisters get it that this is about them too." It was a whole different issue, but she had moved so far in the course of this campaign that ... she was going against what she was hearing in church.

From Harriet's perspective when the campaign began, Latinos were "moving in" and crossing borders into a polity where they had no right to a livelihood. Through her experience in the living wage campaign, however, she came to see that it was "about them too": Latinos, too, had rights; they, too, could legitimately make demands on the state through protest in the public sphere.

Ron, an African American, described how there had been tension between African Americans and Latinos in his high school. But through the experience of joint mobilization in the campaign, he came to see the state as responsible for the plight of his Latino "brothers and sisters":

> Looking at some of our Latinos that were working for Farley [Candy Company], and their pay scales was minimum wage with no benefits, and found out the city was giving Farley money to do this – become a outrage to us. It's like – hey, they can just do that to any company, say, "well, you stay here, we'll give you some money and we'll keep you operating." ... So we, as Afro-Americans, know what "no-match" letters[13] mean now. And we know how our government allows certain industry to do certain things to our Latino brothers and sisters. So there's no problem for us loading up on the bus. Experience takes the place of ignorance. ... Hey, you messing with our brothers and our sisters, you messing with us. So we're going to actions together.

Although "no-match" letters are intended to rout out immigrants who are employed "illegally," Ron came to sympathize with the plight of such workers and take on their cause. Like Harriet, he came to embrace the view that Latinos had rights within the polity and developed expectations that the government should protect those rights, whether social security numbers were "matching" or not. His became a vision of African Americans and Latinos, documented and undocumented alike, acting collectively to affect political and social change: "Working together on [the living wage] issue let us see that, okay, if we work together, we can really get some power and get some things done. *We can take over city hall! We started really thinking and started expanding our minds.*"

Just as African Americans came to embrace a more inclusive notion of citizenship, Latinos also came to feel more included in the polity and felt more able to exercise their rights. This sentiment was articulated by Marisol, the homemaker, who was a Latino ACORN member:

> We got along very well because we helped each other in the sense that the African Americans know the laws of their country very well and the Latinos are waking up and learning about their rights. Therefore fighting together, African Americans and Latinos to attain a living wage, we went to City Hall to protest for our rights. ... I'm very happy because, just imagine - have you ever seen an African American fighting on behalf of my people? My people were asleep. There were very few of us when I joined ACORN. So I'm very proud and very thankful to them, because they know the laws here, and us, well, at least now I've learned about the laws here. People spread the word, you know? You can do this and that. But how is it that these African Americans are fighting on behalf of my people? What about my people? So we too are going to fight, because we too need to come together.

Through their common experience in the living wage campaign, African Americans and Latinos alike carved out a more broadly defined arena of rights and a more expansive sense of who should have them. Miguel, a young Latino participant, described how things were before the campaign and how they changed:

> [Before the campaign] there was a group of African Americans over here, a group of Latinos over there, and there was never a way the two would crossover or a way to bring the two together. More than anything, the Latino didn't want to go out and protest because he was afraid and would say: "I'm an immigrant, they're going to throw me to the immigration officials." But when they saw that the African Americans were supporting them, they felt more secure. ... I think this created a stronger relationship between the two. This time, when we go to the convention, a ton of Latinos and African Americans are going to represent Chicago. ... More than anything else, we're creating a huge base, without color, just with a common cause. That's what we're creating here now.

The insecurities of undocumented status that underwrite exclusion from the polity began to be ameliorated. And despite the traditional boundaries of nation, immigration, ethnicity, and language, the living wage campaign united participants in "common cause."

With the development of more inclusive notions of citizenship, the living wage campaign inspired a new and inclusive political agenda. Chicago saw subsequent mobilizations around such issues as drivers' licenses for immigrants, employment concerns around social security "no-match" letters, and immigrant amnesty. What is particularly noteworthy is how this political agenda was adopted by campaign participants who were not themselves immigrants. African American participants who previously had little understanding or sympathy for immigrants – and even animosity toward them – enacted their newfound active citizenship in struggles on behalf of their Latino immigrant comrades. As described by Miguel:

> Now you can see that the driver's license campaign is taking place. Thousands of African Americans came for this campaign. More than 2,500 African Americans came in support of the amnesty program. This program did not have anything to do with them, but they came just the same to support us. "United we stand," that's the message we wanted to send.

Particularly in the U.S. context where the immigration issue is intensely polarizing and where low-wage and unemployed workers are marshaled in support of anti-immigrant agendas, this shift in ideology and political commitments is remarkable.

The shift was a product of the broad-based nature of the campaign and the mobilization of the most marginalized segments of Chicago's working class. Sassen (2009) has argued, in this vein, for the privileged role of "the outsider" and "the excluded" in the "making" of citizenship, and in potential challenges to existing citizenship arrangements. That such a broad mobilization of "the excluded" took place in a local context diverges from what dominant conceptualizations of collective action would lead us to expect.

CITIZENSHIP IDENTITIES IN CONTEXT

In assessing participants' newfound ideas about citizenship and the state, it is instructive to reflect on their place within a larger context. In particular, ideas about an expansive state and an active, inclusive citizenry run counter to the "new authoritarianism" in which the eviscerated Keynesian nation state (and rescaling of state power toward both supra- and subnational levels) has undermined citizenship rights and democratic participation (Swyngedouw, 1996). They also present a challenge to the dominant ideology underwriting the erosion of citizenship: market fundamentalism (Soros, 2000; Stiglitz, 2003).

In *Genealogies of Citizenship*, Somers examines market fundamentalism as "the drive to subject all of social life and the public sphere to market mechanisms" (2008, p. 2). Working within the legacy of Polanyi (2001 [1944]) and his critique of market encroachment on society, market fundamentalism appears hegemonic in Somers' account. It is, as she calls it, an "ideational regime," which is "comprised of those public narratives and assumptions that have become widely taken for granted in the political culture" (2008, p. 2). As an ideational regime, market fundamentalism serves to undermine the public sphere and the "right to have rights" (Somers, 2008).

Market fundamentalism has roots in classical economic theory and Adam Smith's ideas about the "invisible hand" of the market. On this view, markets operate like a law of nature:

> It is easy to understand how important a cultural construct social naturalism is for market fundamentalism's effort to delegitimate the political interventions of socially inclusive citizenship. The natural law that government interference always threatens liberty reinforces the default position that market solutions are in conformity with the laws of nature, and are therefore always the preferable ones. ... Social naturalism has for two centuries been giving cover to a story about how marketization is a natural, necessary, and inevitable process beyond our control. (Somers, 2008, p. 54; also see pp. 50, 75)

So thoroughly and carefully documented by Somers, the naturalization of market fundamentalism, along with its deep historical and philosophical roots, make it seemingly impenetrable. Alternative visions of citizenship and the state, such as those exhibited by living wage campaign participants, are thus all the more meaningful.

Such alternative visions are especially meaningful in the U.S. context where market fundamentalism is particularly entrenched and virulent. This is reflected in political and economic structures: the U.S. has historically had one of the weakest welfare states and the least "de-commodification" compared to other Western countries (Esping-Andersen, 1990). Somers' (2008) account of Hurricane Katrina and the "left-behind" of New Orleans demonstrates in stark terms how market fundamentalism operates in the contemporary United States. She examines the human disaster, which ensued in the aftermath of the natural one, to uncover what it signified in terms of working-class African Americans' long-term exclusion from the polity.

The American labor movement has, by and large, operated within this market fundamentalist paradigm. It has historically focused less attention on the political sphere compared to its counterparts in Western Europe, and American workers have expected less in the way of benefits from the state. Health care, in particular, stands out as something that, while assumed to be the jurisdiction of the state in many other Western industrialized countries, in the American context has been acquired primarily on the job. The controversy around the establishment of state-run programs during recent debates about health care reform (despite the significant costs of the existing system in both human and financial terms) is indicative of the strong ideological bent in the United States toward market-based solutions to social problems – a bias that unions and their members have often shared. With the exception of a few long-standing programs such as Social Security, American labor has put all their eggs in the union contract basket.

It is certainly the case that the strength of market fundamentalism shifts over time. As suggested by Polanyi (2001 [1944]), when civil society pushes back against increasing market encroachment, states and institutions recalibrate in an effort to maintain legitimacy and equilibrium. Nevertheless, given the historical dominance of market fundamentalism, along with its legacy of an eviscerated American welfare state and a de-politicized labor movement, the findings uncovered in this study are all the more puzzling. Under such circumstances, how was political culture transformed? In particular, how was political culture transformed among people for whom market fundamentalism was as natural as the air they breathe? Scholars of social class have argued that class consciousness emerges in the course of struggle, through experiences of collective action and in confrontation with elites (Fantasia, 1988; Kimeldorf, 1988; Marshall, 1983; Przeworski, 1985). Here I suggest that so, too, does a consciousness of the rights of citizenship develop through on-the-ground struggle.

As discussed at the outset, social movement scholars have for some time understood that subjectivities and ideologies can be created through experiences of collective action, generatively, from the "bottom-up." This insight begs for elaboration, however, with respect to how specific forms of collective action lead to particular kinds of ideologies. Here I have taken these general understandings about subjective transformation in social movements and applied them to the specific case of local political mobilization. In uncovering how the seemingly unshakable ideology of market fundamentalism was challenged on-the-ground through experiences of collective action in the local political arena, the literature on citizenship and on social movements are brought together in a new way.

Johnston has conceptualized these new forms of labor mobilization as "the resurgence of labor as a citizenship movement" (2001; also see Johnston, 2000). He points to a number of recent trends, including the rise of low-wage and immigrant workers' movements, and temporary workers' unions:

> Our argument is that despite the diversity, the different labor movements emerging in each of the circumstances we have discussed all seek to defend, exercise, and extend the boundaries of citizenship, and all these labor movements converge with other citizenship movements that seek to develop public institutions that defend and rebuild local communities in an increasingly globalized public order. (Johnston, 2001, p. 35)

If these different kinds of labor mobilizations are indeed coalescing around the articulation of citizenship rights as Johnston suggests, perhaps the challenge to market fundamentalism can be found elsewhere, beyond Chicago and beyond the fight for a living wage.

RECONCEPTUALIZING COLLECTIVE ACTION

The narratives of citizenship uncovered in this study are all the more surprising given their roots in a locally based mobilization, since theorists from a variety of scholarly traditions view local movements as exhibiting defensive or reactionary tendencies. My argument about why these findings diverge from existing conceptualizations of collective action and identity formation revolve around three trends in the literature with respect to ideas about (1) local versus transnational collective action, (2) social movement goals/tactics versus outcomes, and (3) "new" versus "old" social movements.

The findings of this study, first, point to a need to reconceptualize collective action and identity formation at various scales. There is in the social movement literature a kind of romanticization or idealization of transnational activism that complements the denigration of the local already outlined. It certainly might appear on the surface that transnational organizing – since it involves, literally, the crossing of national boundaries, along with concomitant ethnic, racial, linguistic, and religious ones – holds the most potential to offer a fundamental critique of the current citizenship regime. It might be assumed, in a similar vein, that transnational labor activism holds the potential to offer the broadest vision of worker solidarity, and thus an inclusive notion of citizenship. This study has uncovered the less obvious, but arguably more potent, capacity of locally based political mobilization to produce an active and inclusive citizenship identity. And there are reasons to believe that transnational activism can be limiting in this regard despite suggestions to the contrary in the literature.

It is crucial to keep in mind that transnational social movements have no global governmental entity to appeal to. Although discussions of global governance appear in academic discussions and some segments of the global justice movement (Stevis & Boswell, 2008), such ideals are relatively abstract to most rank-and-file workers on the ground and so they are difficult to organize around. Transnational activism has thus responded to globalization with a focus on multinational corporations (as with anti-sweatshop campaigns) and the creation of alternative civil society spaces (such as the World Social Forum). In either case, these foci have had the effect of deemphasizing the question of government accountability. In comparison, locally based political mobilization targets a tangible, palpable state entity: local government. In Chicago, it was city council and the mayor. As such, local political mobilization holds the potential to reinvigorate notions of state responsibility.

The development of an active citizenship in particular may be bolstered more by local, compared to transnational, activism. At the transnational level activism is often characterized by "transnational advocacy networks" in lieu of grassroots mobilization (see, for example, Evans, 2000 and also Keck & Sikkink, 1998). Although advocacy networks are at times capable of effecting social change and public policy, they have certain limitations:

> Transnational networks normally involve a small number of activists from the organizations and institutions involved in a given campaign or advocacy role. The kinds of pressure and agenda politics in which advocacy networks engage rarely involve mass mobilization .... (Keck & Sikkink, 1998, p. 18)

Given the substantial limits on the mobility of poor and working-class people, transnational approaches can end up relying heavily on paid staff and professional or semi-professional activists. Such professional activists act *on behalf of* the marginalized in lieu of grassroots mobilizations for self-determination. This has consequences for movement leadership development and democracy, as well as for the capacity to energize and politicize the rank-and-file. Transnational networks, in short, most often involve top-down advocacy rather than the kind of on-the-ground struggle that underwrote the emergence of active citizenship Chicago.

It is for this same reason that transnational activism is arguably less inclusive than locally based organizing. Although the language of "transnationalism" has an inclusive ring to it, the reality on the ground can look quite different. Bridging boundaries of nation, language, and culture is far from easy, especially under conditions of extensive geographic dispersal (Johnston & Laxer, 2003, pp. 46, 47). The costs of travel to attend events such as the Battle in Seattle or the World Social Forum are prohibitive for most rank-and-file workers and the poor, and so access is limited. While these are historic, momentous events, it is nevertheless important to recognize the ongoing problems of inclusion that plague such efforts. Most salient in this regard are the power differentials and inequalities between those in the global north and south and how transnational social movements often reproduce them (see, for example, Bandy & Smith, 2005, pp. 8, 11). Even mobilizations that have been held up as exemplars of transnational collaboration, such as Zapatismo and the World Social Forum, have proven unable to overcome these inequalities (Khasnabish, 2008, pp. 214–232; Smith et al., 2008, pp. 49–56). Local community-based mobilizations also struggle with inclusion and overcoming boundaries of race, ethnicity, language, gender, etc. But, as we have seen in Chicago, local campaigns have significant potential to include the most marginalized and disenfranchised since they do not have to grapple with the myriad of problems that come when inequality is coupled with geographic dispersal.

Importantly, the kinds of "marginal" workers that constituted the core of the Chicago living wage campaign and similar efforts tend not to be at the forefront of transnational labor organizing. Transnational organizing certainly has the potential to cross a variety of social boundaries and to bridge divisions between workers internationally. It tends, however, to involve traditional, formal-sector workers from large multinational corporations – in particular those affiliated with traditional trade unions who coordinate such cross-border efforts (Gordon & Turner, 2000).

When taken together, these dynamics point to a common misconceptualization of transnational social movement strategies whereby scholars put more stock in them than is warranted. Transnational activism is glorified as the "new great counter-movement" (Munck, 2007) for "global democracy" (Smith, 2008). But there has been scant recognition of the pitfalls and limitations of transnational activism such as those documented by Seidman (2007) in her study of transnational consumer boycotts around labor rights. As Burawoy (2010) has recently argued, there is a "false optimism" that plagues scholarly accounts of the "global counter-movement." Similarly, Johnston and Laxer critique the "idyllic landscape" and "orthodox narrative" of a global civil society that is based more on first world utopian ideals than the experience of those in the periphery who are on the receiving end of global inequalities (2003, pp. 41, 45).[14] This romanticization of transnational activism undoubtedly serves to obscure some of its problems.[15] The strength of this false optimism, along with the denigration of the local among social theorists, accounts for the apparently anomalous nature of this study's findings, where the subjective consequences of local action fail to match up to theoretical expectations.

These theoretical expectations are not met for a second reason, I argue: a conceptual confusion between movement goals and tactics, on the one hand, and ideological outcomes on the other. In short, tactics that appear narrow or parochial do not necessarily lead, in some linear fashion, to narrow ideological consequences. In the Chicago living wage campaign, both the goals (the focus on wages) and tactics (the focus on individual politicians) had something of a defensive or narrow quality to them. Targeting Ed Burke's house is not apparently as visionary or ambitious as pressing for a global democratic governing body, or traipsing halfway across the globe for an international forum or protest. Why, then, did these tactics not lead to a parallel narrowing of political vision?

The answer to this question can be found in the potentially paradoxical nature of "defensive" actions. Social theorists, most prominently Scott (1985) and Thompson (1991), have portrayed them as something of a double-edged sword such that even seemingly reactionary demands that seek to maintain the status quo can have radical implications. There is, in short, a disjuncture between means and ends such that mere "bread-and-butter" concerns can hold revolutionary potential (Scott, 1985). Without glorifying the potential of reformist political programs or the defense of traditional social arrangements, the theoretical point is that the means and ends of social movements are conceptually distinct.

To some extent this begs the question, though, of why this is the case. I would suggest that the roots of this apparent paradox – of expansive political vision stemming from local, parochial goals and tactics – can be found in the experience of collective action. Local tactical maneuvers are particularly amenable to being accompanied by grassroots mobilization. And so when campaigns are successful as the living wage campaign was (and local campaigns are arguably more winnable) participants discover that they can have a role in creating social change. This sense of collective efficacy can underwrite a continued activist stance, as it did in this study. The sense that common people have some actual leverage and power is, however, a more remote possibility as social movements "scale up" to national or transnational levels.

Despite the findings presented here, the fact remains that some locally based subjectivities are indeed defensive or introverted. Reactions to globalization are of course going to be multiple and varied and will depend on the context. In *Grounding Globalization* (2008), for example, Webster, Lambert, and Bezuidenhout offer a comparative analysis of Australia, South Korea, and South Africa and suggest that the insecurity created by globalization leads communities to either "retreat" – at times to xenophobia and support for right-wing parties – or to various kinds of mobilization (2008, p. 158). The key question that looms then is: when do these reactions amount to a defensive retrenchment versus a challenge to global capitalism or market fundamentalism?

The answer to this question lies beyond the scope of this project, but an examination of the literature offers a possibility worth noting for future research. This third and final argument about existing theories of identity relates to the kinds of social movements being studied. Castells and Touraine can be broadly located within the tradition of scholarship on "new" social movements revolving around lifestyle, personal fulfillment, and, ostensibly, "post-materialist" values (Buechler, 1995). The defensive identities found in Castells thus spring from very particular kinds of movements: religious, ethnic, national. The labor movement, in fact, is noticeably absent from these scholars' work except to be dismissed as an "old" modernist movement. Supposedly no longer relevant in our postmodern or postindustrial age, the labor movement is seen as having been "historically superseded" (Castells, 2010 [1997], p. 425; also see Touraine, 2000, pp. 98, 101, 102). This perspective exemplifies a general trend in which "the labor movement was abandoned by most social movement theorists of the mid-twentieth century" (Evans, 2005, p. 660). Goodwin and Hetland (2011) note the "strange disappearance of capitalism" from social movement scholarship over the last few decades and argue that analyses of social movements have suffered as a result. In line with this observation, I suggest that the findings of the present study appear anomalous precisely because they are found within the labor movement. While labor has turned to local action just as other groups have when facing the insecurities of globalization, this study suggests that labor's experience of local action may be distinct.

Why would local action be so different in the case of the labor movement? Arguably, organizing on a class-wide basis holds the potential to undermine the very kinds of divisions (racial, ethnic, religious, national) that are pointed to as the basis of defensive, introverted identities. Perhaps, also, the specific basis of workers' common ground – their similar locations in a political economic system – might be likely to underwrite a macro-structural critique even when constrained strategically by the use of local action. The crucial point, though, is that the consequences of local action may depend to some extent on the kind of social movement involved.

In any case, it is worth reexamining the privileged status of transnational collective action. It may be that some transnational strategies could also engender a critique of the current citizenship regime despite the limitations outlined here, although such a critique would probably look different from those generated at the local level.[16] Examining the subjective consequences of transnational activism, especially with respect to citizenship identities, could prove to be a fruitful route for future research and could lead to better assessments of different organizing strategies employed in response to the current political economic juncture.

CONCLUSION

In the United States the living wage movement has lost some momentum in recent years, but this has been due to its success as much as anything else, since those municipalities that would be candidates for such campaigns now have living wage legislation on the books. In any case, labor's embrace of local political mobilization has taken off in many directions. Worker centers have emerged as a particularly prominent and potent example (Fine, 2006). In Chicago, the living wage fight led to a "big box" campaign that sought to require Wal-Mart-like stores to maintain certain levels of wages and benefits. In fact, while Wal-Mart has dominated large sectors of the economy and proven virtually unshakable from the perspective of workers on the big box shop floor, it is only through various kinds of community-based political campaigns (to ensure living wages at such stores, or to prevent their presence in communities all together) that the company's dominance has been curtailed in any notable way (Parks & Warren, 2010; Warren, 2005). Clawson (2003) has argued that such community-based labor initiatives, particularly those rooted in communities of color, are the foundation of what could become "the next upsurge" of labor revival.

The strategic importance of these local political mobilizations has been well documented, but this study has demonstrated the importance of the subjective changes they engender as well. In particular, my findings here indicate that these mobilizations have the potential to lead to more expansive notions of state accountability and the development of a more active citizenry. As a form of collective action that mobilizes "marginal" workers largely left out of workplace-based and transnational organizing alike, they have the potential to engender a particularly inclusive vision of citizenship – much broader than what is usually implied by "local" when it is juxtaposed with "global."

While contributing to theories of identity, citizenship, social movements, and globalization as outlined thus far, these findings, finally, speak also to paradigmatic assumptions about working-class conservatism in the United States, which pervade scholarly and popular discussions alike. These assumptions underwrite the long-standing American exceptionalism paradigm and scholarly approaches to American class formation more generally (for an overview of this literature, see Kimeldorf, 1999, pp. 7–11). And they are reflected, as well, in journalistic accounts focused on the trope of working-class "cultural conservatism" as an explanation for each Republican electoral victory (see, for example, Kristof, 2004; Seelye, 2004). Despite this ongoing mantra about the conservatism of American working-class subjectivity, there are indications from the grassroots in Chicago of countervailing trends that push the boundaries of our empirical and theoretical understanding of class formation in the United States.

Uncovering these countervailing trends in participant narratives requires a conceptualization of subjectivity that moves beyond traditional notions of radicalism/reformism/conservatism that have long shaped scholarship on working-class formation. Following in the footsteps of those who have recognized the varieties of working-class formation, I sought to examine, in an inductive fashion, how subjectivity emerged on the ground. Although not reflective of any socialist party platform, nor of some ideal of cultural liberalism, the ideas about citizenship embraced by participants in the living wage campaign present their own potent critique of the contemporary political economy.

Their significance stems as much from context as content. An active and inclusive citizenship emerged in Chicago in the context of a long history of market fundamentalism, which continues to infuse American culture and politics to the present day. This citizenship identity likewise diverged from a xenophobic, anti-immigrant cultural milieu which has characterized American politics for some time and been punctuated by a series of repressive state policies – from California's Proposition 187 in 1994 to Arizona's anti-immigrant law in 2010. The significance of these emergent citizenship ideals stems, then, from their counter-hegemonic characteristics – in particular, an implicit critique of market fundamentalism, an expansive vision of the state's role in meeting social needs, an inclusionary vision of the citizenry, and a recognition that some voices will not be heard without ongoing struggle.

NOTES

1. Note the intellectual legacy of Polanyi (2001 [1944]) here with respect to his recognition of how market encroachment can lead to progressive countermovements but also to fascism.

2. The perspective of Castells and Touraine is similarly echoed in Melucci who states: "Faced with highly impersonal social relationships governed by the logic of organizations, traditional solidarity, ethnic identification, and the particularism of language may constitute a response to the need of individuals and groups to assert

their difference. ... Ethnicity, above all when referring to a real territory, to a 'motherland', is brought back to life as a source of identity because it corresponds to a collective need in information societies to lend certainty and meaningfulness to action" (1996, p. 158).

3. See Mayo (2006) for a summary of some of these perspectives.

4. Home care workers are personal assistants for the elderly and people with disabilities. Clients, requiring assistance with personal care and other basic needs, are cared for in their own homes in lieu of being institutionalized.

5. The final ordinance, subject to last minute negotiations, required at least $7.60 an hour and included the following job categories: home and health care workers, security guards, parking attendants, day laborers, cashiers, elevator operators, custodial workers, and clerical workers.

6. The findings, moreover, can be seen as reliable by the standards of qualitative research – that is, "saturation" occurred such that there was a redundancy to the data being gathered by the end of the data collection process.

7. This material was drawn from both the mainstream and alternative press including metropolitan area, local, community, and union publications. In addition to newspaper and magazine articles, the data include organizational meeting minutes, leaflets, newsletters, educational materials, and internal memos.

8. On the uses and benefits of retrospective accounts, see also Portelli (1991).

9. Early in the campaign, Burke publically signed a petition supporting a living wage when under pressure at large rally. He subsequently withdrew his support.

10. In order to maintain confidentiality, pseudonyms have been used instead of respondents' real names.

11. Social movement scholars have recently revisited the crucial role of emotions in mobilization processes (see, for example, Goodwin, Jasper, & Polletta, 2001). Gould (2002) offers an account of how anger, specifically, underwrote the sustainability of activism within the AIDS protest organization ACT UP.

12. See Meyer and Kimeldorf (2012) on the development of solidarity in the context of broad-based collective action in the Chicago living wage campaign.

13. These are letters received by employers from the federal Social Security Administration outlining discrepancies between the social security numbers and names of their employees. The practice threatens job loss for the workers involved.

14. Johnston and Laxer have suggested that the concept of civil society is applicable to politics at the nation-state level but questionable when it comes to the global level where it has operated primarily as a normative assertion (2003, pp. 43–45). Murphy and Pfaff (2005), in a similar vein, question the very idea of "global" social movements, arguing that their foundations have been local and national.

15. This romanticization is arguably related to the "mythology about globalization" articulated by Ferguson (1992) along with Swyngedouw's similar account of "globalization as ideology" (2004, p. 27).

16. Della Porta (2005) has written about "tolerant identities" that have emerged from the social forum process in Italy, although the extent to which these are related to citizenship is unclear. And while the social forums have a kind of global reach, the data presented on the topic of identity is focused on local social forum participants in Florence and so it may serve to support the argument made here about the

consequences of local mobilization. Also see della Porta and Mosca (2010) on tolerant identities being rooted in local social forums specifically.

ACKNOWLEDGMENTS

I am grateful to have received very helpful comments from Howard Kimeldorf, Dan Cornfield, and Mayer Zald on earlier versions of this manuscript. I would also like to thank the faculty of Rutgers' Labor Studies and Employment Relations Department and of Harvard University's Department of Sociology for very constructive discussions of this project, along with the three reviewers and the PPST editor whose feedback served to strengthen the piece. Research for the project was supported by a Doctoral Dissertation Research Improvement Grant from the National Science Foundation (grant # SES 0424768). I am deeply grateful to the people whose testimony underlies this analysis, and wish to thank everyone who shared their stories with me. Although they will remain nameless in the interest of confidentiality, their honesty, openness, and insight were very much appreciated.

REFERENCES

Amenta, E. (2006). *When movements matter: The Townsend plan and the rise of social security*. Princeton, NJ: Princeton University Press.
Andrews, K. T. (2004). *Freedom is a constant struggle: The Mississippi civil rights movement and its legacy*. Chicago, IL: The University of Chicago Press.
Bandura, A. (1982). Self-efficacy mechanism in human agency. *American Psychologist, 37*, 122–147.
Bandy, J., & Smith, J. (2005). *Coalitions across borders: Transnational protest and the neoliberal order*. Lanham, MD: Rowman & Littlefield.
Bauman, Z. (2000). *Liquid modernity*. Cambridge: Polity Press.
Black, S. (2005). Community unionism: A strategy for organizing in the new economy. *New Labor Forum, 14*, 24–32.
Blackburn, R. M., & Mann, M. (1975). Ideology in the non-skilled working class. In M. Bulmer (Ed.), *Working-class images of society* (pp. 131–160). London: Routledge & Kegan Paul.
Brenner, N. (1998). Global cities, glocal states: Global city formation and state territorial restructuring in contemporary Europe. *Review of International Political Economy, 5*, 1–37.
Brenner, N. (2003). "Glocalization" as a state spatial strategy: Urban entrepreneurialism and the new politics of uneven development in Western Europe. In J. Peck & H. W.-C. Yeung (Eds.), *Remaking the global economy: Economic-geographical perspectives* (pp. 197–215). London: Sage.

Brenner, N., Jessop, B., Jones, M., & MacLeod, G. (Eds.). (2003). *State/space: A reader.* Malden, MA: Blackwell.
Bronfenbrenner, K. (Ed.). (2007). *Global unions: Challenging transnational capital through cross-border campaigns.* Ithaca, NY: ILR/Cornell University Press.
Buechler, S. (1995). New social movement theories. *The Sociological Quarterly, 36,* 441–464.
Burawoy, M. (2010). From Polanyi to Pollyanna: The false optimism of global labor studies. *Global Labor Journal, 1,* 301–313.
Castells, M. (2010 [1997]). *The information age, Volume II: The power of identity.* Malden, MA: Wiley-Blackwell.
Clawson, D. (2003). *The next upsurge.* Ithaca, NY: ILR/Cornell University Press.
Dean, A. B., & Reynolds, D. B. (2009). *A new new deal: How regional activism will reshape the American labor movement.* Ithaca, NY: ILR/Cornell University Press.
della Porta, D. (2005). Multiple belongings, tolerant identities, and the construction of "another politics": Between the European social forum and the local social fora. In D. della Porta & S. Tarrow (Eds.), *Transnational protest and global activism* (pp. 175–202). Lanham, MD: Rowman & Littlefield.
della Porta, D. (Ed.). (2007). *The global justice movement: Cross-national and transnational perspectives.* Boulder, CO: Paradigm.
della Porta, D., & Mosca, L. (2010). Build locally, link globally: The social forum process in Italy. *Journal of World-Systems Research, 16,* 63–81.
della Porta, D., & Tarrow, S. (Eds.). (2005). *Transnational protest and global activism.* Lanham, MD: Rowman & Littlefield.
Dobbie, D. S. (2008). *More than the sum of their parts? Labor-community coalitions in the rust belt.* Ph.D. dissertation, Social Work and Sociology, University of Michigan, Ann Arbor, MI.
Esbenshade, J. (2000). The "Crisis" over day labor: The politics of visibility and public space. *WorkingUSA, 3,* 27–70.
Esping-Andersen, G. (1990). *The three worlds of welfare capitalism.* Princeton, NJ: Princeton University Press.
Evans, P. (2000). Fighting marginalization with transnational networks: Counter-hegemonic globalization. *Contemporary Sociology, 29,* 230–241.
Evans, P. (2005). Counterhegemonic globalization: Transnational social movements in the contemporary global political economy. In T. Janoski, R. R. Alford, A. M. Hicks & M. A. Schwartz (Eds.), *The handbook of political sociology: States, civil societies, and globalization* (pp. 655–670). Cambridge: Cambridge University Press.
Fantasia, R. (1988). *Cultures of solidarity: Consciousness, action, and contemporary American workers.* Berkeley, CA: University of California Press.
Fendrich, J. (1993). *Ideal citizens: The legacy of the civil rights movement.* Albany, NY: State University of New York Press.
Fendrich, J., & Turner, R. (1989). The transition from student to adult politics. *Social Forces, 67,* 1049–1057.
Ferguson, M. (1992). The mythology about globalization. *European Journal of Communication, 7,* 69–93.
Fine, J. (2005). Community unions and the revival of the American labor movement. *Politics & Society, 33,* 153–199.
Fine, J. (2006). *Worker centers: Organizing communities at the edge of the dream.* Ithaca, NY: ILR/Cornell University Press.

Freyberg, M. S. (1995). *Constructing the UAW dodge local 3: Collective identity, collective efficacy, collective action*. Ph.D. dissertation, Department of Sociology, University of Michigan, Ann Arbor, MI.
Gamson, W. (1990). *The strategy of social protest* (2nd ed.). Belmont, CA: Wadsworth.
Gaventa, J. (1980). *Power and powerlessness: Quiescence and rebellion in an Appalachian valley*. Urbana, IL: University of Illinois Press.
Giugni, M. (1998). Was it worth the effort? The outcomes and consequences of social movements. *Annual Review of Sociology, 98*, 371–393.
Giugni, M., McAdam, D., & Tilly, C. (Eds.). (1999). *How social movements matter*. Minneapolis, MN: University of Minnesota Press.
Glaberman, M. (1980). *Wartime strikes: The struggle against the no-strike pledge in the UAW during World War II*. Detroit, MI: Bewick/Ed.
Goodwin, J., & Hetland, G. (2011). The strange disappearance of capitalism from social movement studies. In J. Goodwin (Ed.), *How to explain a social movement*. Boulder, CO: Paradigm Publishers.
Goodwin, J., Jasper, J. M., & Polletta, F. (2001). *Passionate politics: Emotions and social movements*. Chicago, IL: University of Chicago Press.
Gordon, M. E., & Turner, L. (Eds.). (2000). *Transnational cooperation among labor unions*. Ithaca, NY: ILR/Cornell University Press.
Gould, D. (2002). Life during wartime: emotions and the development of ACT UP. *Mobilization, 7*, 177–200.
Gramsci, A. (1971). *Selections from the prison notebooks*. New York, NY: International Publishers.
Grele, R. J. (2006). Oral history as evidence. In T. L. Charlton, L. E. Myers & R. Sharpless (Eds.), *Handbook of oral history* (pp. 43–101). Lanham, MD: Altamira.
Harvey, D. (1996). *Justice, nature and the geography of difference*. Cambridge: Blackwell.
Hathaway, D. (2000). *Allies across the border: Mexico's "Authentic Labor Front" and global solidarity*. Cambridge, MA: South End Press.
Herod, A. (2003). Geographies of labor internationalism. *Social Science History, 27*, 501–523.
Hirsch, E. (1990). Sacrifice for the cause: Group processes, recruitment, and commitment in a student social movement. *American Sociological Review, 55*, 243–254.
Jennings, M. K. (1987). Residues of a movement: The aging of the American protest generation. *American Political Science Review, 81*, 367–382.
Jessop, B. (1994). Post-Fordism and the state. In A. Amin (Ed.), *Post-Fordism: A reader* (pp. 251–279). Oxford: Blackwell.
Johnston, J., & Laxer, G. (2003). Solidarity in the age of globalization: Lessons from the Anti-MAI and Zapatista struggles. *Theory and Society, 32*, 39–91.
Johnston, P. (2000). The resurgence of labor as citizenship movement in the new labor relations environment. *Critical Sociology, 26*, 139–160.
Johnston, P. (2001). Organize for what?: The resurgence of labor as a citizenship movement. In L. Turner, H. C. Katz & R. W. Hurd (Eds.), *Rekindling the movement: Labor's quest for relevance in the 21st century* (pp. 27–58). Ithaca, NY: ILR/Cornell University Press.
Juravich, T., & Bronfenbrenner, K. (1999). *Ravenswood: The steelworkers' victory and the revival of American labor*. Ithaca, NY: ILR/Cornell University Press.

Katznelson, I. (1986). Working-class formation: Constructing cases and comparisons. In I. Katznelson & A. R. Zolberg (Eds.), *Working-class formation: Nineteenth-century patterns in Western Europe and the United States* (pp. 3–41). Princeton, NJ: Princeton University Press.
Kay, T. (2005). Labor transnationalism and global governance: The impact of NAFTA on transnational labor relationships in North America. *American Journal of Sociology, 111*, 715–756.
Kay, T. (2011). *NAFTA and the politics of labor transnationalism*. Cambridge: Cambridge University Press.
Keck, M., & Sikkink, K. (1998). *Activists beyond borders: Advocacy networks in international politics*. Ithaca, NY: Cornell University Press.
Kelley, R. (1997). The new urban working class and organized labor. *New Labor Forum, 1*, 7–18.
Khasnabish, A. (2008). *Zapatismo beyond borders: New imaginations of political possibility*. Toronto: University of Toronto Press.
Kimeldorf, H. (1988). *Reds or rackets?: The making of radical and conservative unions on the waterfront*. Berkeley, CA: University of California Press.
Kimeldorf, H. (1999). *Battling for American labor: Wobblies, craft workers, and the making of the union movement*. Berkeley, CA: University of California Press.
Klandermans, B. (1997). *The social psychology of protest*. Oxford: Blackwell.
Klatch, R. (1999). *A generation divided: The new left, the new right, and the 1960s*. Berkeley, CA: University of California Press.
Kristof, N. (2004). Living poor, voting rich. *The New York Times*, November 3.
Langford, T. (1994). Strikes and class consciousness. *Labour/Le Travail, 33*, 107–137.
Living Wage Resource Center. (2007). Living wage wins. Retrieved from http://www.living wagecampaign.org. Accessed on November 13, 2007.
Luce, S. (2004). *Fighting for a living wage*. Ithaca, NY: ILR/Cornell University Press.
Mann, M. (1973). *Consciousness and action among the Western working class*. London: Macmillan.
Markowitz, L. (2000). *Worker activism after successful union organizing*. Armonk, NY: M.E. Sharpe.
Marks, G., Mbaye, H. A. D., & Kim, H. M. (2009). Radicalism or reformism? Socialist parties before World War I. *American Sociological Review, 74*, 615–635.
Marshall, G. (1983). Some remarks on the study of working-class consciousness. *Politics & Society, 12*, 263–301.
Marwell, G., Demerath, N. J., III., & Aiken, M. T. (1993). 1960s civil rights activists turn forty: A generational unit at mid-life. *Research in Political Sociology, 6*, 175–195.
Maynes, M. J., Pierce, J. L., & Laslett, B. (2008). *Telling stories: The use of personal narratives in the social sciences and history*. Ithaca, NY: Cornell University Press.
Mayo, M. (2006). Building heavens, havens or hells? Community as policy in the context of the post-Washington consensus. *Critical Studies, 28*, 387–400.
McAdam, D. (1988). *Freedom summer*. New York, NY: Oxford University Press.
McAdam, D. (1989). The biographical consequences of activism. *American Sociological Review, 54*, 744–760.
Melucci, A. (1996). *Challenging codes: Collective action in the information age*. Cambridge: Cambridge University Press.

Meyer, R., & Kimeldorf, H. (2012). Experiential sources of solidarity: Events and subjective transformation. Unpublished manuscript.

Munck, R. (2007). *Globalization and contestation: The new great counter-movement.* New York, NY: Routledge.

Murphy, G. H., & Pfaff, S. (2005). Thinking locally, acting globally? What the Seattle WTO protests tell us about the global justice movement. *Political Power and Social Theory, 17,* 151–176.

Nash, B., Jr. (Ed.). (1998). Special issue: Global labor movements. *Journal of World-Systems Research, 4*(1).

Nissen, B. (2000). Living wage campaigns from a "social movement" perspective: The Miami case. *Labor Studies Journal, 25,* 29–50.

Olesen, T. (2005). *International Zapatismo: The construction of solidarity in the age of globalization.* London: Zed Books.

Parks, V., & Warren, D. (2010). Race, labor and the Wal-Mart economy: Grassroots political responses to economic inequality in Chicago. Unpublished manuscript.

Penney, R. (2002). *Organizing the unorganized: The construction of consciousness and action in worker mobilization.* Ph.D. dissertation, Department of Sociology, University of Michigan, Ann Arbor, MI.

Polanyi, K. (2001 [1944]). *The great transformation: The political and economic origins of our time.* Boston, MA: Beacon Press.

Polletta, F. (2002). *Freedom is an endless meeting.* Chicago, IL: University of Chicago Press.

Portelli, A. (1991). *The death of Luigi Trastulli and other stories: Form and meaning in oral history.* Albany, NY: SUNY Press.

Przeworski, A. (1985). *Capitalism and social democracy.* Cambridge: Cambridge University Press.

Reynolds, D. (1999). Coalition politics: Insurgent union political action builds ties between labor and the community. *Labor Studies Journal, 24,* 54–75.

Reynolds, D. (Ed.). (2004). *Partnering for change: Unions and community groups build coalitions for economic justice.* Armonk, NY: M.E. Sharpe.

Rhomberg, C., & Simmons, L. (2005). Beyond strike support: Labor-community alliances and democratic power in New Haven. *Labor Studies Journal, 30,* 21–47.

Sassen, S. (2009). Incompleteness and the possibility of making: Towards denationalized citizenship? *Political Power and Social Theory, 20,* 229–258.

Schwartz, M., & Paul, S. (1992). Resource mobilization versus the mobilization of people: Why consensus movements cannot be instruments of social change. In A. D. Morris & C. M. Mueller (Eds.), *Frontiers in social movement theory* (pp. 205–223). New Haven, CT: Yale University Press.

Sciacchitano, K. (1998). Finding the community in the union and the union in the community: The first-contract campaign at Steeltech. In K. Bronfenbrenner, S. Friedman, R. W. Hurd, R. A. Oswald & R. L. Seeber (Eds.), *Organizing to win: New research on union strategies* (pp. 150–163). Ithaca, NY: ILR/Cornell University Press.

Scott, J. C. (1985). *Weapons of the weak: Everyday forms of peasant resistance.* New Haven, CT: Yale University Press.

Seelye, K. Q. (2004). Moral values cited as a defining issue of the election. *The New York Times,* November 4.

Seidman, G. (2007). *Beyond the boycott: Labor rights, human rights, and transnational activism.* New York, NY: Russell Sage Foundation.

Sennett, R. (1998). *The corrosion of character: The personal consequences of work in the new capitalism.* New York, NY: W.W. Norton.
Smith, J. (2008). *Social movements for global democracy.* Baltimore, MD: Johns Hopkins University Press.
Smith, J., Karides, M., Becker, M., Brunelle, D., Chase-Dunn, C., della Porta, D., ... Vazquez, R. (2008). *Global democracy and the world social forums.* Boulder, CO: Paradigm Publishers.
Somers, M. R. (1997). Deconstructing and reconstructing class formation theory: Narrativity, relational analysis, and social theory. In J. R. Hall (Ed.), *Reworking class* (pp. 73–105). Ithaca, NY: Cornell University Press.
Somers, M. R. (2008). *Genealogies of citizenship: Markets, statelessness, and the right to have rights.* Cambridge: Cambridge University Press.
Soros, G. (2000). *Open society: Reforming global capitalism.* New York, NY: Public Affairs Press.
Stevis, D., & Boswell, T. (2008). *Globalization and labor: Democratizing global governance.* Lanham, MD: Rowman & Littlefield.
Stiglitz, J. E. (2003). *Globalization and its discontents.* New York, NY: W.W. Norton.
Stillerman, J. (2003). Transnational activist networks and the emergence of labor internationalism in the NAFTA countries. *Social Science History, 27,* 577–601.
Swyngedouw, E. (1996). Reconstructing citizenship, the re-scaling of the state and the new authoritarianism: Closing the Belgian mines. *Urban Studies, 33,* 1499–1521.
Swyngedouw, E. (2004). Globalisation or "glocalisation"? Networks, territories and rescaling. *Cambridge Review of International Affairs, 17,* 25–48.
Tarrow, S. (2005a). *The new transnational activism.* Cambridge: Cambridge University Press.
Tarrow, S. (2005b). The dualities of transnational contention: "Two Activist Solitudes" or a new world altogether? *Mobilization, 10,* 53–72.
Thompson, E. P. (1991). *Customs in common.* London: Merlin Press.
Touraine, A. (2000). *Can we live together?: Equality and difference.* Cambridge: Polity Press.
Turner, L., & Cornfield, D. B. (Eds.). (2007). *Labor in the new urban battlegrounds: Local solidarity in a global economy.* Ithaca, NY: ILR/Cornell University Press.
Warren, D. T. (2005). Wal-Mart surrounded: Community alliances and labor politics in Chicago. *New Labor Forum, 14,* 17–23.
Webster, E., Lambert, R., & Bezuidenhout, A. (2008). *Grounding globalization: Labour in the age of insecurity.* Malden, MA: Blackwell.
Whalen, J., & Flacks, R. (1989). *Beyond the barricades: The sixties generation grows up.* Philadelphia, PA: Temple University Press.
Zald, M. N., Morrill, C., & Rao, H. (2005). The impact of social movements on organizations: Environment and responses. In G. F. Davis, D. McAdam, W. R. Scott & M. Zald (Eds.), *Social movements and organization theory* (pp. 253–279). Cambridge: Cambridge University Press.
Zolberg, A. R. (1972). Moments of madness. *Politics & Society, 2,* 183–207.

POLITICAL FIELDS AND RELIGIOUS MOVEMENTS: THE EXCLUSION OF THE AHMADIYYA COMMUNITY IN PAKISTAN

Sadia Saeed

ABSTRACT

This paper examines the Pakistani state's shift from the accommodation to exclusion of the heterodox Ahmadiyya community, a self-defined minority sect of Islam. In 1953, the Pakistani state rejected demands by a religious movement that Ahmadis be legally declared non-Muslim. In 1974 however, the same demand was accepted. This paper argues that this shift in the state's policy toward Ahmadis was contingent on the distinct political fields in which the two religious movements were embedded. Specifically, it points to conjunctures among two processes that defined state–religious movement relations: intrastate struggles for political power, and the framing strategies of religious movements vis-à-vis core symbolic issues rife in the political field. Consequently, the exclusion of Ahmadis resulted from the transformation of the political field itself, characterized by the increasing hegemony of political discourses referencing Islam, shift toward electoral politics, and the refashioning of the religious movement through positing the "Ahmadi issue" as a national question pertaining to democratic norms.

In 1953, a group of prominent *ulema*[1] in Pakistan launched a social movement demanding that the state forcibly declare the heterodox Ahmadiyya community (in short Ahmadis) a non-Muslim minority. At this moment, state authorities explicitly rejected this demand. In 1974, Pakistan's National Assembly responded to the same demand by constitutionally declaring Ahmadis a non-Muslim minority. This paper addresses the following question: why did the Pakistani state shift from including all sections of self-identifying Muslims into the boundaries of Muslim community to forcibly evicting some from the novel legal category of "Muslim"? Relatedly, how can we account for the failure of the religious movement in the first moment and its success in the second?

The genealogy of the Pakistani state's relationship with the Ahmadis raises a number of intriguing issues. First, it is far from clear why the Pakistani state did not declare Ahmadis non-Muslim in 1953 since the very basis of the creation of Pakistan in 1947 was premised on the "two-nation theory" – the idea that the Muslims and Hindus of the Indian subcontinent constituted two separate nations in every sense of the word. This paper addresses this issue by positing both the moments of accommodation and exclusion of Ahmadis as sites of critical inquiry. Both moments pose questions about the historically fluid ways in which the Pakistani state has constructed its national identity over time through shifting interpretations of the functions of the state and the role of Islam in the political and juridical life of the "imagined political community" of the nation (Anderson, 1991; Brubaker, 2002, 2004; Chatterjee, 1993; Zubrzycki, 2006). Furthermore, this paper approaches these moments both as loose comparative cases (Haydu, 2010) and as events (Sewell, 2005) in the trajectory of consolidation of a Muslim nationalist discourse in Pakistan.

Second, the "Ahmadi issue," as it is popularly referred to in Pakistan, is a local manifestation of a global turn toward increased importance of religion in public life (Casanova, 1994). This is especially visible with the rise of "political Islam," a phenomenon referring to the proliferation of Islamic social movements that aspire toward a greater fusion of religion and the state, particularly in the sphere of law (Fuller, 2003). This shift has led to an increasing reliance on "Muslim politics" characterized by "the competition and contest over both the interpretation of [religious] symbols and control of the institutions, formal and informal, that produce and sustain them" (Eickelman & Piscatori, 1996, p. 5). This phenomenon has been directly addressed by scholars of Islamic social movements who have highlighted the importance of the rich cultural and mobilizational work done by religious leaders on the ground (e.g., Bayat, 2007; Davis & Robinson, 2009; Mahmood, 2005; Tugal, 2009; Wickham, 2002). However, this paper suggests that religious movement outcomes are equally contingent on how religious actors engage in practical politics with state and other political actors.

Using Pierre Bourdieu's field theory and interventions from social movement theory, particularly frame theory, this paper develops a political fields framework for examining state–religious movement relations to account for politics of nationalist policy formation in Pakistan.[2] This framework allows an examination of the historical struggles over, and interactions among, political and symbolic power that shaped the contexts in which the two anti-Ahmadi religious movements were embedded. Frame theory allows an examination of the processes through which religious actors fashioned and refashioned themselves across time to acquire symbolic capital at the level of the state. Combining insights from these two approaches, this paper argues that nationalist policies toward Ahmadis were contingent on conjunctures among two processes within historically specific political fields in Pakistan: first, intrastate struggles for political power, and second, the extent to which religious actors aligned their anti-Ahmadi movement frames with core symbolic issues rife in the political field. Consequently, the shift in the state's nationalist policy toward Ahmadis resulted from a transformation of the political field itself. This transformation was characterized by the increasing hegemony of political discourse referencing Islam, shift toward electoral politics, and the refashioning of anti-Ahmadi religious movement through positing the "Ahmadi issue" as a *national* question pertaining to *democratic* norms. These findings are developed through drawing on government publications, newspapers, and personal interviews conducted with key political actors involved in the exclusion of Ahmadis in 1974.

In what follows, I first elaborate how this paper builds on field theory and frame theory to develop a political fields framework for examining practical politics in Pakistan. I also lay out the main empirical arguments of this paper. The next section gives a brief background of the Ahmadiyya community in Pakistan. The analyses of religious movements and political fields at two main historical junctures follow in which I flesh out my main analytic arguments.

POLITICAL FIELDS AND RELIGIOUS SOCIAL MOVEMENTS IN PAKISTAN

A social field is a space of objective positions held by individuals, groups, or institutions determined by the distribution of combinations of various capitals – economic, political, cultural, and symbolic (Bourdieu, 1993a, p. 72; Bourdieu & Wacquant, 1992, p. 97). Each field is the site of struggle over these different forms of capital that can be potentially converted into each other. At stake is "the legitimate principles of the division" of that particular field (Bourdieu, 1985, p. 734). How individual actors act in this framework is determined both by their objective positions in the field and the habitus, that is, the subjectively held meanings and dispositions that produce "regular" practices. In other words, practices are a product of the relation between the habitus and the specific social contexts or fields in which the action takes place. Habitus structures practices through the fuzzy realm of socially agreed upon "practical schemes" specific to a particular field (Bourdieu, 1990, p. 12; also see King, 2000). All members of the field share a belief and an interest in upholding the value of the field-specific capital. Thus, the field is akin to a gaming space such that even when the game takes a highly antagonistic turn, players remain wedded to the game itself and resist attempts at its subversion (Bourdieu, 1993b, p. 74). However, because fields are sites of struggle with different actors having different aims, practices are strategically deployed to shape distribution of capitals and occasionally even the *doxa*, that is, the fundamental rules of the game of that particular field.

Building on field theory, Bourdieu argues that the political field is the social space in which struggles over political power take place[3] (Bourdieu, 1991). Bourdieu uses the term "political" to refer to democratic politics and "political field" to the social space in which political parties vie with each other. It constitutes the space in which the act of *delegation* takes place whereby professional politicians are entrusted with the task of expressing the will of their constituents. At stake is the acquisition of political capital, or the ability to win votes (Kauppi, 2003). This in turn allows the acquisition of "objectified political power," or administrative control over public powers such as law, army, police, finances, etc. This is accomplished through struggles over mobilization of groups, a process that entails creation of competing "political products, issues, programmes, analyses, commentaries, concepts and events" among which citizens choose (Bourdieu, 1991, p. 172; also see Bourdieu, 1999). Thus, the political field is the site in which both symbolic struggles over representation and classification of politically salient categories and political struggles over formal state power are carried out. Both these forms of capital in the political field are potentially convertible into each other.

While these struggles in consolidated democracies are organized around established political parties as Bourdieu maintains, those in postcolonial contexts such as Pakistan routinely include multiple and shifting state and social actors such as bureaucratic elite, military leaders, and religious groups in addition to traditional political parties (e.g., see Alavi, 1972; Wedeen, 1999). Political fields in such contexts are less "settled" (Steinmetz, 2007) on the distribution of political and symbolic power. For example in Pakistan, as I discuss below, the very boundaries of the political field are a recurring object of contestation since diverse actors such as Islamists, military rulers, and democratic political parties often hold distinct and antagonistic visions about what constitutes legitimate political authority. Contentious issues pertaining to both formal political power (i.e., which actors and institutions can legitimately hold formal state power) and symbolic power (which actors can legitimately pronounce hegemonic citizenship classifications) have got resolved in different ways at different historical junctures, depending on the very configuration of the political field. It is then not surprising that political fields in Pakistan have undergone frequent transformations. Another significant feature of Pakistan is that elongated periods of military rule[4] have resulted in periods of highly diminished formal political activity with routine episodes of banning of political parties and detainment of political opposition. However, the very logic of the political field entails that even authoritarian leaders routinely engage in symbolic struggles to acquire political capital, which I define more broadly as political legitimacy.

Because a political fields framework offers a fundamentally relational perspective, it brings to fore the importance of the institutional and discursive relations between different parts of the state. Specifically, it decentralizes the state both into its component institutional parts (e.g., military, bureaucracy, politicians) and distinct imperatives (territorial, coercive, and symbolic) (Abrams, 1988; Loveman, 2005; Migdal, 2001). In contrast to advanced democracies in which the relative functions of the different branches of the state are clearly demarcated and adhered to, postcolonial state fields are characterized by overlapping of functions and powers across formal institutional lines (Hansen & Stepputat, 2001; Mamdani, 1996). As a result, different statist interest groups possessing distinct dispositions struggle over the distribution of political capital. At stake is the articulation of the *doxa* through institutionalizing practices and classifications based on the habitus of the "winners" in a bid to settle the boundaries of the political field (Bourdieu 1993b, p. 74).

A political fields framework also incorporates state–society interactions. State actors in the political field engage in acquisition of symbolic capital through which politically salient collectivities and categories such as family, classes, national groups, ethnicities, etc., are defined (Anderson, 1991; Brubaker, 2002; Corrigan & Sayer, 1985). However, politicized social groups such as religious movement actors also have huge stakes in imposing their own visions of legitimate classifications in the body politic. Although they usually do not possess the resources to directly capture state power, they are centrally invested in directing cultural policies of the state. The aim is to carve out and monopolize a discursive space of political claims-making in order to acquire symbolic capital. Thus, these social actors are players in the political field by virtue of engaging in symbolic struggles with state actors.

As noted above, this paper investigates how anti-Ahmadi religious movements have fared in political fields in Pakistan over time. Of central importance is an examination of social movement repertoires, both practical and discursive, within the political field (McAdam, Tarrow, & Tilly, 2001). Social movement theorists have underscored *framing* processes as acts of construction of meanings through which movement leaders create "resonance" with potential participants. It is through concrete acts of framing that problems are diagnosed, solutions proposed, and potential participants motivated to undertake action (Snow, Rochford, Worden, & Benford, 1986). In similar vein, a growing number of studies are investigating the conditions under which Islamic religious movements have mobilized citizens, successfully made political claims, and achieved cultural hegemony (e.g., Bayat, 2007; Davis & Robinson, 2009; Mahmood, 2005; Snow & Byrd, 2007; Tugal, 2009; Wickham, 2002; Wiktorowicz, 2004). However, one important dimension that remains underexamined is the congruence of the habitus of religious actors with the accepted practical schemes that define the implicit "rules" of the political field at any given time.

Below, I show that it is through interactions and conjunctures among two processes that unfold within the political field – one of intrastate struggles for political power and the other of framing strategies of religious movement actors *vis-à-vis* the political field itself – that determined how and why Ahmadis were accommodated by the state in 1954 and excluded in 1974. I argue that in the first moment, the political field was characterized by intrastate struggles among bureaucratic elite and politicians for political power *and* state–society struggles over the constitutional relationship between Islam and the Pakistani state. The anti-Ahmadi religious movement was unsuccessful in aligning its movement frames with this core constitutional issue, instead adopting violent anti-Ahmadi and anti-state frames. This enabled bureaucratic elite to wrest political power away from the politicians. The accommodation of Ahmadis emerged from the distinct habitus of the bureaucratic elite which was characterized by authoritarian tendencies and distrust of mass politics and politicized religion.

Subsequently, the boundaries of the political field were transformed through the general elections of 1970 that ushered in the democratically elected regime of Zulfiqar Ali Bhutto (1971–1977). Gaining political power through electoral means and turning the Ahmadi issue into a constitutional debate placed Islamist political parties in a favorable position to push for the nationalist policy of exclusion of Ahmadis. By engaging in framing strategies that appropriated a Muslim nationalist discourse and democratic norms, the religious movement effected the exclusion of Ahmadis, in the process acquiring significant symbolic capital and transforming the *doxa* itself by making Muslim politics hegemonic in the political field.

THE AHMADIYYA COMMUNITY IN PAKISTAN

Pakistan came into existence in 1947 following British colonial rule in India on the basis of the two-nation theory. This idea purports that Muslims of India constituted a separate nation and thereby deserved a separate homeland to safeguard the interests of the Muslim community. Despite this ideological valorization of a Muslim nationalist ideology, the triangular relationship between the state, religion, and the nation is far from straightforward and has been the site of continual contestation and negotiation among key state and social actors (Binder, 1961; Nasr, 1994; Zaman, 2002). Social movements organized around the issue of the religious status of the Ahmadis have been a principal mode of acquisition of symbolic power for many religious groups (Kaushik, 1996; Saeed, 2007). The two moments of accommodation and exclusion thus present an exciting empirical opportunity for inquiring both into politics *of* nationalism and nationalism *in* politics.

The Ahmadi issue has theological, economic, and symbolic dimensions. In terms of Islamic doctrine, the most pivotal point of controversy rests on the issue of the status of the founder of the Ahmadiyya sect Mirza Ghulam Ahmad (1835–1908) who had lived in colonial India and claimed the status of Prophet but while upholding the supremacy of Prophet Mohammad (Friedmann, 1989). Traditionally, Muslims believe that the Prophet Mohammad is the last prophet to be sent on earth by God and regard Mirza Ghulam Ahmad as an apostate. Furthermore, the Ahmadi conception of the meaning of *jihad* (Holy War) as conducted through the pen (i.e., through arguments and proofs) and not through warfare is viewed suspiciously by orthodox Muslims. Also, Ahmadi leadership openly professed loyalty to British during the colonial era, leading to popularization of (unsubstantiated) claims by religious groups that Ahmadis have historically been disloyal to Pakistan (Lavan, 1973).

The exact number of Ahmadis in Pakistan is an issue of contention. According to the 1998 census conducted by Government of Pakistan, around 96% of the population is Muslim and 0.22% is Ahmadis.[5] In general, Ahmadis enjoy greater economic well-being than non-Ahmadis because of their higher educational achievements. However, these differences are blown out of proportion by orthodox religious groups as part of their anti-Ahmadi polemics. Hence, perceptions of the wealth of Ahmadis must be regarded as a significant cause of anti-Ahmadi sentiments. That the 1974 Amendment did not subsequently open up jobs for ordinary Muslims in any substantive way is hardly surprising given the extremely small number of the community. Being declared a non-Muslim minority in 1974 essentially barred Ahmadis from occupying the posts of the Prime Minister and President of Pakistan since the Constitution of 1973 declared that only a Muslim could occupy these posts. It further meant that Ahmadis would be able to gain admissions for government jobs, public educational institutions, and federal and provincial legislatures on the basis of their numerical strength, determined by quotas reserved for minorities.

I contend that the most significant dimension of the Ahmadi issue is the nationalist, symbolic one. The term "Muslim" was defined by anti-Ahmadi movements in both time periods to *specifically* exclude Ahmadis on the grounds that Ahmadi theological tenets defied a core Islamic belief in the finality of prophethood. For religious groups in Pakistan, the non-Muslimness of Ahmadis is always-already a "fact." The core political issue lodged in the Ahmadi issue by these religious groups is the symbolic relationship between religion and the state in Pakistan. Hence, the categorization of Ahmadis as non-Muslim in 1974 did not become a means for the state to undertake moral regulation of its citizens in their day-to-day life. In terms of practicing Islam in the public space, the Amendment had no practical effects on religious freedoms of Ahmadis who continued to practice and preach their religion with impunity. This situation changed in 1984 when the military ruler General Zia-ul-Haq promulgated an Ordinance that makes it a criminal offense for Ahmadis to refer to themselves as Muslim or to practice Islam in public. It explicitly renders these as acts of "posing as Muslims" and makes any Ahmadi who "outrages the religious feelings of Muslims" liable to fines and imprisonment.[6] Thus, the 1974 Amendment laid the groundwork for the moral regulation and state policing of the Muslim/non-Muslim distinction. In this paper, however, the core symbolic issue that I discuss is the contested issue of the Pakistani state's relationship with Islam.

THE POLITICS OF ACCOMMODATION OF AHMADIS

In this section, I will explain the nationalist policy of accommodation of Ahmadis by the Pakistani state in 1953. My analysis proceeds in three parts. First, I analyze debates on the constitutional relationship between Islam and the Pakistani state between 1947 and 1952. I depict the symbolic centrality of this issue in the political field and lay out the central political and religious interlocutors and their position-takings in this debate. Next, I analyze the anti-Ahmadi movement and show that not only did it remain unsuccessful in creating resonance among its anti-Ahmadi demands and the issue of the relationship between religion and state but it also unwittingly became the means for bureaucratic elite to wrest formal political power from politicians. Last, I examine the habitus of the bureaucratic elite and its relationship with the accommodation of Ahmadis.

Constitutional Debates Over Religion and the State, 1947–1952

A significant geopolitical feature characterizing the Pakistani state at the time of independence in 1947 was the territorial structure of the Pakistani state, consisting of two "wings" – East and West Pakistan – and separated by some 1,000 miles with India lying in between. While the East wing, which emerged as independent Bangladesh in 1970, was ethnically homogenous, the West wing was composed of four provinces that were constituted along ethnic lines. Ethnic tensions resulting from such divisions have been endemic since the formative postcolonial period and have necessitated attempts at a centralizing ideology for central state actors (Baxter, 1997). Inevitably, the issue of the Pakistani state's relationship with Islam has been central to these recurring ideological debates.

The political field in the immediate postcolonial period was characterized by multiplicity of nationalist discourses on the relationship between religion and the state in Pakistan. The most significant site in which this debate took place was the Constituent Assembly that was given the task of framing a constitution. Its members had been determined through indirect elections held in 1946 under British colonial rule. There were only two political parties in the Constituent Assembly – the Muslim League Party (ML) that had spearheaded the Muslim nationalist movement in British India under the leadership of Mohammad Ali Jinnah and the Congress Party representing Hindu and other religious minorities. Jinnah was appointed as the first President of the Constituent Assembly.

Within the Constituent Assembly itself, two prominent narratives emerged during this time – a liberal-secular discourse and a Muslim nationalist discourse. Both of these positions emerged as opposing conceptions of the national community during the course of constitutional debates. The first narrative was issued by Jinnah in the first session of the Constituent Assembly four days prior to the independence of Pakistan. Here, Jinnah explicitly held that the basis of inclusion in Pakistan was political citizenship and not religion. For the "Father of the Nation," as Jinnah is referred to in Pakistan, religion and the state were two separate entities (Constituent Assembly of Pakistan Debates (henceforth CAP), August 11, 1947, p. 20). However, in subsequent debates in the Constituent Assembly on the preamble of the constitution termed the Objectives Resolution that took place in 1949 following Jinnah's death, a Muslim nationalist discourse was given political salience by ML. Of the 11 clauses of the Objectives Resolution, explicit reference to Islam appears in 3. For example, while not declared an Islamic state in which the law of the land would be based on *shari'a*,[7] its first clause poses a hierarchy of sovereigns for the new polity – Allah, the State, and the People:

> Sovereignty over the entire universe belongs to Allah Almighty alone and the authority which He has delegated to the State of Pakistan, through its people for being exercised within the limits prescribed by Him is a sacred trust.

The non-Muslim, Congress members of the Constituent Assembly rigorously opposed the Objectives Resolution on ground of its religious character, noting that its adoption may hinder the development of democracy in Pakistan by giving way to repressive interpretations of Islam (CAP, March 8, 1949, pp. 13–14). Instead, they argued for a more universal basis for protection of citizenship rights such as found in the United Nations Charter (CAP, March 9, 1949, p. 36). However, these minority voices were marginalized and the Objectives Resolution adopted through a majority ML vote.

Although the members of the Constituent Assembly were split along religious lines with Muslim members voting unanimously for the Resolution and non-Muslim members objecting to it on liberal-secular grounds, the Muslim members of the Constituent Assembly held radically different conceptions of the relationship between religion and the state. On the one end of the spectrum was Maulana Shabbir Ahmad Uthmani, perhaps the most prominent member of the *ulema* in Pakistan at the time. Uthmani supported the Objectives Resolution by maintaining that Islam did not accept "the view that religion is a private affair between man and his creator and as such has no bearing upon the social or political relations of human beings" (CAP, March 9, 1949). Uthmani made a case for the complete fusion of religion and state in his speech even though the Objectives Resolution did not explicitly endorse such a position. On the other end of the spectrum was Mian Iftikharuddin, an ardent socialist and the only Muslim member of the Constituent Assembly to express disapproval of the Objectives Resolution for falling short in "the field of political, economic and social justice" (CAP, March 10, 1949, p. 52). Iftikharuddin concurred with Congress Party members that the first clause of the Resolution could be readily construed as vesting sovereignty in the state and not directly in the representatives chosen by the people. However for Iftikharuddin, the crucial question was how to turn Pakistan into a "dynamic democracy" and the answer was to be found in socialism and not Islam (p. 53). In between these two positions lay other ML members such as Zafrullah Khan, the first Foreign Minister of Pakistan and the only Ahmadi in the Constituent Assembly. Zafrullah Khan defended the Objectives Resolution's clause that requires the state to make provisions enabling Muslims to order their lives in accordance with principles of Islam, maintaining that such provisions would not be binding on the non-Muslim minorities (CAP, March 12, 1949, p. 67). Zafrullah Khan argued that democracy entailed that "political authority should be exercised through representatives freely chosen by the people" (p. 68). As long as this condition was met, Islam could only aid the quality of democracy.

That these widely different personalities with distinct and differing visions of the relationship between religion and the state could agree on the Objectives Resolution is only explicable when one considers that all the clauses referencing Islam were only nominal in nature. More significantly, the adoption of the Objectives Resolution as the unified voice of the ML consolidated the party's political standing as well as conferred significant symbolic capital to it, as was witnessed by the wide praise with which the Resolution was met across the country.

The Islamists constituted another site of agency within the political field and were crucial in shaping the content of the Objectives Resolution.[8] Here, I want to note the influence of one of the most influential Islamist of Pakistan Sayyid Abu'l-A'la Maududi (1903–1979) who founded the Islamist political party *Jamaat-e-Islami* (JI) in colonial India in 1941. While initially ambivalent about the creation of Pakistan, Maududi subsequently undertook a campaign for an "Islamic Constitution." This became an increasingly public project and a concerted effort under independent Pakistan, routinely arousing the ire of state authorities who periodically banned the JI's publications and detained Maududi in the years between 1947 and 1958 (Nasr, 1994, pp. 103–146). While Uthmani was led toward constitutional debates because of his political position as a member of the Constituent Assembly, Maududi's entire political project in these years rested on proposing a blueprint for the Pakistani constitution that would make *shari'a* the law of the land and crucially transform the entire social fabric of Pakistan (Maududi, 1980, p. 101). Maududi was also an avid critic of ML politicians who, he claimed, used Islamic rhetoric for political ends and thereby lacked commitment to the demands of a genuine Islamic state.

In the time period preceding the Constituent Assembly debates, JI made overtures to the *ulema* through Uthmani in a bid to join hands in the struggle to influence the content of the Objectives Resolution. Uthmani became the medium through which Maududi sought to legitimize his own vision of Pakistan's future constitution in the political field. It was through these combined efforts that references to Islam came to occupy such a central place in the Objectives Resolution. When the Objectives Resolution was passed, JI proclaimed it as a victory for itself, implicitly suggesting that Uthmani had served as a conduit for Maududi's vision (Nasr, 1994, p. 124). One ML politician subsequently observed that references to Islam were made solely to satisfy Uthmani (Hyat Khan, 1995, p. 220).

However, debates on the constitutional relationship between Islam and the state were far from over with the passing of the Objectives Resolution. This crystallized most starkly during public debates on the constitution of Pakistan. In December 1952, the Basic Principles Committee (BPC), a Committee set up by the Constituent Assembly of Pakistan to work out the details of the Constitution, presented a second draft of its Report.[9] This report was scrutinized by publics across the country. While several aspects of it were heatedly discussed in the press, the issue that centrally concerns us here is its proposal about the formation of a Board composed of *ulema*. It was proposed that this Board be charged with the task of determining whether the bills passed in Federal and Provincial Legislatures were "repugnant to the Holy Quran and *Sunnah*." If yes, the Board would suggest the proper lines along which the Bill should be reframed. It would then be necessary for the Legislature to incorporate the changes in the Bill.

The *Ulema* Board clause met with huge outcry from different sections of the population, both from those in favor of the presence of religion in politics and those against it. For the former group, the BPC Report was not Islamic enough. Thus in response, a group of *ulema* and Islamists including Maududi held a convention and presented their own model of BPC Report. A few of the amendments proposed were compulsory education of Quran and Islamic teachings in the educational system; prohibition through legislation of "the propagation of atheism and infidelity and the insulting or ridiculing of the Holy Qur'an or the *Sunnah*"; "the Quran and the *Sunnah* be the chief source of the law of land"; and that the name of the state be changed from Pakistan to the "Islamic Republic of Pakistan" (Maududi 1980, p. 348). On the other end, liberal-seculars expressed their discontent with the religious character of the BPC Report. For example, the editorial of *Dawn* warned that the country was in danger of slipping into "Ulemacracy" (*Dawn*, Karachi, January 24, 1953). Political leaders such as Khan Abdul Qayyum Khan, Chief Minister of NWFP Province, rejected the BPC Report for taking power away from the people and putting it in hands of *ulema* (*The Pakistan Times*, Karachi, January 1, 1953). In response to these critiques, the Constituent Assembly moved to adjourn consideration of the BPC Report to a later date. When the first Constitution of Pakistan was finally approved in 1956, it contained no reference to *Ulema* Boards.

This discussion gives a snapshot of the symbolic terrain on which the constitutional issue of the relationship between religion and Islam was contested in the political field in Pakistan. It characterized the discursive space in which the anti-Ahmadi religious movement, to which I turn next, was launched. In the next section, I argue that the failure of the anti-Ahmadi movement to discursively align its movement frames with this core symbolic issue and its adoption of violent anti-Ahmadi and anti-state frames enabled bureaucratic elite to wrest political power from ML politicians in a struggle to reconfigure the very boundaries of the political field.

The Anti-Ahmadiyya Movement

Anti-Ahmadi movements have a long history in Pakistan. Even before the creation of Pakistan, right-wing religious groups, most notably the *Majlis-e-Ahrar-Islam* (in short, *Ahrar*), a Muslim political organization formed in 1931, were agitating against the Ahmadis, portraying them as heretics (Jalal, 2000; Lahore High Court (henceforth LHC) 1954; Lavan, 1973). In Pakistan, the demand that Ahmadis be declared a non-Muslim minority was first made by *Ahrar* in 1949. The passing of the Objectives Resolution gave the *Ahrar* leadership impetus to make their anti-Ahmadi demands public (Nasr, 1994). As early as 1950, state executive authorities began paying attention to the content of anti-Ahmadi rhetoric that was being spread across Punjab by *Ahrar* leaders. Typically in these meetings, writings of Mirza Ghulam Ahmad, founder of the Ahmadiyya community, were misquoted and "twisted and obscene and indecent inferences drawn"; he and other community leaders described as "adulterers and given to unnatural indulgences"; Ahmadis described as traitors to Pakistan; Zafrullah Khan verbally abused and "often described as an 'ass' and as a 'knave'"; and lists of Ahmadi army and civil officers handed out (LHC, 1954, p. 20). Especially alarming for state authorities were statements that could readily be interpreted as incitements toward anti-Ahmadi violence. For example, one *Ahrar* leader often said in his speeches that if Mirza Ghulam Ahmad had claimed prophethood in his lifetime, he would have killed him with his own hands. It was also noted that on a few occasions, such statements led to audience members volunteering to kill prominent Ahmadi members.

As more and more *ulema* began to be sympathetic to the *Ahrar* cause, Punjab politicians began taking notice of the movement. With Punjab provincial elections approaching in March of 1951, prominent politicians such as Mumtaz Daultana, the Chief Minister of the province, began to use anti-Ahmadi propaganda as a platform for winning support among the electorate (Nasr, 1994). Furthermore, with economic crises and food shortages rampant in the summer of 1952, religious groups became active in channeling the social unrest into religious grievances. In May of 1952, *Ahrar* and some prominent *ulema* formed a *Majlis-e-Amal* (Council of Action) and formally adopted the demand that Ahmadis be declared a non-Muslim minority, Zafrullah Khan removed from his post, and Ahmadis be removed from all key government jobs.

During this time, *Ahrar* enlisted the support of JI. Maududi entered into an alliance with the *Ahrar* reluctantly and cautiously since his own Islamist project of a constitutional Islamic state militated against the passionate and violent denunciations by *Ahrar* leaders against Ahmadis and eventually state authorities. The involvement of Maududi can be explained by the symbolic struggles over the relationship between religion and the state in the political field that I have recounted above. In order to capitalize on the anti-Ahmadi movement but without aligning his JI too closely with the *Majlis-e-Amal* dominated by *Ahrar*, Maududi incorporated the demand that Ahmadis be declared a non-Muslim minority into his constitutional blueprint that was developed in response to the second BPC Report that I have discussed above (Maududi, 1980, p. 362). According to Maududi, the issue was to be decided through constitutional means and not through staging riots or partaking in violent actions. Here, the movement came the closest to aligning its demands with the core symbolic issue of the constitutional relationship between Islam and the state that was rife in the political field at that time.

Between July of 1952 and January of 1953, the *Ahrar*-led agitation became more confrontational toward the state despite public statements by Punjab ML leaders and Prime Minister Nazimuddin that they were sympathetic to the *Ahrar* cause (LHC, 1954). Increasingly, the *Ahrar* began to undertake violent and disruptive activities, utilizing newspapers and pamphlets as mediums for coordinating riotous large-scale meetings, issuing threats to state authorities, and inciting violence against Ahmadis. As the movement proceeded, it turned from an agitation directed against the Ahmadis into one directed against the state. The significant shift that took place at this time was the employment of the trope of "direct action," a euphemism for large-scale riots that were eventually staged. Daily reports appeared in newspapers such as the *Zamindar* (Lahore) to the effect that all efforts were being made and volunteers being recruited in thousands to march to Karachi, the capital of Pakistan, on a certain date, so as to give public demonstrations and picket the residences of the Governor-General and Prime Minister of Pakistan (e.g., *Zamindar*, Lahore, February 19, 1953). The government was quick to respond by arresting prominent leaders of *Ahrar* and declaring Martial Law in Lahore to quell the movement.

In face of *Ahrar's* violent movement repertoires and framing strategies, JI disassociated itself formally from the *Majlis-e-Amal* in February of 1953. Sympathetic politicians such as Prime Minister Nazimuddin increasingly started taking a hardened position toward *Ahrar*. With their anti-Ahmadi and anti-state framing strategies, the *Ahrar* placed themselves in direct opposition to executive state authorities. While Maududi did attempt to articulate the anti-Ahmadi demands as a constitutional issue, ultimately

Maududi adopted the anti-Ahmadi rhetoric of the *Ahrar* through the publication of a pamphlet titled "*Qadiani Masalah*" or the "Ahmadi Problem" (Maududi, 1953) for which he was ultimately charged and given the death sentence for inciting "feelings of enmity and hatred between different groups in Pakistan."

As I have noted above, Pakistan came into existence under the leadership of Jinnah who was elected as the first President of the Constituent Assembly. While Jinnah was alive, he also held on to the position of Governor-General, a colonial office that was retained in Pakistan to serve a ceremonial function in order to preserve a symbolic continuity with the authority of the British colonial state. However, Jinnah invested this office with considerable executive powers (Khan, 2005). When the anti-Ahmadi movement was launched, the position of Governor-General was occupied by a powerful bureaucrat Ghulam Mohammad. At this moment, the bureaucrats as an interest group were players in the political field and were in the process of consolidating a powerful bureaucratic-military oligarchy in direct opposition to the elected politicians (Jalal, 1991; Talbot, 1998).

The anti-Ahmadi movement brought to fore the unsettled issue of which state actors within the political field held legitimate authority to decide the religious status of Ahmadis. In the context of the Constituent Assembly's failure to frame a constitution that could meet a broad consensus in Pakistani society and the absence of general elections that would have determined who the legitimate legislative state actors were, the movement became a means through which different state actors in the political field vied for formal state power. As the movement started becoming more violent, Ghulam Mohammad ordered the Army to impose Pakistan's first Martial Law over the city of Lahore. Ghulam Mohammad also made Nazimuddin government's inability to deal decisively with movement agitators the pretext for dismissing it in April of 1953. The arrests of prominent *ulema* and Islamists, the dissolution of central government and the imposition of Martial Law became events in the reconfiguration of the political field by the bureaucratic elite. Subsequently in October of 1954, after the religious movement had been suppressed by executive state authorities, Ghulam Mohammad dismissed the Constituent Assembly altogether. This move was eventually challenged in the Federal Court of Pakistan where Chief Justice of Pakistan Mohammad Munir declared this act of dissolution legal.[10] The new Cabinet set up by Ghulam Mohammad contained several high-level military officials, thus paving the way for the Army's eventual ascendancy in Pakistani politics (McGrath, 1996).

The political field on the whole was severely compromised by these usurpations of political power which reconfigured the political field by criminalizing *ulema* and Islamists and marginalizing politicians. Furthermore, the Ahmadi issue provided the bureaucratic elite with a discursive space to impose their own symbolic vision of the relationship between religion and the state in Pakistan. The most salient document here is the Report of the Inquiry Commission formed in 1953 to probe into the anti-Ahmadi agitation to which I turn next. The Inquiry Commission was led by Justice Munir and provides a core document for inquiring into the habitus of the bureaucratic elite.

Habitus of the Bureaucratic Elite and the Accommodation of Ahmadis

Although bureaucrats did not participate in popular constitutional debates in the political field, they eventually advanced their own vision of the relationship between religion and the state from which the nationalist policy of the accommodation of Ahmadis emerged. These bureaucrats, both civil and military, possessed a distinct habitus that took shape under the British colonial regime. The relationship between military and civilian establishment in Pakistan was strikingly similar to the one that had existed between the British Indian Army and the British colonial state. According to one historian of the Pakistani army, "the (British) Indian Army, from its very inception, was trained to be the 'custodian of law and order' and to promote colonial interests at the cost of different indigenous and regional interests within the subcontinent" (Hashmi, 1983, p. 149). This relationship continued into the immediate postcolonial period, with the Pakistani Army remaining predisposed toward maintaining internal order at the behest of executive authorities in addition to tasks of defense and external security.

Furthermore, the structure of the bureaucracy in the immediate postcolonial period was a continuation of its colonial predecessor (Alavi, 1983). Postcolonial state elite often remain imbued with colonial dispositions about local populations as subjects to be ruled over rather than citizens to which they are responsible (Mamdani, 1996). Indigenous members of the colonial bureaucracy who opted to join Pakistan upon independence continued to enjoy discretionary, arbitrary powers in collusion with the provincial and local police. Hamza Alavi has noted that these "bureaucrats were brought up on the myth of 'guardianship,' the idea that it was their mission to defend the interests of the people as against the supposed partisanship of and personal ambitions of 'professional' politicians"

(Alavi, 1983, p. 66). That the bureaucrats could undermine the authority of politicians by overstepping their traditional roles as administrators was noted by contemporaries such as the socialist Mian Iftikharuddin who during the course of Constituent Assembly debates in 1952 explicitly critiqued the presence of bureaucrats in ministries formed by the Muslim League, noting that those charged with matters relating to defense and internal affairs in Pakistan had served under the British colonial state and were administrators rather than politicians (Toor, 2011, p. 40).

The Munir Inquiry Report led by Justice Munir combines the secular dispositions of the higher judiciary of Pakistan at that time (Lau, 2006) with the authoritarian ones of the bureaucrats. The Report states at the beginning that it uses the term "Muslim" to refer to "the general body of Muslims who do not believe in Mirza Ghulam Ahmad" and "Ahmadi" to those "who believe that Mirza Ghulam Ahmad was a prophet" (LHC, 1954, p. 9). This politics of naming suggests that the judges deliberately distanced themselves from the issue of the religious status of the Ahmadis. During the course of the judicial inquiry, the *ulema* brought before it argued that their anti-Ahmadi demands were based on the promise of an Islamic state contained in the Objectives Resolution. This, according to the judges, was an erroneous assumption since the Objectives Resolution was equally premised on two mutually contradictory principles: first, democratic ideals that vest sovereignty in the people, and second, on the ideals of an Islamic state that vests sovereignty in Allah. The state could either be Islamic or it could be democratic (p. 210). The judges drew on Jinnah's historic speech before the Constituent Assembly to espouse liberal-secular ideals: "The future subject of the State is to be a citizen with equal rights, privileges and obligations, irrespective of colour, caste, creed or community" (p. 203). Consequently, "faith is a matter for the individual and however, false, dishonest or ridiculous it may appear to be to another, it may still be held sincerely and honestly by the person who professes it" (p. 279).

Politicized religion, on the other hand, is a vehicle for disorder and "an embodiment of complete intellectual paralysis" (p. 220). The judges questioned a host of *ulema* on their views on what constitutes an Islamic state and what defines a Muslim. Based on a range of differing opinions that were put forth, judges concluded that the *ulema* "were hopelessly disagreed among themselves" on the very important question of who was a Muslim (p. 36). Furthermore, the judges linked their distrust of politicized religion with populism, noting that "the masses" can be set on "any course of action, regardless of all considerations of discipline, loyalty, decency, morality or civic sense" if convinced on religious grounds (p. 231). This narrative about politicized religion was woven into a specific colonialist view of the people as devoid of "intelligence," without "a sufficiently developed mind" and to be "led" by "the leaders" (p. 275). But these leaders cannot be the politicians. The Report strongly reproached politicians for their failure to deal firmly with the Islamist movement. Political parties and leaders are characterized as exploiters of religion. The Report distinguishes between the legislative functions of the politicians and the governance functions of the executive, explicitly privileging the latter over the former. The Ahmadis emerge as the victims, the silent minority being used by corrupt political and Islamist parties to further selfish and politically motivated interests. The outcome then was what I have termed the accommodation of Ahmadis.

In short, this period in Pakistan was defined by a political field characterized by embedded struggles between various state and social actors over the symbolic, religious dimensions of the state. The anti-Ahmadi movement remained unsuccessful in aligning its movement frames with these symbolic struggles. Unwittingly, it created the space for the bureaucratic elite to deploy coercive tactics both *vis-à-vis* the politicians and the anti-Ahmadi movement in a bid for political power through reconfiguring the boundaries of the political field at that time. They then proceeded to legitimate their dispositions about religion, mass politics, and politicians through an illiberal, secular nationalism in an attempt to convert political power into symbolic capital.

BETWEEN ACCOMMODATION AND EXCLUSION

A number of significant shifts took place in the period between the two moments of accommodation and exclusion that were crucial for setting the stage for the transformation of the political field in Pakistan. The most significant trajectory constituting this shift was the one spanning the consolidation of military authoritarianism in the 1960s and the emergence of the democratically elected regime of Zulfiqar Ali Bhutto in 1971. The military regime of Ayub Khan (1958–1969) witnessed attempts at distancing of the state from popular expressions of religion. In line with the military habitus of those times, Ayub Khan was highly suspicious of what he perceived as the use of Islam by political and Islamist parties (Khan, 1967). The constitution of 1962 dropped "Islamic" from the country's name, thereby renaming Pakistan the "Republic of Pakistan." On the political front, it instituted a Presidential system through a system of local representation termed Basic Democracies. Political parties were thereby banned. However, both these moves came under heavy criticism and had to be quickly remodified. The Political Parties Act of 1962 removed the ban on political parties, while the First Constitutional Amendment Act of 1963 re-inserted the term "Islamic" in Pakistan's name. The Ayub regime, however, witnessed the promulgation of the *Muslim Family Laws Ordinance, 1961*[11] (MFLO) that explicitly brought the laws governing the domestic space of marital and other familial relationships under state regulation. Overall, the Ayub regime was decisive in pointing toward the failure of the "secular" project in Pakistan as Ayub Khan increasingly began to rely on "Islamic modernism" (i.e., state-directed liberal Islam as, for example, envisioned in MFLO) and associate with Islamist parties to manage political opposition from popular, leftist, and secular groups (Nasr, 1994, pp. 152–155). In other words, Muslim politics as a form of practical politics began gaining increasing legitimacy in the political field as military elite under the leadership of Ayub Khan began abandoning their earlier dispositions about expelling religion from politics. Essentially, this meant the legitimization of practical politics associated with mobilization of citizens.

Because of increasing discontent among the citizenry about the undemocratic structure of the state, manifested among other things through the student and labor demonstrations of 1968 and opposition in East Pakistan to West Pakistan's disproportionate share of economic and political capital, President Ayub Khan turned over power to his trusted General Yahya Khan in 1969 who proceeded to hold Pakistan's first general elections in 1970 (Talbot, 1998, pp. 179–188). In the closing years of 1960s, leftist parties such as Bhutto's Pakistan Peoples Party (PPP) and Wali Khan's National Awami Party (NAP) emerged as prominent contenders for political power. As elections of 1970s neared, Bhutto's PPP emerged as the major national party with a popular manifesto of *"Islam is our faith; Democracy is our Polity; Socialism is our Economy."* During the election campaign, PPP identified itself as a mass populist party with its election slogan of *"roti, kapra aur makan"* (Bread, cloth and home). Furthermore, to counter claims by religious groups that socialism was fundamentally in contradiction with religion, Bhutto espoused a discourse of "Islamic socialism," arguing that Islamic egalitarian principles were in perfect accord with those of socialism (Burki, 1988, p. 53).

Eventually, the socialist government of Zulfiqar Ali Bhutto came to office in 1971 in the wake of Pakistan's war with India and following the loss of significant territory through the creation of the independent state of

Bangladesh. While elected, the regime's claim to being democratic remained tenuous because of the conditions under which Bhutto's PPP came to power. If the postelection period had not resulted in the independence of Bangladesh, Bhutto would not have enjoyed the majority that he did after 1971. However, that he was the most popular leader in what remained of Pakistan is uncontested.

When the second anti-Ahmadi movement was launched in 1974, the political field was centered on the democratically elected National Assembly and did not include military or bureaucratic elite, who had for various historical reasons stepped away from claims to state power at this time (Alavi, 1983, p. 76; Ziring, 1980, p. 105). This Assembly contained a broad spectrum of political parties and ideological positions. The ruling party was the PPP that held around 60% of the seats. The various Islamist parties in the opposition together held around 12% of the seats. The main opposition was formed by an alliance between NAP and the Islamist party *Jamiat-ul-Ulema-e-Islam* (JUI) with NAP's leader Wali Khan elected as the leader of the opposition.

The reconfiguration of the political field through the entry of elected political parties, including Islamist parties committed to the game of electoral politics, redefined practical politics in the political field. One of the most salient features of this changed political field was the acceptance of the symbolic relevance of "Islam." The loss of Bangladesh was a significant intervening event in legitimating Islam *in its nominal capacity* within the political field in the 1970s. It posed the fundamental question about whether a common Islamic identity could transcend provincial and ethnic identities. Furthermore, with the break-up of Pakistan, both Bangladesh and India had a greater number of Muslims within their individual territories than Pakistan. One scholar observes that "now that Pakistan ... [was] no more the 'national homeland' for all, or even most, Muslims of the subcontinent, its raison d'etre must be that it is the home of the good Muslims" (Ahmad, 1983, p. 116). Thus, Islam was to continue to provide a "centralizing ideology" through playing a more prominent role in the state. This is reflected in the Constitution of 1973 in which Islam was declared the "state religion." While no legislative measures were taken, the fact that Islam had to be increasingly referenced to make claims to political authority meant that the political field was ripe for exercise of agency that could push Islam from having a nominal to an institutional role. The first manifestation of this shift was the enactment of a constitutional amendment rendering Ahmadis a non-Muslim minority to which I turn next.

THE POLITICS OF EXCLUSION OF AHMADIS

The Anti-Ahmadiyya Movement

The "Ahmadi question" emerged on the national scene in 1974 following a scuffle between non-Ahmadi and Ahmadi students in the city of Rabwah, a predominantly Ahmadi town. According to popular newspaper accounts, the Ahmadi "crowd" was armed with sticks, knives, and swords, and proceeded to attack and beat the "Muslim" students, injuring 30 in the process. The state immediately appointed a High Court judge, K. M. A. Samdani, to investigate the incident and submit his findings, thus instituting what is popularly termed the "Rabwah Tribunal." It was subsequently determined by this Tribunal that claims of violent beatings of non-Ahmadi students by Ahmadi students were wildly exaggerated and mostly inaccurate.[12] However, the immediate response to the incident was that acts of violence against the Ahmadis started (*Dawn*, Karachi, June 23, 1974). While these were curbed by the state within a week, a nation-wide movement spearheaded by religious groups was launched that advocated the social boycotting of Ahmadis and demanded that the state declare Ahmadis non-Muslim. A minor skirmish thereby provided a political opening that was seized upon by religious leaders to relaunch an anti-Ahmadi movement.

While initially silent on the question of the religious status of Ahmadis, prominent leaders of PPP including Bhutto publicly declared their faith in the doctrine of the finality of Prophethood and affirmed the Islamic identity of Pakistan. In a speech in the National Assembly, Bhutto referred to the Ahmadi issue as a "problem" that dated back to 1953 but noted that the categories of minorities had been defined in the 1973 constitution and that no party or individual had raised the issue of the minority status of Ahmadis at that point. Bhutto concluded that the Ahmadi issue was being used by his political opponents to ignite trouble and weaken Pakistan. The government, he declared, "had no vested interest in the problem," was taking a "rational view" and "trying to apply universal morality to the issue" (*Dawn*, Karachi, June 4, 1974). Soon thereafter, however, Bhutto announced that the Ahmadi issue would be placed before the National Assembly for deliberation.

In order to understand the shift in Bhutto's inclinations, we must examine the framing strategies of the religious movement in 1974. First, this movement was national in scope and included a wide array of social and political actors including Islamist parties in the National Assembly, student unions, trade unions, *petit-ulema* in local mosques across the country who sent in petitions to national newspapers to express support with the movement, *Aalmi Majlis Tahaffuz Khatm-e-Nubuwwat* ("International Association for the Protection of the Finality of Prophethood," henceforth MTKN) and prominent political leaders. Furthermore, some of these groups had been dedicated to the movement goals even prior to the Rabwah incident. For example, MTKN was formed in 1949 as a religious platform for those members of the *Ahrar* who sought to undertake the anti-Ahmadi "cause" but in the capacity of their religious and not political identities.[13] The emphasis on the religious/political dichotomy is meant to underscore the purity of the religiously motivated individual in contrast to the conniving of the politically motivated individual. Even before 1974, prominent members and supporters of MTKN propagated anti-Ahmadi rhetoric through print media. For example, Agha Shorash Kashmiri, a highly prominent Urdu journalist and *Ahrar* member used his weekly Urdu magazine *Chattan* as a vehicle for keeping the anti-Ahmadi movement alive. While the first anti-Ahmadi movement had utilized public meetings and fiery orators to incite orthodox Muslims against Ahmadis and draw the attention of politicians, the refashioned MTKN confined its violence to the print media, carefully skirting the thin line between freedom of speech and hate speech.[14]

Second, the country was gripped in anti-Ahmadi fervor and the pressure on the state to act according to "popular" demand was intense. Anti-Ahmadi demands were couched within public narratives about the state's responsibility toward Islam. For example, an editorial referred to Bhutto not only as a politician but also as a "religious representative" (*Nawa-e-Waqt*, Lahore, June 14, 1974). The celebrated journalist Z. A. Suleri celebrated the Rabwah incident as "a blessing in disguise" for throwing into "bold relief the truly religious character of Pakistani society" (*Nawa-e-Waqt*, Lahore, June 23, 1974). Furthermore, the demands were couched within rhetoric of democracy, with various organizations, opposition members, and newspapers demanding that the state act in a democratic manner. An editorial in *Dawn* argued that the Islamist opposition in the National Assembly was within its democratic right to express dissent and canvass popular support for its demands (*Dawn*, Karachi, June 7, 1974).

Third, the state response in 1954 was cited as an instance of state repression (Saeed, 2007). As anti-Ahmadi agitation continued to grow in 1974, Bhutto was confronted with a choice: revert to the historical precedent of cracking down on religious movement to thwart anti-Ahmadi demands, or to engage somehow with the demands. Certainly, Bhutto routinely engaged in highly draconian measures to repress oppositional movements.

For example in 1973, Bhutto carried out an extremely violent military operation in the province of Baluchistan to curb a movement demanding greater regional autonomy (Jaffrelot, 2002, pp. 28–32). Subsequently in 1975, Bhutto would dissolve NAP and arrest Wali Khan. During this time, Bhutto cracked down not only on regional movements but also on labor movements (Ali, 2010), and his particularly feudalistic modes of torturing and humiliating opposition are well documented (e.g., Burki, 1988; Wolpert, 1993).

However, suppression of the anti-Ahmadi movement was not undertaken as a matter of considered policy toward religion. First, the PPP had aligned itself with popular religious sentiments through its discourse of Islamic socialism. It was precisely because Bhutto combined authoritarianism with religious populism that his regime defies the democracy/authoritarian distinction. While nominal, this identification with Islam was symbolically potent, circumscribing the range of actions available to Bhutto. More significantly, Bhutto came to dominance in the political field through a populist mode of electoral campaign that was novel in Pakistani politics. Bhutto emerged as a charismatic leader through "a folksy and colorful campaign" in which large portraits of Bhutto, Bhutto's performative theatrics during public rallies (such as passionate shouting accompanied with rolling up his sleeves, opening his shirt front), catchy slogans centered on Bhutto ("Our Bhutto is truly a lion while the others are merely devious"), etc., were the norm (Syed, 1992, pp. 68–79). This extreme self-posturing as a man of the people meant that while Bhutto could take radical steps to repress political opponents, he was compelled to engage with a truly nation-wide religious movement making demands on his government.

According to Sahabzada Farooq Ali, the Speaker of National Assembly in 1974, Bhutto had received a lot of support from the Ahmadis during his election campaign of 1970 and enjoyed close ties with several Ahmadis.[15] Farooq Ali also had close ties with the Ahmadis that had organically emerged over time because of a huge presence of Ahmadis in his electoral constituencies of cities of Sialkot and Gujarat. However, for both Bhutto and himself, the core issue was not one of religion but of a popular demand that had to be met. Similarly, Raja Tridev Roy, the Minister of Minority Affairs and Tourism at that time, maintains that Bhutto's acquiescence on the Ahmadi issue was not reflective of Bhutto's personal views or wishes but arose from "a misplaced sense of self-preservation" and as a means to neutralize the Islamic rhetoric of opposition parties.[16]

The particular frames adopted by the anti-Ahmadi religious movement and the mutual legibility between these frames and Bhutto's nationalist discourses led to the issue of the religious status of Ahmadis being placed before the National Assembly. A motion passed by the Law Minister Abdul Hafeez Pirzada "to discuss the question of the status in Islam of persons who do not believe in the finality of Prophethood of Mohammad" was adopted in the hope to arrive at "an effective, just and final solution" (National Assembly of Pakistan Debates (henceforth NAPD), June 30, 1974, pp. 1302–1303). The National Assembly was subsequently converted into a Special Committee to debate the religious status of Ahmadis. Bhutto himself employed discursive frames of democracy and Muslim nationalism to laud the Amendment. In his speech in the National Assembly on the day the Amendment was passed, Bhutto maintained that the resolution of the Ahmadi question was fundamentally a religious issue that required a "genuine resolution" because

> Pakistan came into creation for the Muslims to have a homeland; and if a decision is taken which the body of Muslims in this country feel to be against the tenets of the fundamental beliefs of Islam, it would dangerously affect the rationale and raison d'etre of Pakistan. (NAPD, September 7, 1974, p. 566)

Bhutto hailed the decision as one of democratic triumph, maintaining that the decision could not have been taken "without democratic institutions." The editorial of the English daily *Dawn* echoed this sentiment:

> The manner in which the decision was taken augers well for the growth of democracy in the country. Constitutionality is the breath of life in a democracy. The same decision coming as an official decree would not have meant the same thing. (*Dawn*, Karachi, September 10, 1974)

Thus "democracy" and a Muslim nationalist discourse formed the central symbolic contours of the political debate on the religious status of the Ahmadis in 1974. It is within this symbolic terrain that Members of National Assembly (MNAs) engaged with the issue of the religious status of Ahmadis. Next, I analyze the habitus of these actors that led to the nationalist policy of exclusion of Ahmadis.

Habitus of Political Actors and the Exclusion of Ahmadis

During the proceedings in the National Assembly, the Ahmadi leadership was invited to present their views and to answer questions posed by MNAs. The crucial issue at this moment was not the definition of a Muslim but the specific issue of whether the Ahmadis were Muslim according to an accepted definition of a non-Muslim as any person who does not believe in the unqualified finality of prophethood in the person of Prophet Mohammad. Pamphlets and books were distributed by Islamist parties in the National Assembly to give an "authentic" description of the Ahmadiyya community's "political history" (a creation of the British colonial state "to disintegrate the unity of the Muslims"); religious precepts (false and doubly dangerous because they are presented as true Islam); social organization (self-separatist), its political ambitions (take over Pakistan); and its practices as citizens (disloyal and traitorous toward Pakistan) (Usmani, 1977, p. 125). However, as noted above, such discourses were not novel and had been disseminated widely during the first anti-Ahmadi movement as well. The crucial difference however was that in 1974 these were aligned with democratic procedures, thereby finding legitimacy within the political field at large.

During the proceedings, Ahmadi representatives were asked if they regarded non-Ahmadis as non-Muslims. Ghafoor Ahmed, an MNA belonging to JI, maintains that the response of the Ahmadis was an unequivocal yes, which had the effect of angering even the more secularly inclined MNAs who had been wary of the Ahmadi issue being brought to the National Assembly.[17] According to Sherbaz Mazari, an independent MNA, Ahmadi leaders in the National Assembly said "extremely provocative" things and that perhaps if they had been more tactful, some people might have felt differently about the proposed Amendment.[18] Another MNA Gul Aurangzeb maintains that during the course of the inquiry, Ahmadi representatives maintained that the founder of the community and his descendants were incapable of any physical ailment, thus portraying their leaders as superhuman. This irked MNAs antagonistic toward Ahmadiyya religious beliefs.[19] Sahabzada Farooq Ali maintains that the Ahmad representatives referred to Ahmadis as "the truly faithful and true ones" and to non-Ahmadis as Muslims who were *gumrah*, or deviants from the true path.

Additionally, there were a number of factors that delimited the autonomy MNAs had about voting for the Amendment. Before the proceedings began, Bhutto publicly declared that MNAs would enjoy complete freedom to vote for or against the Constitutional Amendment as they saw fit (*Dawn*, Karachi, June 14, 1974). Personal interviews conducted with a number of MNAs contradict this. They also suggest other opportunities and constraints perceived by MNAs. Together, these varied stories reveal a significantly transformed political field and a concomitant and gradual shift in the *doxa* of the political field in Pakistan. I characterize this shift as the acceptance of a new rule that popular religious sentiments cannot be legitimately marginalized by any section of the political elite.

Gul Aurangzeb, an MNA belonging to Muslim League (Qayyum), was given the directive by his Party Head to vote against the Ahmadis as Bhutto wanted the Amendment to go through in order to gain popularity among the people. According to Aurangzeb, "We, the members of ML (Q) were sold by Qayyum *Sahib* [Mr. Qayyum] to Bhutto." Furthermore, he held, "In the parliament there was no question of anybody opposing Bhutto's orders and nobody was willing to face the public outside." Aurangzeb proceeded to tell me of the difficulties he would have faced from the electorate when he would have returned from the capital to his home constituency of Swat, an increasingly Islamicized area in the northern areas of Pakistan. According to Aurangzeb, "In my country if you do not agree with the mobs, you are declared a traitor." He added that if he had a free choice, he would have abstained from voting. A very similar story was related to me by another MNA Sherbaz Mazari, an Independent in the 1974 Assembly. With misting eyes, Mazari told me that he had erred in not taking a stance at that moment and that he had voted with the crowd in fear of Bhutto. According to Mazari, MNAs from Islamist parties and Bhutto himself personally approached and asked him to vote for the Amendment.

Other MNAs had other motivations. Ahmad Raza Kasuri, an Independent and an ardent critic of Bhutto both inside and outside the Assembly, was the first MNA to raise the Ahmadi issue in the National Assembly immediately in the aftermath of the May 29 events.[20] He had had a two-fold motivation for raising the Ahmadi issue in the National Assembly: one, to put political pressure on Bhutto, and second, because of his personal religious convictions about Ahmadiyya faith, which he regards as heretical. For Kasuri, the defining feature of a Muslim is the love and affection they have for Prophet Mohammad. Because Islam is the official religion of Pakistan, it was wholly lawful to make this definition legal and thereby exclude Ahmadis.

If Kasuri was unambiguous about the primacy of religion in justifying the Amendment, others such as Justice Samdani, head of the Rabwah Tribunal, were conflicted about making religion central to public, political life. On the one hand, Samdani clearly referred to the Second Constitutional Amendment as akin to "persecution" of a vulnerable minority. Equally unambiguously, Samdani acknowledged the centrality of *fiqh* (Islamic jurisprudence) traditions[21] that are intolerant toward heresy and apostasy and render non-Muslims as second-class citizens. Yet at the same time Samdani argued that he was in favor of a "true Islamic state" based on principles of justice and equality. However, because of the impossibility of realizing such a state, he was "in favor of secularism." In other words, for Samdani, the egalitarian ethos of Islam stood in opposition to socially constructed *fiqh* norms that punish apostasy. Even in Samdani's rejection of an "Islamic state," the perfection of such a state was affirmed.

Raja Tridev Roy, a Buddhist hailing from Chittagong Hill Tracks in Bangladesh was the Minister of Minority Affairs at the time. He maintains that he was personally not in favor of the Amendment but as a non-Muslim felt that "this is a matter of theology and dictation of Islam and ... beyond my ability and my responsibility." That Roy felt that his religious status excluded his voice in the national debate on the religious status of Ahmadis itself points to a fundamental transformation of the political field, especially when we recall the role played by non-Muslims members of the Constituent Assembly during debates on the Objectives Resolution in 1949.

Ghafoor Ahmad, an MNA belonging to JI, voted autonomously and consistently with JI's political project of Islamic constitutionalism within a democratic framework. He maintains that he voted for the Amendment on the basis of his religious beliefs and because the 1973 Constitution declared Islam the state religion of Pakistan. According to Ahmad, it is of utmost importance to determine who is and is not a Muslim since only a Muslim can be the Head of an Islamic State.

In short, the above interviews suggest a radically different habitus of the political field than that of the bureaucratic elite in the 1950s. My analysis reveals a multiplicity of dispositions about democracy, nationalism, and religion, all of which together cohered to produce the nationalist policy of exclusion of Ahmadis. Bourdieu has aptly used the notions of signifier and signified to capture the particular force through which groups are formed in a democratic system: the delegate serves as a signifier that signifies to the group that it exists, and the act of delegation enables an act of political transcendence whereby "what was merely a collection of several persons" emerges as "a social body" (Bourdieu, 1991, p. 208). The year 1974 constituted just such a moment in which the delegate and the delegated referenced each other within an authoritarian-populist regime to reconstitute the symbolic boundaries of the nation through the exclusion of Ahmadis from the body politic.

CONCLUSIONS

This paper has argued that the Pakistani state's shift from the accommodation to exclusion of Ahmadis was contingent on struggles for political and symbolic power within historically specific political fields. In 1953, the anti-Ahmadi movement played right into the dynamics of intrastate competition for state power among bureaucrats and politicians. The movement eventually became the means for the institutionalization of the authoritarian military regime of Ayub Khan. The nationalist policy of accommodation of Ahmadis in 1953 was constituted through this political trajectory, with the anti-Ahmadi and anti-state framing strategies employed by the religious movement providing further ammunition. In 1974 however, the demand that the Ahmadis be declared a non-Muslim minority was framed as democratic and nationalist. This narrative was accepted by Bhutto and MNAs to acquire symbolic capital, and because of the imperatives of electoral politics and the salience of Muslim politics in the political field. The transformation of the political field that I have analyzed attests to the ways in which religious actors refashioned themselves across the two moments through becoming central players in electoral politics, denouncing violence, and aligning their movement frames with democracy and a Muslim nationalist discourse.

The usefulness of the concept of political field lies precisely in the way it alerts us that "political ideologies do not simply 'reflect' the social bases of political action – if anything, the opposite is true: political struggle is precisely a fight over the capacity to impose a legitimate vision of social space and its relation to the political field, i.e., to convert political capital (control over the instruments of political representation) into symbolic power (the prestige of being the effective 'delegate' of a social group" (De Leon, Desai, & Tugal, 2009; Eyal, 2005, p. 153). Both moments of accommodation and exclusion of Ahmadis depict that citizenship classifications are a function of interactive politics in which religious and political signifiers are contested and strategically deployed to constitute political practices. Furthermore, the framework of political fields that I have employed depicts that these practices were a product of the relation between the habitus of political actors and the historically specific political fields in which they were embedded. Political dispositions structured practices of nationalist policy formation through historically concrete political and symbolic struggles, in turn producing nationalist policies that were strategic and contingent.

In conclusion, the present paper offers following directions for future research. First, it provides an opportunity to enhance our understandings of politics in Muslim societies through its examination of state–religious movement interactions undertaken through a comparative/historical analysis of two outcomes in a single national case. Second, insights from this paper are relevant for scholars of nationalism interested in the nation/ religion/state nexus. The present analysis of nationalist shifts within the single case of Pakistan clearly shows that boundaries of signifiers of the nation such as religion are fluid and open to multiple and contested definitions. Finally, one of the central concerns occupying many analysts (e.g., Casanova, 1994; Hefner, 2001; Kymlicka, 1985) is the fate of national minorities in political orders that may be procedurally democratic yet pave the way for majority groups to strip minorities of their social and political rights. By looking at a similar transition in Pakistan, the findings of this paper can be used to theorize the dangers of majoratarian democracy in contexts where constitutions are stripped of liberal rights and made subservient to popular will.

NOTES

1. The term *ulema* refers to traditional Muslim authorities trained in Islamic jurisprudence.
2. I define nationalist policy as the set of institutional practices through which states attempt to normalize particular nationalist discourses by reifying specific practical categories of classification.
3. Political sociologists have increasingly begun to highlight the relevance of Bourdieu's sociology for exploring political processes through which classifications among citizens (or subjects) are managed (e.g., Eyal, 2005; Go, 2008; Ray, 1999; Steinmetz, 2007, 2008; Wacquant, 2005).
4. For example, the military regime of Ayub Khan (1958–1969), Zia-ul-Haq (1977–1988), and Pervez Musharraf (1999–2008).
5. http://www.statpak.gov.pk/depts/pco/statistics/other_tables/pop_by_religion.pdf. Accessed on July 26, 2010. Personal interviews reveal that Ahmadis consider their numbers significantly underrepresented by the Government.
6. The 1984 Ordinance has led to a huge number of Ahmadis being charged and punished on grounds of defiling Islam, blasphemy, and similar charges. A number of international and local NGOs (including Human Rights Watch, Amnesty International, and the Human Rights Commission of Pakistan) and the Ahmadi-run website http://www.thepersecuton.org routinely document instances of human rights abuses.
7. *Shari'a* refers to the law of Islam, which has roots in Qur'an and in accounts of the life of the Prophet Mohammad.
8. Although *ulema* and Islamists oftentimes overlap in religious ideology, the two groups constitute distinct religious groups. In general, *ulema* are trained in traditional sites of learning, or *madrassas*, where they receive instruction through a study of foundational religious texts on *fiqh* (Islamic jurisprudence) in addition to Quran and *Sunnah* (sayings and habits of Prophet Mohammad) (Zaman, 2002). For *ulema*, traditional religious learning and personal conduct are the central modes through which a Muslim religious identity is realized and perfected. Islamists differ markedly in their political orientations in that while wedded to the same sources of

religious learning as the *ulema*, they seek to restore the primacy of Islamic norms through applying them to contemporary social and political realities. Hence, while the *ulema* may be politically indifferent, Islamists are "explicitly and intentionally political" (Euben & Zaman, 2009, p. 4).

9. The first draft, presented in 1950, was severely criticized across Pakistan, but particularly in East Pakistan, for reducing the numerical majority of East Pakistan in the legislature by giving East Pakistan the same representation as the four provinces of West Pakistan. In response to the outcry, it was decided that suggestions and proposals would be solicited from the public until January 1951, after which a second draft would be prepared and submitted.

10. *The Federation of Pakistan v. Moulvi Tamizuddin Khan*. PLD 1955 Federal Court 240.

11. Some of the changes included state permission for Muslim men to undertake more than one marriage, changes in divorce laws as a result of which men could not divorce women arbitrarily, and increase in the legal age at which girls could marry from 14 to 16 (Ansari, 2009).

12. Interview with K. M. A. Samdani. Islamabad, Pakistan, January 30, 2008.

13. My discussion of MTKN draws from personal interview conducted with Maulana Allah Wasaya, presently belonging to the top leadership of the MTKN. Islamabad, Pakistan, March 5, 2008.

14. For example, *Chattan* was banned by Punjab provincial authorities in 1968 because of the intensity of its anti-Ahmadi rhetoric. *Abdul Karim Shorish Kashmiri v. The State of West Pakistan*. PLD 1969 Lahore 289.

15. Interview with Sahabzada Farooq Ali. Multan, Pakistan, April 8, 2008.

16. Interview with Raja Tridev Roy. Islamabad, Pakistan, April 4, 2008.

17. Interview with Ghafoor Ahmad. Karachi, Pakistan, March 8, 2008.

18. Interview with Sherbaz Mazari. Karachi, Pakistan, March 9, 2008.

19. Interview with Gul Aurangzeb. Islamabad, Pakistan, March 4, 2008.

20. Interview with Ahmad Raza Kasuri. Islamabad, Pakistan, January 30, 2008.

21. See Friedmann (2003) for a discussion of heresy in Islamic history.

ACKNOWLEDGMENTS

An earlier version of this paper was presented at the Annual Meeting of the American Sociological Association in 2011. I would like to thank Julia Adams, Avi Astor, Baris Buyukokutan, Fatma Muge Gocek, Ho-fung Hung, Robert Jansen, Howard Kimeldorf, Charles Kurzman, Patricia McManus, Rob Robinson, George Steinmetz, Nick Wilson, Akbar Zaidi, three anonymous reviewers, and Julian Go for their helpful comments, questions, and suggestions. Thanks are also due to the participants of: Power, History and Social Change Workshop at the Department of Sociology at the University of Michigan; Politics, Economy and Culture Workshop at the Department of Sociology at Indiana University, Bloomington; and

Comparative Research Workshop at the Department of Sociology at Yale University.

REFERENCES

Abrams, P. (1988). Notes on the difficulty of studying the state. *Journal of Historical Sociology*, *1*(1), 58–89.
Ahmad, A. (1983). Democracy and dictatorship. In H. Gardezi & J. Rashid (Eds.), *Pakistan: The roots of dictatorship* (pp. 40–85). London: Zed Press.
Alavi, H. (1972). The state in post-colonial societies: Pakistan and Bangladesh. *New Left Review*, *I*(74), 59–81.
Alavi, H. (1983). Class and state. In H. Gardezi & J. Rashid (Eds.), *Pakistan: The roots of dictatorship* (pp. 40–93). London: Zed Press.
Ali, K. A. (2010). Strength of the state meets the strength of the street: The 1972 Labour Struggle in Karachi. In N. Khan (Ed.), *Beyond crisis: Re-evaluating Pakistan*. London: Routledge.
Anderson, B. (1991). *Imagined communities: Reflections on the origins and spread of nationalism*. London: Verso.
Ansari, S. (2009). Polygamy, Purdah and political representation: Engendering citizenship in 1950s Pakistan. *Modern Asian Studies*, *43*(6), 1421–1461.
Baxter, C. (1997). *Bangladesh: From a nation to a state*. Boulder, CO: Westview Press.
Bayat, A. (2007). *Making Islam democratic: Social movements and the Post-Islamic turn*. Stanford, CA: Stanford University Press.
Binder, L. (1961). *Religion and politics in Pakistan*. Berkeley, CA: University of California Press.
Bourdieu, P. (1985). Social space and the genesis of groups. *Theory and Society*, *14*(6), 723–744.
Bourdieu, P. (1990). *The logic of practice*. Palo Alto, CA: Stanford University Press.
Bourdieu, P. (1991). *Language and symbolic power*. Cambridge, MA: Harvard University Press.
Bourdieu, P. (1993a). *Sociology in question* (R. Nice, Trans.). Thousand Oaks, CA: Sage.
Bourdieu, P. (1993b). *The field of cultural production*. New York, NY: Columbia University Press.
Bourdieu, P. (1999). Rethinking the state: Genesis and structure of the bureaucratic field. In G. Steinmetz (Ed.), *State/culture: State formation after the cultural turn* (pp. 53–75). Ithaca, NY: Cornell University Press.
Bourdieu, P., & Wacquant, L. J. D. (1992). *An invitation to reflexive sociology*. Chicago, IL: The University of Chicago Press.
Brubaker, R. (2002). Ethnicity without groups. *European Journal of Sociology*, *43*(2), 163–189.
Brubaker, R. (2004). Rethinking nationhood: Nation as institutionalized form, practical category, contingent event. *Contention*, *4*(1), 3–14.
Burki, S. J. (1988). *Pakistan under Bhutto, 1971–1977*. London: Macmillan.
Casanova, J. (1994). *Public religions in the modern world*. The University of Chicago Press.
Chatterjee, P. (1993). *The nation and its fragments: Colonial and postcolonial histories*. Princeton, NJ: Princeton University Press.
Constituent Assembly of Pakistan Debates. (1947). Karachi: Government of Pakistan Press.
Constituent Assembly of Pakistan Debates. (1949). Karachi: Government of Pakistan Press.
Corrigan, P., & Sayer, D. (1985). *The Great Arch: English state formation as cultural revolution*. Oxford: Blackwell.

Davis, N. J., & Robinson, R. V. (2009). Overcoming movement obstacles by the religious orthodoxy: The Muslim brotherhood in Egypt, Shas in Israel, Comunione e Liberazione in Italy and the Salvation Army in the United States. *American Journal of Sociology*, *114*(5), 1302–1349.

De Leon, C., Desai, M., & Tugal, C. (2009). Political articulation: Parties and the constitution of cleavages in the United States, India, and Turkey. *Sociological Theory*, *27*, 193–219.

Eickelman, D., & Piscatori, J. (1996). *Muslim politics*. Princeton, NJ: Princeton University Press.

Euben, R. L., & Zaman, M. Q. (Eds.). (2009). *Princeton readings in Islamist thought: Texts and contexts from al-Banna to Bin*. Princeton University Press.

Eyal, G. (2005). The making and breaking of the Czechoslovak political field. In L. Wacquant (Ed.), *Pierre Bourdieu and democratic politics*. Polity Press.

Friedmann, Y. (1989). *Prophecy continuous: Aspects of Ahmadi religious thought and its medieval background*. Berkeley, CA: University of California Press.

Friedmann, Y. (2003). *Tolerance and coercion in Islam: Interfaith relations in the Muslim tradition*. Cambridge University Press.

Fuller, G. (2003). *The future of political Islam*. New York, NY: MacMillan.

Go, J. (2008). Global fields and imperial forms: Field theory and the US and British empires. *Sociological Theory*, *26*(3), 201–229.

Hansen, T. B., & Stepputat, F. (Eds.). (2001). *States of imagination. Ethnographic explorations of the postcolonial state*. Durham, NC: Duke University Press.

Hashmi, B. (1983). Dragon seed: Military in the state. In H. Gardezi & J. Rashid (Eds.), *Pakistan: The roots of dictatorship*. London: Zed Press.

Haydu, J. (2010). Reversals of fortune: Path dependency, problem solving, and temporal cases. *Theory and Society*, *39*(1), 25–48.

Hefner, R. F. (2001). Public Islam and the problem of democratization. *Sociology of Religion*, *62*(4), 491–514.

Hyat Khan, S. S. (1995). *The nation that lost its soul*. Lahore: Jang Publishers.

Jaffrelot, C. (2002). *A history of Pakistan and its origins*. London: Anthem Press.

Jalal, A. (1991). *The state of martial rule: The origins of Pakistan's political economy of defence*. Lahore: Vanguard.

Jalal, A. (2000). *Self and sovereignty: Individual and community in South Asian Islam since 1850*. Routledge.

Kauppi, N. (2003). Bourdieu's political sociology and the politics of European integration. *Theory and Society*, *32*, 775–789.

Kaushik, S. N. (1996). *Ahmadiya community in Pakistan: Discrimination, travail and alienation*. New Delhi: South Asia Publishers.

Khan, H. (2005). *Constitutional and political history of Pakistan*. Karachi: Oxford University Press.

Khan, M. A. (1967). *Friends not masters: A political autobiography*. London: Oxford University Press.

King, A. (2000). Thinking with Bourdieu against Bourdieu: A 'practical' critique of the Habitus. *Sociological Theory*, *18*(3), 417–433.

Kymlicka, W. (1985). *Multicultural citizenship: A liberal theory of minority rights*. Oxford: Oxford University Press.

Lahore High Court. (1954) *Report of the Court of Inquiry constituted under Punjab Act II of 1954 to enquire into the Punjab disturbances of 1953*. Superintendent, Government Printing, Lahore.

Lau, M. (2006). *The role of Islam in the legal system of Pakistan*. Leiden, The Netherlands: Martinus Nijhoff Publishers.
Lavan, S. (1973). *The Ahmadiyah Movement: A history and perspective*. Delhi: Manohar Book Service.
Loveman, M. (2005). The modern state and the primitive accumulation of symbolic power. *American Journal of Sociology, 110*(6), 1651–1683.
Mahmood, S. (2005). *Politics of Piety: The Islamic revival and the feminist subject*. Princeton University Press.
Mamdani, M. (1996). *Citizen and subject: Contemporary Africa and the legacy of Late Colonialism*. Princeton, NJ: Princeton University Press.
Maududi, S. A. (1953). *The Qadiani problem*. Lahore: Islamic Publications Ltd.
Maududi, S. A. (1980). *Islamic law and constitution*. Lahore: Islamic Publications Ltd.
McAdam, D., Tarrow, S., & Tilly, C. (2001). *Dynamics of contention*. Cambridge: Cambridge University Press.
McGrath, A. (1996). *The destruction of Pakistan's democracy*. Karachi: Oxford University Press.
Migdal, J. (2001). *State in society: Studying how status and societies transform and constitute one another*. Cambridge: Cambridge University Press.
Nasr, V. (1994). *The vanguard of the Islamic revolution: The Jama'at-i Islami of Pakistan*. The University of California Press.
National Assembly of Pakistan Debates. (1974). *Islamabad*. Government of Pakistan Press.
Ray, R. (1999). *Fields of protest: Women's movement in India*. University of Minnesota Press.
Saeed, S. (2007). Pakistani nationalism and the state marginalization of Ahmadiyya community in Pakistan. *Studies in Ethnicity and Nationalism, 7*(3), 132–152.
Sewell, W. H. (2005). *Logics of history: Social theory and social transformation*. The University of Chicago Press.
Snow, D. A., & Byrd, S. C. (2007). Ideology, framing processes, and Islamic terrorist movements. *Mobilization, 12*(2), 119–136.
Snow, D. A., Rochford, E. B., Jr., Worden, S. K., & Benford, R. D. (1986). Frame alignment processes, micromobilization, and movement participation. *American Sociological Review, 51*, 464–481.
Steinmetz, G. (2007). *The Devil's handwriting: Precoloniality and the German Colonial State in Qingdao, Samoa, and Southwest Africa*. The University of Chicago Press.
Steinmetz, G. (2008). The colonial state as a social field: Ethnographic capital and native policy in the German Overseas Empire before 1914. *American Sociological Review, 73*, 589–612.
Syed, A. K. (1992). *The discourse and politics of Zulfikar Ali Bhutto*. New York, NY: St. Martin's Press.
Talbot, I. (1998). *Pakistan, a modern history*. New York, NY: St. Martin's Press.
Toor, S. (2011). *The state of Islam: Culture and cold war politics in Pakistan*. London: Pluto Press.
Tugal, C. (2009). Transforming everyday life: Islamism and social movement theory. *Theory and Society, 38*(5), 423–458.
Usmani, M. T. (1977). *Qadianism on Trail: The case of the Muslim Ummah against Qadianis presented before the National Assembly of Pakistan* (Mohammad Wali Ra'zi, Trans.). Karachi: Maktaba Darul Uloom.
Wacquant, L. (2005). *Pierre Bourdieu and democratic politics: The mystery of ministry*. Polity Press.

Wedeen, L. (1999). *Ambiguities of domination: Politics, rhetoric, and symbols in contemporary Syria*. University of Chicago Press.
Wickham, C. R. (2002). *Mobilizing Islam: Religion, activism, and political change in Egypt*. New York, NY: Columbia University Press.
Wiktorowicz, Q. (Ed.). (2004). *Islamic activism: A social movement theory approach*. Bloomington, IN: Indiana University Press.
Wolpert, S. (1993). *Zulfi Bhutto of Pakistan: His life and times*. New York, NY: Oxford University Press.
Zaman, M. Q. (2002). *The Ulama in contemporary Islam: Custodians of change*. Princeton, NJ: Princeton University Press.
Ziring, L. (1980). *Pakistan: Enigma of political development*. Boulder, CO: Westview Press.
Zubrzycki, G. (2006). *The crosses of Auschwitz: Nationalism and religion in post-communist Poland*. Chicago, IL: University of Chicago Press.

RACIALIZED CLASS FORMATION: BLACKS IN THE PROFESSIONAL MIDDLE CLASS IN THE POST-CIVIL RIGHTS ERA

Eric S. Brown

ABSTRACT

Racialized class formation is a process in which both racial formation and class formation shape the experiences of African Americans in the stratification system. This occurs for blacks in differing social classes. However, this chapter focuses on African Americans in the professional middle class. The professional middle class as a whole has grown substantially under postindustrialism. Racialized class formation has been greatly shaped by the nature of state policy regarding citizenship rights and has varied in the transition from the pre-civil rights era to the post-civil rights era. This chapter utilizes historical, interview, and secondary data to analyze experiences of the "first generation" of black professionals to integrate employment in mainstream institutions after the Civil Rights Act of 1964. The focus is on the processes of recruitment, hiring, and promotion, as well as relations with clientele among those black professionals and how their middle class employment experiences are racialized.

INTRODUCTION

William Julius Wilson's *Declining Significance of Race* is a seminal work on the contemporary black middle class – setting the parameters of academic and policy debates – despite the fact that it is only indirectly about the black middle class (Fainstein, 1993). Rather, Wilson's real scholarly and policy interests lie with the difficult conditions faced by the black urban poor (Wilson, 1987, 1996). In many ways the black middle class is merely a backdrop for the "underclass" debate that he became deeply embroiled in (Gans, 1996).

Wilson actually expands on the prior work of Moynihan (1972) and Freeman (1976) in building a class-based argument about racial inequality. Moynihan of course was on the academic and political front lines battling race-based arguments during the 1960s and 1970s. Wilson goes further than his predecessors by proposing a powerful thesis about the increasing importance of class *supplanting* race in the life chances of African Americans since the civil rights era. For this reason, I term the theoretical approach that Wilson champions *class-determined racial inequality* theory. His work (following Moynihan) begins largely as an argument with 1970s-era scholars and activists, working within black-nationalist and internal colonial frameworks, who gave primacy to race-based factors.[1] It is in this context that Wilson came to see class and race as increasingly oppositional constructs. In actuality, his work focuses on groups that are identified and structured by *both* race and class characteristics: the black middle class and the black urban poor.

The class-determined approach became a meteoric paradigm in the 1980s that sharply shifted discussion of racial inequality to the "underclass" debate and away from the black middle class (Fainstein, 1993; Patillo-McCoy, 1999, pp. 13–30; Steinberg, 1995, pp. 137–155). Consequently, the class-determined approach is not represented by a demonstrable number of empirical studies of the status of the black middle class – particularly the kinds of monograph length works that extend findings and theory. Nevertheless, it remains the sociological benchmark when it comes to analyses of the black middle class. However, a number of anomalies have been explored by researchers looking at least in part at the status of the black middle class, which illustrate the complex relationship between race and class and challenge basic assumptions of the Wilson paradigm. While the fortunes of the black middle class and the black urban poor have unquestionably diverged, even *before* the civil rights era, middle class life chances still vary along racial lines for blacks and whites. This can be found in patterns of residential segregation (Fainstein, 1993; Massey & Denton, 1993), wealth accumulation (Conley, 1999; Oliver & Shapiro, 2006; Shapiro, 2004), employment discrimination (Collins, 1997; Feagin & Sikes, 1994; Reskin, McBrier, & Kmec, 1999), and patterns of white privilege in general (Bonilla-Silva, 2006; Brown et al., 2003).

This chapter will respond to the recent literature on the black middle class, as well as the assumptions of the Moynihan–Wilson thesis. One problem is the vagueness of what – or who – comprises the black middle class. Many studies have overstated the parameters and size of the African American middle class. Nevertheless, this chapter will not seek to provide a holistic definition or analysis of the black middle class(es). That is a task beyond the scope of this chapter. Rather, I want to focus on a segment of the black middle class(es) that is clearly "middle class" and provides a useful empirical and theoretical analysis of the status of that group: professionals Most studies of the black middle class focus more on segments of the "lower middle" class and do not focus on professionals. What can we learn about the black middle classes from examining the experiences of members of the relatively privileged black professional middle class specifically? Much has been written about the role of civil rights policy and changing opportunities for the new black middle class. What can interview data help us to understand about the effect of these "macro" policies at the "micro" level? What happens to African Americans during recruitment, hiring, and promotion into professional positions? Does "race" affect the experiences of black professionals in their relationships with clients? Does it matter whether black professionals deliver professional services?

BUILDING ON THE RECENT LITERATURE ON THE BLACK MIDDLE CLASS

Direct comparison of the "new" black middle class and their white counterpart finds continuing racial inequality regarding income differences, more black income earners per household, continued discrimination, and greater relative black job losses during periods of recession (Landry, 1987). For members of the black middle class, racism is a lived experience that permeates all spheres of life including work, neighborhood, school, and public places (Feagin & Sikes, 1994). Black corporate managers are shunted off into racialized positions within large corporations with lesser opportunities for advancement and salary increases (Collins, 1997). More work will have to be done on the black middle class in coming years, but they will be guided by the shifts in the literature that are characterized by these and other works. In this section, I briefly consider the contributions of four monograph length urban case studies on the black middle class. The work of these scholars illustrates a further methodological and conceptual break with the Moynihan–Wilson thesis regarding the black middle class. The works discussed below complement the work cited above, which were not urban case studies but provided new primary data on the complexities of the interaction between race and class in "lived experience."

As far as the conceptualization of social class is concerned, Steven Gregory argues for a neo-Marxist approach that emphasizes the role of praxis and empirically situates this idea in the lived social relations of Corona. For Gregory, the middle class is not a mere "reflection" of occupational status, but based on the interaction of social, political, and economic forces of daily life. In further elaborating his own praxis-oriented theoretical approach to the black middle class, Gregory highlights the tension between the East Elmhurst section of Corona – which is substantially black middle class – with that of the neighboring North Corona neighborhood, which is also predominantly black, but not middle class (Gregory, 1998).

Mary Patillo-McCoy categorizes the black middle class in Groveland based on both "behavioral" and conventional "objective" gradational conceptions of the middle class. In terms of behavior, the black middle class in Groveland, "mow their lawns, go to church, marry, vote (they really vote), work, own property, and so on" (Patillo-McCoy, 1999, p. 15). Patillo-McCoy notes the "income-to-needs ratio" used by economists, as well as occupational and educational criteria generally summoned by sociologists and demographers to ascertain the middle class (Patillo-McCoy, 1999, pp. 15, 16). In her more recent work, she illustrates some further issues that revolve around race and class – illustrating the contradictory status of the black middle class between a sponsoring white elite and the mass of working class and poorer blacks that they must "lead" (Patillo, 2007, pp. 81–87).

Bruce Haynes' historically grounded study of the black middle class suburban neighborhood of Runyon Heights in Yonkers provides an historically oriented conception of the changing foundation of the black middle class. For Haynes membership in the black middle class is arguably double-sided: founded on occupational status but grounded in home ownership. In the pre-World War II era, the black middle class was small but relatively elastic (Haynes, 2001). By contrast, in the postwar period a "new" black middle class arrived in Runyon Heights with a different occupational basis and relatively higher incomes (Haynes, 2001, p. xx). They also brought a strong commitment to home ownership and promoting a black version of gentrification (Haynes, 2001, p. 96).

Karyn Lacy has also published an important case study of black middle class neighborhood life in the suburbs. Her recent book entitled *Blue Chip Black* raises insightful questions about the variegated experiences of suburban middle class blacks. She examines the Washington, DC suburbs of Maryland and Virginia. Her focus is on questions concerning culture and identity among middle class blacks in different types of suburban settings. Lacy is critical of earlier studies that focused exclusively on middle class African Americans living in central city neighborhoods amongst, or in close proximity to, poor and working-class blacks. In her research, she finds important kinds of variation (Lacy, 2007, p. 23).

Lacy defines the middle class on a gradational basis, determined primarily on an *individual* income threshold of $50,000. This threshold basically distinguishes the upper and lower middle classes. This is an effort by Lacy to factor out the "blue collar aristocracy" that is apparently overrepresented in analyses of the black middle classes. Once distinguishing the lower middle class, Lacy further establishes a distinction between the "core" and "elite" middle classes. The core black middle class consists of individuals who earn between $50,000 and $100,000 annually, the elite those who earn more than $100,000 (Lacy, 2007, pp. 39–42). This conception of a black middle class "structure" corresponds to the concepts used by Lloyd Warner's Yankee City studies that proclaimed "upper middle," "middle middle," and "lower middle" classes.

This chapter is certainly informed by, and benefits from, the important recent work on the black middle class(es) cited above. However, I seek to move the analysis of the African American middle class in new directions. There are four factors that distinguish my work from the Moynihan–Wilson thesis, as well as more recent studies. The first distinction involves the region and locality. This chapter analyzes the experiences of the black middle class on the *West Coast*. The region has its own unique history, migration patterns, and social dynamics that make it a necessary piece of the larger geographic puzzle for this topic.

Second, this chapter focuses on the black *professional* middle class. Indeed, professionals are an important and distinguishable segment of the middle class. Studies of the middle class often provide definitions or conceptions of the black middle class that do not clearly distinguish them from the "lower" middle classes or the working class (Lacy, 2007, pp. 30–41). However, professionals are "indisputably" middle class on the one hand, because they fulfill all of the criteria of *gradational* definitions of middle class (income, educational attainment, and occupational status). In addition, professionals also have a relatively unique position in the class structure considering the *relational* aspects of the middle class debate. As Erik Olin Wright suggests, professionals control key "assets" in terms of knowledge and credentials that correspond with relatively high amounts of independence and decision-making in their work. This helps to construct the "boundary" that separates them from the "lower" middle classes (Wright, 1997, pp. 149–168).

A third contribution is that while this chapter is derived from a larger "urban case study" of Oakland, it focuses on *multiple sites* of the black professional middle class. It provides an analysis of black professionals in three separate but interrelated social arenas. These sites include the workplace, community, and local politics. In terms of work, African American professionals are divided on the one hand, into a *traditional* group that primarily delivers services to a segregated clientele within segregated local institutions and small private practices. On the other hand, the post-civil rights era has also seen the continued movement of black professionals into the *mainstream* (i.e., predominantly white) workplace of corporations, nonprofit organizations, and government agencies, which is the primary focus of this chapter. A second site for analyzing the experiences of black professionals is that of the *community*. Black professionals live in different neighborhood types that feature different kinds of race and class composition and degrees of proximity to poorer black neighborhoods. A third site involves the participation of the black professional middle class in local *politics*.

Finally, this chapter seeks to further problematize basic concepts of "class" and "race." I will focus my analysis on one social class – the professional middle class. As Charles Derber indicates, professionals form a social class based on their ability to produce and distribute a key social resource: professional *knowledge*. This shapes their *intermediate* position within the class structure of postindustrial society because they primarily contribute neither capital nor mass labor power as such (Derber, 1990, pp. 11–24). Furthermore, development of professional occupations is one of historical class formation that can be traced through preindustrial, industrial, and postindustrial society. This approach to class promotes the construction of a relational rather than a gradational conception of the middle classes.

Professional middle class formation is "racialized" in large part because of formal and informal patterns of *segregation* – or "dual society" – that

Racialized Class Formation   231

have long been part of the African American experience.[2] This is found not only in terms of residential segregation but also in local political life and occupational segregation. In terms of the basic problem of occupational segregation, black employees are generally pushed into particular niches in the labor market.[3] Black mainstream managers and professionals fill niches concerned with mediating relations between private firms or government and the black community (Collins, 1997, pp. 17–27). "Traditional" black professionals fill niches in which they are involved in providing professional services directly to the black community (Brown, 2009, pp. 263–291). The black professional middle class is a distinct (and internally differentiated) entity, not merely a subset of a larger professional middle class.

PROBLEM AND METHOD

The Moynihan–Wilson theoretical and methodological approach to analyzing the black middle class produced a framework that has emphasized the use of aggregate and *secondary* data, and the primacy of "class over race." Ironically, Wilson's research on the black "underclass" promotes a case study approach utilizing multiple methods that generate *primary* data (Wilson, 1987, 1996). In this sense, there was a need for a new round of social science research that could provide new empirical and theoretical insights specifically into the status of the black middle class(es). In response to these anomalies, a new literature – partly cited above – has emerged in the last decade or so that has highlighted these theoretical and methodological problems regarding the "new" black middle classes.

My research benefits from the methodological insights of recent studies of the black middle class. One of my goals is to apply the insights of the secondary sources and to push for the development of new theory that can fruitfully examine the past and present status of the black middle classes. However, I am particularly concerned to develop new data through *primary* research. I make use of qualitative methods – traditionally used to study poor and working-class urban neighborhoods – and apply them to the study of the black *professional* middle class. This effort emphasizes a *multiple method* approach that includes interview research, historical-archival research, and collection of secondary data from the census and other sources. Moreover, these varied methodologies have been embedded in an *urban case study*. A case study helps to highlight important similarities and differences that can be found in different kinds of local communities or neighborhoods where the black middle class(es) reside.[4]

While I am concerned with the substantial quantitative growth of black professionals, I am particularly interested in the immense qualitative changes that resulted for both African Americans and the larger society. My data comes from three basic sources. First, I conducted historical-archival research concerning the development of the black community in Oakland and the place of the black middle classes within that community. Some of that research, only partly incorporated here, includes an analysis of the development of black urban communities in Oakland since the nineteenth century. This data also looks at the changing class dynamics and institutional patterns of black neighborhoods in Oakland since the 1960s that correspond with the local growth of the black middle classes. The historical research was mostly conducted in two important archives: the Bancroft Library at the University of California, Berkeley and the archived material on African American history at the Oakland Public Library.

Second, I have also collected aggregate secondary data from the census. I have made use of this data to analyze national and local (Oakland metropolitan area) trends regarding occupational and residential changes. Most of this aggregate data is concerned with social and demographic changes in Oakland between 1940 and the present. This census data provides a useful backdrop for basic trend analysis that serve as a reference point for the findings of the qualitative data. It helps to provide a link between relevant national and local demographic changes.

Finally, a central source of evidence for this chapter is derived from the 30 interviews that were conducted with African American professionals. These interviews were conducted with professionals from Oakland and the East Bay metropolitan area as part of the case study. The interviewees are treated as both subjects and local key actors in the black professional middle class. I asked them about (1) their social backgrounds (family status, education, etc.), (2) their employment history, (3) community life and social networks, and (4) their political attitudes and practices as they related to their experiences as African American professionals.

For this chapter, the main source of data is derived from the interviews. Interviewees were coded as either "mainstream" or "traditional" members of the black professional middle class. *Mainstream* black professionals – the subject of this chapter – are those who work in predominantly white institutional settings (for-profit firms, nonprofit organizations, or government agencies). *Traditional* black professionals are those that serve black clientele in individual (e.g., private practice attorneys or physicians) or institutional (e.g., teachers or clergy in segregated school and church) settings.

The selection of local interview subjects for this study was based on a *snowball sample* of black professionals from the Oakland metropolitan area, who entered their professional careers between the mid-1960s and the end of the 1970s. This was the first cohort to enter such positions after the passage of the 1964 Civil Rights Act. The 30 years of the experience of this "new" black middle class is readily contrasted with that of the "old" black middle class that was created, nurtured, and confounded by formal segregation (Frazier, 1957). A snowball sample is consistent with the methodology of case studies (Feagin, Orum, & Sjoberg, 1991).

The snowball sample for this chapter was developed after identifying initial African American professional subjects in the Oakland and East Bay metropolitan area. Other subjects were identified by suggestion of those already interviewed. While "network analysis" is not part of this study, I was able to note overlapping connections among different groups of black professionals. Key actors were subjects who were frequently named by other subjects, and who often played key "nodal" roles in formally and informally connecting black professionals through institutional settings. These black professionals were generally connected through a particular profession itself, or through civic or political organizations in which they were involved. The discussion of civic and political activities is part of a larger research project and not included here.

My effort in collecting this sample of interview subjects was to capture a cross-section of black professionals in the Oakland/East Bay metropolitan area. This sample is certainly not a random sample. No claim of constituting a "scientific sample" is made by the researcher. However, my interest is in capturing a broad selection of professionals rather than focusing on a single profession. Seventeen professions are represented in the sample.[5] My effort is to understand the process of racialized class formation in one place, and I limit my claims about the representativeness of the sample. More work will be needed on the subject of the black professional middle class, including aggregate research. I encourage others to carry out research on the black professional middle class and other racialized classes of differing "racial groups" including white racialized class formation.

The interview subjects for this research project included 20 men and 10 women. Women were underrepresented in the sample. This partly reflects a gender bias in the social networks of the predominantly black male subjects that I interviewed in my snowball sample. The black professionals that I interviewed entered their professional careers between the mid-1960s and 1980. This reflected a time period when there was less public (i.e., male) recognition of gender inequality and policy efforts to ameliorate it. There was also less focus on recruitment and hiring of women, and less overall opportunity for women because of overt sexism. I originally planned to add the gender dimension to the study and interview more women. However, I think that the intersection or race, class, and gender is a larger subject unto itself and deserves its own focus (Collins, 2000). In the current generational cohort, women – blacks and others – are having somewhat increased success in higher education and hiring, but women in the workforce – including women professionals – still face overt discrimination, glass ceilings, and "salary gaps" (McCall, 2001; Reskin, 1999).

This study may be seen, along with the other case studies, as part of "multiple observations" of research on the black middle classes. Analysis of the interviews and the other data (i.e., historical and observational) in my study, allows for qualitative analysis of dimensions of the "racialized class formation" process experienced by these Oakland-area black professionals since the civil rights era. This is captured in the conflict over their presence in once nearly all-white occupational preserves and the civil rights policies that have shaped the opportunity structure and processes of recruitment, hiring, and promotion, and the relationship of black professionals to their clients in the post-civil rights era.

Both blacks and whites in California, in the Bay Area as a whole, and the East Bay in particular, have higher incomes than members of the same groups in other parts of the country (Table 1). Poverty rates are also

Table 1. Median Household Income and Poverty Rates by Race and Place in 1989 and 1999.

Place	Black Median Income ($)		Black Poverty Rate (%)		White Median Income ($)		White Poverty Rate (%)	
	1989	1999	1989	1999	1989	1999	1989	1999
United States	19,758	24,423	29.5	24.4	31,435	44,687	9.8	9.1
California	26,079	34,956	21.1	22.4	37,724	51,279	9.1	10.5
Oakland (PMSA)	25,444	NA	21.1	NA	43,904	NA	5.9	NA
Alameda County	24,480	35,909	21.3	21.2	41,740	62,181	6.4	7.2
Oakland City	21,771	31,184	23.9	24.9	34,623	54,076	9.0	11.5
Oakland suburbs[a,b]	32,201	44,270	17.0	17.2	45,299	67,829	5.2	5.4

Source: U.S. Bureau of the Census (1990 and 2000).
[a]Based on category of "not in central cities" for the Oakland primary metropolitan statistical area.
[b]For 1999, the data refers to Contra Costa County.

relatively lower. The relatively higher standard of living experienced by blacks in the East Bay makes it an important area to investigate. Relatively greater incomes reflect the higher cost of living (i.e., greater demand for housing, food and services, etc.) in the Bay Area as well as the greater demand for labor in service industries (including professional labor) in the region. The higher standard of living experienced by blacks in Oakland and the East Bay makes it an important and instructive area to investigate. This is the case given the apparent racial inequalities that remain locally manifest despite the relatively greater growth and prosperity of this region.[6]

As seen above, basic disparities between blacks and whites in median income and poverty rates remain evident at both the national and local levels. Therefore, local historical and interview data collected from Oakland is appropriate for augmenting available aggregate data and survey research on race and class inequalities. It should be noted that no one urban area – neither the great city of New York, nor the important contributions of the Chicago School – can capture all of the complexities of qualitative changes in urbanized race and class inequalities. In this sense I have also chosen Oakland as a research site because it is a West Coast city – and there is a dearth of research on the black middle class on the West Coast. In addition, Oakland as the greatest proportion of black population of any of the large West Coast cities and the influence of the local black middle class is reflected in this fact. Nevertheless, local and qualitative studies are still needed (in addition to aggregate and quantitative research) to capture the broader context of changes in race and class inequalities since the civil rights period. This study makes a contribution to this larger research agenda by analyzing the case of black professionals in Oakland and the East Bay.[7]

THEORIZING RACIALIZED CLASS FORMATION

While class-determined theory sees "racial inequality" as largely reducible to class inequality, an alternative approach analyzes the *interactive* relationship between race and class factors more closely (Pettigrew, 1981). That is, race *and* class not race *or* class. Race and class both "cast shadows" on the other and both affect the life chances of blacks of differing class backgrounds (Franklin, 1991). Omi and Winant (1994) are highly instructive in this regard by offering their conceptions of racial formation and "racialization." These concepts can be applied to the particular processes of "class formation" experienced by black professionals. I will term this alternative approach *racialized class formation*. This approach argues that while class formation is a fundamental and ongoing process in capitalist societies it is shaped by, or sometimes superseded by other material and ideological sources of conflict including "race." Other sources of conflict that tend to confound straightforward class analysis in various societies include: nationality, ethnicity, religion, language, sexual orientation, and, of course, gender. Class-determined arguments – whether "Marxist," or not – frequently miss these "complicating" factors. Several theoretical approaches have tried to amend the limitations of more narrow class analyses including some neo-Marxism, neo-Weberianism, and, of course, intersectionality. In the United States, "race" has been an enduring aspect of inequality not reducible to class, but interfacing with it in social structure and social (inter)action. Another way to put it is that, historically, class formation for African Americans has never been a race-neutral process. *Class formation* in the United States is tempered by *racial formation*.

The racial formation theory produced by Omi and Winant has been an important contribution to the literature. As with other sociological approaches, "race" is a social (not biological) construction. Moreover, like social class, race "is a concept which signifies and symbolizes social conflicts and interests by referring to different types of human bodies" (Omi & Winant, 1994, p. 55). For them race is neither an essentialism, nor an illusion. That is, like social class, race is a "sociohistorical process by which racial categories are created, inhabited, transformed, and destroyed" (Omi & Winant, 1994, p. 55). Further, race operates at both macro (social structure) and micro (identity and interaction) levels of society. Race is both a structural and cultural (ideological) phenomenon. Many aspects of social relations become *racialized* because of both the ideological and structural significances of race in the United States (and in other societies). Race (like class and gender) plays a role in shaping the perceptions and actions of citizens in regard to things that they may or may not perceive that they have in common, such as the issues of equality and opportunity, the proper exercise of power, political ideology, and the goals of social policy (e.g., welfare, health, and education).

One of the most useful contributions of Omi and Winant is the concept of *racial projects*. Racial projects illustrate the reflexive relationship of race in social structure to cultural or ideological formulations of race. Racial projects are ongoing in societies that feature racial formation. These projects are generally proposed and implemented by core institutions and organizations in the society. The *state* would, of course, be such a key institution in generating racial projects in the United States. One example of a racial project that is relevant for this chapter concerns the state and the events surrounding, and the responses to, the civil rights movement. Other key organizations involved in civil rights policy dynamics include civil rights organizations, civic and nonprofit groups, corporations, and unions. This important racial project was a result of the federal government response to civil rights movement in the 1960s. It led to new "political processes" and the "institutionalization" of several civil rights movement goals (Bloom, 1987; McAdam, 1999).

The racial project of civil rights policy – or seeing that the state provides a formal delineation and recognition of basic citizenship rights for groups historically denied them – has played a central role in promoting expanded black entrance into mainstream middle class occupations. Racialized class formation has been a constant in U.S. history. Indeed, racialized class formation is a process that is not exclusive to the black middle class, but is a generalized process for African Americans (Wilson, 2007). Racialization shapes class formation among all the social classes in the United States due significantly to basic patterns of residential segregation (Massey & Denton, 1993) and disparities in the accumulation of wealth (Shapiro, 2004). African Americans in the working class, the "underclass," the capitalist class, and the middle classes can all be seen as affected by processes of racialization in the class structure (Wright, 1997, pp. 52–55).

HISTORICIZING RACIALIZED CLASS FORMATION: FROM THE PRE-CIVIL RIGHTS ERA TO THE POST-CIVIL RIGHTS ERA

Racialized class formation as it has affected African Americans in the professional middle class can be seen taking fundamentally different forms before and after the civil rights era – but not disappearing. It is useful to elaborate three periods of citizenship status for African Americans. These three periods are: the *pre-civil rights era* (until 1964), the *civil rights era* (1964–1980) and the *post-civil rights era* (1980–present). The civil rights movement reached its apex with the passage of the Civil Rights Act in 1964. The post-civil rights era emerged with the rise of conservative political forces and the Reagan Administration in effectively challenging and curtailing (but not yet eradicating) the institutionalized status of "liberal" civil rights policies. The tension between liberal and conservative political ideologies has helped to shape the context and debate about racialized class formation in the post-civil era.

Initial racialized class formation of the African American professional middle class took place under conditions of formal and semi-formal (i.e., in the North) segregation in the *pre-civil rights era*. This produced a petite bourgeois black middle class that provided direct and indirect professional (and business) services to segregated black communities in the Northern and Southern cities (Frazier, 1957, pp. 43–59). While black-owned businesses provided business services (e.g., barbershops, beauty salons, corner stores, bars, and restaurants) to virtually exclusive black customers, black professionals did the same (Drake & Cayton, 1945, pp. 398–469). Lawyers, physicians, dentists, clergy, journalists, teachers, social workers, and college faculty, among others, provided professional services almost exclusively to black clients, patients, students, and parishioners under a regime of formalized and semi-formalized segregation in the South and North, respectively.

These pre-civil rights era professional services were provided through black-owned professional practices, segregated black-owned firms and institutions (e.g., historically black colleges and universities and black-owned newspapers), and through the state itself (e.g., public schools and social services). Racialized class formation of the black professional middle class came into play mostly after the turn of the last century, and especially since the Great Migration. This pattern expanded with the increased ghettoization of Northern and Southern cities. These events produced the conditions for the slowly expanding numbers of black professionals throughout the pre-civil rights era (Edwards, 1959, pp. 23–25). This group of black professionals operating under formalized and semi-formalized segregation was a relatively small grouping with relatively small numbers of clients. Many had to have second "working class" jobs (Landry, 1987). They were financially strapped, and socially and politically marginal in the context of the larger society (Frazier, 1957).

Despite the significant political constraints that this segregated black professional middle class faced they were also a politically mobilized group – especially in the South. There the black middle class formed the leadership of the civil rights movement that effectively challenged the injustices of formalized segregation and compelled the federal government to enact civil rights laws – with new enforcement mechanisms – that changed the social and political terrain for African Americans as a whole (Bloom, 1987; McAdam, 1999; Morris, 1986). Key pieces of legislation in this regard included the 1964 Civil Rights Act, the 1965 Voting Rights Act, and the 1968 Fair Housing Act.

These pieces of legislation helped to constitute the construction of a *civil rights policy regime* that coincided with the civil rights era and promoted formal equality of citizenship for blacks, particularly in the realms of employment, higher education, accommodations, voting, political representation, housing, etc. The emergence of the civil rights policy regime codified a federal government shift from *exclusionary* policy (pro-segregation) to *inclusionary* policy (pro-integration) that corresponds with a transition from the pre-civil rights era to the civil rights era. Worth considering is that in the post-civil rights era there are increasing voices among policy advocates and the general public arguing for a *seclusionary* policy. That is, policies (thus far only partly successful) that advocate the withdrawal of the state from the promotion of civil rights laws and policies (including affirmative action). Under seclusionary policies the problems of discrimination and racial inequality are concealed or "secluded" under the rubric of "color blindness."[8]

As far as access to mainstream (i.e., predominantly white) occupations in the private, public, and nonprofit sectors is concerned, new rights under the Civil Rights Act and 1964 and affirmative action policies were key. The civil rights policy regime – including both civil rights laws and affirmative action policies – provided a new opportunity structure for African Americans who were able to move up and into professional jobs in mainstream institutions. Thus, during the civil rights and post-civil rights eras, respectively, an alternative type of racialized class formation has taken place. This involves large-scale entrance of black professionals into mainstream job opportunities for the first time during the period of the mid-1960s and 1970s.

WHY THE PROFESSIONAL MIDDLE CLASS?

One of the most dynamic social changes in postwar American society has been the formation of a significant black professional middle class. This process of racialized class formation entails, on one hand, the quantitative growth in the overall number of blacks who are members of professional occupations and also increasingly integrated into "mainstream" (i.e., predominantly white) firms, nonprofit agencies and government employment. Nevertheless, African American members of the professional middle class frequently find themselves facing tangible barriers and "ceilings" in the labor market and within the institutions that employ them. That is, they often find themselves excluded or diverted from the conventional opportunity structures of recruitment, hiring and promotion despite their greatly increased representation in mainstream institutions since the 1960s.

On the other hand, these African American professionals are conscious social actors, aware of their relatively privileged status as well as their particularly racialized status and identity as *black* professionals. They experience this at work, as well as in the other components of their public and private lives (Cose, 1993; Feagin & Sikes, 1994).

In the contemporary period, blacks in the professional middle class can be divided into two substantial groupings: (1) professional employees and (2) self-employed professionals. The focus of this chapter is on the former group. They are most representative of the entrance of African American professionals into the *mainstream* of the public and private sectors of the economy. On the other hand, self-employed black professionals retain many similarities with the old black middle class from the era of formal segregation. This includes the direct provision of many basic professional and social services that are often, otherwise, unavailable to the black poor. Nevertheless, self-employed black professionals (e.g., lawyers and doctors) continue to play a vital role within the larger black community.

In terms of understanding the status of the black middle class as such, this chapter focuses on the *professional* middle class for pragmatic theoretical and methodological reasons. First, as Erik Olin Wright and other scholars have found, operationalizing the concept "middle class" is difficult.[9] Definitions of the "middle classes" are often inconsistent and are based variously on constructions based on educational attainment, occupational status, or income. In self-report surveys about class background, the majority of Americans define themselves as "middle class" (Jackman & Jackman, 1982). Clearly, not everyone, or nearly everyone, is in the "middle class." A number of studies of the black middle class include broad segments of the workforce, many of whom might be considered members of the working class (Zweig, 2001, pp. 9–38). The size of the *black* middle class in particular might be overstated. This study chooses a simpler route-to look at professionals because they are (for the most part) unambiguously middle class. They tend to correspond with both "gradational" and "relational" aspects of defining the middle class.[10] Additionally, secondary data from the census concerning this group is readily available.

Second, professionals play a central role in the expanding service sector of the United States – the world's most advanced postindustrial economy. Professional work is one of the more prestigious examples of the way in which services have replaced manufacturing as the mainstay of employment in the U.S. economy. Professionals require significant personal investments in higher education and social capital. They are purveyors of specialized knowledge that is demonstrated by the possession of university degrees, licenses, and other difficult to obtain credentials. Professionals provide many of the vital services that are utilized by the public in the course of contemporary social life. They are a relatively autonomous and self-directed occupational grouping. Furthermore, professionals represent a significant contemporary employee "organizing strategy" to improve their relative conditions in the services-based postindustrial labor market: the process of expansive *professionalization*. This strategy is geared toward increasing the share of the social surplus available to professionals relative to other kinds of workers. It is distinct from the earlier (and now declining) efforts at mass *unionization* that dominated the earlier periods of industrialization.

Assessing whether or not the degree to which black entrance into the ranks of the professional middle class has been equitable is one important indicator of the degree of integration of African Americans as a group into one of the most basic U.S. social institutions: the labor market. The net growth of U.S. employment since the 1970s has been virtually 100% in the service sector (Noyelle, 1987). As part of this process of "postindustrialization," the growth of professional jobs has been tremendous in the postwar period (Table 2). Thus, the access of blacks to such positions is an important barometer of the genuine national pursuit and achievement of equal opportunity in the larger society.

Table 2. Percentage of Blacks by Occupational Category in Oakland, 1960–2000.

Occupation	1960	1970	1980	1990	2000
Professional	5.1	8.4	9.3	12.4	17.7
Managers	3.3	2.5	8.5	13.2	11.9
Clerical	10.4	20.8	29.1	26.4	23.5
Sales	3.0	3.3	7.3	10.9	8.2
Craftsmen	7.5	10.4	9.8	8.1	7.6
Operatives	16.6	18.3	7.9	4.0	9.3
Private Household	9.4	4.8	1.6	0.9	NA
Service Workers	16.1	20.7	20.1	19.4	18.7
Laborers	14.0	10.5	6.5	4.8	3.1
Other	14.7	0.2	NA	NA	NA
Total	100.0	100.0	100.0	100.0	100.0

Source: U.S. Bureau of the Census (1950–2000).

POSTWAR RACIALIZED CLASS MOBILITY IN OAKLAND

When African Americans from the South migrated to Oakland and the East Bay in large numbers before and during World War II, they were mostly a population of recent sharecroppers, farmers, and domestic workers (and their children) from Southern states (especially Louisiana, Arkansas, and Texas). As across the bay in San Francisco, most black migrants came to the East Bay cities of Oakland and Richmond looking for jobs in the expanding arms producing industries (Daniels, 1991, pp. 165–166). Shipbuilding – especially in the Kaiser plants – was a major draw for migrant workers looking for work (Johnson, 1993, pp. 60–82). Most of these workers (black and white) were from the South. Blacks who migrated to the East Bay had the added incentive of escaping the formalized racial segregation of the South, as well as finding new employment opportunities in the manufacturing and government sectors of the economy.

One African American attorney described the process that brought him to leave his Arkansas home as a teenager to live with his sister in Oakland:

> My parents are still in Arkansas. I came to live with my sister – who had come out here, as had my older brother. When they were – I guess my sister came out here immediately after she graduated from high school. My brother, who's next to me, came out during his senior year to live with relatives out here. Primarily to escape the cotton patches of Arkansas. And that's definitely the reason I came too, was to escape the cotton patches. It's hot out there picking 300 pounds of cotton. Oh, it's quite different. You had to pick cotton. It wasn't a matter of choice. You had no option. And that was good. It taught the work ethic [laugh]!

The process of migration of blacks from the South produced, for the first time, the prospect of substantive aggregate inter-generational upward mobility. Moving from caste-like conditions in the "Jim Crow" South introduced many African Americans to the manufacturing sector of the modern capitalist economy for the first time. These linked factors – *geographic* mobility and cross-generational *social* mobility – were both key elements of tremendous social changes during the unfolding of the civil rights era. Many of the children of these World War II-era black Southern migrants would have opportunities for further mobility into professional and other white-collar occupations.

Nevertheless, racial exclusion was a constant in the collective social experience of black migrants. As with earlier black ghettoes that formed in the World War I era in Northeastern and Midwestern cities, black migrants to the East Bay were also forced into crowded ghettoes in the neighborhoods of West Oakland, South Berkeley, and Richmond during World War II (Brown, 1998, pp. 267–272). A similar process took place across the bay in the Hunters Point neighborhood of San Francisco (Broussard, 1993, p. 175). As with Northeastern and Midwestern cities, these segregated Bay Area black ghettoes became a contradictory source of both black hopes for opportunity and social mobility, as well as entrenched urban poverty.

Not all blacks worked in the shipyards, of course. Domestic and other service jobs remained a significant area of employment for many first-generation blacks.[11] Other blacks were able to move into government related, and other civilian, jobs that sprang up in relation to local military bases and defense-related production. As a general rule, government employment has been more readily accessible to blacks than work in the private sector (Carnoy, 1994, pp. 150–194). One African American woman, who later became a teacher, school administrator, and earned a Ph.D., started out as a clerk at the Oakland Naval Supply Center. After obtaining her B.A. in English in 1965, she found it difficult to find a "suitable" job. Married and with a newborn baby, she needed a job nonetheless, and a friend suggested she apply for "something" at the Naval Supply Center:

> Well my first full-time job was working for the government for the Naval Supply Center in Oakland for two years. I had just had my baby in April and then I graduated that June. And so the care that she needed at the beginning-but I found that-and I don't know if it was because I didn't know how to look for a job – but I found it difficult to find a job. And I'm sure it's not just my ability to look for one, but the fact that there was still a good deal of overt racism which would prevent a [black] person with a degree from still getting a job. So anyway I worked for the Naval Supply Center for two years [before] I left there.

In addition to the children of migrants, younger black adults who moved to Oakland during the 1960s and 1970s also benefited from the expanding local opportunity structure that was shaped by the civil rights policy regime. Their opportunities for membership in the growing black professional middle class would result, in part, from fortunate historical timing. They would be coming of age during the civil rights movement and its aftermath. They would, thus, be in a position to experience educational and career opportunities that were largely closed to the previous generation. The changing access to the upper tiers of the occupational structure for blacks in Oakland can be glimpsed in Table 2. Between 1960 and 1990, the number of black professionals in Oakland increased by more than a fourfold rate, and managers by a rate of nearly seven times.

The (trans)formation of the black middle class in the 1960s and 1970s was, unquestioningly, one of unprecedented *structural* class mobility

(Blau & Duncan, 1967). More specifically, it represented a new process of *racialized* class formation. The black professional middle class was greatly expanded and restructured from a smaller grouping trapped in segregated institutions and suddenly given access to mainstream labor markets. Bart Landry found in his 1976 data that more than 70% of middle class blacks in his survey came from working-class or poor backgrounds (Landry, 1987, pp. 98–100).

RACIALIZED RECRUITMENT AND HIRING: CIVIL RIGHTS POLICIES AND THE "INTEGRATION" OF THE PRIMARY LABOR MARKET

One of the most important new opportunities for blacks in the 1960s was expanded access to higher education-especially admission to predominantly white "mainstream" colleges and universities. This dramatic change corresponds with what I would term the development of the *civil rights policy regime*. New civil rights law provided a new legal infrastructure to promote a "rights revolution" especially for racial minorities and women (Skrentny, 2002). The other dimension of the civil rights policy regime included "proactive" policies in the form of affirmative action and other "interventionist" policies. Indeed, the development of these policies during the 1960s – in response to the civil rights movement – represents the defining characteristic of the *civil rights era* as such. They represent the development of *inclusionary policies* designed to promote access to mainstream institutions and opportunity structures for racial minorities and women. These changes can be readily contrasted with the entrenchment of *exclusionary policies* during the *pre-civil rights era*.

These policy changes ultimately affected higher education admissions, employment hiring and promotion, and business contracts. In the case of higher education, the weight of federal government sanction under Title VII of the Civil Rights Act of 1964 (i.e., the threatened loss of substantial federal research funds and federal student financial aid) led both public and private institutions of higher education to open their doors to prospective black students. Increased access to higher education for blacks has been both a key outcome and an essential underpinning of the civil rights policy regime.

With increased undergraduate admission of historically underrepresented groups came programs designed to meet the needs of these new students. The new programs included retention programs, Educational Opportunity and Affirmative Action (EOP/AA) programs and grants, scholarships, fellowships and other such financial aid targeted to underrepresented minorities. The implementation of these programs (with federal government support) have been central to the process of promoting greater inclusion of racial minority groups and students from low-income backgrounds into institutions of higher education since the civil rights era of the 1960s and 1970s (Bowen and Bok, 1998; Freeman, 1976).

However, the expansion of the black professional middle class during the civil rights era has also been mediated by the implementation of affirmative action in higher education at the *graduate and professional level*. Increased access to mainstream higher education institutions at the graduate level made opportunities for access to "mainstream jobs" and upward mobility possible for many more women and minorities. For example, in 1965 the percentage of all law students that were black was only 1%, for medical school only 2%. By 1975, these figures had climbed to 4.5% and 6.3%, respectively (Blackwell, 1987, p. 103). However, despite the rapid upward trend in graduate school matriculation during the 1960s and 1970s, "significantly fewer blacks than whites are likely to be found in most graduate-level fields for several decades" (Freeman, 1976, p. 56).

Correspondingly, the particular role of outreach and opportunity for admission to graduate and professional schools cannot be underestimated. This is the case regarding not only the structural foundation of affirmative action that has brought blacks into these programs in the first place, but also for providing the evidence that African Americans *could* be a part of these historically exclusionary institutions and have bona fide professional careers when they graduated. One interview subject described the opportunity for social mobility that was provided by his affirmative action-based admission to the (Boalt Hall) Law School at Berkeley. He placed his experience in the social and political context of the times:

> As a result of being a probation officer I got exposed to the legal system. And certainly that helped to shape my interests in law. And then, of course, opportunity presented itself. 1968 was when Martin Luther King was killed, and there was a great awakening on the part of some institutions in that they wanted to get a more diverse student body. And Boalt Hall did some affirmative outreach. And they were fortunate enough to get me [laugh]. So I started school there in 1969, August of 1969.

Similarly, an African American woman describes the experience that led her transition from "settling" for a B.S. degree in nursing to the realization that she could pursue a medical degree. Working with self-employed black doctors in a community clinic setting was a transformative experience.

Having a supportive, informal professional social network complements formally inclusive recruitment policies:

> I think that, looking back, I must have had some reservations as to whether or not I really had the brains to be a physician. I think I had always admired or secretly wanted to be a physician. But there was no one in my family who was a physician. I didn't have the role models. And it really wasn't until my last year of nursing school. And in my last year of nursing school, just before I got my bachelors, I found myself with physicians because the last year is mostly [spent in the clinic]. When you're in the hospital actually taking care of patients. You're no longer in the classroom. You're spending most of your time actually doing nursing, on site. I started working around physicians and it was really the first time I've had close contact with physicians. And I was lucky to also be very close to some black physicians who were very supportive of me. ... So I started to take some premed courses, to see how I would do. And I did very well in them. And the nurses, who were black, had always been supportive. And I had talked with them about maybe going on. And again I think it was those role models, the black nurses, as well as the black physicians that I had talked with, that really encouraged me.

In addition to recruitment to higher education, recruitment by employers is itself an interrelated step in the process of the development of the black professional middle class. Reversing the patterns of the historic exclusion of blacks from access to primary labor markets, and correspondingly from incorporation into the mainstream of the professional middle class, has been no small matter. It has entailed federal government oversight and enforcement, as well as demonstrable efforts by companies to break down exclusionary barriers in order to bring blacks, and other underrepresented groups, into the professional and managerial opportunity structures of their firms. This development illustrates the integration of federal policy with the internal bureaucratic and legal dynamics of private companies that is at the core of the civil rights policy regime.

The layers of management found within corporations and government agencies are key arenas of employment for professionals. Most professionals can also be classified as managers.[12] Providing access for black professionals to these sources of professional employment is key to implementing civil rights policies. Human resource managers and executives carry out the bureaucratic details of this process within private companies concerning responsibility for civil rights regulations and legal oversight for micro-level implementation of affirmative action policies. One such example was the "director of Corporate Equal Employment Opportunity" at a California-based corporation. She was hired in 1964, specifically, to oversee the conformity of the company with federal civil rights law. She described the general changes over a period of nearly 30 years:

> When I got to [the company] in 1964, there were no blacks in management. And at that time they made an effort of going out and recruiting blacks. They went back to all [of the historically] black colleges. Recruiting engineers – there was a big push at that time. They brought in about 20 or 30 [black engineers] at that time. In some other areas like customer service, human resources, there [were] only one or two black [employees] within that area. Hardly any other minorities – almost known as totally white male throughout that company. I saw lots of changes with the [proportion] going from less than one percent to maybe up to about 20 percent were minorities [in 1993]. The management groups that you report to the Equal Employment Opportunity Commission (EEOC), there was a huge increase.

California is the first state in which racial minorities outnumber whites.[13] Nevertheless, the growth from 1% to about 20% nonwhite representation in the management fields in this firm over a thirty-year period is a noteworthy transformation. This is particularly the case since corporate management is a less hospitable area of employment for black professionals than similar positions in government employment (Collins, 1997, pp. 49–57). Regardless, large core sector corporations, nonprofits, and government – the institutions most directly covered by civil rights laws – are the major source of employment growth for black professionals since the civil rights era (Freeman, 1976; Smith, 2001). This would be expected if civil rights policies (including affirmative action) had been effective in creating the new employment opportunity structure for African Americans (Holzer, 2001; Leonard, 1990).

In the firm mentioned above, most of the senior management positions are drawn from the professional ranks of engineers, and to a lesser degree, attorneys. It should also be noted that this particular company has won awards from the Civil Rights Division of the Justice Department and has been known as one of the best companies in the country at "promoting diversity" and has presumably been more successful than most firms in doing so. Recruitment prospects for black professionals vary depending on industrial sector (e.g., public vs. private), by type of firm, and over time. Nevertheless, multiple studies utilizing both aggregate-level data (Bound & Freeman, 1990; Brown et al., 2003; Carnoy, 1994; Harrison & Gorham, 1992; Holzer, 2001; Smith, 2001; Turner, Fix, & Struyk, 1991) and qualitative case study data (Bonilla-Silva, 2006; Collins, 1997; Cose, 1993; Feagin & Sikes, 1994) demonstrate continued patterns of racial discrimination and disparity in labor market outcomes.

A combination of "legal ambiguity" in the original writing of Title VII of the Civil Rights Act of 1964, and institutional pressures to reduce compliance with Equal Employment Opportunity/Affirmative Action (EEO/AA) mandates dating back at least to changes made during the Reagan administration, may explain part of the continuing income gap facing black workers (Edelman, 1992). There are a couple of general qualifying points to be made here. Research indicates that blacks fare better in the public sector than in the private sector (Reskin, 1999). On the one hand, black professionals are represented in greater proportions in the public sector relative to their employment in the private sector (where the bulk of overall employment exists). Additionally, black professionals working for government are also relatively better paid than are blacks in the private sector (Wilson, 1997). On the other hand, black professionals are also concentrated – or occupationally "segregated" – in qualitatively different (less mobile) kinds of jobs than their white counterparts (Reskin, 1999).

In her research on black managers, Sharon Collins found two basic routes to the jobs held by those employees. *Racialized* jobs are those that "indicated an actual and/or symbolic connection to black communities, to black issues, or to civil rights agencies at any level of government." *Mainstream* jobs are those that "relate to total constituencies, and neither explicit nor implicit connections to blacks could be found in the job description" (Collins, 1997, pp. 73–77). Blacks tend to be favored for *racialized* professional and managerial jobs. These jobs tend to have short promotional ladders because they don't connect "racialized" employees to the "mainstream" social networks and internal labor markets that generate mobility within the firm. By contrast, job opportunity and mobility for black professionals and managers is greater in the public sector, where formal or "meritocratic" criteria are used more stringently. In the private sector, employers are more likely to rely on informal methods of evaluation to hire and promote employees (Granovetter, 1974).

In general, blacks, as the racialized, low-status "other" are judged more on the basis of formal (objective) criteria, including educational credentials, tenure of employment, and experience. By contrast, white males are more likely to be evaluated on the basis of informal (subjective) criteria. That is, white male professionals are presumed to have greater amounts of "loyalty, good character, sound judgment and leadership potential" (Wilson, 1997, p. 39). On the whole, the evaluative process for prospective professional employees tends to produce a "racial (and gender) preference" for white males. This was clearly illustrated in the case of an interview subject. He is a full professor in the social sciences at a public university in Northern California. Indeed, he is a dignified and straightforward man of rural Southern black origin. His blunt style of personal expression, and his unapologetic views on issues of race, apparently rubbed many colleagues the wrong way. In his first search for an academic position in the 1970s, he landed a position at an elite Ivy League institution. He had been there briefly when he received the unofficial verdict delivered by the Provost (also black). As he put it:

> I didn't fit into Yale. I got a job at Yale, but I didn't fit into Yale. I was told by the Provost [that I wouldn't be tenured]. I liked him – but ... I was told by him that I didn't have the "social graces" to be there at Yale.

Those judged more on the basis of "informal" criteria (those deemed to be more like those doing the judging) are always at an advantage over those judged primarily on the basis of "formal" criteria. Perhaps, a white male exhibiting the same blunt personal qualities would have been considered "refreshingly honest." However, neither formal, nor informal evaluative criteria are ironclad. For prospective professional employees, these criteria are often shifting, variable, and inscrutable. Racial minorities and women (who generally operate as the other) are more likely to be excluded from professional-level hiring and promotion opportunities due to the unequal application or indetermination of fair evaluative criteria. The result is that employers can find justification, as needed, to get rid of "undesirable" employees. This becomes more apparent as we look at the process of promotion.

RACIALIZED PROMOTION AND THE PARAMETERS OF BLACK PROFESSIONAL OPPORTUNITY

In contrast to working-class jobs (i.e., jobs in the secondary labor market), the concept of "promotion" is central to middle class occupations and to the process of professional middle class formation. The ability to advance, over time, is a key indication of whether or not one is truly experiencing professional opportunities. On the other hand, African Americans who are promoted into mainstream institutional positions of expertise and authority may find themselves as "fish out of water" with little support from the company management, or respect from the employees he or she is supposed to supervise. One of my interview subjects-a banker from Oakland-provides a clear example. He previously worked for a major Midwestern-based bank but did not receive promotion opportunities accorded to white colleagues of the same initial rank. Many of the bank managers at this company were allowed to go overseas to study European banking, an opportunity that would greatly enhance their global banking knowledge and increased their future prospects for promotion. Being selected for this program was an indication that one was on the "fast track" at the company. As the interviewee elaborated:

> I felt that there was a fair amount of racism at [the bank] and it was at the top as well as at the bottom. Part of the routine was that a lot of the guys got a chance to go to Europe [to study European banking]. I remember being flat out told that blacks couldn't be successful in Europe. Which I thought was a way projecting their racism on a whole continent.

He finally left the bank in the late 1970s, because he concluded that he had no future there. He had an offer from a bank in Northern California, but his wife was reluctant to move and leave behind family and friends. Ironically, he subsequently took a job at a branch of a European (i.e., French) bank located in the large Midwestern city where he lived. He was hired to oversee the day-to-day operations of the bank. He had the infuriating experience of being offered the position, and then having it retracted because his future employees refused to work for a black bank manager:

> I interviewed with [that bank] for about six months. After six months they made me an offer, it was a super offer. A lot of money, mortgage subsidy, trips. They made me an offer that morning and they wanted me to meet the people who were going to work for me. And I was taken to my office and ... later I got a call from them, and they told me there was a problem. The people that met you ... are rebelling. They're saying that they won't work for you, that you're not qualified to be their boss. This means that we need to extend the process a little longer. We want to rescind the offer and extend this process and we'd like to get samples of your writing. And I said, let's have a meeting and talk about that. And at the meeting I said, What you've done is wrong. You know it's wrong. You've probably violated some laws here. I said, but I'm not going to sue you, it's over. I'm really qualified to be manager of this office. And I went home and told my wife, we're going to California.

The case of an African American corporate attorney from Oakland provides further illustration of this "racialized mobility" phenomenon. He started out in the legal department of a large California-based company in the early 1970s and worked there for 17 years. Most of his work was in the area of the legal relations between corporations and state and local governments. He also became involved in the legal issues of "corporate free speech." These legal issues concerned efforts by California consumer groups to force disclosure of sensitive company information deemed relevant to the public. He eventually argued, successfully, for the company in a landmark Supreme Court case concerning that issue. It was virtually unprecedented for an "in house" lawyer to argue such an important legal case. Usually these types of cases are "farmed out" to major law firms kept on retainer by such companies. His tremendous success in this case put him on the immediate "fast track" in the company. Like some others on the rise, he was sent to Harvard for advanced management training. Upon return to the Bay Area he was named a division manager of East Bay operations based in Oakland, where he lived. My interview with him revealed the racial dynamics of his increased corporate responsibilities as a division manager in terms of the locality:

> The East Bay division is the most diverse division in our territory. And by all measurements it's one of the toughest divisions. It's right in the middle of an urban center that is noted for its many challenges that you have in the East Bay. The same challenges that you have in the streets of East Oakland you have in the workforce. And you're confronted with all of the urban issues that you can think of, right there in the East Bay. Even today the East Bay still presents a major challenge for anybody, no matter what the situation is.

And in terms of the racialization of the local workforce, and managing its "diversity":

> You look at the diversity of the workforce. You have more minorities in that division than in any other division. No matter how you may want it or not, the challenge is different in an "inner city" than in some remote suburb. It's just a different challenge, you've just got to have different skills.

He was then named an executive assistant to the president of the company. This meant that he was being groomed for a stepping-stone to a top position in the firm. A year later he was promoted to executive vice president for community relations. The irony is that the great success that got him promoted was based on involvement in important and precedent-setting "mainstream" legal issues. His success before the Supreme Court probably saved the company tens of millions of dollars in potential lawsuits and consumer-related compliance costs. Yet, when he was promoted it was into a "community relations" position. That is, he was promoted to the conventional type of "racialized" position reserved for black professionals at the top levels of the corporate hierarchy. Presumably, these are actually worthwhile positions. Unfortunately, these jobs are not truly valued by the companies when compared to positions that are more directly related to "bottom line" profit concerns (Collins, 1997).

Alternatively, there are the outcomes in which mobility for black professionals is blocked. There are only so many such positions at the top of the hierarchy. Too many blacks in high-level positions might send a "negative message" to white male professional employees and undermine the perceived status of many such professional positions. This is similar to the case of "too many" blacks moving into a neighborhood and leading to its "decline." As another corporate attorney described it:

> Promotions. What I've noticed about promotions with the company was one thing and with me it was something else. For the most part, I saw that they allowed blacks to get to a certain level and then you had a glass ceiling. Not with everyone, but for the most part. Some were able to make higher ranks.

The same attorney described the manner in which his opportunity for mobility and those of a white female attorney colleague were curtailed by the informal workings of the "old boys network" of middle management in the legal department of his firm:

> There was another white woman who trained with me around that same time in 1980 and the [man] that we worked under ... he treated her just as bad as he did me, meaning that they did not try to show you anything to help you out – which was the purpose of us working under them. So they could help train us. They did their best to show us ... as little as possible and then when any inquiry was made as to how we were performing they could report it as basic. But then others, you'd note that they'd take them under their wing and provide them as much assistance as they can even though some of those [white male] individuals may have less ability to learn and to grasp. They take them under their wing and assist them and I saw that even more in the department in which I worked.... They found ways to give them higher salaries than me, and a few others who were working as attorneys. So it boiled down, quite often, to favoritism and economic gain – not gain but more economic benefit to those who I don't think deserved it any more than myself.

Ultimately, this African American attorney left the firm in order to start a small joint law practice (with another black attorney). His future in the corporate legal department was basically null and void. He described the process by which "undesirables" were pushed out of their positions at the company. These companies may generally prefer to not fire women and racial minority professionals because they are presumably under the eye of federal civil rights oversight. Rather, creating an increasingly inhospitable working environment was a very effective method for encouraging them to resign:

> One of the means of letting you know that they don't want you, is by affecting the performance evaluations. They began to do things on performance evaluations that were unjustified. They make your performance much poorer, refuse to give you pay increases, increase the workload, and there's only so much of that that you can take. You find that either you're going to accept it, and you can only accept so much, and then find other means. That was their way of doing it, not just for me, but for several of the attorneys that were there that they were determined that they wanted to replace.

Chief executive officers (who represent the financial and legal interests) of large companies may come under the scrutiny of the EEOC and the Civil Rights Division of the Justice Department. Representing the company, they tend to take affirmative action laws fairly seriously. They are concerned about the unpleasant possibilities of legal sanction, bad publicity, demonstrations, or boycotts led by civil rights or other protest groups. These can hurt the bottom-line financial interests of the company. Consequently, corporate leadership is often motivated to express some concern about issues of discrimination or to officially promote "diversity." If not motivated by true concern, they are at least worried about the legal, financial, and publicity ramifications of civil suits. In either case, top corporate leadership can make some degree of difference in the relative volume of employment opportunities offered to "underrepresented" racial minorities and women (when compared to companies not covered by the EEOC or Office of Federal Contracts Compliance Programs (OFCCP)).[14]

Within private companies and government agencies, there is more employee-generated conflict over affirmative action policy when applied to *promotions* than with *hiring*. Some white males looking to move from middle management to upper management apparently feel that they are victims of "reverse discrimination," even though as a group they are clearly collectively advantaged in the aggregate promotion process. The EEO director at a large company described the conflict over affirmative action-based management training programs for women and minorities this way:

> We started the officer of management training program where we would take minorities and women [who] had excellent potential and did not have the seniority, and put them through an accelerated training program. Give them so long to be a manager, give them so long as to be an officer. Send them to the accelerated schools like UC Berkeley's MBA program and things like that so they would be ready at a faster rate. Were there people upset over it? Yes. A lot of white males were upset about the accelerated training program. But it had the support of the chairman of the board, vice chairman of the board, the president, and all the officers. It had their support. They were going to make it work, because they wanted those numbers changed.

More specifically that more conflict about affirmative action arises in reference to promotions than to hiring, because of the narrowing of the management "pyramid." There are simply fewer jobs as one moves up the bureaucratic hierarchy of a firm or government agency:

> Yes. If you got above a level 10, then people became concerned, especially white males because the number of jobs decreases. ... They saw the training programs as taking away some of their opportunities.

Black population and political presence play an important role in cities like Oakland (as compared with cities with little black political presence) in providing a larger pool of potential black professional candidates for professional jobs in the *public* sector. Black political presence also provides a pressure point to employ blacks in local government, although the days of the old ethnic urban political machines died before the emergence of black city administrations since the 1970s. One black urban planner described the effects on his department:

> This being a "majority minority" city – I hate the [phrase] – but [with Oakland having] a majority [of] African American, and other non-white communities ... made the department try to create some semblance of balance. There's still a lot of discrimination here in this situation, there's still a lot of racism and problems even within the city government. However, certainly the demands of the public in the African American community here and through some of the council people, and [former] mayor and so forth that they put in place, have made it necessary that they have some black involvement.

As in the private sector, problems of promotion for black professionals occur in the public sector as well. The limited number of higher-level professional positions available in public bureaucracies plays havoc with the prospects of black professional mobility. Even in local government services where blacks are very well represented (as compared to the corporate world), promotions can be as strongly contested along racial lines as they are in the private sector. The same urban planner described his experience with blocked mobility in both the old "seniority" system and the more contemporary "civil service" testing system. Whites have been able to maintain a privileged status under both systems:

> Well it has to do with promotions. You're not judged by your experience or your capabilities, but you're judged by how it makes the demographics look. For example, just recently promotions came up here for a person to be a Planner III, to head major projects. And now here we've got – I've been here the longest. When I came here, seniority was a major issue. In other words, many whites for whom I tested against – where I did better than them – were given promotions over me because they had more seniority and that was the rule. But now – when I became – when the African Americans became the majority in seniority – seniority no longer plays a role. So new whites come – which has happened right here in this department – they're promoted over us because all of a sudden seniority doesn't matter.

Thus, in both the private and public sectors, promotion of professional employees is a racially contested terrain. Indeed, the gulf in perception between blacks and whites about the degree of racial inequality and the prevalence of discrimination in American society is generally quite large (Blauner, 1992; Hochschild, 1995). "Institutional discrimination" can become widespread within organizations, with or without sanction from the executive leadership. The response by those experiencing discrimination in situations where executive leadership is indifferent or hostile, is sometimes a class action civil suit. An engineer at a large company based in Northern California described an unsuccessful class action suit in the 1970s that alleged widespread discrimination in promotions among other things:

> [The suit concerned] promotions, different things, racial epithets, I forget all they based it on. But we fought it, we called the NAACP and we got documentation of instances where people had been affected in hiring, promotion, training, firing. So we documented this. There were about 160 of us who were involved in this lawsuit. We put up a very good fight. We lost. Well, [the company] had an army of lawyers. There was no way we could we could win. But at least we did prove to the company that there was in fact discrimination at all levels. Even though we didn't win the case I think we opened their eyes and let [the company] know that things were not as they should be. And so [some blacks] were suddenly reclassified and given promotions and some were even given management positions. In fact we even had – and still have – a vice president of the company who is black. We fared much better after the lawsuit than we did before. So it's kind of strange that four people who initiated something that involved all of us, and we in turn by our efforts improved things for ourselves, and I think for others who came along later.

Indeed, recent cases of employee class action race and sex discrimination lawsuits against major corporations give insight into the institutionalized patterning of employment discrimination. A recent report disclosed that more than 100,000 employees were covered in recent class action lawsuits under the 1991 Civil Rights Act. The defendants included large employers such as Texaco, State Farm, Shoney's Inc., Lucky Stores, Motel 6, Smith Barney, and Dun and Bradstreet, among others (Myerson, 1997). The issues of recruitment, hiring and promotion are very contentious, and much is at stake for blacks seeking professional opportunities. Despite prestigious credentials and accomplishments, black professionals are often treated as though they are not adequately qualified for such opportunities. Most of my interview subjects participated in the civil rights or black power movements as students or young adults in the 1960s and 1970s. This seems to have played a role in their willingness to actively contest what they perceive as discriminatory behavior in the workplace and other settings.

PROFESSIONAL WHILE BLACK: CLIENTELE ISSUES

The traditional work of professionals involves the delivery of services directly to clients, patients, patrons, parishioners, and students. These clients are the consumers of services produced by professionals. The delivery of professional services by black professionals is "complicated" by the factor of race. Black professionals face two particular issues that revolve around the race and class for their would-be clients. First, black professionals are far less likely (than white professionals) to deliver professional services to white clients. Even in the post-civil rights era, African American professionals are much more likely to deliver professional services to other blacks, including the black poor. Thus, racialized class formation is exhibited in the professional service delivery process as well.

In this regard, what the neoclassical economist Gary Becker has casually referred to as "discriminatory taste" is largely beyond the scope of antidiscrimination law. Previous research has documented the "preference" of white consumers for the delivery of their professional and business services from whites, or at least, a preference that the deliverers of these services not be black (Feagin & Sikes, 1994, pp. 164–180; Waldinger & Aldrich, 1990, pp. 58–64). As a result, corporate firms are usually reluctant to assign black professionals such as lawyers and brokers to deal with white clients. This is also why self-employed black professionals (e.g., lawyers and doctors) have difficulty finding white clients. The preference of white consumers of professional services to receive those services from white professionals still occurs because those consumers prefer not to relate to blacks possessing a relatively superordinate occupational status:

> In all these cases, consumption of the service is connected with personal characteristics of the suppliers of the service. In the words of one West Coast personnel officer, the problem with respect to some kinds of jobs is not that the black employee lacks skills, "but that he is aesthetically objectionable – he spoils the decor, so to speak." This "spoilage" is rarely noted in situations where the black relation to whites is subordinate. In the business decision, the personal views of the employer may become irrelevant; the concern is the loss of sales by putting black workers in positions that reverse the lines of authority when dealing with consumers (Franklin, 1991, p. 122).

Thus, "racial preference" remains a prevalent factor in limiting black opportunities to serve a wide range of clients. This is particularly true when the provision of professional services entails direct, face-to-face interaction between a black professional and a white client (Franklin, 1991, p. 73). As a result, black professional employees are likely to be limited in their opportunities to work directly with white clients in substantively important ways. The result is a segregated, racially stratified market for professional services in which black professionals are "ghettoized" in the delivery of their services disproportionately to black and poorer clients. This tends to lower their incomes, curtail their potential client base, and lessen the range of their professional social networks.

On the other hand, however, my interviews indicate that black professionals generally want to provide services to "underserved" black clients, including the poor. This finding is contrary to the assertions of some that the black middle class seeks to abandon the black poor in their professional and civic efforts. Thus, an important area of difference between black and white professionals – particularly those in the areas of social or medical services – is in their clientele bases. An African American social worker with nearly 30 years of experience discussed her career with me. She has had a strong sense of wanting to help others facing difficult social and personal problems. She started as a "community mental health worker" without a college degree, but ultimately earned an M.S.W. from Berkeley. In her professional journey from caseworker to case management, she has seen many sides of the social work profession while focusing on particular needs of minority communities:

> I worked primarily with disturbed kids. As I went through my career – I came in with a high school diploma – and as I began to get more and more into my craft, I found that I had to go back to school. So I went back to school and received my BA in psychology ... and through that time I continued to work with kids who were severely emotionally disturbed, and they were primarily kids of color. And ... after I went to graduate school [for the MSW] I came back and started doing school social work. So I've consistently been working in the social services area and working primarily with kids of color – kids and families of color – and also in mental health, so it's been ... for the past 28 years.

As her social work career developed after completing graduate study, she was able to pursue new professional opportunities with colleagues. Her opportunities developed as part of social networks that primarily involved other black women social workers. They are collectively concerned with "minority community issues." As she elaborated on a sense of African American cooperation and obligation to the "community":

> You have an obligation. And most of these kids were of color. So, that was very revealing in itself.... [A]fter I got out of graduate school, my supervisor ... was a partner in a group [social work] practice in the community. She offered me a position to come in with her in this group practice. And the group practice at that time consisted of three African American women who were social workers. They were all licensed clinical social workers. And their specialty was working with kids of color who were victims of physical and sexual [abuse].... The significance? I was an intern [then] and now I'm a partner in a group practice.

In fact, research findings indicate that black social work students are much more likely to want to provide services to poor and racial minority communities than are white social work students. In urban areas, much of the service provision to the poor is through government agencies (directly or indirectly through government contracts). This is of particular concern given that the field of social work is rapidly moving toward an emphasis on privately delivered services (e.g., counseling and psychiatric social work) to predominantly white middle class clients (Specht & Courtney, 1994). The devolution of Aid to Families with Dependent Children (AFDC) in 1996 as a federal entitlement program to one of "temporary assistance" via welfare reform and the overall diminution of social services to the poor is instructive in this regard.

As with social work, the delivery of medical services to black urban neighborhoods is shaped by the availability of African American doctors. The experience of an African American doctor that I interviewed illustrates the role that black professional service providers play in black neighborhoods. She has held two primary medical practice positions during her medical career. The first position was in private practice and she is currently employed in a nonprofit agency that contracts with the state government of California. She disbanded her private practice because she didn't like dealing with the tedious paperwork and "business aspect" (e.g., figuring expenses, accounting, and quarterly taxes) of private practice that took time away from delivering actual medical services to her patients. In both positions, she has preferred to serve poor and minority communities despite the relatively lower remuneration. I asked her about her experience in private practice:

> It was in East Oakland. I had mainly [Medicaid] patients. Mainly black patients. Mainly low income patients. Which I didn't mind. I felt as a black person that I needed to give something back. I think it made me feel good to be in the black community. I realized that I would not make as much with the clientele that I had that I could make somewhere else but I was, again, satisfied. But I'll admit I was not a business person. To be quite honest, I don't think I had been prepared in medical school for that end of it .... I just did not like the business aspect of it.

And she describes the positive impact that she was able to make serving the same kinds of clients, after becoming an employee of the nonprofit agency:

> I had a lot of autonomy. I was able to do training programs and work with the operators. From being a staff physician, I became the chief physician and the director of clinical services here. I am probably only one of – well actually I'm the only black physician. All of the psychologists are white. Most of the people in the prevention unit that deals with the children from fetal to three are white. In that unit are speech therapists, nurses, infant specialists who are at a masters degree level, but they're all

white. But they're working with a black community. And there were some issues going on. So I saw some possibilities for me really having some input, such as training, like how to deal with black clients and issues that happen with the population that we see. And I've enjoyed that because I think it really has made a difference.

In the field of medicine, Black and Latino doctors are much more likely to serve racial minority patients than are white doctors. In fact, communities that are disproportionately white and poor have significantly more doctors per capita than black and Hispanic communities regardless of their status as poor or nonpoor. Reduction in the supply or availability of minority doctors may correspond with reduced health in minority communities (Komaromy et al., 1996). Moreover, continuing political attacks on civil rights and affirmative action policies will likely have the long-term effect of further reducing the supply of doctors serving poor and minority communities.

CONCLUSION

Despite the institutionalization of civil rights and affirmative action policies for two generations, African Americans remain greatly underrepresented in professional occupations and in other high-status middle class occupations. This is a problem of unequal hiring and promotion processes into such professional (and related managerial) positions. Furthermore, there are deep, socially reproduced structural inequalities of race (and class and gender) that civil rights laws and affirmative action policies alone cannot resolve (Bonilla-Silva, 2006; McCall, 2001). This includes the dynamic of "informal" evaluation and decision-making that frequently leads to a "preference" by white employers for white employees to be hired in positions of authority or expertise (Wilson, 1997).

The partially realized project of integrating blacks into "mainstream" professional occupational opportunities since the zenith of the civil rights movement has led to a new process of *racialized class formation* in the post-civil rights era. Occupational segregation hasn't been eliminated but exists in altered forms (McCall, 2001). As we have seen, members of the black professional middle class are racialized. As a result they are likely to (1) be employed in affirmative action-defined positions, (2) be hired in positions that mediate relations between firms and/or government and the black community, (3) serve predominantly or disproportionately (read segregated) black clientele as either self-employed professionals or professional employees of predominantly white firms, nonprofit organizations, or government agencies, and (4) be subject to evaluation by informal rather than formal job performance criteria in comparison to white colleagues. Moreover, the controversial oversight of civil rights laws and affirmative action policies has played a central role in the presence of blacks in mainstream institutions of higher education at the undergraduate, graduate, and professional levels (Bowen & Bok, 1998). Indeed, higher education provides the vital "pipeline" for black professional employment opportunity (Freeman, 1976).

Thus, recent and future political and judicial efforts to eradicate key civil rights and affirmative action policies (e.g., Proposition 209 in California) at the national and state levels, as well as overall economic decline in the United States, will likely have serious implications for the continued social reproduction of the black professional middle class. Efforts to incorporate racial minorities into the mainstream of primary labor markets – especially African Americans and probably Latinos as well – will face serious challenges. The exclusionary barriers posed by race and other forms of social status serve to reduce aggregate-level access for blacks and other underrepresented groups to professional occupations. Thus, the likely forthcoming dismantling of basic civil rights policies and affirmative action will likely hurt both the social reproduction of the black middle class and the professional service needs (e.g., educational, medical, and legal) of blacks (especially the poor) by reducing the pool of professionals interested in serving poor and racial minority communities.

Ironically, there is evidence that the life chances of blacks vis-à-vis occupational mobility is shifting back toward increased "racial significance" in the contemporary *post-civil rights era*. Research on the era of the 1980s has found that the children of middle class whites were nearly twice as likely to improve their occupational status as the children of middle class blacks (Duncan, Smeeding, & Rodgers, 1993). Downward mobility is also much more prevalent among African American men than among their white counterparts (Davis, 1995). Furthermore, a study conducted by the Brookings Institution found a clear trend of downward mobility for blacks of *middle class background* born in the late 1960s (Isaacs, 2007). The combination of these shifting trends raise questions about the continuing viability of the cross-generational social reproduction of the black professional middle class in the ongoing post-civil rights period.

African Americans have entered the mainstream professional middle class later, in smaller relative numbers and at lower occupational status levels than have whites (Freeman, 1976; Jaynes & Williams, 1989). Indeed, until the passage of the Civil Rights Act of 1964, black professionals (as in other areas of public life) existed as virtually segregated subset of the professional middle class. They were mostly isolated in black colleges, teaching in segregated public schools, providing legal, medical, and spiritual advice to underserved black clients and patients. In fact, a mitigated pattern of segregated professionalization arguably remains the predominant form for most black professionals even while in "mainstream" institutional settings. Despite having a black president in the United States, there is continued "underrepresentation" of blacks in professional occupations, and the "integration" of blacks into the professional middle class remains an incomplete project at best. What happens in this regard to the contemporary process of racialized class formation of black professionals in the long term will depend on what happens in the debate about racial inequality in the larger society.

NOTES

1. Race-based constructs utilized by scholars in the internal colonial tradition included the now standard concept of "institutional discrimination" utilized initially by iconoclastic radical activist-theorist Kwame Ture (Stokely Carmicahael). See Ture and Hamilton (1992 [1967]). In the 1970s, Bob Blauner tried to work out basic intellectual problems such as the necessary differentiation between ethnic vs. racial minorities and the concept of racial privilege, which are standard in the sociological literature today. See Blauner (2001).
2. See the sociological and historical overview offered on the "dual society" and the long-term entrenchment of segregation in U.S. society. See Ringer (1983).
3. The "ethnic niches" can vary from city to city. Waldinger found that blacks in New York never had much of a hold on the manufacturing sectors and were concentrated in the service economy early on. He found that working class blacks were pushed out of hotel service and replaced by immigrants of color. Subsequently, blacks became increasingly concentrated in the government sector. Black professionals are also relatively overrepresented in the public sector. See Waldinger (1995).
4. As Charles Ragin suggests, when aggregate data has been used to paint a particular analytic framework for a research problem, it may be necessary to utilize case studies or "in-depth" analyses of the research problem. This may require multiple studies by different scholars to establish important empirical findings. See Ragin (1994).
5. The professions represented are attorneys (6), physicians (3), clergy (3), teachers (3), academics (2), politicians (2), engineer, urban planner, banker, public health official, journalist, social worker, industrial psychologist, librarian, nurse, demographer, and artist.
6. This finding is similar to research that indicated that despite substantial sunbelt economic growth, increasing employment opportunities, and the ascendancy of local black political leadership in Atlanta, the substantive socioeconomic status of blacks locally remained notably poorer relative to their white peers. That is, general

economic growth, in and of itself, doesn't readily alter entrenched patterns of racial inequality. See Orfield and Ashkinaze (1991).

7. See, for example, Feagin et al. (1991).

8. Eduardo Bonilla-Silva has characterized "color blindness" as the dominant racial ideology of the post-civil rights era – utilized by conservatives and liberals. Underlying "color blindness" are *frames* that mask the material benefits of white racial privilege. These frames form the basis of *color-blind racism* that preserves a structured system of racial inequality by promoting "racism without racists." See Bonilla-Silva (2006, pp. 1–49).

9. For example, Erik Olin Wright and other scholars have invested much intellectual effort to get a grasp on the essential bases of the contemporary middle class or middle classes. Wright has introduced analytic concepts like "contradictory class locations" (see Wright, 1978) and later, the construction of models built around skills and credentials as exploitable assets (see Wright, 1985). Most recently, variables of skill, authority, and property have been analyzed by Wright (1997).

10. Professionals are mostly unambiguous middle class for a number of conventional reasons. They tend to rate highly on the three key *gradational* criteria: occupational status, income, and educational attainment. They also fulfill the *relational* dimensions of middle class position identified by Erik Olin Wright and others including the categories of skill and authority (clear correlations with managers) in the postindustrial advanced capitalist class structure. See Wright (1997, pp. 79–111).

11. Nationally, in 1940, over 70% of black women and about 15% of black men worked in such positions. In 1950, the comparable figures were 61% of black women and 14% of black men in domestic service occupations. See U.S. Bureau of the Census. (1952). *Census of the Population.* Washington, DC: U.S. Government Printing Office.

12. Eliot Friedson writes that "it is no accident that Wright, Costello, Hachen, & Sprague (1982, p. 719) found that by their 'class location' criteria, conventionally classified 'professionals' were 'managerial' in 52 percent of the cases." See Friedson (1986).

13. Based on the 1990 Census, the state of California had a population that was 53% white and 47% "minorities" (African Americans, Asian Americans, Latinos, and Native Americans). By 2000, California achieved a "majority of minorities." According to the 2000 Census, the state was only 46.7% (non-Hispanic) white. Latinos were 32.4%, Asian Americans 12.3%, blacks 7.4%, and Native Americans 1.9% of the state's population. Accordingly, California is much more "multiracial" than any other state.

14. Larger companies that have contracts with the federal government tend to be core sector firms and also tend to provide higher wages, salaries, and benefits. The primary labor market jobs they provide are most in demand from prospective employees. They are also the firms scrutinized more closely for patterns of discrimination, and most affected by affirmative action policies during the heyday of civil rights enforcement. Between 1974 and 1980 in firms covered by the OFCCP, the employment growth rate for black men was 3.8%, faster than in non-covered firms. For other minority men (e.g., Asian American and Latino), it was 7.9% faster. It was 13.2% faster for black women, and 2.8% faster for white women. By contrast,

employment growth for white men was 1.2% slower for white men. See Leonard (1986, p. 359).

ACKNOWLEDGMENTS

The research for this chapter was made possible, in part, by a graduate fellowship from the National Science Foundation. The author has benefited from the suggestions of several readers. I wish to thank Troy Duster, Mike Hout, Bob Blauner, Michael Omi, Judith Blau, and Dave Brunsma for comments on earlier versions of this chapter. I also greatly appreciate the helpful comments of the anonymous reviewers and the editor.

REFERENCES

Blackwell, J. (1987). *Mainstreaming outsiders: The production of black professionals* (2nd ed.). Dix Hills, NY: General Hall.

Blau, P., & Duncan, O. D. (1967). *The American occupational structure*. New York, NY: The Free Press.

Blauner, B. (1992). Talking past each other: Black and white languages of race. *The American Prospect, 10*, 55–64.

Blauner, B. (2001). *Still the big news: Racial oppression in America*. Philadelphia, PA: Temple University Press.

Bloom, J. M. (1987). *Class, race and the civil rights movement*. Bloomington, IN: Indiana University Press.

Bonilla-Silva, E. (2006). *Racism without racists: Color blind racism and the persistence of racial inequality in the United States* (2nd ed.). Lanham, MD: Rowman & Littlefield.

Bound, J., & Freeman, R. (1990). What went wrong?: The erosion of relative earnings and employment among young black men in the 1980s. *The Quarterly Journal of Economics, 107*(1), 201–232.

Bowen, W., & Bok, D. (1998). *The shape of the river: Long-term consequences of considering race in college and university admissions*. Princeton, NJ: Princeton University Press.

Broussard, A. S. (1993). *Black San Francisco: The struggle for racial equality in the West, 1900–1954*. Lawrence, KS: University Press of Kansas.

Brown, E. S. (1998). Black ghetto formation in Oakland, 1852–1965: Social closure and African American community development. *Research in Community Sociology, 8*, 255–274.

Brown, E. S. (2009). The black professional middle class and the black community: Racialized class formation in Oakland and the East Bay. In K. L. Kusmer & J. W. Trotter (Eds.), *African American history since World War II* (pp. 263–291). Chicago, IL: University of Chicago Press.

Brown, M. K., Carnoy, M., Currie, E., Duster, T., Oppenheimer, D. B., Shultz, M., & Wellman, D. (2003). *White-washing race: The myth of a color-blind society*. Berkeley, CA: University of California Press.

Carnoy, M. (1994). *Faded dreams: The politics and economics of race in America*. New York, NY: Cambridge University Press.

Collins, P. H. (2000). *Black feminist thought: Knowledge, consciousness, and the politics of empowerment* (2nd ed.). New York, NY: Routledge.

Collins, S. (1997). *Black corporate executives: The making and breaking of a black middle class.* Philadelphia, PA: Temple University Press.

Conley, D. (1999). *Being black, living in the red: Race, wealth, and social policy in America.* Berkeley, CA: University of California Press.

Cose, E. (1993). *The rage of a privileged class.* New York, NY: HarperCollins.

Daniels, D. H. (1991). *Pioneer urbanites: A social and cultural history of black San Francisco.* Berkeley, CA: University of California Press.

Davis, T. J., Jr. (1995). The occupational mobility of black men revisited: Does race matter? *Social Science Journal, 32,* 121–135.

Derber, C., Schwartz, W. A., & Magrass, Y. (1990). *Power in the highest degree: Professionals and the rise of a new Mandarin order.* New York, NY: Oxford University Press.

Drake, St. C., & Cayton, H. R. (1945). *Black metropolis.* Chicago, IL: University of Chicago Press.

Duncan, G., Smeeding, T., & Rodgers, W. (1993). Whither the middle class? A dynamic view. In D. Papadimitriou & E. N. Wolff (Eds.), *Poverty and prosperity in the USA in the late twentieth century* (pp. 202–271). New York, NY: St. Martin's Press.

Edelman, L. B. (1992). Legal ambiguity and symbolic structures: Organizational mediation of civil rights law. *American Journal of Sociology, 97,* 1531–1576.

Edwards, G. F. (1959). *The Negro professional class.* Glencoe, IL: The Free Press.

Fainstein, N. (1993). Race, class, and segregation: Discourses about African Americans. *International Journal of Urban and Regional Research, 17,* 384–403.

Feagin, J. R., Orum, A., & Sjoberg, G. (Eds.). (1991). *A case for the case study.* Chapel Hill, NC: University of North Carolina Press.

Feagin, J. R., & Sikes, M. (1994). *Living with racism: The black middle class experience.* Boston, MA: Beacon Press.

Franklin, R. S. (1991). *Shadows of race and class.* Minneapolis, MN: University of Minnesota Press.

Frazier, E. F. (1957). *The black bourgeoisie: The making of a middle class.* New York, NY: The Free Press.

Freeman, R. (1976). *Black elite: The new market for highly educated black Americans.* New York, NY: McGraw-Hill.

Friedson, E. (1986). *Professional powers: A study of the institutionalization of formal knowledge* (p. 60). Chicago, IL: University of Chicago Press.

Gans, H. (1996). *The war against the poor: The underclass and antipoverty policy.* New York, NY: Basic Books.

Granovetter, M. (1974). *Getting a job: A study of contacts and careers.* Cambridge, MA: Harvard University Press.

Gregory, S. (1998). *Black corona: Race and the politics of place in an urban community.* Princeton, NJ: Princeton University Press.

Harrison, B., & Gorham, L. (1992). Growing inequality in black wages in the 1980s and the emergence of an African American middle class. *Journal of Policy Analysis and Management, 11,* 235–253.

Haynes, B. (2001). *Red lines, black spaces: The politics of race and space in a black middle class suburb.* New Haven, CT: Yale University Press.

Hochschild, J. L. (1995). *Facing up to the American dream: Race, class, and the soul of the nation.* Princeton, NJ: Princeton University Press.

Holzer, H. J. (2001). Racial differences in labor market outcomes among men. In N. J. Smelser, W. J. Wilson & F. Mitchell (Eds.), *America becoming: Racial trends and their consequences, 2 vols* (pp. 98–123). Washington, DC: National Academy Press.

Isaacs, J. (2007). *Economic mobility of black and white families.* Washington, DC: The Brookings Institution.

Jackman, M. R., & Jackman, R. W. (1982). *Class awareness in the United States.* Berkeley, CA: University of California Press.

Jaynes, G., & Williams, R., Jr. (Eds.). (1989). *A common destiny: Blacks and American society.* Washington, DC: National Academy Press.

Johnson, M. S. (1993). *The second gold rush: Oakland and the East Bay in World War II.* Berkeley, CA: University of California Press.

Komaromy, M., Grumbach, K., Drake, M., Vranizan, K., Lurie, N., Keane, D., & Bindman, A. B. (1996). The role of black and Hispanic physicians in providing health care for underserved populations. *The New England Journal of Medicine, 334*(20), 1305–1310.

Lacy, K. R. (2007). *Blue chip black: Race, class, and status in the new black middle class.* Berkeley, CA: University of California Press.

Landry, B. (1987). *The new black middle class.* Berkeley, CA: University of California Press.

Leonard, J. S. (1986). What was affirmative action? *The American Economic Review, 76*(2), 359–363.

Leonard, J. S. (1990). The impact of affirmative action and equal employment opportunity law on black employment. *Journal of Economic Perspectives, 4,* 145–174.

Massey, D., & Denton, N. (1993). *American apartheid: Segregation and the making of the underclass.* Cambridge, MA: Harvard University Press.

McAdam, D. (1999). *Political process and the development of black insurgency, 1930–1970* (2nd ed.). Chicago, IL: University of Chicago Press.

McCall, L. (2001). *Complex inequality: Gender, class, and race in the new economy.* New York, NY: Routledge.

Morris, A. (1986). *Origins of the civil rights movement.* New York, NY: The Free Press.

Moynihan, D. P. (1972). The schism in black America. *The Public Interest, 27,* 3–24.

Myerson, A. R. (1997). Workers unite, take job bias to the courts. *The New York Times,* January 12.

Noyelle, T. J. (1987). *Beyond industrial dualism.* Boulder, CO: Westview Press.

Oliver, M. L., & Shapiro, T. M. (2006). *Black wealth, white wealth: New perspectives on racial inequality* (2nd ed.). New York, NY: Routledge.

Omi, M., & Winant, H. (1994). *Racial formation in the United States: From the 1960s to the 1990s* (2nd ed.). New York, NY: Routledge.

Orfield, G., & Ashkinaze, C. (1991). *The closing door: Conservative policy and black opportunity.* Chicago, IL: University of Chicago Press.

Patillo, M. (2007). *Black on the block: The politics of race and class in the city.* Chicago, IL: University of Chicago Press.

Patillo-McCoy, M. (1999). *Black picket fences: Privilege and peril among the black middle class.* Chicago, IL: University of Chicago Press.

Pettigrew, T. (1981). Race and class in the 1980s: An interactive view. *Daedalus, 110*(2), 233–255.

Ragin, C. C. (1994). *Constructing social research: The university and diversity of method* (pp. 81–103). Thousand Oaks, CA: Pine Forge Press.
Reskin, B. F., McBrier, D. B., & Kmec, J. A. (1999). The determinants and consequences of workplace sex and race composition. *Annual Review of Sociology, 25*(1), 335–361.
Ringer, B. (1983). *We the people and others: Duality and America's treatment of its racial minorities.* New York, NY: Tavistock.
Shapiro, T. (2004). *The hidden cost of being African American: How wealth perpetuates inequality.* New York, NY: Oxford.
Skrentny, J. D. (2002). *The minority rights revolution.* Cambridge, MA: Belknap Press of Harvard University Press.
Smelser, N. J., Wilson, W. J., & Mitchell, F. (Eds.). (2001). *America becoming: Racial trends and their consequences, 2 vols.,* Washington, DC: National Academy Press.
Smith, J. P. (2001). Race and ethnicity in the labor market: Trends over the long and short term. In N. J. Smelser, W. J. Wilson & F. Mitchell (Eds.), *America Becoming: Racial trends and their consequences, 2 vols* (pp. 52–97). Washington, DC: National Academy Press.
Specht, H., & Courtney, M. E. (1994). *Unfaithful angels: How social work has abandoned its mission.* New York, NY: The Free Press.
Steinberg, S. (1995). *Turning back: The retreat from racial justice in American thought and policy.* Boston, MA: Beacon Press.
Ture, K., Hamilton, C. (1992 [1967]). *Black power.* New York, NY: Vintage.
Turner, M. A., Fix, M., & Struyk, R. J. (1991). *Opportunities denied, opportunities diminished: Discrimination in hiring.* Washington, DC: The Urban Institute Press.
U.S. Bureau of the Census. (1950–2000). *Census of population housing. Population and housing characteristics for census tracts and block numbering areas.* Oakland, CA: PMSA. Washington, DC: Bureau of the Census.
U.S. Bureau of the Census. (1990 and 2000). *Metropolitan areas. Summary of social and economic characteristics for persons and for households and families.* Oakland, CA: PMSA. Washington, DC: Bureau of the Census.
Waldinger, R. (1995). *Still the promised city?: African Americans and new immigrants in postindustrial New York* (pp. 240–253). Cambridge, MA: Harvard University Press.
Waldinger, R., & Aldrich, H. (1990). Trends in ethnic business in the United States. In R. Waldinger, H. Aldrich, R. Ward & Associates (Eds.), *Ethnic entrepreneurs* (pp. 49–78). Newbury Park, CA: Sage.
Wilson, G. (1997). Pathways to power: Racial differences in the determinants of job authority. *Social Problems, 44*(1), 38–54.
Wilson, G. (2007). Racialized life-chance opportunities across the class structure: The case of African Americans. *Annals of the American Academy of Political and Social Science, 609*(1), 215–232.
Wilson, W. J. (1987). *The truly disadvantaged.* Chicago, IL: University of Chicago Press.
Wilson, W. J. (1996). *When work disappears.* New York, NY: Alfred E. Knopf.
Wright, E. O. (1978). *Class, crisis and the state.* London: New Left Books.
Wright, E. O. (1985). *Classes.* London: Verso.
Wright, E. O. (1997). *Class counts.* New York, NY: Cambridge University Press.
Wright, E. O., Costello, C., Hachen, D., & Sprague, J. (1982). The American class structure. *American Sociological Review, 47,* 709–726.
Zweig, M. (2001). *The working class majority: America's best kept secret.* Ithaca, NY: Cornell University Press.

PART III
SCHOLARLY CONTROVERSY: VARIETIES OF CAPITALISM

PART III

VARIETIES OF WHAT? SHOULD WE STILL BE USING THE CONCEPT OF CAPITALISM?

Fred Block

ABSTRACT

This article argues that social scientists should reconsider the analytic value of the term "capitalism." The paper argues that the two most coherent definitions of capitalism are those derived from classical Marxism and from the World System theory of Immanuel Wallerstein. Marx and Engels' formulation was basically a genetic theory in which the structure of a mode of production is determined by the mode of surplus extraction. During the course of the 20th century, however, Marxist theorists had to modify this framework and the result has been an uncomfortable hybrid. Wallerstein resolved these tensions by redefining capitalism in terms of the logic of a world system. However, his argument has difficulty in explaining the consequential variations over time in the specific rules and institutional structures that operate at the global level. The article goes on to argue in favor of Karl Polanyi's concept of market society because it focuses attention on the political governance of market societies at both the national and the global levels.

In the Fall of 2011, the Occupy Wall Street movement galvanized the long-dormant left in the United States by reframing politics as a battle between the 99% and the 1% of the population that had seen huge income and wealth gains over the previous 30 years. For the first time in decades, issues of economic inequality became topics of daily conversation. Frank Luntz, the Republican wordsmith and strategist, announced that he was "frightened to death" by this new movement's impact on public opinion, and when the Republican Governor's Association met in late November in Florida, he offered his 10 commandments on how Republicans should respond to this challenge.[1]

His first commandment to the governors was: "Don't say 'capitalism.'" He elaborated: "I'm trying to get that word removed and we're replacing it with either 'economic freedom' or 'free market.' The public ... still prefers capitalism to socialism, but they think capitalism is immoral. And if we're seen as defenders of quote, Wall Street, end quote, we've got a problem."

It is hard to tell whether Luntz' advice was a deliberate feint to trick the left or actual political malpractice, but I have been arguing exactly the opposite point for more than a decade (Block, 2000, 2002; see also Graham & Gibson, 1996). My point is that at least since the 1970s, the political right has been strengthened by using the term capitalism and the left has been weakened. Luntz' argument is certainly correct for the earlier period; for roughly a century from the Paris Commune to the rebellions of 1968, rallying against capitalism gave the international left the moral high ground, and defenders of existing property arrangements were well advised to talk instead about economic freedom or free markets. But in the 1970s, things changed because under the intellectual leadership of Irving Kristol (1978), the right self-consciously appropriated the term capitalism and insisted that they were pro-capitalist and proud.

Kristol's maneuver helped create the context in which Margaret Thatcher could insist that: "There is no alternative" – meaning that we live in a capitalist society and we have to accept rules that require that we be extremely kind to the rich and cruel to the poor or we will destroy the incentive system that brings forth new investment from the former and greater work effort from the latter.[2] And the right continues to use this rhetoric down to the present. In 2009, for example, the most conservative Republican members of the U.S. House of Representatives introduced a proposed constitutional amendment entitled the "Preserving Capitalism in America Amendment." The measure was in response to the bailout of the U.S. auto industry; the proposal would prohibit the government from owning stock in any company. In a word, when the right transitioned from a defense of "free markets" to a defense of "capitalism," they gained the critical leverage of invoking a global system that would not tolerate deviations from its founding principles.[3]

Over these last 30 years of increasing economic strains in the developed market societies, this rhetoric worked very well to dampen challenges from the left. The right would repeatedly argue that the reason that the economy was not performing up to its potential was that there had been too many deviations from core capitalist principles – too much taxation, too much government regulation, too much welfare. Only when these were cut back sufficiently would prosperity return. At the same time, they could remind people that the only known alternative to capitalism was socialism and that system had failed spectacularly in the Soviet Union and its allies.

Moreover, during this same period, the left tended to gain the greatest political advantage precisely when it avoided invoking the duality of capitalism versus socialism. So, for example, the anti-globalization movement that produced the massive demonstration in Seattle against the World Trade Organization and that organized itself globally through the World Social Forum emphasized the slogan: "Another World Is Possible" – deliberately leaving ambiguous whether that other world was socialist or capitalist. That ambiguity allowed the movement to gather extremely diverse constituencies behind its banners (Santos, 2008).

Similarly, while some of the militants in the Occupy Wall Street movement talk about capitalism and socialism, the movement's main rhetoric avoids those terms and focuses on the clash between the 1% and the 99%.[4] Since many moderate and conservative citizens are disturbed by the deepening inequalities of income and wealth in the United States (Page & Jacobs, 2009), this has allowed the movement to generate a sympathetic response from people who have not the slightest affinity for socialism. In short, focusing attention on the greed and immorality of Wall Street operatives – rather than a label for the entire system – helped Occupy Wall Street to tap into deeply rooted distrust of economic elites.

But beyond the question that Luntz raises as to which term gives which political groups the most strategic leverage, there is also an urgent question for social scientists – what is the analytic value of "capitalism" as a concept? Does it help to illuminate key features of existing societies or does it carry with it burdensome associations from earlier historical periods? The question is complicated because the analysis of capitalism was pioneered by the Marxist tradition and the socialist movement.

And this legacy is itself complex. Marx began his career elaborating a critique of political economy that was intended to overthrow the categories and assumptions of classical political economy – including the claim that society's choices were dictated by the demands of an economic mechanism. But Marx is now largely remembered for developing his own political economy that he used to explain the internal contradictions of the capitalist mode of production. A number of insightful analysts have questioned whether the shift from the critique of political economy to a new political economy might have subverted that initial project (Gouldner, 1980; Polanyi, Arensberg, & Pearson, 1968; Sahlins, 1976). So for all social scientists – both those who simply want to understand contemporary societies and those who share the emancipatory aspirations of critical theory – there is an urgent need to interrogate the concept of capitalism.

"CAPITALISM" AND THE SOCIAL SCIENCES

In the decades right after World War II, the term "capitalism" had only a marginal existence in academic discourse in the United States; it was used by a relatively small number of scholars on the left whose views had been shaped by the socialist tradition. While such influential Central European thinkers as Max Weber (1998 [1904–1905]) and Schumpeter (1942) used the word in the titles of famous books in the first half of the 20th century, their example was not followed by most academics in the United States. Even those who celebrated the contributions of Weber and Schumpeter tended to avoid this terminology because it had been tainted by the Cold War. Capitalism was the epithet that the international communist movement used to denounce the United States.

This situation changed as a consequence of the New Left inspired revival of Neo-Marxism in the 1960s.[5] Books such as Immanuel Wallerstein's *The Modern Capitalist World System* (1974), Anthony Giddens', *Capitalism and Modern Social Theory* (1971), and the edited volume by Edwards, Reich, and Weisskopf, *The Capitalist System* (1972), gave new legitimacy to the term. It was this new-found respectability that made Kristol's initiative to appropriate the term for conservatives successful. Two radical defenders of free markets, Milton Friedman (1962) and Ayn Rand (1966), had anticipated Kristol's move in the 1960s by using capitalism in the title of key works, but their effort was unsuccessful because the term was still so strongly associated with the communist left. Even New Leftists were initially reluctant to use the term; in his speech in 1965 at the first SDS March on Washington against the Vietnam War, SDS President Paul Potter proposed to "name the system" that had produced racism and the Vietnam War, but he still did not actually say the word capitalism (Potter, 1965).

The irony is that Kristol's move to appropriate the term proved more durable than the efforts of academic Neo-Marxists. The influence of Neo-Marxism receded in most social science disciplines by the 1980s as the Thatcher–Reagan "Right Turn" came to dominate both political and scholarly debates. The term "capitalism" did not gain academic respectability until the 1990s when a number of scholars began to argue that capitalism was not homogenous, and that there were instead distinct types or varieties of institutional arrangements that fit under this rubric. This new perspective was a reaction to the Thatcher–Reagan rhetoric that claimed that there was just one set of options on offer and that every country had to put on what the *New York Times* columnist Thomas Friedman (1999) would later dub the "golden straitjacket." An early contributor to this variety approach was Esping-Andersen's influential 1990 book, *Three Worlds of Welfare Capitalism*, which documented the very substantial variations in public provision across Western Europe and North America. Another important strand was the body of scholarship that sought to make sense of the rapid economic rise of Japan and other East Asian economies that clearly diverged sharply from the Anglo-American economic model (Orru, Biggart, & Hamilton, 1997; Wade, 1990).

By the end of the 1990s and the early 2000s, this body of work had been consolidated under the framework of "varieties of capitalism" scholarship producing careful documentation of the ways that welfare systems, financial systems, corporate governance, employment relations, and innovation systems differed across market democracies. Important contributions to this body of literature were made by sociologists, political scientists, economists, and other scholars (Berger & Dore, 1996; Crouch & Streeck, 1997; Gray, 1998; Hall & Soskice, 2001; Hollingsworth & Boyer, 1997; Lundvall, 1992).[6]

But what is striking about this significant body of work is that virtually all of the emphasis was on "variety" and there was very little discussion of why it made sense to see these all as variations of a single type – namely capitalism. This omission is understandable since this body of work was a response to the right's embrace of the concept of capitalism and its insistence that there was one single model of how to organize an efficient and effective society. By stressing that there were "varieties of capitalism," these scholars were challenging the right and arguing that there was significantly more policy space available to governments than free market theorists were willing to admit.

But at a certain point, it becomes necessary to ask: are these all varieties of the same species or could these be different species that have distinct internal processes and are on quite different historical trajectories?[7] The question is important because for both Marxists and for capitalism's conservative defenders, the term capitalism retains an irreducible teleology or belief about the direction of history. For Marxists, capitalism is an absolute constraint on human possibilities; it must be ended to create a just social order. For right-wing defenders of capitalism, eventually all societies will recognize the need for social arrangements that prioritize the accumulation of wealth and limit governmental "interference" in the operations of an autonomous economy.

In short, the term capitalism invokes the ideas of a system that has a fundamental unity or coherence (Graham & Gibson, 1996). And this, in turn, produces specific predictions about paths of development that are necessarily closed off because they are inconsistent with the system's defining features. This is apparent when we look both at the classical theory of capitalism developed by Marx and Engels and at the work done by their theoretical followers in the 20th century. The stark reality is that there really is no widely influential theory of capitalism outside of those developed within the Marxist tradition,[8] so it is only logical that the term still carries with it meanings that derive from that long history.

BACK TO MARX

In Marx and Engels' theorization of capital, the class relationship between capitalist and worker in which surplus value is appropriated is the key driving mechanism. This is central to the way in which they understand both the rise of capitalism and the accumulation of contradictions that would ultimately bring capitalism to an end. It is after all the pressure on each particular capitalist to continue extracting more and more surplus value that explains both the extraordinary dynamism of capitalist enterprise and the emergence of periodic crises when the system's ability to produce an avalanche of new commodities exceeds society's ability to purchase them. But Marx and Engels also insist that the powerful force field created by the everyday process of appropriating surplus works to reshape ideology, culture, law, and politics to reproduce this core class relationship.

Let us call this argument a genetic theory of capitalism because it is fundamentally similar to the idea that the DNA encoded in each cell shapes the structure and development of the entire organism. Rather than the cell, the basic unit is the production unit where surplus value is extracted. The dominant mode of surplus extraction, in turn, shapes the structure and development of the entire society. This kind of genetic theory can be elaborated in ways that look like crude economic determinism in which culture and politics play no independent role and in very sophisticated versions that recognize that culture and politics have a significant degree of autonomy. To avoid beating at straw men, we can stipulate that it is only the more sophisticated versions of this genetic argument that are being considered here.

Marx and Engels used this way of defining capitalism as a way to separate their politics and theories from those of their contemporaries. Specifically, they were differentiating themselves from both reformists and from "utopian socialists" and anarchists who, they thought, lacked a persuasive theory of how radical change would occur. The genetic theory insisted that reformism was doomed to failure; unless capitalism was torn up by its roots, the genetic code would continue to reassert itself. This required destroying the reign of private property, which could only occur when the working class had developed sufficiently. A proletarian revolution that abolished private ownership of the means of production was the only way to keep capitalism from reproducing itself.

This version of the theory was compelling during Marx's lifetime since this new form of social organization was still reasonably young. But the persistence of these social relations created a problem for subsequent Marxist theorists who had to explain both the continued existence of capitalism and the expanding role of government in managing the tensions created by market economies.[9] These theorists began to emphasize the strand in Marx and Engels' work that described how problems generated by the accumulation process are ultimately managed by and through the state.

Marx and Engels had insisted, after all, that when capitalist class relations were developing within feudalism, there were growing tensions and conflicts that could only be resolved through state action. The bourgeois revolution used the state to dismantle feudalism and institute a new property regime that supported and encouraged the core process of accumulating surplus value from free laborers. Similarly, in *Capital*, Marx describes how the state intervenes to place limits on the length of the working day and that creates the critical turn to continuous technological improvement as the way to squeeze more surplus value from each worker.

Building on these arguments, subsequent Marxists have argued that the state imposes a variety of "fixes" that solve one set of problems in the capitalist economy, but these fixes invariably generate new contradictions and tensions. While David Harvey (2006, 2010) has developed his own taxonomy of these different types of fixes, his theoretical move is characteristic of virtually all Marxist theorizing in the 20th century (from Lenin, Luxemburg, and Hilferding to Baran and Sweezy, Ernest Mandel, Arrighi, and the French regulation theorists). All of them seek to delineate different stages or phases of capitalist development by analyzing the different ways in which the state seeks to resolve and manage the underlying contradictions of the system. These analysts differ in how much they emphasize the complex process of political maneuvering through which these fixes come about, but none of them treat the solutions as emerging automatically from the contradictions. They also suggest that each particular fix or solution sets capitalist development along a particular path that will generate new contradictions and a need for new fixes. Solutions are only temporary; the fundamental contradictions will reassert themselves at one time or another.

But when they get to this point, these theorists are no longer working with the pure genetic theory of capitalism elaborated by Marx and Engels. What they have instead is a hybrid theory that says that at any moment in time, the structure of a given capitalist society will be determined by a combination of the fundamental class relations and the state-imposed fixes designed to contain the contradictions generated by those fundamental class relations. Moreover, it would seem that as time goes on, and a continuing series of new fixes have been attempted, the genetic theory – by itself – would account for a diminishing proportion of the institutional forms of any given capitalist society.

There is nothing, in principle, wrong with hybrid theories, but the problem here is that the process of theoretical fusion leaves the theorist with a very serious contradiction. One possibility is that the political fixes could actually change the underlying class relationships. So, for example, if a particular nation pursued a financial fix where capital is increasingly directed into acquisition of stocks, bonds, derivatives, and other types of paper and that process actually displaced the primacy of accumulation through the direct expropriation of surplus value, this would fundamentally alter the nature of capitalism. But this would eliminate the unifying element that Marx and Engels gave to their account of capitalism as a system; each of the different phases or different fixes could give you societies with different class structures, different dynamics, and different contradictions.

But most of these theorists steadfastly refused to follow this argument to its logical conclusion. Instead, they continued to invoke the classical argument that underneath all of the diverse fixes, there are the same fundamental class relationships and the same core contradictions. In other words, the only fixes that are possible within capitalism are those that are consistent with the underlying laws of accumulation. But these claims seem more like declarations of loyalty to a dogma than analytically powerful arguments about the actual development of societies.

In sum, by the last decades of the 19th century, it was no longer possible to adhere to Marx and Engels' initial genetic theory of capitalism in which the process of appropriation of surplus value in the wage relationship shapes the entire social order. But the later hybrid formulations by Marxist theorists fail to provide a persuasive explanation for the unity of the capitalist mode of production. It would seem that different fixes could allow societies to develop along different lines. In analogy with biological evolution, there could be the emergence of a new species of social order that was no longer capitalist and yet did not have the collective ownership of the means of production that defines socialism.[10]

THE WALLERSTEINIAN MOVE

With these theoretical tensions within the Marxist tradition, the concept of capitalism appeared on ever shakier ground as the 20th century progressed. However, a novel theoretical move gave the concept of capitalism a new vitality and coherence in the last decades of the 20th century. This was the appearance of Immanuel Wallerstein's multivolume study of the modern world system that provided a way out of the theoretical dilemmas faced by Marxist theorists in the 20th century (1974, 1980, 1989). Wallerstein's key move was to redefine the essential features of capitalism. While he followed Marx and Engels in emphasizing the initial importance of employers appropriating surplus value through the wage relationship, Wallerstein made the emergence of a global trading system the essential feature and principal disciplinary mechanism of capitalism. Wallerstein dispensed with the genetic theory of capitalism and solved the problem of the unity of capitalism by shifting the unit of analysis from nations to the capitalist world system itself.[11]

Wallerstein follows Marx in arguing that the initial breakthrough was the invention of capitalist agriculture in Northwest Europe that significantly increases agricultural productivity and profits. But the increased output creates the pressure for increased trade and this leads both Holland and

England to pursue overseas commercial advantage. These early capitalist powers build a world system that then transforms every society that is brought into it. European expansion imposes coerced labor on people in the Americas, Africa, and Asia, and the profits from plantations and mines then accelerate economic development in Europe.

Wallerstein's innovation solves the problem that had plagued 20th century Marxists – how to resolve the tension between continuity and change. For Wallerstein, the continuous unchanging feature of capitalism is a world system that exerts unrelenting pressure on societies to obey its commands. While the nature of production can shift from agriculture to manufactured goods to services and global leadership can shift from Holland to England and then to the United States, the unchanging feature is that there is a capitalist world system that puts nations in a zero-sum competition with each other to squeeze more wealth out of their workers. Moreover, that world system will continue to be divided between a core of the richest countries, a periphery of poor nations, and a semi-periphery of those who are in between even though some of the incumbents of those different positions will change over time.

Wallerstein's reformulation of the theory of capitalism preceded the greatly increased public consciousness of "globalization" that occurred in the 1980s and 1990s. As a consequence, his ideas very quickly turned into a common sense description of reality. People who have never heard of Wallerstein now routinely use the term capitalism to describe the core logic of a competitive world economy. Whether they are on the left, the right, or the center, they insist that nations are competing with each other for advantage in trade and capital flows, and this system then places dramatic constraints on what policies could and should be pursued at the national or even supranational level.

In fact, this is essentially the theoretical apparatus that is used – explicitly or implicitly – by most variety of capitalism analysts. They generally use capitalism not as a description of the economic arrangements of the individual cases, but of the competitive world economy in which nations are situated. It is this environment that is seen as placing distinct limits on how far they might evolve in one direction or another. While there are different institutional configurations that can lead to certain kinds of success in the world marketplace, it is extremely unlikely that any society will deliberately choose an institutional configuration that produces failure in the global competitive struggle. The collapse of the Soviet Union and the radical transformation of the Chinese Communist regime testify to the seriousness of these global pressures.

PROBLEMS WITH THE WALLERSTEIN SOLUTION

The idea that different nations are competing for advantage in the global economy which systematically rewards certain types of policies and practices and metes out pain and austerity to others is indisputable. But the question remains what makes these global structures capitalist? Would it still be a capitalist world system, for example, if the global trading rules required that all products be priced in accordance with their environmental impact?

This question is important because scholarship in political economy stresses the variability over time of the specific arrangement that governs global capital flows and global trade flows. For example, there is considerable consensus that the severity of the global crisis of the 1930s had everything to do with the breakdown of the 19th century gold standard because Great Britain was no longer able to fulfill the responsibilities of a global hegemon (Kindleberger, 1973; Block, 1977; Polanyi, 2001 [1944]). Similarly, the shift from the Bretton Woods regime of fixed exchange rates to the floating exchange rates agreed to in 1973 is generally seen as marking the shift from an era of "embedded liberalism" to the new era of unfettered neo-liberalism (Ruggie, 1982).

But if there are a wide variety of possible global regimes that depend on historical contingencies such as the rise and fall of certain global powers and there are a wide variety of national adaptations to these global rules, the idea that there is some unchanging capitalist essence to this global system becomes problematic. For example, it has been argued that the Bretton Woods era was a "golden age" for social democratic regimes because of the fixed exchange rates and institutionalized limits on capital controls, and that the demise of Bretton Woods placed severe strains on social democratic arrangements (Scharpf, 1991). This suggests that there might be an achievable global regime that would be even more favorable to social democratic policies than Bretton Woods had been. In short, without a genetic theory and with high degrees of contingency in the construction of the global regime, it is no longer apparent what makes the whole thing capitalist.

To be sure, Wallerstein also argues that the world system at any point in time rests on the power of a singular global hegemon (see also Arrighi, 1994; Arrighi & Silver, 1999). To be sure, there is a process of hegemonic succession with England succeeding Holland, and the United States succeeding England, and the period in which the hegemon begins to decline is generally a period of greater global conflict and instability. But part of what assures that it remains a capitalist world system is that this hegemonic power is the most economically advanced nation and it needs to make the world safe for its own business firms.

Yet the precise way in which the economy of that dominant power connects with the rest of the global economy is variable over time. England began as "the workshop of the world" sending a flood of exports overseas, but with rapid industrialization in Germany and the United States in the late 19th century, England increasingly sent capital abroad. The United States followed the English model beginning with export dominance then turning to capital outflows, but in the most recent period, it has used its global dominance to be the world's greatest debtor nation. Since hegemons will attempt to modify the global rules to fit their domestic economic needs, it follows that the mere fact of "capitalist" hegemony is consistent with there being considerable space for variation in the nature of the global regime.

It is also important to consider that in the 20th century constructing and maintaining a global regime has became a political problem that requires complex negotiations among multiple nations. In the same way that national states have a significant degree of autonomy from the existing class structure, global institutions and rules also can be expected to have some degree of autonomy from the interests of the hegemonic power. Shifting alliances within the state system might facilitate or block changes in particular rules and variations in institutional capacity and resources will have an impact on the ability of a global organization such as the International Monetary Fund or the World Trade Organization to exert pressure for a particular policy outcome.

In sum, Wallerstein is certainly correct to emphasize that nations must contend with an already existing world system that places limits on their options. But he gives insufficient attention to the way that the operation of the world system at any particular moment depends on the particular global regime or regimes that have emerged from the power relations among nations. As an activist and as a commentator on political struggles, he has embraced the fight for particular reforms of the global rules that would provide, for example, more policy space for developing nations to accelerate their economic development. But in his theory, there is no real acknowledgment that under a particular hegemon, there is a possibility of a variety of different regimes that would provide different levels of constraint on governmental choices. And some of these regimes could open up space for some societies to pursue greater equality and greater democratization of economic decision making than anyone associates with the idea of capitalism.

ANALYZING THE LOGIC OF FINANCIALIZATION

Whether we draw on the classic Marxist definition of capitalism or Wallerstein's relocation of the capitalist imperative to the operation of a world system, the concept of "capitalism" has two connected weaknesses. First, it leads us to think that economic dynamics and processes are the key to understanding what is going on at any given moment. Second, it leads us to imagine that there is immense power behind that existing set of arrangements rather than understanding those arrangements as the contingent product of a particular historical moment. We can see this deficiency most clearly if we examine the process of financialization that led up to the 2008 financial meltdown on Wall Street.

We know that the dominant U.S. model of business made a significant shift toward finance in the three decades from 1978 to 2008 (Krippner, 2011). There was very substantial growth of employment and profits in the banking sector and related businesses, and many of the largest non-financial corporations expanded the share of their business that consisted of financial activities – lending money or investing in unrelated enterprises. Arrighi (1994, 2007), in particular, has emphasized that this is an expected pattern for a declining hegemon; it uses the power accumulated in the previous period to extract profits around the world through financial channels.

But how do we understand this accumulation of power and profits in the financial sector of the economy? In classical accounts of "finance capital," people like J. P. Morgan accumulated vast amounts of wealth through exerting control over large industrial empires, and then were able to exert considerable additional power by either lending or withholding lending from potential borrowers in different parts of the world. In a situation where there was a scarcity of global financing, someone like Morgan was able to make his lending contingent on a significant share of the profit stream and that further enhanced his wealth and power.

Today, however, the figure who seems closest to the Morgan model is Warren Buffett who sits atop an empire of productive enterprises that generates enormous wealth which allowed him to bail out Bank of America and Goldman Sachs at the peak of the 2008 crisis. But Buffett has remained a critic of financialization famously denouncing derivatives as "financial weapons of mass destruction." The remarkable thing about big commercial banks and big investment banks in the United States is that they maintain a considerable degree of distance from productive enterprises; they generally do not own them nor do they have direct ways to share in their profit streams.[12] To be sure, they make some money from big corporations by handling their commercial paper and merger deals, by selling them complex derivatives, and managing their foreign exchange needs, but this represents a small share of corporate revenues.

In this recent period, it would also be mistaken to attribute the vaunted power of Wall Street to its stranglehold on the scarce supply of global financing. On the contrary, the distinguishing feature of this era has been huge pools of capital generated in other parts of the world such as the sovereign wealth funds of the oil-producing nations and the vast currency reserves accumulated by China, Japan, and other exporting nations in Asia. A significant share of Wall Street's enormous profits came from borrowing or recycling these foreign flows of capital, most notoriously, by selling foreign financial institutions' dubious bond instruments based on subprime mortgage loans.

In a word, it is difficult to trace Wall Street's power directly to production relations in the United States or even to some durable features of the world system. On the contrary, this very real process of financialization seems to be dependent on a series of contingent political choices. First, the enormous size of the largest commercial banks can be traced to their ownership of a disproportionate share of domestic deposits which resulted from government policies that simultaneously privileged certain banks as "too big to fail" and encouraged a 30-year process of financial consolidation through mergers (Dymski, 2011). Second, extremely cozy relations between financiers – commercial bankers, investment bankers, as well as hedge fund and private equity managers – and government officials were driven by a campaign finance system that gave Wall Street unprecedented political influence (Hacker & Pierson 2010b). Third, when the U.S. government chose to force other nations to lend us money to finance our chronic current accounts deficit, they had no attractive alternative. This meant that it was an exertion of geopolitical power by the United States in defense of the dollar's central role in the global system that pushed foreign capital into Wall Street's hands (Krippner, 2011; Schwartz, 2009).

Furthermore, there are historical examples where the exercise of this kind of disproportionate power by financial institutions proved to be transitory. For example, the combination of New Deal reforms, World War II, and the Bretton Woods agreements significantly diminished the clout of U.S. internationally oriented banking institutions for a period of almost 40 years. Japanese banks dominated the rankings of the biggest global banks in the 1980s, but the bursting of Japan's real estate bubble in the 1990s led to a rapid retreat in their global influence. And, of course, England's great banking houses that flourished under the 19th century gold standard shrank in power and influence as British global power receded.

In short, we simply do not know at this point whether the 2008 financial crisis will be followed by a reconsolidation of the power of U.S. finance or by a significant contraction of the financial sector's power and influence. That will depend on a series of complex political dynamics both within the United States and between the United States and other nations. But if we define the financialization of the U.S. economy as the emergence of a new type of financial capitalism, it attributes to this development a power and permanence that might not be merited.

THE POLANYIAN ALTERNATIVE

A framework derived from Karl Polanyi's book, *The Great Transformation*, is a much better analytic starting point than the concept of capitalism for social scientists to analyze dynamics within both national societies and the global economy. Polanyi had been deeply immersed in Marxist theorizing in the 1930s, but when he wrote the book in the early 1940s, he eschewed Marxist terminology and generally substituted the term "market society" for capitalism (Block, 2003). He did this, I think, precisely to emphasize the hugely consequential political choices that the world faced in shaping the post-World War II world. *The Great Transformation*, in fact, highlighted the mistakes that had been made by global leaders and diplomats in shaping the post-World War I world, and Polanyi was determined that the same mistakes not be repeated.

Polanyi's theoretical orientation can be aptly summarized in the phrase – "the primacy of politics."[13] While much Marxist theorizing emphasizes the primacy of economics or of the accumulation process, Polanyi saw significant problems with this approach. His view was that Marx had begun by advancing a critique of political economy, but then had himself become a political economist, which meant that he became trapped within a set of ideas that attributed to the economy far too much influence in shaping social life. Polanyi's alternative was to return to the critique of political economy, which meant liberating people from the belief that the economy should dictate how we live our lives.

For Polanyi, this meant challenging the view that socialism was only possible after decades of capitalist development had greatly expanded society's productive capacity. Polanyi's insisted that even in the period of England's rapid industrialization, a more humane and decent society had been possible. It was for this reason that he elevated Robert Owen, the English industrialist and theorist, whom Marx and Engels had derided as a "Utopian Socialist." By making Owen the hero of *The Great Transformation*, Polanyi was signaling that the obstacle to creating a society in which the economy was subordinated to democratic rule has always been politics – not the maturation of the productive forces.

Finally, Polanyi agreed with Max Weber's argument that Marx and Engels were mistaken in imagining that political power was ultimately reducible to class power. Weber's understanding of the autonomy of state power had led him to predict that the Bolshevik Revolution would end in dictatorship (see his essay on "Socialism" in Weber, 1978). It was for this reason that Polanyi believed that the only path to a more humane society was through making democratic self-governance more effective, and this required a commitment to reformist politics. But recognizing the autonomous power of the state also led him to see that government could be used to tame the worst features of market society by protecting people from the market and by reducing the inordinate power of property holders.

The basic outlines of a Polanyian theory of market societies can be conveyed in three theses.[14]

Thesis 1. *Market economies are always and everywhere embedded.*

In order to return to the *critique* of political economy, Polanyi stressed that it was an illusion that modern societies were shaped by the logic of an economy that had become autonomous. He insisted that in both premodern and modern societies, economic arrangements were embedded in politics, the law, and culture. This was his way of escaping from the tendency toward economic determinism that he saw in the Marxist tradition; he preferred a more complex way of thinking that saw economic processes, cultural processes, and political processes as intertwined.

But he also put enormous weight on the project of creating a self-regulating market economy that was inspired by the writings of the classical economists in the late 18th and early 19th century. This project envisioned the creation of a "market society" whose structure and institutions would be built around a fully self-regulating set of markets for capital, for labor, and for products. Polanyi stressed that this project was inherently utopian; it could not possibly be realized since there can be no such thing as an autonomous economy. But he also emphasized that the pursuit of this project was hugely consequential; it would wreak havoc on nature and society and generate tensions that would lead to two World Wars.

At the time that Polanyi was writing *The Great Transformation*, he believed that this project of creating a self-regulating market economy had finally been defeated. But Polanyi's analysis is so relevant today precisely because these ideas were effectively revived by Hayek and Friedman in the 1950s and 1960s and ultimately came to dominate U.S. foreign and domestic policies in the 1980s, 1990s, and 2000s (Mirowski & Plehwe, 2009; Phillips-Fein, 2009). As in the earlier period, it is not that the project came anywhere near succeeding; it is that policies derived from the project had disastrous consequences.

Thesis 2. *Market society and the contemporary world economy are shaped by an ongoing double movement.*

One side of the double movement is the effort to expand the scope of markets in allocating resources and organizing economic activity. It is often fueled by firms that are trying to find new markets for their products and work to eliminate overseas barriers to sales or push to dismantle regulations that interfere with their sales. But Polanyi stresses that other interests in society might periodically push in the same direction, especially to weaken the position of firms that have become entrenched through government subsidies or other types of support. So, for example, consumers might want to open a market to more competition to avoid paying a premium price to a firm that had won a government-enforced monopoly to sell a given medication.

But the project of creating a self-regulating market society gives this side of the double movement vastly enhanced power and influence. Specific policy debates shift from nuanced discussions of the costs and benefits of a particular proposal to highly polarized choices between free markets and heavy-handed government. This is precisely what happened in the United States from the late 1970s onward in debates about changing the regulations governing financial institutions. At almost every juncture, there was not a serious discussion of the merits of a particular policy proposal; choices were made on the basis of an ideological commitment to a financial marketplace that would be regulated by market forces.

However, Polanyi also insists that the movement in favor of expanded markets generates a countermovement that seeks to protect society from the market by using government to limit and restrict the scope of markets or to provide resources directly to citizens. Participation in this movement is also heterogeneous; it can include businesses that seek protection from foreign competition or from aggressive domestic competitors, professionals who employ the state to carve out monopolies, as well as farmers who seek protection from the volatility of agricultural markets. But it has often been trade unionists and neighborhood-based activists who provide the backbone of the protectionist countermovement as they express a need to be insulated from a variety of market pressures.

For Polanyi, the emergence of a strong countermovement is not inevitable; he emphasizes that in the case of European colonialism, political repression effectively blocked the path to such movements. But when the project of imposing a self-regulating market creates greater turbulence and uncertainty for large portions of the population and there is an opportunity for political mobilization, Polanyi anticipates that people's effort to protect themselves will generate pressures for new government policies. But he is also explicit, that the protective countermovement can generate either deeply reactionary state policies or policies that expand democratic control of the economy. In the 1930s, fascist mobilizations were part of the protectionist countermovement and put societies on a path that destroyed both democratic institutions and civil liberties.

Thesis 3. *Political contestation at multiple levels – local, regional, national, and supranational – shapes the economic paths that are available to societies at any given moment.*

Polanyi emphasizes that there is a global system that constrains the choices available within societies, and he stresses the central role that England played in shaping that order in the 19th century. But he also insists that there is a high level of contingency in constructing and maintaining this global system. England was not compelled to impose free trade and the gold standard on the rest of the world; it was rather the outcome of intense struggles in which the movement for laissez-faire was enormously strengthened by the arguments of Malthus and Ricardo that self-regulating markets were the only rational way to structure an economy. Moreover, rising powers such as the United States and Germany challenged some of these claims and did not hesitate to use government power to accelerate their industrial development (Chang, 2002). Moreover, geopolitical tensions and accumulating economic contradictions created a series of windows when the rules governing the global system could have been restructured.

In short, just as competing political forces struggle within nations to shape their institutions and their economic trajectory, so, also, there is an ongoing global struggle to shape and reshape the institutions that govern the global system. At the time that Polanyi was writing, the debate over the structure of the post-World War II order was still largely an elite conversation. But over the last three decades as the discourse of globalization has spread, significant global publics now recognize that the specific rules of the global regime have deep consequences for both their immediate well-being and their long-term prospects (Evans, 2008). So we increasingly see political parties, such as the Workers Party that has governed Brazil for the last decade, engaged in a multilevel struggle that involves both transforming Brazil's economy and creating international alliances to change the governance arrangements for the global system.

CONCLUSION

This discussion has come back to questions of politics and political choices. This is inevitable because the concepts that social scientists use have real consequences in the social world. As C. Wright Mills (1959) defined it, part of the sociological imagination is to explain what kind of society we live in, where it stands in history, and where it is going. The answers that social scientists give to these questions help to inform the way both citizens and elites think about the choices they confront.

Over the past three decades, as inequality of income, wealth, and power increased dramatically in the United States and as processes of financialization careered out of control, the social science community failed to provide the citizenry with the tools they needed to understand what was happening or give them appropriate warnings of impending dangers.[15] This failure cannot be attributed to the concept of capitalism alone but to the broader weakness of the critique of political economy within the social sciences.

Since we are now living in the immediate aftermath of a financial crisis that brought the global economy to the brink of disaster in 2008 and 2009, the urgency of reviving the critique of political economy should be obvious. The aftershocks of that crisis continue to reverberate through the global economy in 2011 and 2012, and it is uncertain when – if ever – the global economy might return to a path of stable and predictable growth. In a word, we are living through one of those historical moments when it is no longer possible to ignore the operations of the world system or to sidestep questions about how that system should be governed.

Collectively, the world faces a series of urgent questions. Can agreement be reached to replace the dollar with a new global reserve currency that would be managed by the International Monetary Fund or a successor institution? Can global institutions expand the supply of capital to finance green energy projects and other productive investments across the world economy? Should there be an international financial transaction tax to dampen global capital flows and slow the growth of financial derivatives? How should the system of financial regulation be restructured to keep banks and other financial institutions from taking on system-destabilizing levels of risk? Can the rules governing the global trading system be revised to expand the capacity of governments to increase employment and build new economic capacities? And ultimately, can we shape global institutions and global rules that are both democratically accountable and consistent with stronger democratic decision making within nations?

Suffice it to say that the Polanyian framework gives us much greater leverage on these questions than the concept of capitalism that we have inherited either from Marxism or market liberalism. Our urgent task is to analyze the strengths and weaknesses of the varieties of global regimes that could replace the failed system that was based on the theory of market self-regulation. In contemplating these choices, the key issues are how those different possible regimes would block or enable different varieties of market societies and might some open a path to the creation of societies that subordinate markets to democratic control.

NOTES

1. Chris Moody, reporting for Yahoo News, was at this session. His piece, "How Republicans are being taught to talk about Occupy Wall Street" appeared on December 1, 2011.
2. For an account of how this rhetoric played out in shifting welfare policy in the United States, see Somers and Block (2005).
3. For example, in the 2012 Presidential campaign, when Mitt Romney faced criticism for the predatory practices of the private equity firm that he had headed, his main defense was that his critics did not understand how capitalism works.
4. A rough indicator is provided by a Google search for "occupy wall street" that produced 838 million hits. When both "occupy wall street" and "capitalism" were put in the search, the number fell to 21 million hits – a decline of 97.5%.
5. Some of my own contributions to this current of thought are in Block (1987).
6. For a different critique of this body of work, see Block (2007).
7. Other scholars, of course, have recognized the importance of this question. See especially Streeck (2011) for an argument that goes in a different direction.
8. While other important theorists such as Weber, Schumpeter, Sombart, and Veblen used the concept of capitalism, it seems fair to argue that they retained significant elements of the Marxist analysis and they did not elaborate a systematic alternative conceptualization (Marx, 1963).
9. In his writings on France, particularly the *18th Brumaire*, Marx was acutely aware of the overdevelopment of the French state whose tentacles reached into every

corner of the economy. But he tended to see this as an anomaly with England's less developed state representing the purer case of a capitalist society.

10. It is beyond the scope of this paper to address the ambiguities of the concept of socialism. But since Marxism posits socialism as the negation of capitalism, it follows that if the concept of capitalism has lost its coherence, then we have little guidance as to what constitutes a socialist society.

11. It was precisely this move that led Robert Brenner (1977) to label Wallerstein as a neo-Smithian because he had shifted the central mechanism from production to the circulation of commodities.

12. The exception here are the private equity funds that routinely buy up productive enterprises, reorganize them, and then sell them back to others. But even they generally make their money not by exploiting workers but by firing them – they make businesses leaner and then sell them at a profit.

13. This is the title that Berman (2007) gives to her important account of the development of European social democracy. See also Mason (1968).

14. This is a modification of the theses offered in Block (2007). See also Schrank and Whitford (2009).

15. For some discussion of this neglect, see Hacker and Pierson (2010a) and Piven and Block (2010).

ACKNOWLEDGMENTS

I am grateful to Matthew Keller and Magali Sarfatti Larson for comments on an earlier draft.

REFERENCES

Arrighi, G. (1994). *The long twentieth century*. New York, NY: Verso.
Arrighi, G. (2007). *Adam Smith in Beijing*. New York, NY: Verso.
Arrighi, G., & Silver, B. (1999). *Chaos and governance in the modern world system*. Minneapolis, MN: University of Minnesota Press.
Berger, S., & Dore, R. (Eds.). (1996). *National diversity and global capitalism*. Ithaca, NY: Cornell University Press.
Berman, S. (2006). *The primacy of politics*. New York, NY: Cambridge University Press.
Block, F. (1977). *The origins of international economic disorder*. Berkeley, CA: University of California.
Block, F. (1987). *Revising state theory*. Philadelphia, PA: Temple University Press.
Block, F. (2000). Deconstructing capitalism as a system. *Rethinking Marxism, 12*(3), 83–98.
Block, F. (2002). Rethinking capitalism. In N. W. Biggart (Ed.), *Readings in economic sociology* (pp. 219–230). Walden, MA: Blackwell.
Block, F. (2003). Karl Polanyi and the writing of *The Great Transformation*. *Theory and Society, 32*, 275–306.
Block, F. (2007). Understanding the diverging trajectories of the United States and Western Europe: A Neo-Polanyian analysis. *Politics & Society, 35*(3), 3–33.

Brenner, R. (1977). The origins of capitalist development: A critique of Neo-Smithian Marxism. *New Left Review, 104*(July/August), 25–92.
Chang, H.-J. (2002). *Kicking away the ladder*. London: Anthem Press.
Crouch, C., & Streeck, W. (Eds.). (1997). *Political economy of modern capitalism*. Thousand Oaks, CA: Sage.
Dymski, G. (2011). *Genie out of the bottle: The evolution of too-big-to-fail policy and banking strategy in the U.S.* Unpublished paper. UC Riverside, Riverside, CA.
Edwards, R., Reich, M., & Weisskopf, T. (Eds.). (1972). *The capitalist system: A radical analysis of American society*. Englewood Cliffs, NJ: Prentice-Hall.
Esping-Andersen, G. (1990). *The three worlds of welfare capitalism*. Princeton, NJ: Princeton University Press.
Evans, P. (2008). Is an alternative globalization possible? *Politics & Society, 34*(2), 271–305.
Friedman, M. (1962). *Capitalism and freedom*. Chicago, IL: University of Chicago Press.
Friedman, T. (1999). *The Lexus and the olive tree*. New York, NY: Farrar, Straus & Giroux.
Giddens, A. (1971). *Capitalism and modern social theory*. Cambridge: Cambridge University Press.
Gouldner, A. (1980). *The two Marxisms*. New York, NY: The Seabury Press.
Graham, J., & Gibson, K. (1996). *The end of capitalism (as we knew it)*. Cambridge, MA: Blackwell.
Gray, J. (1998). *False dawn*. London: Granta Books.
Hacker, J., & Pierson, P. (2010a). Winner-take-all politics. *Politics & Society, 38*(2), 152–204.
Hacker, J., & Pierson, P. (2010b). *Winner-take-all politics*. New York, NY: Simon & Schuster.
Hall, P. A., & Soskice, D. (Eds.). (2001). *Varieties of capitalism*. Oxford: Oxford University Press.
Harvey, D. (2006). *The limits to capital*. New York, NY: Verso.
Harvey, D. (2010). *The enigma of capital and the crises of capitalism*. Oxford: Oxford University Press.
Hollingsworth, J. R., & Boyer, R. (Eds.). (1997). *Contemporary capitalism: The embeddedness of institutions*. Cambridge: Cambridge University Press.
Kindleberger, C. P. (1973). *The world in depression, 1929–1939*. Berkeley, CA: University of California Press.
Krippner, G. (2011). *Capitalizing on crisis*. Cambridge, MA: Harvard University Press.
Kristol, I. (1978). *Two cheers for capitalism*. New York, NY: Basic Books.
Lundvall, B.-A. (Ed.). (1992). *National systems of innovation*. London: Pinter Publishers.
Marx, K. (1963 [1852]). *The 18th Brumaire of Louis Bonaparte*. New York, NY: International Publishers.
Mason, T. (1968). Primacy of politics: Politics and economics in national socialist Germany. In S. J. Woolf (Ed.), *The nature of fascism* (pp. 165–195). New York, NY: Random House.
Mills, C. W. (1959). *The sociological imagination*. New York, NY: Oxford University Press.
Mirowski, P., & Plehwe, D. (Eds.). (2009). *The road from Mont Pelerin*. Cambridge, MA: Harvard University Press.
Orru, M., Biggart, N. W., & Hamilton, G. (1997). *The economic organization of East Asian capitalism*. Thousand Oaks, CA: Sage.
Page, B., & Jacobs, L. (2009). *Class war*. Chicago, IL: University of Chicago Press.
Phillips-Fein, K. (2009). *Invisible hands: The making of the conservative movement from the New Deal to Reagan*. New York, NY: Norton.
Piven, F. F., & Block, F. (2010). Déjà vu, all over again. *Politics & Society, 38*(2), 205–211.

Polanyi, K. (2001 [1944]). *The great transformation.* Boston, MA: Beacon Press.
Polanyi, K., Arensberg, C. M., & Pearson, H. W. (1968). The place of economies in societies. In G. Dalton (Ed.), *Primitive, archaic and modern economies: Essays of Karl Polanyi* (pp. 116–138). Boston, MA: Beacon Press.
Potter, P. (1965). *Naming the system.* Retrieved from http://www.antiauthoritarian.net/sds_wuo/sds_documents/paul_potter.html
Rand, A. (1966). *Capitalism: The unknown ideal.* New York, NY: New American Library.
Ruggie, J. (1982). International regimes, transactions, and change: Embedded liberalism in the postwar economic order. *International Organization, 36,* 379–415.
Sahlins, M. (1976). *Culture and practical reason.* Chicago, IL: University of Chicago Press.
Santos., Boaventura de Sousa (2008). The World Social Forum and the Global Left. *Politics & Society, 36*(2), 247–270.
Scharpf, F. (1991). *Crisis and choice in European social democracy* (R. Crowley & F. Thompson, Trans.). Ithaca, NY: Cornell University Press.
Schrank, A., & Whitford, J. (2009). Industrial policy in the United States: A Neo-Polanyian interpretation. *Politics & Society, 37*(4), 521–553.
Schumpeter, J. (1942). *Capitalism, socialism, and democracy.* New York, NY: Harper & Bros.
Schwartz, H. (2009). *Subprime nation.* Ithaca, NY: Cornell University Press.
Somers, M., & Block, F. (2005). From poverty to perversity: Ideas, markets, and institutions over 200 years of welfare debate. *American Sociological Review, 70,* 260–287.
Streeck, W. (2011). Taking capitalism seriously: Towards an institutionalist approach to contemporary political economy. *Socio-Economic Review, 9,* 137–167.
Wade, R. (1990). *Governing the market.* Princeton, NJ: Princeton University Press.
Wallerstein, I. (1974). *The modern world-system: Capitalist agriculture and the origins of the European world-economy in the sixteenth century.* New York, NY: Academic Press.
Wallerstein, I. (1980). *The modern world-system II: Mercantilism and the consolidation of the European world economy, 1600–1750.* New York, NY: Academic Press.
Wallerstein, I. (1989). *The modern world-system III: The second era of great expansion of the capitalist world-economy, 1730–1840s.* New York, NY: Academic Press.
Weber, M. (1978). *Selections in translation* (W. G. Runciman, Ed. and E. Matthews, Trans.). Cambridge: Cambridge University Press.
Weber, M. (1998 [1904–1905]). *The Protestant ethic and the spirit of capitalism* (T. Parsons, Trans.). Los Angeles, CA: Roxbury Press.

A POLANYIAN ANALYSIS OF CAPITALISM: A COMMENTARY ON FRED BLOCK

Nina Bandelj

ABSTRACT

This chapter responds to Fred Block's article about the weaknesses of the concept of capitalism because of its close association with Marxism, and his proposal for a Polanyian analysis of political economy. In this chapter, I interrogate what may be the commonalities as opposed to divergences between Marx and Polanyi, and I question whether the concept of capitalism is really so wedded to Marxism so as to loose its analytic value, and be better replaced by notions such as market society, or political economy, as used by Polanyi. I agree with Block that a Polanyian analysis importantly widens our view beyond economic reductionism to an understanding of economy and society as co-constitutive. However, I see utility in adding the qualifier "capitalist" to "political economy" to differentiate between socialist and capitalist political economies, for instance, and to properly characterize a system based on private property rights, guided by pursuit of material gain, which advantages some strata in society more than others, leading to endemic social inequality. I propose that a Polanyian focus on society and economy as co-constitutive is more effectively coupled with an analysis that considers capitalism not as a self-driven system of surplus extraction and accumulation, but as an institutional order dependent on political choices. Such a perspective would advance a Polanyian analysis of capitalism.

"What is the analytic value of 'capitalism' as a concept?" asks Fred Block in his thought-provoking essay. "Does it help illuminate key features of existing societies, or does it carry with it burdensome associations from earlier historical periods?" By earlier historical periods, Block means the historical materialist analysis offered by Karl Marx of the "genetic theory of capitalism" that "retains an irreducible teleology about the direction of history." Block first argues that the term capitalism is inextricably intertwined with the Marxist conceptualization and, second, he points to the weaknesses of the Marxist perspective. Mostly, according to Block, Marxist analysis has been undermined because of its inability to account for the expanding role of government in managing the tensions created by capitalist accumulation. He also notes that efforts, like the Wallersteinian move to take the analysis of capitalism to the world-system scale, have its own problems. This leads Block to conclude that capitalism has lost its analytic value. Instead, he urges us to revive a critique of political economy and replace the concept of capitalism with the framework proposed by Karl Polanyi (1944) in his book *The Great Transformation*, which "generally substitute(s) the term 'market society' for capitalism," and brings to the forefront politics and political choices, rather than insists on the primacy of the economic in a Marxist fashion.

I should disclose from the start that I am very sympathetic to the Polanyian perspective. My own work in economic sociology and about postsocialist transformations finds inspiration in Polanyi's ideas of the always-embedded economy. For one, in my research on the social foundations of foreign direct investment markets in Central and East European countries after 1989, I argue that one can draw parallels between the institutionalization of self-regulating markets in the 19th century England, that Polanyi discusses in *The Great Transformation*, and postsocialist economic transformations after 1989 where, contrary to the neoliberal emphasis on the importance of state withdrawal from economy to free markets, postsocialist states were crucial in building market institutions and creating demand for foreign capital (Bandelj, 2008, 2009). Further, my short book on *Economy and State* theorizes the relationship between these two spheres as that of state-economy embeddedness, which is grounded in the Polanyi's notion of fictitious commodities (Bandelj & Sowers, 2010). Recently, with two graduate student collaborators, we reviewed the literature on the impact of neoliberal globalization on work, and applied the Polanyian double movement dynamic at the global level to understand this relationship (Bandelj, Shorette, & Sowers, 2011). Finally, in an analytical piece debating the utility of the concept of relational work (Zelizer, 2005, 2012) in economic sociology, I distinguish between the Polanyian notion of embeddedness from the one more widely adopted in contemporary economic sociology, namely the Granovetterian embeddedness (Granovetter, 1985). Here I pinpoint the crucial difference in how the relationship between the economic and the social is understood in these two traditions, as co-constitutive and analytically separate, respectively, which has serious implications for the understanding of relationality in economic processes and the theory of economic action (Bandelj, 2012; see also Krippner & Alvarez, 2007).

This said, simply concluding that I agree with Fred Block's key point about the utility of a Polanyian analysis would not provide for much of an intellectual exercise that I was asked to engage in by writing a response to his essay. Therefore, I want to question Fred Block's conclusion about the obsolescence of the concept of capitalism as much as I want to be critical about his (and my own) embrace of a Polanyian perspective. I do this by asking (a) what may be the commonalities as opposed to divergences between Marx and Polanyi, and (b) whether the concept of capitalism is really so wedded to Marxism so as to lose its analytic value, and be better replaced by market society or political economy.

My position is that a Polanyian analysis indeed importantly widens our view beyond economic reductionism and teleological view of history toward the analysis of economy and society that treats these two spheres as co-constitutive. However, embracing the term *market* over capitalism can also dangerously reinforce the rightist views that markets are benevolent, and enable anyone who tries to get ahead. I also want to point to the vagueness hidden in the concept of political economy, proposed as an alternative by Block, which does not distinguish between particular types of social organization of the economy beyond broadly characterizing that political choices dictate economic arrangements. From this perspective, socialism and capitalism are both types of political economies, as they are both sets of institutional arrangements about economic production, distribution, consumption, and exchange that result from political choices on how economy should be governed. But no one will argue that socialism and capitalism are not crucially distinct. We need to retain the qualifier "capitalist" in the "capitalist political economy" to denote that the vast majority of the contemporary economic systems are heavily privatized, and guided by pursuit of material gain, which advantages some strata in society more than others, leading to endemic social inequality. In fact, one might expect that in advancing the Polanyian alternative, Block would discuss Polanyi's mosaic typology of the types of social organization of economy-market exchange, reciprocity, and redistribution. In my view, this typology is very useful in describing how different forms of the social organization of economy can coexist, but we need to be able to emphasize that the system where market-exchange strongly prevails over other forms is analytically distinct from other possible combinations of these three economic arrangements. To capture the characteristics of such a system, in my view, the qualifier "capitalist" in front of political economy is necessary.

DIVERGENCES AND COMMONALITIES BETWEEN MARX AND POLANYI

Block proposes that Polanyi's notion of political economy as laid out in *The Great Transformation* is a better starting point to analyze the contemporary societies and the global economy than the (Marxist) concept of capitalism is. Polanyi, writes Block, was influenced by Marx in the 1930s, but in *The Great Transformation*, he "eschewed Marxist terminology and generally substituted the term 'market society' for capitalism." Moreover, Polanyi diverged from Marxist historical materialism to emphasize "the primacy of politics" over the primacy of the economy. Nevertheless, both Marx and Polanyi were keenly interested in interpreting the transformations in the economic systems brought about by industrial revolution. While Marx has a clear view of the direction of history through different stages that all have to deal with their inherent contradictions, Polanyi's perspective more closely approximates a cyclical movement, with politics dictating the type of economic system on the one hand, and the societal reaction potentially changing the existent system on the other, as captured in the notion of a "double movement." Polanyi also puts more emphasis on the power of the state as a change agent, rather than on class dynamics that stands as a central revolutionary force in the Marxist account. This is consistent with Polanyi's view that state can play a crucial role in protecting society from market forces, rather than, to use a famous quote from Marx, functions as "but a committee for managing the common affairs of the whole bourgeoisie." Block summarizes the key tenets of the Polanyian framework, including that "market economies are always and everywhere embedded," that "market society and the contemporary world economy are shaped by an ongoing double movement," and that "political contestation at multiple levels – local, regional, national, and supranational – shapes the economic paths that are available to societies at any given moment." All in all, the Marxist analysis retains economy as a sphere analytically separate from society and state, while the Polanyian approach insists on co-constitution between economy and society.

Given Block's rightful reputation as the authoritative interpreter of Polanyi's work, it comes as a surprise that in discussing these tenets Block does not mention Polanyi's central notion of fictitious commodities of labor, land, and money. Polanyi argued that land, labor, and money are not commodities in the same sense as these things are produced by firms to be sold on the market. For one, it is a fiction that land, labor, and money are inherently produced with the intention to be supplied for sale on the market, thus state action is needed to constitute them as commodities, in the push to create a market system. In another sense, it is also illusory that land, labor, and money can be easily multiplied should demand increases, as could other "proper" commodities. In fact, state action is needed to constrain their full-blown commodification and prevent the complete exhaustion and consequent destruction of these resources, and this represents the "countermovement" in the Polanyian double movement logic.

Focusing on the commodification of labor, land, and money is not only central for understanding the logic of the double movement, but also important for drawing comparisons between Marx and Polanyi. For Polanyi, commodification of labor is central to his arguments about the rise of market society. For Marx, the necessity of the proletariat to sell their labor as a commodity is the crux of Marxist capitalism. While Marxist and Polanyian accounts may diverge on the "fictitiousness" of labor and the role of the state in labor commodification and decommodification, the pressures to commodify labor are central to both of their analyses, as is the concern with social inequality. Even in global financial capitalism, class distinctions are not eradicated. On the contrary, one could say that they are resurfacing with potency in the times of crises, as we can see in the Occupy Wall Street movement. Protesters may not use the word capitalism, but their collective action is nevertheless propelled by the clash between the 1% and the 99%, a clash resulting from patiently obvious social inequality. Block suggests that Polanyi envisions various actors as participants in a protective countermovement but he, nevertheless, singles out trade unionists as those "who provide the backbone of the protectionist countermovement." Labor remains an integral, if not the only, actor. In this sense, the Polanyian and Marxist analyses share some common concerns, even if they diverge on identifying the source of these concerns. This is important for the discussion of the relevance of the concept of capitalism. As much as the Marxist version of capitalism is defined by its historical materialist teleology, it is also characterized by the focus on the need to sell labor on the market and consequent social inequality. One could argue that the use of the term market society instead of capitalism masks this inherent inequality between market participants, albeit inequality that transcends just class lines.

A case in point is the much more frequent use of the word "market" rather than "capitalism" to characterize the transformation of the economic systems after the fall of communist regimes in Central and Eastern Europe.[1] Block's point on how the word capitalism fell out of favor in the United States because it was too closely associated with the communist left is telling. One wonders whether in describing the transformations after the fall of communist regimes in Central and Eastern Europe, the word capitalism was eschewed because it smacked too much of the opposite of socialism. "Market transition" and "democratic transition" were more palatable descriptions of the systemic transformations than "transition to capitalism." But the systems put in place in Central and Eastern Europe after dismantling command economy are nothing but capitalist if capitalism denotes an economic system based on private property rights in which economic activity, including the production, distribution, consumption, and exchange, is basically determined through market operation where private actors can exchange their property rights with other private actors for material gain. Differences between owners and non-owners are endemic to the capitalist system, and they bring with them significant inequalities. While it is true that the classifications of owners and non-owners are more blurred in contemporary times of shareholder capitalism and certainly not confined to production given the rise of financialization, in practice the system retains clear divisions between "haves" and "have-nots." This is in contrast with the expectations associated with the notion of "a market," "free-market," or "emerging-market," which in their neoliberal interpretation by-and-large describe a form of individual choice and freedom that everyone has in succeeding economically only if they try. This kind of understanding of markets was very appealing in promoting market reforms in the postcommunist context, while the "downsides of markets" have been largely underplayed in political discourse, even if they represent an integral part of the postsocialist experience, as also evidenced in analyses of rising inequality in Central and Eastern Europe after 1989 (Bandelj & Mahutga, 2010).

CAPITALISM AS INSTITUTIONAL ORDER BASED ON PRIVATE PROPERTY RIGHTS AND MARKET COMPETITION

After interrogating whether Marx and Polanyi provide divergent frameworks, as intimated by Block,[2] I want to also question Block's conclusion that the analysis of capitalism is so wedded to the Marxist framework that it has lost its value. While I am sympathetic to Block's critiques of "the genetic theory of capitalism," I am not so ready to dismiss the notion of capitalism altogether. First, what to make of the fact that over the past couple of decades it was the literature with the word capitalism in its name that gained quite some traction, namely the "varieties of capitalism" perspective. As Block himself notes, this literature largely moved away from the Marxist analysis to emphasize that there is no one single (or right) way of organizing the capitalist economy. Block acknowledges the value in making this point against "the Right's embrace of the concept of capitalism and its insistence that there was one single model of how to organize an efficient and effective society."

I agree with this conclusion as I also agree with the point that the analysis of the "varieties" detracted from the analysis of "capitalism." Indeed, the main distinction delivered in the varieties of capitalism literature was that between the liberal *market economies* (LME) and coordinated *market economies* (CME) (Hall & Soskice, 2001), to differentiate between economies where markets and competition are the primary way of coordinating economic action from those where firms depend more on non-market modes of coordination, relational contracting, network monitoring, and a greater reliance on collaboration than on competition. Although the LME vs. CME distinction refers to the macro-organization of the economy, it was derived from the analysis that takes firms as central actors and questions what firms need to do in different systems to exploit their core competencies in the areas of industrial relations, vocational training and education, corporate governance, relations with employees, and interfirm relations. With firms as the focal units of analysis, it is not surprising that the literature lost sight of the macro-systemic properties of capitalism, and that, indeed, by using the LME and CME designations, the varieties of capitalism perspective practically replaced the word "capitalism" with "market economy."

This move is not unlike the one that Block suggests was done by Polanyi in substituting the term capitalism with market society in *The Great*

Transformation. However, it is precisely the loss of historical specificity in the analysis of the varieties of market/political economy, generally, that has been a point of critique of the varieties of capitalism perspective, recently launched by Wolfgang Streeck, and Dorothee Bohle and Bela Greskovits. These scholars have argued for "bringing capitalism back in" (Streeck, 2010a), understanding "capitalism *tout court*" not only its varieties (Bohle & Greskovits, 2009) and for "taking capitalism seriously" (Streeck, 2010b). Interestingly, their analyses have found inspiration in Polanyi, just as Block's has. Still, these scholars have reached the opposite conclusion from Block, in that they not only retained but even emphasized the value of calling the object of their analysis capitalism, and not just political economy, or market society. This is because they approached capitalism "not as a self-driven mechanism of surplus extraction and accumulation governed by objective laws, but as a set of interrelated social institutions, and as a historically specific system of structured as well as structuring social interaction within and in relation to an institutionalized social order" (Streeck, 2010b, p. 1). Moreover, among key defining feature of the capitalist social order are "legitimate greed" and "differential endowment of social classes with agentic capacities" (Streeck, 2010b, pp. 7, 11). Even more basically, for Bohle and Greskovits (2009) at the core of the understanding of capitalism lie two fundamental motives of action, fear and greed, and their dynamic interplay. Interestingly, referencing Polanyi's use of the notion of "satanic mill," the title of section one of part two in *The Great Transformation*, Bohle and Greskovits (2009, p. 374) note that in any variety of a capitalist system "workers are anxious about the 'satanic mill' (Polanyi, 1944) that undermines the stability of their existence by abruptly and permanently changing their professional and social status and identity."

This brings us back to the commonalities between Polanyi and Marx that I discussed earlier. The countervailing forces of workers' fear and capitalists' greed can be well imagined in a Polanyian analysis, even if class conflict is not at the crux of a Polanyian political economy. Nevertheless, attention to class inequality is not completely foreign to a Polanyian perspective, given that labor is one central fictitious commodity. In fact, to understand the countermovement better, one may need to theorize the political action that happens outside of the state purview more forcefully than Polanyi does. In my reading of Polanyi, the emergence of the countermovement is rather under-theorized; it seems to appear quite spontaneously and it is confined to state institutions. A Marxist analysis gives us potential insights into how labor becomes a political actor, even if the result is not a proletarian revolution, nor is labor the only civil society actor that participates in the countermovement dynamic.

In sum, Block makes a persuasive and important argument for an analysis of political economy that considers society and economy as densely intertwined and not as separate spheres, and I am fully on board with this. Still, I think that such an analysis should call historically particular kinds of political economy by their rightful name. That name is capitalism if the system is based on private property rights and market competition for material gain. In my reading, a Polanyian analysis, which treats capitalism as an institutional order, has great promise. It would be worthwhile to advance a Polanyian theory of capitalism along these lines.

NOTES

1. Doing a simple search in Sociological Abstracts with the words "capitalism" or "market" or "democracy" in the title, and "Central and Eastern Europe" in keywords, yields nearly twice as many articles with the word market and 60% more articles with the word democracy than those with the word capitalism in the title.

2. It should be noted that in his other work Block (2003) does discuss the Marxist influences on Polanyi more explicitly.

REFERENCES

Bandelj, N. (2008). *From communists to foreign capitalists: The social foundations of foreign direct investment in postsocialist Europe*. Princeton, NJ: Princeton University Press.

Bandelj, N. (2009). The global economy as instituted process: The case of central and Eastern Europe. *American Sociological Review, 74*(1), 128–149.

Bandelj, N. (2012). Relational work and economic sociology. *Politics and Society. 40*(2), 175–201.

Bandelj, N., & Mahutga, M. C. (2010). How socio-economic changes shape income inequality in central and Eastern Europe. *Social Forces, 88*(5), 2133–2161.

Bandelj, N., Shorette, K., & Sowers, E. (2011). Work and neoliberal globalization: A Polanyian synthesis. *Sociology Compass, 5*(9), 807–823.

Bandelj, N., & Sowers, E. (2010). *Economy and state: A sociological perspective*. Cambridge, UK: Polity Press.

Block, F. (2003). The writing of the great transformation. *Theory and Society, 32*, 245–306.

Bohle, D., & Greskovits, B. (2009). Varieties of capitalism and capitalism tout court. *European Journal of Sociology, 50*, 355–386.

Granovetter, M. (1985). Economic action and social structure: The problem of embeddedness. *The American Journal of Sociology, 91*, 481–510.

Hall, P., & Soskice, D. (2001). *Varieties of capitalism: The institutional foundations of comparative advantage*. Oxford, UK: Oxford University Press.

Krippner, G., & Alvarez, A. (2007). Embeddedness and the intellectual projects of economic sociology. *Annual Review of Sociology, 33*, 219–240.

Polanyi, K. (1944). *The great transformation: The political and economic origins of our time.* Boston, MA: Beacon Press.

Streeck, W. (2010a). Institutions in history: Bringing capitalism back in. In G. Morgan, J. Campbell, C. Crouch, O. K. Pedersen & R. Whitley (Eds.), *The Oxford handbook of comparative institutional analysis* (pp. 659–686). Oxford, UK: Oxford University Press.

Streeck, W. (2010b). Taking capitalism seriously: Towards an institutionalist approach to contemporary political economy. *Socio-Economic Review*, 1–31.

Zelizer, V. (2005). *The purchase of intimacy.* Princeton, NJ: Princeton University Press.

Zelizer, V. (2012). How I became a relational economic sociologist and what does that mean? *Politics & Society, 40*, 145–174.

MARX, WEBER, AND THE "CEASELESS ACCUMULATION OF CAPITAL"

Ho-Fung Hung

ABSTRACT

Seeing capitalism as a system defined by the imperative of the ceaseless accumulation of capital, instead of using the definition based on wage labor or international trade as Block questions, I argue that the concept of capitalism is still too useful to be abandoned, and cannot be replaced by the Polanyian concept of market in our critique of political economy. As Fernand Braudel and Giovanni Arrighi contend, the capitalist logic of capital accumulation, which is affined to monopoly and state power, is antithetical to the logic of market exchange, which is decentralized and prioritizes livelihoods over profits. Historically, capitalism sometimes made use of the market and sometimes subjugated the market to facilitate accumulation. Likewise, globalization today is a combined movement of expanding free market in certain aspects of life through financial deregulation, privatization, trade liberalization, etc. on the one hand, and exclusion of various processes and costs outside the market through revival of extra-economic coercion, externalization of environmental costs, etc., on the other hand. The imperative of capital accumulation drive capitalists and capitalist states to foster marketization and demarketization in different times and spaces. The critique of and resistance to our capitalist system needs to be antimarket in some instances and pro-market in others. A Polanyian critique of the free market is surely powerful and helpful, but it is not enough for our full understanding of the economic malaises of our times. It is at best counterproductive to throw away the concept of capitalism altogether.

Fred Block has dropped a bombshell to all critical social scientists by suggesting we all should abandon the concept of capitalism as an analytic category, replacing it with Polanyi's concept of the market in our diagnosis of contemporary and historical political economy.

His suggestion is based on both political and intellectual grounds. Politically, the term "capitalism" used to be a word of the left in their critique of the status quo, while the defenders of the status quo preferred the term "market." But recently, the right becomes increasingly open to refer to the existing system as capitalism in a triumphalist way. The critical connotation of "capitalism" is therefore lost, and there is little reason that critical intellectuals should hold on to a term that is contaminated and stolen by the enemy.

Intellectually, Block critiques both orthodox Marxist definition of capitalism as a wage-labor-based economic system and world-systemist definition of capitalism as a world trading system. He points out that over time, both wage-labor class relation and world trade has been put under different regulations and hybridized with other types of economic relations, so much so that characterizing different hybridized forms of economic systems as an essentially unchanging capitalist system could become increasingly dubious. Block sees the Polanyi's concept of market as a viable alternative. According to Polanyi, market is always embedded in different social, political, and ideological settings. Hence, examining different types of market embeddedness across space and time could better capture the diversity of economic systems of our times without the need to assume some unchanging essence of the system. And the left's critique of the status quo can be grounded on the denunciation of only one form of market system, namely, the socially destructive "self-regulatory market" that the neoliberals installed over the last 30 years.

Leaving aside the content and analytic prowess of the Polanyian view for the moment, Block's critique of the conception of capitalism in fact focuses only on the weaker definitions of capitalism and leaves out stronger ones. What is neglected is the Weberian conception of capitalism. As a historical sociologist most well-known for his state theory nowadays, Weber has not been particularly reputed for this theory of capitalism ever since his culturalist explanation of the rise of capitalism as presented in the *Protestant Ethic and the Spirit of Capitalism* had been discredited by many critical political economists. But his conception of capitalism in the book continues to prevail, influencing many Marxian analyses.

To Weber, what is characteristic of a capitalist economic system is the domination of the capitalist spirit, under which the urge to accumulate money for the sake of accumulating more money in rational and methodical manners overrides all other imperatives. This spirit was represented by Benjamin Franklin's saying that "[r]emember, that money is of the prolific, generating nature. Money can beget money, and its offspring can beget more, and so on. Five shillings turned is six, turned again it is seven and three pence, and so on, till it becomes a hundred pounds. The more there is of it, the more it produces every turning, so that the profits rise quicker and quicker" (cited in Weber 1992 [1930], p. 50). This logic is contrary to most if not all religious-moral systems preceding, and outside of, capitalism:

> In fact, the *summum bonum* of this ethic, the earning of more and more money, combined with the strict avoidance of all spontaneous enjoyment of life, ... is thought of so purely as an end in itself, that from the point of view of the happiness of, or utility to, the single individual, it appears entirely transcendental and absolutely irrational. Man is dominated by the making of money, by acquisition as the ultimate purpose of his life. Economic acquisition is no longer subordinated to man as the means for the satisfaction of his material needs. This reversal of what we should call the natural relationship, so irrational from a naive point of view, is evidently as definitely a leading principle of capitalism as it is foreign to all peoples not under capitalistic influence. (p. 53)

This very unusual capitalist logic could not emerge by itself because of the widespread hostility of preexisting moral norms. Its emergence in certain part of early modern Europe was aided by certain extra-economic forces that happened to dominate and help clear its way. According to Weber, such extra-economic force in question is the Calvinist conception of predestination, under which the anxiety to have a glimpse of God's grace urged Calvinist merchants to see the wealth they accumulated as an indicator of such grace. Although this cultural explanation of the rise of capitalism is denounced by most Marxian scholars, Weber's definition of capitalism as a system with the "ceaseless accumulation of capital" as its *modus operandi* can be found throughout Immanuel Wallerstein's and Giovanni Arrighi's works.

To Wallerstein, what drives the genesis of an international division of labor in the "long sixteenth century" is the rise of the logic of ceaseless accumulation of capital under an interstate system. This logic creates and sustains the exploitative unequal exchanges among core, periphery, and semi-periphery of the system, as well as its geographical expansion to incorporate new periphery zones. To be sure, the whole range of Wallerstein's works is mostly about how the international division of labor developed, while little has been said with respect to how exactly the logic of ceaseless capital accumulation drives such development.

What is left unsaid in Wallerstein is elaborated in Arrighi's Braudelian re-reading of Marx. It is remarkable that Marx's *Capital*, Vol. 1, starts with a discussion of "generalized commodity exchange," or the economic activity characterized by C-M-C, in which two commodity producers exchange their goods with money as a medium. In this situation, money is a tool of exchange, and the acquisition of commodity's use value is the end. When Marx moves on to part two of *Capital*, he starts to discuss the rise of capitalist activity as characterized by M-C-M', in which M' equals M plus an increment, or M + ΔM. In such activity, the commodity involved is just a mean in the pursuit of increase in monetary wealth, or capital. Like Weber, Marx sees the pursuit of profit for the sake of making more profit as an end in itself under capitalism. But unlike Weber, Marx does not see such profit orientation as the defining characteristics of the capitalist system. Instead, he sees it as no more than epiphenomenal to the system. He then sets out to exposit capitalism's essence by looking into the labor process, where all the increment to M allegedly originates as surplus value extracted from wage labor.

Whether ΔM originates from surplus value in the labor process is debatable. What is more important but is neglected by Marx and many of his followers is how exactly the C-M-C process and the M-C-M' process is related. Are they linked logically and the latter is a natural, spontaneous outcome of the former? Marx seems to suppose so in *Capital*. But if we look back to history across civilizations, we will readily find a lot of cases in which C-M-C prevailed but did not lead to M-C-M'. The question is therefore how and why the transition from C-M-C to M-C-M' happened in early modern Europe but not in other times and places.

The merging of Braudel's and Marx's insights in Arrighi's *The Long Twentieth Century* (1994) and *Adam Smith in Beijing* (2007) offers us hints to the answer. For Braudel, market and capitalism are not to be confounded and should be examined empirically as two distinct patterns of economic activities. While market economy is grounded on exchange and competition among small producers, concerning more about livelihood than profit, capitalism is driven by profit maximization and wealth accumulation that historically required state support and monopolistic economic organizations, as exemplified by chartered companies in early modern Europe. Braudel sees that market is anticapitalist and vice-versa, as the logic of the two types of economic activities are not only incompatible but also contradictory. It is the logic of farmer market vis-à-vis the logic of large grocery chain.

Arrighi sees Braudel's distinction between market and capitalism as the same as the distinction between C-M-C and M-C-M' as captured by Marx. He argues that the dominance of the capitalist logic and the subjugation of the market logic should not be seen as natural outgrowth of market development, as he, resonating with a new historiography of the early modern world, finds ample evidence of advanced market system without capitalism, with Qing China in the seventeenth and eighteenth centuries as the most cited example (e.g., Pomeranz, 2001). Arrighi makes use of Charles Tilly's theory of state formation to argue that the very unusual interstate system and incessant international conflict in early modern Europe urged state makers to compete for internationally mobile capital, forging a state-capital alliance that is unseen anywhere else and enabled the rise of M-C-M' to dominance. Under this capital-state alliance, western European states became well known in their one-sided support of merchants amid the latter's conflict with lower classes pauperized by profit-making activities. A case in point is the suppression of food riots by the English and French states, which had eschewed authorities' medieval pledge to protect subjects' subsistence right and become steadfast defenders of capital's profitability (Tilly, 1975).

While Europe witnessed the rise of a state-capital alliance fostering the rise of capital accumulation to dominance, early modern China, which too witnessed market expansion resulting from the influx of American silver as a much more stable and valuable medium of exchanges than preceding mediums like paper money and copper coins, also saw the emergence of entrepreneurs engaged in M-C-M' activities. The Confucianist state of the time was supportive to these entrepreneurs' role in facilitating the growth of the market economy, but it was also anxious to prevent the social dislocation that unchecked profit-making activities would entail. Consequently, despite the many favorable policies to mercantile activities in general (such as low commercial taxes and government loans to merchants), the imperial state never hesitated to side with the laboring classes whenever those entrepreneurial activities went too far and disrupted local livelihoods, as shown in many cases when the authorities penalized grain merchants for invoking food riots. Mercantile elite and profit-making activities in China, therefore, never grew as strong as their counterparts in western Europe, and hence the "advanced market without capitalism" in Qing China (Hung, 2008).

Transcending the labor theory of value, we can see capitalism as not necessarily tied to wage labor but to diverse forms of economic processes, so far as the pursuit of profit remains central to the economic system. In other words, as far as the profit motivation is concerned, there is only one variety of capitalism. What vary is the actual activities that are involved to create ΔM in different times and places of the system. It can be through long-distance trade, wage-labor-based manufacturing, slave-based plantation, household factory harnessing unpaid familial labor, or even financial speculation without any material mediation, hence compressing the M-C-M's into M-M'. Under this definition of capitalism, we would not have the problem of not being able to characterize hybridized systems composed of different modes of labor controls and economic regulations, as critiqued by Block regarding other definitions of capitalism. We could unambiguously identify an economic system as capitalist so far as its dominant economic units are driven by the pursuit of profit, which is then plowed back to fuel the further expansion of the units and the system at large, generating even more profit. This process is the foundation of all economies seeking endless GDP growth.

This Weberian-Marxist conception of capitalism not only does not share the problem of other conceptions that motivates Block's critique of the concept, but also addresses issues that the Polanyian conception of market could not deal with effectively. The analytic power in understanding the peril of neoliberalism and market fetishism at the zenith of Pax Britannica and our contemporary times notwithstanding, the Polanyian critique of "self-regulating market," which is seen as the mother of all social evils, falls short of making sense of many nonmarket and even antimarket processes that are also integral to the dominant economic system and are as polarizing and dislocating to people's livelihoods as the self-regulating market itself.

One key Polanyian critique of the nineteenth-century self-regulating market was its creation of fictitious commodities through such processes as commodification of labor that created pauperization and chronic unemployment of the working classes. It is surely true to England, where the rise of a modern economy was inseparable from the violent separation of direct producers from their land since the great enclosure. But integral to this self-regulatory market was an array of extra-economic coercions that helped create and sustain the self-regulating market in England and the world. The deindustrialization of India through administrative coercion destroyed the native textile industry, clearing the way for the conquest of the Indian market by British textiles, as well as periodic looting of China in the form of war indemnity and literal plundering as in the 1900 invasion of Beijing by eight Western powers are cases in point. The booty generated from such extra-economic violence has been a significant source of wealth that fueled Britain's great transformation and the reproduction of the global free market. This violence is a constitutive part of the normal functioning of the "self-regulating market," not outside of it.

In our times of neoliberalism, the self-regulatory market did not dominate every aspect of life everywhere. Low-cost labor from the developing countries is a key foundation of the global neoliberal order. But most of the labor involved in the process was far from fully commodified. A large portion of this low-waged labor were reliant on nonmarket activities – such as subsistence farming back in the village of the laborers' origins – for their reproduction, and the externalization of the cost of reproduction outside of the market is essential to the global low-wage manufacturing regime. Concurrent with the de-marketization of labor reproduction is the de-marketization of labor process itself here and there around the world. The decline of formal wage labor and revival of indentured labor and human trafficking are good examples.

What we know of as globalization today is in fact a combined movement of expanding free market in certain aspects of life through financial deregulation, privatization, trade liberalization, etc. on the one hand, and exclusion of other aspects of life, such as reproduction of labor and the labor process itself in select locations, out of the market on the other hand. While a Polanyian critique of globalization addresses the dynamics of the first movement, it does not address the second. In this regard, the Weberian-Marxist conception of capitalism is helpful. Under the logic of the ceaseless accumulation of capital, dominant economic actors, including both capitalists and capitalist states, would resort to whatever means beneficial to the accumulation in different spaces and times. This can be marketization, demarketization, and the employment of extra-economic means of exploitation. It follows that the Polanyian remedy for our failed system through social protection against the freewheeling market can only be part of the solution. In response to the dislocations and destructions that global capitalism brought to our society and nature via extra-economic exploitation, marketization could be a remedy, at least in some cases and under certain conditions. One example would be the movement that seeks to free indentured labors, bringing them into waged employment. Another example would be the establishment of a global carbon trading system that will marketize the cost of greenhouse gas emissions that has been so far externalized from the capitalist system to the whole humanity and our future generations.

In light of the above, the critique of and resistance to our dominant economic system – which is by definition capitalist provided with its accumulation imperative – need to be antimarket in some instances and promarket in others. A Polanyian critique of the free market is surely powerful and helpful, but it is not enough for our full understanding of the economic malaises of four times. It is at best counterproductive to throw away the concept of capitalism altogether – so far as we understand that the very foundation of the capitalist system is the ceaseless accumulation of capital and nothing else.

REFERENCES

Arrighi, G. (1994). *The long twentieth century: Money, power, and the origins of our times.* London: Verso.
Arrighi, G. (2007). *Adam Smith in Beijing: Lineages of the twenty-first century.* London: Verso.
Hung, H.-F. (2008). Agricultural revolution and elite reproduction: Transition to capitalism debate revisited. *American Sociological Review, 73*(4).
Pomeranz, K. (2001). *The great divergence: China, Europe, and the making of the modern economy.* Princeton, NJ: Princeton University Press.
Tilly, C. (1975). Food supply and public order in modern Europe. In C. Tilly (Ed.), *Formation of national states in Western Europe.* Princeton, NJ: Princeton University Press.
Weber, M. (1992 [1930]). *The protestant ethic and the spirit of capitalism.* London: Routledge.

ON FRED BLOCK, VARIETIES OF WHAT? SHOULD WE STILL BE USING THE CONCEPT OF CAPITALISM?

Wolfgang Streeck

ABSTRACT

There are good reasons for preferring the concept of capitalism over that of "market economy." A capitalist economy is one that depends on the commercialization-through-monetarization of ever more social relations. The result is disequilibrium as the normal condition of a society placed under pressure by its "economy" for continuous reorganization in line with a need for ongoing capital accumulation. A capitalist society enlists the possessive individualism of its members as its principal vehicle of social progress, measured as an increase in wealth-as-money. While Polanyian theory has pointed out important features of advanced capitalist societies, there is no need to sacrifice core Marxian concepts for it. Marxian theory helps avoid the trap of political voluntarism, which stipulates a priority of politics in the capitalist political economy or a fundamental difference between "varieties" of capitalism. Moreover, rather than regarding the capitalist economy as by definition "always embedded," political-economic theory must allow for a self-destructive, and indeed socially destructive, tendency of capitalist political economies to "disembed" themselves by struggling free from social controls and dictating to social life the imperatives of market efficiency and a market-conforming distribution of life chances.

Capitalism – the thing, not the name – was anything but popular in the years following WWII, and this was so everywhere in the industrialized world, including the United States. Outside of the Communist bloc, free markets and private property had to be made palatable again to a politically empowered working class, by wrapping them into a collection of containing and constraining policies and institutions that were to protect societies from a repetition of the disasters of the 1930s. As we now know, however, the political provisions that were to turn capitalism into something else – called a "mixed economy" or a "social market economy," to make the new appear sufficiently different from the old[1] – lasted only a quarter century. With the end of postwar reconstruction in the 1960s, a grinding process of gradual institutional change set in that insensibly undermined and eventually removed most of the safeguards once devised to make capitalism compatible with then powerful collective demands for security, stability, equal opportunity, shared prosperity, and the like.

Forty years later, we are beholding the results of an extraordinary historical development: a newly liberated capitalism having successfully extricated itself, Houdini-like, from the social fetters it had temporarily had to pretend to be willing and able to live with. Among the collective safety provisions that have fallen victim to capitalism's remarkable escape act are politically guaranteed full employment, economy-wide free collective bargaining, industrial democracy at the workplace, a broad public sector offering secure employment in good jobs, extensive public services, economic planning to prevent the return of business cycles and crises, a social welfare state guaranteeing a general floor of social rights for every citizen and protecting people's lives from the commodifying pressures of market competition, and so on. It is important to note that these developments, and the pressures emanating from them for a deep reorganization of life and society in response to market pressures for competitiveness, flexibility, and profitability, were not at all limited to the United States but appeared in locally diversified forms in all industrial societies, some leading in the breaking of the promises of the postwar era and others lagging, but all of them essentially moving in the same direction.[2]

How is what we have seen in the past four decades to be interpreted? In terms of Fred Block's essay, have we seen the rise of one out of a range of other, equally possible variants of "market society," brought about by wrong-headed theories and bad political decisions, mysteriously synchronized across countries and sectors but in principle open to reversal by better theories and decisions in the future? Or are we witnessing an inherent dynamic of a politically hard-to-govern, self-driven social process – in the words of traditional theories of capitalism: the functioning of an anarchic regime of economic action that is a *problem* for government and politics rather than its *product*? While Block opts for the first answer, inspection of the historical sequence during which capitalism became "unleashed" (Glyn, 2006) from its postwar chains makes me tend toward the second. It is under this impression that I advocate that we stick to the concept of capitalism and some of the theoretical tenets that come with it, rather than abandoning it and instead calling the beast, as Block suggests, "market society."

Why capitalism? *Name ist Schall und Rauch*, as Goethe has it.[3] Still it may be useful to be reminded that it is certainly not *laborism* that we have in mind when referring to contemporary political economy as it is capital, measured in units of money, and not human capacity, that is being accumulated in it – or human capacity only to the extent that it is conducive to capital accumulation. Markets are, as we learn in Economics 101, "where supply and demand meet." But what makes the difference is that under capitalism, supply and demand meet *as commodities* in order to turn money into more money, according to Marx's venerable formula, $M \to C \to M'$.[4] It is here that the peculiar dynamism, the *Eigendynamik*, of the capitalist socioeconomic formation is rooted (Ingham, 2004, 2008). When speaking of capitalism, we have in mind, or at least could and should have, the specific restlessness (Sewell, 2008) of an economic regime that is bent on permanently revolutionizing, not just itself but also the society in which it is located, as a condition of its prosperity and indeed survival (Schumpeter, 2006 [1912]). A capitalist economy, technically speaking, is one that depends on the relentless commercialization-through-monetarization of ever more social relations. The result is disequilibrium as the normal condition of a society placed under continuous pressures by its "economy" for ongoing reorganization in line with a need for continued, maximally efficient capital accumulation. One could also say that the concept of capitalism refers to a society that has enlisted the possessive individualism of its members as its main vehicle of social progress, measured again as an increase in wealth-as-money – a society that has made the amelioration of its collective living conditions and the realization of its core value of personal freedom both dependent on and subservient to successful activation of the profit motive and the maximization of the rate of increase of its capital. With this in mind and in this sense, I do think that, *pace* Block, capitalism as a system *does* have "a fundamental unity,"[5] due to its "economy" extending far into its society and profoundly shaping and conditioning social life.[6]

Practicing Polanyian that I have become, not least under the influence of, among others, Fred Block,[7] I still hesitate to discard the Marxian heritage as light-heartedly as he does. Marx, of course, needs no defense; he is easily recognized as the by far most sophisticated among the nineteenth century founding figures of sociology. While he does not depend on us paying tribute to him, if only because he is no longer alive, exchanging him wholesale even for someone like Karl Polanyi might cut us off from important sources of inspiration, not to mention hiding from us the roots and deeper meanings of core concepts of political economy and economic sociology that we use every day. Examples where we, thanks to Marx, do not have to reinvent the wheel include dialectical figures of thought like the self-undermining of institutions (Greif & Laitin, 2004; Greif, 2006); the notion of historical tipping-points where quantity turns into quality; the memory of the violent roots of modern society including modern capitalism ("primitive accumulation;" Marx, 1967 [1867, 1887], 873 ff.) and of the coercive foundations of apparently voluntary exchange relations (Graeber, 2011); the analysis of the employment relationship as one of domination based on free but asymmetrical contract; the inverse shape of the labor supply curve especially at its lower end, etc. Of course, it has become commonplace to distance oneself from Marxian, or Marxist, "determinism" and, even worse, "historical materialism." But concerning the former, it must be allowed to remember that "determinism" was the hallmark of nineteenth century science, and that it was in any case much more pronounced in, say, Spencer and the young Durkheim because they were ignorant of dialectics and had no concept of "countervailing forces," as offered by Marx in his discussion of the declining rate of profit under the impact of an increasing "organic composition" of capital (Marx, 1981 [1894], chapters 2 and 13). As to historical materialism, one can still be impressed with the caution with which someone like Max Weber avoided challenging the Marxian account of the origin of capitalism directly,[8] just as one must not forget that Marx himself spent much of his time trying to organize a revolutionary political movement, instead of sitting back and waiting until the presumably iron laws of history delivered to mankind a socialist society.[9]

However that may be, it does not seem a good idea to replace Marxian "determinism" with political voluntarism,[10] and be it in the form of a conceptual move to a Polanyian "always embedded" "market society." There simply is no "primacy of politics" under capitalism, and cannot be. Nowhere is this clearer than in the version of the "varieties of capitalism" literature that Block calls upon for support, which attributes the alleged differences between "liberal" and "coordinated" political economies, *not* to the volitions of a democratically organized citizenry, but to different strategies of firms in competitive markets ("firm-centered approach"; Hall & Soskice, 2001; cf. Streeck, 2011). Block, unfortunately, explicitly subscribes to the functionalist economism of that literature when, invoking Wallerstein, he declares it to be "undisputable" that in the global economy, nations compete against nations, and governments exist to improve the "competitiveness" of their national economies.[11] It is interesting to note that in its empirical analyses, the economistic-functionalist strand of what advertises itself as a theory of the "varieties of capitalism" speaks, like Block, not of capitalism but of "market economies" (Hall & Soskice, 2001). In both cases, abandoning the concept of capitalism not only hides its commonalities but also falls in the trap of a functionalist concept of the economy as a politically designed and controlled technical arrangement for consensual wealth creation.

Clearly, there *is* politics under capitalism, and indeed democratic rather than just technocratic politics, but there is also the *Eigenleben* of the capitalist system of action.[12] While highly politically consequential, and in this sense fundamentally political indeed, capitalism is powerfully capable of protecting and extracting itself from political control. In Polanyian terms, while politics may operate as a countermovement to the capitalist market, and sometimes even as a successful one, the market moves on its own, generating the movement to which the countermovement must try to respond. The concept of capitalism, outdated as some may have thought it was, has the important advantage that it reminds us of the fact that the political regulation of economic life in contemporary modern societies is always precarious as it is typically condemned to limping behind the dynamic expansion of commercialized market relations. Speaking of capitalism, that is to say, protects us from forgetting that capitalist land-grabbing permanently imparts Schumpeterian creative destruction, not just on established "economic" practice, but also on social structures and institutions, in particular by replacing the conservatism of social obligations with the voluntarism of free contractual exchange, regardless of the collective consequences (Streeck, 2011).

As I have shown empirically for the German case (Streeck, 2009), the decline of postwar pacified capitalism must primarily be attributed to endogenous subversion and erosion of an institutional framework that had become suboptimal for capital accumulation, rather than, as Block suggests, to the frivolous fancies of neoliberal economists and misled politicians. Postwar democratic capitalism was fragile from its beginning – it only looked stable due to extraordinary political circumstances and the studied optimism of political leaders after the end of the war. In fact it could never hope to last longer than, in historical terms, a very short period. When it began to decay in the 1970s, it was because of the helplessness of democratic politics, organized at and confined to the level of nation-states, against capitalism's new international opportunities for evading the social constraints that had by the 1970s landed it in an increasingly uncomfortable profit squeeze. For a time, the dependence of politics and political success under democratic capitalism on uninterrupted capital accumulation – or in the technocratic language of standard economics: on economic growth – led inevitably optimistic politicians to place their hopes on riding the tiger and jump on the historical bandwagon toward liberalization and deregulation until the re-formed capitalist economic regime almost crashed as a result of its unfettered progress.

It may seem like hairsplitting if I now ask, in Block's terms as he reconstructs the Polanyian conceptual framework, whether the current crisis was due to the capitalist "economy" having become *mis*embedded or *dis*embedded. Block declares the latter to be impossible, due to economic action always and inevitably being social action. But while one can fully and indeed emphatically agree with this, as I do,[13] there is no logical need to conclude from it that a capitalist political economy is governed by a primacy of politics. Instead I believe that a realistic theory of political economy must provide for the possibility that social institutions built to protect society and humanity from the "vagaries of the market" *may be overrun by these* – and that capitalist action may break through its social containment unless that containment is continuously reinforced and vigilantly kept current.

Capitalism, that is to say, is indeed "always embedded" Block (2007) in that it takes place in a society, subject to social constraints and opportunities. Also, capitalism in an important sense depends on remaining so embedded as it thrives on the rule of law, mutual trust, normative coordination and institutionalized cooperation, creative intelligence, and the like. Nevertheless, and at the same time, capitalist actors always struggle to escape from their social containment and free themselves from obligations and controls (Streeck, 2011). Ideas of solidarity and institutions of social regulation are as a result at a permanent risk of erosion, with capitalist patterns of action spreading like cancer (McMurtry, 1999) in the body social. This is so in spite of the fact that capitalism as such, pure and simple and liberated from social constraints, cannot exist. In this sense, capitalism feeds parasitically on the society that it inhabits or befalls, with its expansion ultimately amounting to its self-destruction unless checked by social and political opposition. Sometimes, as in the neoliberal era, the capitalist advance may capture the very politics that should contain it for its own good, and turn it into a vehicle of its own self-destructive progress; this, I believe, is what Polanyi meant when he described the expansion of "market society" as a "frivolous experiment" of states and governments.[14]

Is the state, then, the executive committee of the capitalist class? The answer that does justice to the dialectical, i.e., inherently contradictory nature of capitalism as a social formation is that it *is*, but only to the extent that it is *not*. If government was entirely captured by capitalist interests, it would be unable to protect them from destroying themselves – as none other than Marx himself has indicated in the famous chapter on the working day in Vol. 1 of *Capital* (Marx, 1967 [1867, 1887], 340 ff.). But while capitalism does depend on being saved from itself by a politics that is at least in part responsive to social countermovements, capitalists cannot act on such dependence, if only because they are always irresistibly tempted to gamble on making a last killing before the casino will go bankrupt. So the social countermovement on whose success the survival of capitalism – its sustained "embeddedness" – depends must assert itself against the powerful resistance of its beneficiaries-cum-adversaries, a resistance that is not at all perfunctory or doomed to fail, but is in fact dead serious. There is no functionalism here, and the stabilization of the capitalist system of action is a highly uncertain undertaking whose success is not guaranteed even though it would be in the interest of those working to prevent it. Capitalists can be taught that interest, but whether they will condescend to learn the lesson is up to them (Streeck, 2004). Power, after all, is the ability to refuse to learn (Deutsch, 1963). As we have seen in the current crisis, such ability may require no more than being big enough for one's demise to be a threat to the community at large.

Coming to the end of my comment, I would also like to put in a word for not entirely abandoning concepts like socialism or even communism.[15] As to the latter, David Graeber in his book on the anthropology of debt (2011) has succinctly pointed out the generically communist foundations of economic life, even in advanced capitalism. Concerning socialism, to me the concept is indispensable for connoting the counterpart of – possessive-consumerist – individualism, reminding us against the grain of today's "cult of the individual" that, once again citing Marx, man is an animal that can be an individual only in a society.[16] What other concept is there in any case for the more communal, more other-regarding and more collectively responsible way of life that we today seem to need more urgently than ever, a life with much less license to externalize the costs of private pleasure-seeking to the rest of the world? And how are we to name a social organization with much more shared control over the collective fate and with a strong collective capacity to avoid the unanticipated consequences of freely expanding market relations – consequences that unendingly mystify us today when as individuals we cause effects that we cannot possibly want, not just as a society but also as individuals?

Fred Block's notion of an "always embedded" capitalism subject to a "primacy of politics" radiates an optimism that conspicuously resembles what European Social Democrats have for a long time made themselves believe: that socialism, as defined above, could be had, preserved, and surreptitiously expanded on top of a capitalist economy-cum-society, by serving its inexorably growing functional need for collective governance. Looking back at the past four decades, however, we see a sustained process of institutional transformation, slow but irresistible and driven, not by democratic politics but by the dynamic logic of capitalist development, that has effectively destroyed most if not all of the political safeguards whose establishment had been the very condition for capitalism being allowed to return after the disasters of the first half of the twentieth century. That logic, and the reorganization – or disorganization – of social life that it dictated, culminates today in the dual crisis of the global financial as well as the national democratic state system. Decades of "reform" aimed at meeting the ever more aggressive demands of capitalist markets have only exacerbated the capitalist wear and tear on the social fabric, often with the connivance of blackmailed states and governments, including social-democratic ones. Is this experience really compatible with a theory that considers "market society" to be at the disposition of politics? Or does it not rather speak for attributing to capitalism as a social action system a life, a logic, a power, and a dynamism of its own, on which social-democratic postwar *politics as usual* has more and more lost its grip? If one comes to conclude, as I have, that it is the latter that is the more realistic perspective, is it then still responsible to invest one's time and energy in developing responsible ideas as to how responsible governments may repair "the system" or turn one "variety of capitalism" into another? Or would it not be much more constructive to be less constructive – to cease looking for better *varieties* of capitalism and instead begin seriously to think about *alternatives* to it?

NOTES

1. In postwar Germany, capitalism simply was a no-no word. In Frankfurt where I studied sociology in the late 1960s, Adorno preferred to speak of *Tauschgesellschaft* (catallactic society), perhaps because the notion of capitalism was then too much associated with Communist orthodoxy. On the other hand, the neo-socialist young generation, to which I was proud to belong, spoke of "social market economy" only tongue-in-cheek; to us the term was all-too-obvious capitalist propaganda. If, as Block claims, capitalism has recently become a positive concept in the United States, the same is not true in Europe. Here the word came again in use after the end of Communism when Michel Albert's book, *Capitalism Against Capitalism* (Albert, 1993 [1991]) became a bestseller. The book distinguishes between good and bad capitalisms, the former associated with a widely defined Rhineland and the latter with Anglo-America. It prefigured current dichotomies between "coordinated" and "liberal" capitalisms or indeed "market economies." Since the crisis doubts have been growing whether good capitalism is really so much better than bad capitalism.

2. For the case of Germany, presumably the paragon of a "coordinated," i.e., socially domesticated "market economy" (Hall & Soskice, 2001), see Streeck (2009).

3. In English, approximately: Names are smoke and mirrors. Faust I, Marthens Garten.

4. Financialization, of course, has cut the sequence short, to M → M' (McMurtry, 1999).

5. Which, of course, unlike what Block seems to suggest, does not necessarily imply coherence. In fact an important lesson we can learn from Marx is that unity can be internally contradictory, or dialectical. More on this below.

6. For an elegant "microfoundation" of a theory of capitalism as a social action system, see a recent paper by Jens Beckert, on capitalism's "four C's": credit, commodity, competition, creativity.

7. For proof, see my *Re-Forming Capitalism* (2009), in particular chapter 17, pp. 230 ff.

8. For example: "We have no intention whatever of maintaining such a foolish and doctrinaire thesis as ... that capitalism as an economic system is a creation of the Reformation ...," in view of "the tremendous confusion of interdependent influences between the material basis, the forms of social and political organization, and the ideas current in the time ..." (Weber, 1984 [1904/1905], p. 91). Or: "It is, of course, not my aim to substitute for a one-sided materialistic an equally one-sided spiritualistic causal interpretation of culture and of history. Each is equally possible, but each, if it does not serve as the preparation, but as the conclusion of an investigation, accomplishes equally little in the interest of historical truth" (*ibid.*, p. 183).

9. With the necessary good will, one may read the deterministic language in Marx as rhetorical in nature: as a strategic expression of optimism deployed to encourage readers to join the political countermovement against capitalism and make the theoretical prophecy self-fulfilling in practice.

10. For an example, see Block (2011) on the possible "construction of a new regime of accumulation" by none other than the Obama administration.

11. On why this is mistaken even at the empirical, not to mention the conceptual level, see Streeck (2009, chapter 13).

12. On the proper dynamic of capitalism as an institutional regime, see my essay, "Taking Capitalism Seriously" (Streeck, 2011). On how to study modern capitalism, see Streeck (2012) and Beckert (2012).
13. For why and how, see Beckert and Streeck (2008).
14. For a conclusive critique of the "always embedded" concept of capitalism, see Beckert (2009).
15. Needless to say that I am not here concerned with the technicalities of political salesmanship. My concern is that, if we abandon the terms in order to remain politically inoffensive, we may lose sight of what they signify.
16. "Aber die Epoche, die diesen Standpunkt erzeugt, den des vereinzelten Einzelnen, ist grade die der bisher entwickeltsten gesellschaftlichen (allgemeinen von diesem Standpunkt aus) Verhältnisse. Der Mensch ist im wörtlichsten Sinn ein ζῶον πολιτικόν, nicht nur ein geselliges Tier, sondern ein Tier, das nur in der Gesellschaft sich vereinzeln kann" (Marx, 1953 [1857–1858], p. 6).

REFERENCES

Albert, M. (1993 [1991]). *Capitalism against capitalism: How America's obsession with individual achievement and short-term profit has led it to the brink of collapse.* New York, NY: Four Walls Eight Windows.
Beckert, J. (2009). The great transformation of embeddedness: Karl Polanyi and the new economic sociology. In C. Hann & K. Hart (Eds.), *Market and society: The great transformation* (pp. 38–55). New York, NY: Cambridge University Press.
Beckert, J. (2012). *Capitalism as a system of contingent expectations: On the microfoundations of economic dynamics.* Köln, Max Planck Institute for the Study of Societies, Unpublished manuscript.
Beckert, J., & Streeck, W. (2008). *Economic sociology and political economy: A programmatic perspective.* MPIfG Working Paper No. 08/4. Max Planck Institute for the Study of Societies, Cologne, Germany.
Block, F. (2007). Understanding the diverging trajectories of the United States and western Europe: A neo-Polanyian analysis. *Politics & Society, 35*(3), 3–33.
Block, F. (2011). Crisis and renewal: The outlines of a twentieth-century New Deal. *Socio-Economic Review, 9*(1), 31–57.
Deutsch, K. W. (1963). *The nerves of government: Models of political communication and control.* New York, NY: The Free Press.
Glyn, A. (2006). *Capitalism unleashed: Finance globalization and welfare.* Oxford: Oxford University Press.
Graeber, D. (2011). *Debt: The first 5,000 years.* Brooklyn, NY: Melville House.
Greif, A. (2006). *Institutions and the Path to the Modern Economy.* Cambridge: Cambridge University Press.
Greif, A., & Laitin, D. A. (2004). A theory of endogenous institutional change. *American Political Science Review, 98*(4), 633–652.
Hall, P. A., & Soskice, D. (2001). An introduction to varieties of capitalism. In P. A. Hall & D. Soskice (Eds.), *Varieties of capitalism: The institutional foundations of comparative advantage* (pp. 1–68). Oxford: Oxford University Press.
Ingham, G. (2004). *The nature of money.* Cambridge: Polity.

Ingham, G. (2008). *Capitalism*. Oxford: Polity.
Marx, K. (1953 [1857–1858]). *Grundrisse der Kritik der Politischen Ökonomie (Rohentwurf) 1857–1858*. Berlin: Dietz Verlag.
Marx, K. (1967 [1867, 1887]). *Capital. A critique of political economy* (Vol. 1). New York, NY: International Publishers.
Marx, K. (1981 [1894]). *Capital. A critique of political economy* (Vol. 3). London: Penguin.
McMurtry, J. (1999). *The cancer stage of capitalism*. London: Pluto.
Schumpeter, J. A. (2006 [1912]). *Theorie der wirtschaftlichen Entwicklung*. Berlin: Duncker & Humblot.
Sewell, W. H., Jr. (2008). The temporalities of capitalism. *Socio-Economic Review, 6*, 517–537.
Streeck, W. (2004). Educating capitalists: A rejoinder to Wright and Tsakalatos. *Socio-Economic Review, 2*(3), 425–483.
Streeck, W. (2009). *Re-forming capitalism: Institutional change in the German political economy*. Oxford: Oxford University Press.
Streeck, W. (2011). Taking capitalism seriously: Towards an institutional approach to contemporary political economy. *Socio-Economic Review, 9*(1), 137–167.
Streeck, W. (2012). How to study contemporary capitalism? *European Journal of Sociology, 53*(1), 1–28.
Weber, M. (1984 [1904/1905]). *The protestant ethic and the spirit of capitalism* (T. Parsons, Trans.). Introduction by Anthony Giddens. London: Unwin Paperbacks.

THERE WAS NO BABY IN THIS BATHWATER: A REPLY TO THE CRITICS

Fred Block

ABSTRACT

In response to Bandelj, Hung, and Streeck, I make three basic points. First, while the initial article focused on definitions of capitalism as a system, the critics prefer to see capitalism as a spirit or a tendency that emphasizes the unlimited pursuit of profit. While we are in agreement that such a tendency is destructive, it is confusing to define capitalism this way when most others are using the term to describe a system that they see as coherent. Second, some of the critics question whether efforts to reign in the capitalist impulse can be successful for very long. I argue that the breakdown of restraints in the post-World War II period can be traced to the end of the Bretton Woods regime of fixed exchange rates in 1973. This policy shift was neither inevitable nor the result of political agency by financial or corporate interests. Third, the concept of capitalism fails to illuminate key fault lines in contemporary political economies such as the divide between finance and production or between giant firms and small- and medium-sized enterprises.

FOCUSING ON THE DIFFERENCES

My respondents have also made my task much easier by substantially converging on the argument that we need to hold on to the concept of capitalism to describe a set of social arrangements in which the ceaseless pursuit of profits is not just tolerated but encouraged. They are all suggesting that I am, in effect, discarding something extremely valuable in my haste to clean house. While we disagree on this central point, it is important to note that this is essentially a family squabble; the four of us share a commitment to a Polanyi-inspired political economy that is deeply critical of present economic arrangements. For this reason, my goal is to pinpoint the precise issues on which we see things differently.

The initial piece was aimed at the use of the concept of capitalism to describe a system – a coherent and somewhat unified set of arrangements that is reproduced over time. This is what both Marx and Wallerstein have referenced, and it is also the understanding that has seeped into everyday common sense. When Margaret Thatcher proclaimed: "There is no alternative"; she was invoking the systematic nature of the capitalist order. However, my critics – with slightly varying inflections – are using capitalism to denote something somewhat different, a spirit or a tendency that they see as necessarily destructive. In Streeck's formulation, capitalism is a dangerous beast that was contained in the social democratic decades immediately after World War II, but was then able to slip past all restraints and create in its wake disorder, deepening inequality, and financial crises. For Bandelj, we need to retain the word capitalism to characterize political economies "guided by pursuit of material gain, which advantage some strata in society more than others ...." And Hung invokes the Weberian definition of the capitalist spirit: "under which the urge to accumulate money for the sake of accumulating more money in rational and methodical manners overrides all other imperatives."

I am certainly in agreement that the unconstrained pursuit of wealth is a dangerous and destructive force, but the issue is what name we give to that destructive force. I think that whenever we talk about a capitalist system, we are reinforcing the erroneous claim that the unconstrained pursuit of profit could possibly be the basis for organizing a society. The reality is that any market society that persists for any time at all must combine this pursuit of gain with institutions and practices that restrain greed. It also must find ways to produce and distribute certain critical goods on bases other than profitability, such as reliance on reciprocity and redistribution.

Streeck (2009) has written eloquently against functionalist thinking in the social sciences, and I agree with his critique. He recognizes a strong tendency to take the institutional arrangements at any given moment and reify them into a coherent and durable system rather than recognizing that different institutions tend to have different histories and dynamics that often come together in temporary and fairly unstable configurations. But given that many of our colleagues have this bias toward functionalist thinking, it follows that even if we use the term "capitalism" to connote a destructive demiurge, they might well imagine that we are talking about a smoothly functioning system. To be sure, Humpty Dumpty in *Through the Looking Glass* insisted, "When I use a word, it means just what I choose it to mean – neither more nor less." But as critical social scientists, we have to be very careful that the concepts we use are not being undermined by connotations and associations that influence the way that our students and colleagues interpret what we are saying.

But there is more than just the naming issue. I think of the unconstrained pursuit of wealth as being similar to the drive by some human beings to exercise political authority over their fellow human beings. When this "will to power" is left unconstrained, it produces the oppressive reign of feudal lords, intrusive party bureaucrats, and different styles of authoritarian rule. But humanity has developed over centuries democratic institutions and practices that work – admittedly imperfectly – to channel this impulse in ways that are significantly less destructive. So now, those with the will to power compete for office within democratic structures and even when their campaigns are successful, there are institutionalized limits on the powers they can exercise.

Precisely because the impulse to accumulate huge piles of money is unlikely to disappear any time soon, the issue is how to channel and limit this drive so that it does a minimum amount of damage. In my vision of the good society, most people will have alternatives to working for a profit-oriented firm, and profit-seeking firms would be tightly regulated so that their profits came from increases in efficiency rather than from imposing costs on others. But this brings us to the critical point of disagreement. Streeck argues explicitly that any set of constraints on profit-making will prove to be only a temporary expedient because the capitalist impulse will break through the restraints and will again run wild. But why? Presumably, he is not equally pessimistic that the will to power will inevitably escape constraints and return us to dictatorship. Ho-Fung Hung helps on this by mentioning that in China in the 17th and 18th centuries, the Confucian state successfully supported merchants while keeping them from predatory actions that would have disrupted local economic activity. If the Chinese state could successfully constrain profit-seeking merchants for two centuries, why couldn't it happen again for even longer?

I am arguing that the only durable protection against both the will to power and the will to make obscene profits are democratic practices and widespread understanding of the urgency of maintaining a system of restraints. Streeck suggests in his conclusion that there might be alternatives to capitalism that would durably solve this problem. But the experiences of socialism in the 20th century and particularly the experience of China under the rule of the Communist Party suggests that transformations in property relations can be reversed with surprising rapidity. Despite decades of socialist property arrangements and denunciations of the capitalist road, China still made a U-turn that has allowed the children of the party elite to dispossess other Chinese and accumulate vast fortunes.

And on the other side, the broad strokes with which Streeck describes the recent history of unfettered capitalism leads him to neglect the huge differences that now separate the United States from much of Europe and especially the Nordic social democracies as manifested in such key indicators as child poverty, income inequality, and even literacy (Block, 2011). He argues that all of these nations are moving in the same direction, but isn't it relevant that the United States seems to be hurtling along at 100 miles an hour while Sweden might be moving at something closer to 5 miles an hour? Don't these different rates of speed suggest that there might be different dynamics involved?

But our central disagreement is about interpreting the shifts that have occurred over the last 40 years. Streeck acknowledges that for roughly three decades after World War II, greed was effectively contained by social democratic and New Deal policies in both Europe and the United States. But then policy changes carried out in the mid-1970s effectively undermined the containment structure and those pursuing unlimited profits became ever more powerful and influential in persuading others to let them run riot. The culmination, of course, was the 2008 Global Financial Crisis created by mortgage brokers and investment bankers determined to maximize their bonuses.

Streeck suggests that the failure of this containment structure was both inevitable and was directly caused by "capitalist" agents seeking their freedom. Even though I think we are referencing the same set of events, I see this history differently. For me, the critical decision was the abandonment of Bretton Woods' system of fixed exchange rates in 1973 by the major Western powers and the shift to an international monetary regime based on floating rates that were set by currency traders.

REVISITING THE HISTORY

In designing the post-World War II international monetary system, John Maynard Keynes and Harry Dexter White were trying to increase the policy autonomy of national governments so they would be able to pursue full employment (Block, 1977). Some governments that had tried to pursue expansionary policies in the 1930s suffered capital flight as propertied interests insisted that those policies would inevitably lead to inflation and a falling value for the national currency. This was a classic self-fulfilling prophecy; as long as enough asset holders shifted resources abroad, the currency's value would fall and inflationary pressure would rise as imports became more expensive.

Keynes and White reasoned that if exchange rates were not being set daily by currency traders but were established by governments at a level that could be sustained, this threat would be diminished. Moreover, they also added another layer of protection; the Articles of Agreement of the International Monetary Fund (IMF) gave governments the authority to regulate capital movements so that politically motivated flight of capital could be restricted. It is therefore not accidental that the growth of the welfare state and the pursuit of full employment flourished during the Bretton Woods era of a fixed exchange rate system (Ruggie, 1982).

However, free-market economists also recognized this connection and they polemicized ferociously through this entire period in favor of a return to market-determined exchange rates. They promised that with a shift to market exchange rates, there would be a complete elimination of the occasional disruptions that occurred when a government made a significant upward or downward adjustment of its exchange rate. Instead of sharp jumps, the market would smooth things out and make exchange rates far more predictable.

There was, of course, no empirical foundation for this claim, and when the shift to floating rates occurred in 1973, the consequence was a huge increase in exchange rate volatility because trading currencies suddenly became a lucrative business for banks and other financial institutions and there was nothing to stop sudden and dramatic appreciation or depreciation of any given currency. And this increased volatility of exchange rates, in turn, set off a cascade of consequences. With huge exchange rate swings, asset holders felt the need to protect themselves by shifting assets into appreciating currencies. So they lobbied governments to dismantle capital controls creating an explosion of international capital movements and, of course, even more exchange rate volatility (Block, 1996).

And if these steps were not sufficient to restrict government policy autonomy, the financial engineers then invented and gained approval to sell a variety of derivative instruments designed to protect investors from the heightened volatility of exchange rates and interest rates. These instruments increased volatility even further and made it even easier for herds of investors to put intolerable pressure on governments that were pursuing policies that were at odds with the bankers' deep preference for austerity. This is how we arrived at the recent plight of the Greek government where policy autonomy fell to zero in the face of speculators and the unrelenting demands of the European institutions.

The significance of the cascade set off by the 1973 move to floating exchange rates was recognized by Fritz Scharpf, whose book, *Crisis and Choice in European Social Democracy* (1991), was first published in German in 1987. Scharpf showed systematically the ways in which the post-1973 international monetary environment undermined the effectiveness of social democratic policies. With significant reductions in policy autonomy, measures that had worked in the past were no longer effective and social democratic parties began a long search for new policies – a search that often ended with a capitulation to market liberalism.

In brief, the cumulative impact of the changes that began with floating exchange rates in 1973 was to significantly weaken the restraints that had been placed on unchecked greed in the early decades after World War II. The transformation did not happen overnight, but with each successive step, the forces in favor of even further financial liberalization became even stronger as an economic force, as a political force, and as an ideological force.

But it was not inevitable that this dynamic of financial liberalization occur at all. In 1971, the Nixon administration was facing intensifying conflicts between the dollar's role in the international monetary system and the ability of the United States to pursue its preferred foreign and domestic policies. Both the U.S. trade balance and the current account balance were becoming increasingly negative and this was creating global doubts that the United States would continue to sell gold at the guaranteed rate, which was then $35 an ounce. On the domestic front, the Nixon administration was facing a potentially difficult re-election campaign, especially if the economy did not quickly bounce back from the 1970–1971 recession. In a word, global pressures indicated the need for contractionary policies, while domestic considerations made expansionary policies necessary.

Nixon's surprise announcement in August 1971 that he was closing the gold window and imposing wage and price controls was a deliberate move to negotiate a realignment of currency values that would devalue the dollar relative to other currencies and particularly the German Mark (Gowa, 1983). However, the resulting negotiations failed to reach consensus on a series of reforms that would keep the fixed rate system in place. While some devaluation of the dollar was accomplished, there were a continuing series of dollar crises that extended into 1973. Part of the problem was that Nixon and Kissinger were preoccupied with what they considered to be more urgent geopolitical matters such as the Vietnam War, the overture to China, and the relationship with the Soviet Union. In place of serious high-level negotiations, they simply tried to manage a series of dollar crises. The result was that the United States and the Europeans backed into a system of floating rates in March 1973 without anyone thinking that it was anything but a temporary expedient (Odell, 1982). But once the move had been made, they never got around to negotiating a new monetary agreement.

In fact, there is good reason to believe that Bretton Woods was another accidental victim of the Watergate scandal. In White House conversations with his economic advisors in March 1973, Nixon is very clear that he does not want to be perceived as ignoring the nation's obligation to provide global economic leadership. He repeatedly talks about muddling through the current currency crisis and then launching an initiative to negotiate a broad reform of the Bretton Woods system (U.S. Department of State, 2009). But at the end of the next month, April, Nixon accepts the resignations of Haldeman and Ehrlichman and fires John Dean whose Congressional testimony in early June 1973 dooms his presidency. By the time Gerald Ford succeeds Nixon in 1975, the new administration had to cope with a host of other issues that had more urgency than global monetary reform.

As for the Europeans, they saw a move toward floating rates in March 1973 as a way to develop a higher level of European integration. They hoped that with a coordinated float, they could keep intra-European rates relatively stable and avoid the dramatic shifts that had been occurring since August 1971. In a word, their choice was also tactical; they continued to prefer a world with more stable exchange rates. To be sure, the actions of currency speculators created a series of crises to which the move to floating rates was a partial solution, but there is little evidence that significant sectors of business were instrumental in persuading policymakers to try a floating rate system.

In retrospect, the shift to floating rates was an extremely important historical turning point, but its significance was not readily apparent at the time. On both sides of the Atlantic, discussion and understanding of the architecture of the international financial system was limited to a small group of international economists and even sophisticated political leaders had little idea of what was at stake in these arrangements. In general, the people who had been active in the intense policy debates in the 1930s and 1940s were either dead or retired, and the generation of experts who had come up in the meantime consisted largely of narrowly trained economists with little historical training.

In saying this, I draw on my personal experience; I began studying the international monetary system in the immediate aftermath of Nixon's decision to close the gold window in 1971. Even among left-wing scholars, there was very little knowledge about these arrangements or their significance. In a word, the two-and-a-half decades of prosperity after World War II had produced something akin to amnesia; the intense debates of the 1930s about the gold standard had been almost entirely forgotten outside of a small expert community. Even in Europe, most of the intellectual focus was on the construction of European institutions rather than on international monetary arrangements.

The lesson is that the gradual unraveling of the restraints on profit-seeking activity did not have to happen. Had social democrats in Europe and liberals and progressives in the United States understood at the time that their political projects depended upon keeping the Bretton Woods system of fixed exchange rates in place, they could well have forced the major powers to follow a different path. Had Europe and the United States reached a compromise that left the fixed exchange rates in place, they could have averted the cascade that we have described.

For example, in 1969, the Nixon administration had concurred with the decision to create Special Drawing Rights (SDRs) in the IMF. This was seen by some as a way to gradually reduce the dollar's centrality to the global monetary system by embracing Keynes' idea of an internationally created currency. When the crisis erupted in 1971, had there been different kinds of pressures on political leaders, the resolution might have involved an accelerated transition to SDRs in exchange for a negotiated realignment of exchange rates, and the United States agreeing to a 10 year transition period in which it would bring its current account into balance. In short, had the response to the crisis been to move toward increasing global cooperation and expanding the capacity of the IMF, this could well have given new life to social democratic initiatives within nations and in the European Community.

In sum, the capitalism vs. socialism binary takes our eyes off the prize, which is the actual structure of the global economic regime. Keynes and White understood this and so also have global activists who have waged campaigns in support of the financial transaction tax. There are concrete reforms of the global financial system that could be won, which would significantly change the balance of social forces within nations (Evans, 2008).

A SEPARATE POINT: LOCATING FAULT LINES

Nina Bandelj is certainly correct to argue that we need a category system that allows us to differentiate effectively between different types of political economy. While I am arguing for using market society as the central category, I think we need a lot of different modifiers to differentiate subtypes of that species. I would suggest that we could effectively differentiate between forms of market society that were more or less dominated by financial institutions or more or less oligarchic in their structure.

After all, the best concepts illuminate the key fault lines of a particular social order. For classical Marxism, the concept of capitalism did precisely this by focusing attention on the struggle between workers and employers at the point of production and by highlighting the regularity of crises in which a surfeit of products could not find buyers.

But given that we live in a different era, the key fault lines have changed. It is telling that none of the respondents argue that we should retain the concept of capitalism because it illuminates the class struggle or the emergence of periodic crises. Rather, they emphasize the Polanyian point that when the effort to create a self-regulating market system is pushed too far, then the entire social order will be threatened by crisis. Bandelj makes this point very clearly by arguing that when the commodification of land, labor, and money is stretched to an unreasonable extent, the results will be predictably disastrous. On this point, we are in complete agreement.

But there are two significant fault lines in contemporary political economies that the concept of capitalism does not really help us to understand. The first is the tension between financialization and the actual production of goods and services (Krippner, 2011). To be sure, the former can be designated as M-M as contrasted to M-C-M, but these formulations fail to convey how extraordinarily destructive some types of financial activity can be. Once one defines the pursuit of profit to be inherently problematic, it becomes harder to highlight the critical dividing line between financial activity that actually helps people to make things – like long-term loans to small businesses – and the predatory lending that was at the center of the mortgage crisis.

We could begin to illuminate this fault line by differentiating among levels of financialization within different market societies. Perhaps we could differentiate the degree to which money had been commodified or decommodified within different market societies, and that could be a basis for organizing reform efforts designed to exert more political control over the allocation of finance.

The second key fault line is that which runs between small- and medium-sized businesses on the one hand and the giant corporations – both financial and nonfinancial – on the other. This divide has been a central axis of conflict at earlier points in U.S. history, and it seems to be reemerging as social movements have emphasized the shared interests of 99% against the top 1%. Sure, Marx and Engels acknowledged the existence of the petit bourgeoisie, but that class was doomed to disappear as concentration and centralization advanced. There is little in the Marxist tradition that anticipates the renewed importance of small- and medium-sized enterprises at the current stage of technological development.

Recently, Jeffrey Winters (2011) has proposed that rather than capturing contemporary dynamics through the terminology of capitalism, we might be better off using the concept of oligarchy – a term that was widely used by political analysts until the end of the 19th century. He carefully delineates four distinct types of oligarchy, and he categorizes the contemporary United States as falling under civil oligarchies. In this form, the oligarchs do not exercise violence or political power directly, instead they use their vast wealth to hire agents whose job is to protect their holdings from taxation or other threats. In his analysis, there is no inherent conflict between democracy and oligarchy; the two can co-exist as long as the armies of lobbyists and accountants employed by the very rich are able to protect the needed loopholes and exceptions that allow them to keep their wealth intact.

With the revelation earlier this year that Mitt Romney pays a tax at the rate of only 13.9% on his $21 million of annual income, it is impossible to ignore the specific mechanisms that allow the superrich first to accumulate disproportionate wealth and then to escape the tax rates that ordinary rich people are obliged to pay. It would seem that the concept of oligarchy is much more useful to illuminate this critical fault line than our inherited concepts of capitalism.

Finally, talking about market societies with stronger and weaker oligarchic tendencies is ultimately consistent with Karl Polanyi's (2001, p. 242) definition of socialism as "the tendency inherent in an industrial civilization to transcend the self-regulating market by consciously subordinating it to democratic politics." In the current situation, this means that citizens must understand the need to pay close attention both to the rules governing the international monetary system and the fine points of business, property, and tax laws that protect oligarchic wealth. Helping citizens to understand these issues is the challenge that we face as critical social scientists.

ACKNOWLEDGMENTS

Thanks to Margaret Somers for comments on an earlier draft. I am deeply grateful to Nina Bandelj, Ho-Fung Hung, and Wolfgang Streeck for responding to my provocation in such a generous fashion and with such an admirable absence of polemics. I am also grateful to Julian Go for organizing this conversation and for providing a format that gives me – at least for now – the last word.

REFERENCES

Block, F. (1977). *The origins of international economic disorder*. Berkeley, CA: University of California Press.
Block, F. (1996). Controlling global finance. *World Policy Journal*, *13*(3), 24–34.
Block, F. (2011). Reinventing social democracy for the 21st century. *Journal of Australian Political Economy*, *67*(June), 5–21.
Evans, P. (2008). Is an alternative globalization possible? *Politics & Society*, *36*(2), 271–305.
Gowa, J. (1983). *Closing the gold window*. Ithaca, NY: Cornell University Press.
Krippner, G. (2011). *Capitalizing on crisis*. Cambridge, MA: Harvard University Press.
Odell, J. S. (1982). *U.S. international monetary policy*. Princeton, NJ: Princeton University Press.
Polanyi, K. (2001 [1944]). *The great transformation*. Boston, MA: Beacon Press.
Ruggie, J. G. (1982). International regimes, transactions, and change: Embedded liberalism in the postwar economic order. *International Organization*, *36*(2), 379–415.
Scharpf, F. W. (1991 [1987]). *Crisis and choice in European social democracy*. R. Crowley & F. Thompson (Trans.). Ithaca, NY: Cornell University Press.

Streeck, W. (2009). *Re-forming capitalism*. Oxford: Oxford University Press.
U.S. Department of State. (2009). *Foreign relations of the United States, 1969-1976*, vol. 31, *Foreign economic policy, 1973–1976*. Retrieved from http://history.state.gov/historical documents/frus1969-76v31
Winters, J. A. (2011). *Oligarchy*. Cambridge, UK: Cambridge University Press.